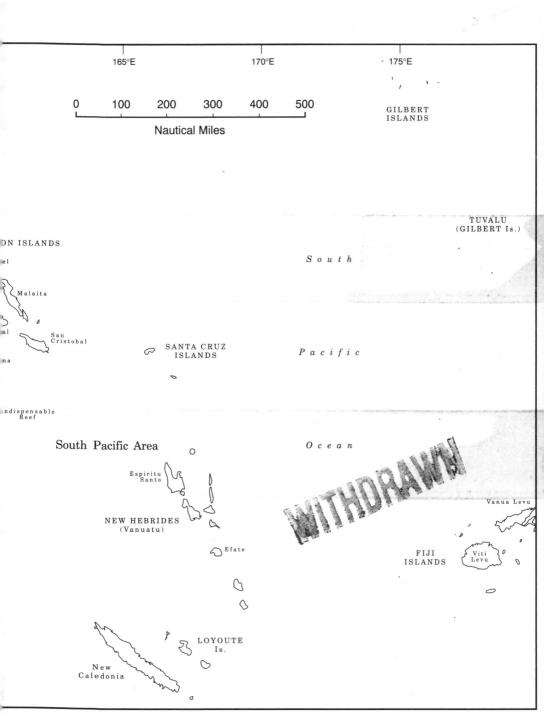

165°E   170°E   175°E

0   100   200   300   400   500

Nautical Miles

GILBERT
ISLANDS

TUVALU
(GILBERT Is.)

ON ISLANDS

South

Malaita

San
Cristobal

SANTA CRUZ
ISLANDS

Pacific

ndispensable
Reef

South Pacific Area

Ocean

Espiritu
Santo

WITHDRAWN

Vanua Levu

NEW HEBRIDES
(Vanuatu)

Efate

FIJI
ISLANDS

Viti
Levu

LOYOUTE
Is.

New
Caledonia

The shame of Savo

The shame of Savo

Anatomy of a naval disaster

Bruce Loxton with
Chris Coulthard-Clark

Naval Institute Press
Annapolis, Maryland

Published and distributed in the United States of America and Canada by the
Naval Institute Press,
118 Maryland Avenue,
Annapolis, Maryland 21402–5035

Library of Congress Catalog Card Number: 94-66596

ISBN 1-55750-763-5

Set in 10/12 pt Times by DOCUPRO, Sydney
Printed by Griffin Press Pty Ltd, South Australia

10 9 8 7 6 5 4 3 2 1

Foreword

The shame of Savo explores the personalities and events associated with that disastrous night of 9 August 1942 when a Japanese cruiser force surprised an Allied fleet off Savo Island. By the end of the night the Japanese had departed intact, having sunk two heavy cruisers (USS *Vincennes* and USS *Quincy*), reduced another two (HMAS *Canberra* and USS *Astoria*) to burning hulks, and hit USS *Chicago* with torpedoes. Over one thousand Allied officers and men were killed. It was, as Commodore Bruce Loxton writes, 'a humiliating defeat'.

Following the disaster, inquiries were held and many books and staff papers were written in an attempt to answer the question: 'How could such a catastrophe occur?' I'll not steal Commodore Loxton's thunder here by giving away his answer.

The idea of a new book on the Battle of Savo came about some four years ago at a luncheon I had with the author. We felt that there had to be more to the battle than had been previously reported, especially with regard to the aerial reconnaissance carried out at the time. At the very least, it was certainly worth reviewing. I must say, however, that back then I could not have envisaged just what a magnificent and important piece of work Commodore Loxton would produce.

It is almost as if Commodore Loxton was fated to write this book. He was at Savo Island as a midshipman in HMAS *Canberra* and he later spent over two years immediately after the war with Rear Admiral Crutchley's operations officer at Savo, Commander Gatacre, when he was captain of the destroyer HMAS *Arunta*. During his time in Navy Office he was able to examine the Board of Inquiry's report into the loss of *Canberra*, and he later attended the United States War College where he was lectured on the subject—much to his displeasure! Finally, Commodore Loxton's time in the intelligence world got him thinking about areas such as reconnaissance, enemy reporting and communications. The result was that he became more and more determined to investigate what really happened at Savo.

This is an important work as it examines the whole fabric of naval operations in the South West Pacific theatre at the time. Commodore Loxton uses his vast naval experience to bring to life the personalities involved and to analyse their decisions. His knowledge of the technology, tactics and conditions that existed in 1942 bring great authority to his arguments. An unusual feature of the book is the generous praise of the Imperial Japanese Navy's professionalism and mastery of the difficult art of night fighting. His perspective is a fresh and vibrant one, and shows through in his writing.

I thoroughly recommend *The shame of Savo* not only as a good read for those with an interest in military history but also, and perhaps particularly, as a book with which commanders at all levels should be familiar.

Vice-Admiral I.D.G. MacDougall, AC
Chief of the Naval Staff

Contents

Illustrations

Maps and diagrams

Dedicated to the memory of
Captain Frank Getting, RAN, of HMAS *Canberra*,
and to those members of his ship's company
who died with him as a result of Allied ineptitude
in the face of Japanese professionalism at the
Battle of Savo Island, 9 August 1942

Acknowledgments

While I am grateful to the many individuals who have helped in the research for and compilation of this book, I owe a very special debt of gratitude to my wife, Dahlis, for her forbearance over more than three years in tolerating a husband whose mind was rarely far away from Savo. I am also very deeply indebted to Chris Coulthard-Clark who, while fully engaged in writing a book on the Royal Australian Air Force's participation in Vietnam, still found the time to assist me in the preparation of what we both hope is a reader-friendly book, free of unnecessary jargon. His task was not made any easier by the tyranny of distance because, while he lives in Canberra, I was rarely closer than Sydney and as often as not in London.

The institutions visited or contacted in Australia, the United States and the United Kingdom were universally helpful, none more so than those in the US: primarily the Naval Historical Collection at the Naval War College, Newport, headed by Dr Evelyn Cherpak, and the Operational Archives Branch of the Naval Historical Center, Washington, where I received every possible help from Miss Kathleen Lloyd. At no time when I was researching matters relating to the United States Navy did I sense that anything was being withheld from me. My American research was greatly facilitated by the willing help of Commodore David Campbell and Commander Bruce Hamilton of the Australian Embassy, and by the search for suitable photographs carried out by Mr Charles Haberlain of the Photographic Section of the Naval Historical Center.

As time went on, I became increasingly aware of the great value of the complete' copy of the War College's Analysis of the Battle of Savo Island which I received as a gift from the Naval Command College of the Naval War College in 1973, when I was assisting Alan Payne in his writing of the history of HMAS *Canberra*. The fact that I am sometimes critical of that document should not obscure my appreciation of its overall value, for it contains an astonishing amount of detail and provided the basis for most of the maps included here.

In London, I enjoyed the facilities offered by the British Library and the National Maritime Museum for my background reading and, for other research, by the Public Record Office where any document asked for was on my desk within twenty minutes. It was in London, too, that the book was named following a suggestion by the Naval Historian at the Ministry of Defence, Mr David Brown, and where I was fortunate in obtaining the services of Mr John Swenke of Stratigraphics, Putney, who drew the maps and diagrams.

In Australia, my thanks go to the research centre at the Australian War Memorial, Canberra, the RAAF Historical Section of the Department of Defence (Air Force Office) also in Canberra and the offices of Australian Archives in Melbourne, Canberra and Sydney. The Archives provided quickly and willingly any material requested—all except the Deck Log of HMAS *Canberra* for August 1942, which survived the ship's sinking and was presented at the Board of Inquiry that followed, but which sadly could not be found.

I am most grateful for the information and opinions offered by many individuals whose readiness to share their special knowledge was crucial to this book. Particular mention must be made of the contributions by Lieutenant Commander William Crutchley regarding the career of his father, Admiral Sir Victor Crutchley, VC, KCB, DSC; Captain Shin Itonaga of the Military History Department at the National Defence Agency, Tokyo, on Japanese naval doctrine, and for clarification of many points of detail; Lieutenant Commander M.J. Gregory (officer of the watch in HMAS *Canberra* when the battle commenced), who carried out a great deal of research on my behalf in Melbourne; Mr Wilbur Courtis, DFC, on Hudson operations, in particular his account as navigator of the sortie of Hudson 218; Mrs Diane Bischer on the sortie of Hudson 185 flown by her father, Squadron Leader Mervyn Willman; Air Commodore Bill Garing, CBE, DFC, and Air Commodore Deryck Kingwell, CBE, DSO, on matters relating to Hudson operations and the Allied Air Forces Command generally; Dr David Medley on the fitting of radar in *Canberra*; Mr Keith Freemantle for a considerable portion of the research which was carried out in Canberra; Captain William Hunnicutt, Commander John Williams, Commander Raymond Orr, Mr Eugene McClarty and Mr George Sallet, all of whom were serving in USS *Bagley* at Savo; Commodore John Snow on naval communications; and Rear Admiral David Holthouse, AO, on naval engineering matters.

Advice and encouragement was received from many people, among whom I particularly wish to mention Lord (Hugh) and Lady Cudlipp, Mr Michael Hill QC, Vice-Admiral Ian MacDougall, Captain N.H.S. White, my brother Alan and last, but by no means least, my family who gave me very considerable support. Others who also have my thanks in this regard are Commander Alex Black, Mr Colin Butterworth, Mrs Peggy Connor, Mr John Date, Captain Peter Goldrick, Commodore Ken Gray, Mr Robert Piper, Mrs Donald Ramsey, Commander Teddy Lesh, Commander Dean Murray, Mr David Vincent and Captain John Wells. Mr Alan Zammit and Mr Jack Langrell are also thanked for the additional photographs provided.

Abbreviations

AA (Canb)	Australian Archives (Canberra)
AA (NSW)	Australian Archives (New South Wales)
AA (Vic)	Australian Archives (Victoria)
AAF	Allied Air Forces
ACH	Area Combined Headquarters
AWM	Australian War Memorial, Canberra
CAP	Carrier aircraft patrol
C-in-C	Commander-in-Chief
CNO	Chief of Naval Operations
CNS	Chief of the Naval Staff
COMAIRSOPAC	Comander Air South Pacific (Area)
COMSOPAC	Commander South Pacific (Area)
CTF	Commander Task Force
CTG	Commander Task Group
DNI	Director of Naval Intelligence
FECB	Far East Combined Bureau
HMAS	His Majesty's Australian Ship
HMNZS	His Majesty's New Zealand Ship
HMS	His Majesty's Ship
IJN	Imperial Japanese Navy
NATO	North Atlantic Treaty Organisation
NHC	Naval Historical Center, Washington
NWC	Naval War College, Newport, Rhode Island
ONI	Office of Naval Intelligence
PRO	Public Record Office, London
RAAF	Royal Australian Air Force
RAF	Royal Air Force

RAN	Royal Australian Navy
RANVR	Royal Australian Navy Volunteer Reserve
RN	Royal Navy
SOPAC	South Pacific (Area Command)
SWPA	South West Pacific Area (Command)
USN	United States Navy
USNI	United States Naval Institute
USS	United States Ship
VHF	Very High Frequency (radio)

Glossary

Action stations: All personnel were allocated positions during various activities like preparing for action, abandoning ship, entering harbour etc. These positions were known as stations, so that hands were sent to action stations, to abandon ship stations and to stations for entering harbour, and so on. Hands at action stations could be either in the first degree of readiness (alert) or the second degree (relaxed). Lower states of readiness were maintained by hands at defence stations, usually on a two-watch basis or, lower still, at cruising stations.

Admiralty: A term originally applied to the British department of state responsible for administering the Royal Navy. With the advent of radio and a centralised naval staff presided over by the First Sea Lord (otherwise known as the Chief of the Naval Staff), however, the Admiralty gained a capability to intervene in operational matters as well—for example, the chase of the *Bismarck*, which was coordinated by the Admiralty. During the Second World War the Admiralty could, and sometimes did, interfere in the activities of the various naval commanders-in-chief, not always to good effect.

ACH: Area Combined Headquarters were responsible to Headquarters Allied Air Forces Command for the conduct of operations in a geographical area.

Allied Air Forces Command: The air component of General MacArthur's South West Pacific Area Command.

Battle ensign: Ships going into action hoisted their ensigns at the mastheads. Australian warships in those days flew the White Ensign at the gaff, but invariably flew the national flag as their battle ensign at the masthead— thus fighting under Australian colours.

Binnacle: A wooden stand for a magnetic compass in and on which were fitted the devices and magnets for countering the effects of a ship's magnetic field on the compass needle.

Chief of Naval Operations (CNO): During the Second World War, Admiral King combined the functions of CNO (the professional head of the Navy Department) with those of the Commander-in-Chief of the United States Fleet (COMINCH), a position which had been rotated before Pearl Harbor between the fleet commanders. As head of the Office of CNO, King did not exercise the same degree of operational control over his subordinate commanders as did his opposite number in London, the Chief of the Naval Staff.

COMDESRON: Each squadron of American destroyers was led by a Squadron Commander (COMDESRON) usually of captain's rank. The responsibilities of this officer, unlike those of a Royal Navy Captain (D), did not usually extend to commanding a ship.

Commander (E): A specialist engineer officer of the rank of commander. Similarly, a lieutenant specialising in supply matters was designated Lieutenant (S). Specialist officers were not eligible to exercise military command, this being the sole prerogative of the seaman or, as it was otherwise known, the executive branch. Seaman officers could sub-specialise in gunnery, torpedoes, navigation, submarines or as aircrew.

Corresponding protection: Cruisers, particularly those constructed under the terms of the Washington Treaty, were not armoured anywhere to withstand the effects of hits from 8-inch shells. Vital areas of battleships, on the other hand, were protected by their armour against the shells of other battleships.

Crossing the 'T': A manoeuvre dearly loved by the naval theorist but virtually impossible to achieve in practice between fleets of roughly equal speed in open waters. The advantage to the crossing fleet was that it could bring its broadsides to bear, while the oncoming fleet was restricted to engaging with only its forward guns. The tactic was first successfully carried out in the days of steam by Admiral Togo at the Battle of Tsushima (1905). Togo was able to achieve this because of his superior speed and manoeuvrability. Admiral Oldendorf was also able to cross Admiral Nishimura's 'T' at the Battle of Surigao (1944) because the Japanese were advancing towards him through a narrow strait. At Jutland (1916) on the other hand, the Germans—enjoying unlimited sea room—countered Jellicoe's threatened deployment across their line of advance by turning away.

D-Day: The day (whether or not specified by date) set for the beginning of a planned operation, usually an attack. In the same way H-Hour represents the time planned for the commencement of an operation.

Director of Naval Intelligence (DNI): The title of the officer on the naval staffs in London and Melbourne and in the office of CNO Washington with responsibility for the collection, evaluation and dissemination of intelligence. During the Second World War this was a single service responsibility, with DNI (London) and DNI (Melbourne) providing the naval input into their respective Joint Intelligence Committees. DNI (Melbourne) controlled the coastwatcher organisation.

Enemy bearing indicator (EBI): A binocular sight used to indicate the bearings of targets to the gunnery control positions. The device could be compass-stabilised once a target was acquired, thus ensuring that it continued to point in the desired direction regardless of how the ship turned.

Far East Combined Bureau (FECB): Formed in Hong Kong in 1934 and later moved to Singapore, this was the centre of British signals intelligence activities against the Japanese.

Form White: A report of the results of a maritime reconnaissance sortie sent in a standardised format. Initially introduced by RAF Coastal Command for the Battle of the Atlantic, it was adopted for use by the Allied air forces on 4 August immediately prior to Watchtower.

General quarters: The USN's equivalent of action stations, with the important difference that American personnel did not remain at general quarters when in the second degree of readiness.

HMAS: A commissioned warship of the Royal Australian Navy.

High frequency (H/F): The radio frequency band between 3000 Khz and 30 Mhz (equivalent to a wave length of between 100 and 10 metres) with a very limited ground wave and propagation worldwide due to reflections off the ionosphere. The result of this characteristic is that H/F signals can be intercepted at long range.

HMS: A commissioned warship of the Royal Navy.

HMNZS: A commissioned warship of the Royal New Zealand Navy.

Joint Planning Committee (JPC): A term common to both Britain and the United States, where JPCs reported to their respective Joint Chiefs of Staff and which were formed to carry out joint rather than single service planning.

Kwantung Army: The Japanese army in Manchuria whose independent frame of mind was often an embarrassment to the Japanese Government, particularly in the 1937 Marco Polo bridge incident.

Lieutenant (JG): An American naval officer was first promoted from ensign to lieutenant (junior grade) before achieving the rank of lieutenant. The time taken to advance from ensign to lieutenant commander was, however, approximately the same as a British counterpart took to move from sub-lieutenant to lieutenant commander—that is, eight years.

Medium frequency (M/F): The radio frequency band between 300 Khz and 3000 Khz (equivalent to a wave length of between 1000 and 100 metres). The extent of the ground wave increases as the frequency decreases, so that the lower frequencies were used for tactical communications before the advent of TBS. During Watchtower, for example, 2058 Khz was used for messages within Crutchley's screening group, while 245 Khz linked the various task group commanders within Turner's amphibious force. *Canberra* attempted to report her situation to Crutchley on the former frequency.

Naval Board: The body responsible for the administration of the RAN. In 1942 it comprised the Minister for the Navy, three Naval Members (serving officers) and the civilian public servant who was Secretary of the Department of the Navy. The First Naval Member was also Chief of the Naval Staff.

Navy Office: The operational and administrative headquarters of the RAN and the Department of the Navy, then situated in Melbourne.

North Eastern Command: A sub-area command of MacArthur's Allied Air Forces. Based on Townsville, it controlled all SWPA aircraft allocated for use in Watchtower, command being exercised through ACH Townsville.

Office of Naval Intelligence (ONI): The division of the Office of CNO headed by DNI.

Port: Left.

Royal Australian Navy Volunteer Reserve: Unlike the militia forces of the Australian Army, officers and men of the RANVR served throughout the world during the Second World War.

RDF: Standing for 'radio direction finding', this term was synonymous with radar, being the name by which radar was known in the Commonwealth navies when first introduced into service in 1939 and prior to July 1943.

Royal Fleet Auxiliary (RFA): A fleet support ship run by the Admiralty but manned by a civilian crew. It was not until towards the end of the Second World War that RFA tankers were built for fuelling abeam. The RFA *Bishopdale*, mined off Noumea, was only capable of fuelling astern by means of a buoyant hose, a method evolved for use by escorts in the difficult weather conditions of the Atlantic but too slow and cumbersome for fuelling a carrier task force.

Search and strike mission: A mission where the strike aircraft were launched at the same time as the search aircraft to reduce the time between the location of and attack on a target.

Snotty: Naval slang for a midshipman.

SOPAC: Vice-Admiral Ghormley's South Pacific Area Command, a sub-area of Admiral Nimitz's Pacific Area Command.

SWPA: General MacArthur's South West Pacific Command.

Starboard: Right.

Task force: A naval force formed for a purpose, made up of either ships or aircraft or a combination of both.

Task group: Part of a task force.

TBS: A VHF radio transceiver.

USS: A ship of the USN manned by naval personnel. Hence fleet tankers like *Platte* were designated USS as were those transports and supply ships which were naval manned.

Washington Treaty: The result of the Washington Conference of 1922 was an agreement which limited, among other things, the displacement of heavy cruisers to 10 000 tons. The characteristics of all six Allied heavy cruisers at Savo were the result of compromises forced on naval designers by that restriction. In *Canberra*'s case, the need to stay within 10 000 tons precluded the fitting of any side armour and diesel generators, and also influenced the arrangement of the boiler rooms. What could have been done once the Washington Treaty's provisions had lapsed was illustrated with *Australia*'s modernisation.

A NOTE ON TIME AND DISTANCES USED IN THIS BOOK

The 24-hour clock system is used throughout. Times based on Greenwich Mean Time (GMT) are suffixed with the letter 'Z' while other letters are used to indicate local time. In the text, except where indicated, all times are eleven hours ahead of GMT (indicated by the suffix 'L') as this time was maintained by the Allied forces off Guadalcanal. Allied forces in New Guinea and eastern Australia maintained their clocks ten hours ahead of GMT (indicated by use of the suffix 'K'). Japanese forces maintained Tokyo time, which was nine hours ahead of GMT and indicated by the suffix 'I'.

In a signal, the time of an event (such as the sighting of Mikawa) was given in GMT. The time of origin of a message was invariably given in GMT prefixed by two figures to indicate the date. Thus the time of origin of a message originated at 1025K on 8 August was 080025Z. The month could be added if desired.

Distances are expressed in imperial measurements rather than metric equivalents. Unless otherwise stated, a mile here refers to a nautical mile (6080 feet, or 1.85318 kilometres).

Introduction

I was an 18-year-old midshipman serving in HMAS *Canberra* when, on 7 August 1942, I took part in Operation Watchtower—the Allied recapture of the southern Solomon Islands from the Japanese invaders who had occupied this portion of the Pacific. In the early morning I stood on the bridge behind our commanding officer, Captain Frank Getting, as the heavy cruiser escorted a group of attack transports, loaded with US Marines, around Savo Island (into what later became known as Iron Bottom Sound) heading for Tulagi, a small island just off Florida Island.

With the first glimmer of dawn, the battle ensigns were hoisted and *Canberra* turned away to allow the transports to make their approach to their anchorages off the beachhead. As it grew lighter we could see the smoke of camp fires ashore and, in the distance, a much larger group of ships approaching Lunga Point on the island of Guadalcanal away to the south. Inshore everything was still.

With dramatic suddenness, fighter aircraft appeared over Tulagi and began strafing Japanese flying boats and float planes moored in the harbour. Plane after plane burst into flames as all fifteen were destroyed. Still there was no reaction from the enemy. I heard Captain Getting exultantly proclaim to anyone within earshot that he would never have believed in that day and age that such complete suprise would be possible. Operation Watchtower was under way.

That was an historic moment, as we were initiating the counterattack against the Japanese which was to proceed, almost without pause, until their unconditional surrender almost exactly three years later. Of particular interest to Australians present was the fact that we were also taking part in the first major opposed amphibious landing since the unsuccessful attempt by a combined French and British (including Australian) force to seize control of the Dardanelles in 1915.

Morale in *Canberra* was high, and we had no thought of possible failure. A week before we had met up with the three US aircraft carriers *Saratoga*, *Wasp* and *Enterprise*. We were aware that the Expeditionary Force also included a modern fast American battleship, *North Carolina*, ten other heavy cruisers, three light cruisers, 35 destroyers, 23 transports and supply ships, and the US 1st Marine Division. Fortunately, we were unaware that both General Douglas MacArthur, the South West Pacific Area commander, and Vice-Admiral Robert Ghormley, the South Pacific Area commander, gave us little chance of success and had strenuously opposed the mounting of the operation at that time. Vice-Admiral Frank Jack Fletcher, the commander of the entire Expeditionary Force, just ten days before our arrival off Tulagi, had told his subordinate task force commanders that he did not think the operation would succeed.

Despite such pessimism at the top, we had made a good start. A large amphibious force and its escort had been assembled from virtually all over the Pacific, had made a passage of seven days from the Fijis and had arrived unheralded on the Japanese doorstep. While good security—including the maintenance of radio silence—undoubtedly had made this possible, we were also lucky with the weather. Poor visibility and heavy cloud cover in the vicinity of the force for the final two days of the approach had prevented our detection by the seven enemy flying boats based on Tulagi. Luck was to stay with us for another two days, during which time we survived three ineffective air raids, the airfield on Guadalcanal was captured with ease and—although the Japanese put up a spirited resistance on small islands in the vicinity—Tulagi itself had been taken.

With his knowledge of the scale of the air reconnaissance planned for Watchtower and of the size of the naval forces in the area, Captain Getting would have felt confident that any Japanese surface force approaching the assault area would be detected and dealt with before it could do any harm. The screening forces would be more than adequate to deal with any ships that survived air strikes from the 231 aircraft in the carriers supporting us. He expected air attacks, but knew that ample warning would be received of their arrival from the Navy's coastwatching organisation for which, as Deputy Chief of the Naval Staff, he had been responsible. Given that warning, the fighter control team in USS *Chicago*, which was fitted with an air warning radar (unusual in cruisers in those days) and the carriers' fighters, would ensure an effective fighter defence of the assault area.

Getting was, no doubt, uneasy about the threat from submarines, for he had once commanded a submarine and was well aware of their ability to create havoc among anchored transports and slow-moving unescorted cruisers. But he must have been reassured by the presence of 23 sonar-fitted destroyers in the sound and the activity overhead of up to five cruiser-borne aircraft on anti-submarine patrol. On the face of it, there was good reason for him to feel that we had more than sufficient naval forces in the area to ensure that the Marines were landed, with all their equipment, and supported for as long as it was necessary to establish themselves ashore and reach their objectives.

Soon after sunset on the 8th, a message was received from General MacArthur's naval headquarters in Brisbane, through the naval radio station in Canberra, that a Japanese force of three cruisers, three destroyers and two seaplane tenders or gunboats had been sighted off Kieta on the east coast of Bougainville Island at 1025 that morning. The Captain, noting the reported composition of the force, assessed that they posed no immediate threat. He expected that the Japanese would be establishing a base from which frequent aerial torpedo attacks could be carried out on the transport area.

Captain Getting would have been aware of the view in the British Admiralty that the Japanese were not good at night fighting, and this undoubtedly strengthened his thinking that they would not attack a markedly superior force—particularly as their reported composition was that of an escort force rather than that of a strike force. He knew that it was planned to carry out long-range air searches during the day. He would have assumed, in the absence of any report to the contrary, that the searches had been flown and that nothing had been found. This negative information would have been an additional reason for believing that the enemy force sighted off Kieta had not continued to close Tulagi and therefore was not a threat that night.

Though tired, Getting was relaxed when he took *Canberra* into her station astern of HMAS *Australia* to commence the night's patrol in the southern entrance to the sound between Florida and Guadalcanal Islands. *Chicago*, the third member of the group, was stationed astern of *Canberra* until *Australia* withdrew inshore to take the screening group commander, Rear Admiral Victor Crutchley, to confer with the amphibious force commander, Rear Admiral Kelly Turner. *Chicago*—whose commander, Captain Howard Bode, was senior to Getting—then made a move to take the lead. When abreast of us, though, Bode had second thoughts and dropped back, explaining as he did so that it would cause less confusion when *Australia* rejoined later in the night if *Chicago* remained astern.

The scene was set for another quiet night on patrol, screened as we were by the US destroyers *Bagley* and *Patterson* on each bow, and with the radar pickets *Blue* and *Ralph Talbot* patrolling to seaward of Savo. Even the unexplained presence of an aircraft soon after midnight did nothing to alert us to the possibility that things were not quite as peaceful as they seemed and that all hell was about to break loose.

Before dawn seven Japanese cruisers and one destroyer were on their way back to Rabaul and Kavieng at high speed having sunk two heavy cruisers, USS *Vincennes* and USS *Quincy*, reduced *Canberra* and the heavy cruiser USS *Astoria* to burning hulks, hit *Chicago* with two torpedoes and damaged two destroyers. Along with those ships, we had lost over 1000 officers and men dead and many wounded. In return, we had inflicted only minor damage to three of the enemy ships and caused less than 100 casualties. It was a humiliating defeat which was exacerbated by the absence of any strikes by our carrier-aircraft against the fleeing enemy.

My experience of the Battle of Savo Island began when I was roused from a deep sleep by a voice in the darkness shouting, 'Come on, wake up—the action alarm is ringing'. I ran out of the charthouse and up two ladders on to the port side of the bridge to my action station, which was the captain's port enemy bearing indicator or EBI (a binocular sight used to indicate the bearings of targets to the gunnery control positions). I was conscious that the ship was swinging rapidly to starboard and accelerating, with the funnels vibrating as the boilers urgently provided the steam necessary to achieve the full power that the Captain had called for. I could see nothing through the binoculars. The night was as black as the inside of a cow and the rapid movement of the ship did not make searching any easier.

The Gunnery Officer, crossing over from the starboard EBI, shouted 'Get out of the way, Snotty [the usual form of addressing one of my lowly rank]—let me have a look!' I stepped back, and almost as I did so there was an explosion close to my left. Thrown backwards against the magnetic compass binnacle, I ended up on the deck. A telephone buzzed and I reached it with difficulty, but no one was on the other end. I let it fall and lay back against the binnacle. Although I knew nothing of my injuries at the time, I had been literally peppered with pieces of metal. While losing a great deal of blood, I was extremely fortunate that nothing vital had been hit.

The Captain and the Gunnery Officer were not so lucky. The latter, Lieutenant Commander Donald Hole, lay still and was in fact dead. Captain Getting, however, was struggling to sit up, telling those about him that he was all right while asking about the state of the ship. I learnt later that his right leg had been almost shot away, both his hands were injured, and that he had shell fragments in his face and other head wounds.

The Surgeon Commander arrived on the bridge to tend to the Captain, who still insisted he was all right and that others should be looked after first. The doctor did as he was told but ignored me, which was not to my liking, and when he stepped over me to leave the bridge, I told him so. As he bent down over me to administer morphia, he explained that he had thought I was dead. I assured him that I was not, and oddly enough at no time did I think that I would die. Pain no longer worried me but I was cold and wet and afraid of shock.

Five weeks later, I was one of a group of wounded survivors who returned to Sydney after a spell in hospital in Auckland. We were met by Rear Admiral George Muirhead-Gould, the officer in charge of the Sydney naval area. In the course of a short address of welcome, he informed us that we should feel ashamed that our ship had been sunk by gunfire without firing a shot in return.

The admiral's words left me with a lasting desire to find out the truth of what had happened that night. We were already hearing a variety of accounts of the battle, and how it was that we had been so quickly immobilised and rendered helpless. The admiral was quite right on one point. We had indeed not fired a shot in our own defence, but should I feel ashamed of this?

Over the past fifty years or so, I have heard and read many accounts of the battle which alleged that our defeat had been in large part due to incompetence of the crews of Australian reconnaissance aircraft, and to mistakes by Rear Admiral Crutchley both in the positioning of destroyers to provide warning of any Japanese approach and in the splitting of the six heavy cruisers into two groups. The loss of *Canberra* was put down to a lack of alertness and the fact that the guns were not loaded. Initially, there seemed to be good reason for the widespread reticence among my fellow officers to discuss the loss of *Canberra*.

As my own career progressed and reports on Operation Watchtower and Savo became available, and as my professional knowledge grew and I gained experience in ship handling, staff work and tactical analysis, it became progressively more apparent to me that the full story had yet to be told. Accounts of the activities of the Australian naval forces involved were based on two reports: one by a Board of Inquiry into the loss of *Canberra* which was held almost immediately after the battle, and the other on a report by Crutchley on Watchtower. The Inquiry was limited to matters related only to the loss of *Canberra*, and its findings were based on the belief that *Canberra* had been opposed by a light cruiser and destroyer force of about three ships. No mention was made of the loss of the American ships, for security reasons. There were also no reports from MacArthur's naval or airforce headquarters, or indeed from any Australian air authority.

It soon became clear that the activities of Australian forces could not be examined in isolation. Watchtower had been an Allied operation involving two areas, both under American control, and any reappraisal had to include an examination of American activities.

I found that authors—mainly American—of accounts of the battle and the operation as a whole, in addition to using the Board of Inquiry and Crutchley reports, had also obtained a great deal of information from a report prepared in early 1943 for Admiral King, Commander-in-Chief US Fleet in Washington, by Admiral Hepburn, a retired officer who had been Chief of Naval Operations in the late 1930s. King had ordered the investigation because he had received no full account of the battle from his admirals; indeed, some had submitted no report at all. Considerable use had also been made of an analysis of the battle of Savo carried out in 1950 by the US Naval War College, which was based on all available American and Japanese information.

Study of the latter analysis finally convinced me of the need for a professional reappraisal of Watchtower and of the Battle of Savo, using primary sources wherever possible. I did not agree with some of the findings in previous studies and reports, since overall there appeared to be inconsistencies not only in the analysis but also in various reports. Several aspects of the operation had not been fully investigated, notably in the areas of command, intelligence, tactical doctrine, aerial reconnaissance and communications. The question as to how it was that *Canberra* had been immobilised in three or four minutes had not, in fact, been answered, and there was a need for an explanation of the poor performance of all four American heavy cruisers.

What follows provides a fuller answer than has hitherto been available and reveals an extraordinary and widespread concatenation of human and systemic errors and shortcomings. Were Muirhead-Gould to ask me now if I, as a member of her ship's company, felt ashamed that *Canberra* was destroyed without firing a shot in her own defence, I would reply that any feeling of guilt on my part has been well and truly exorcised. But were he to ask me if I felt a corporate responsibility for the poor showing of the Allies commands and naval forces I would have to answer in the affirmative. Our showing was not one of which any Allied officer could be proud.

1

The Pacific War to July 1942

In December 1941 Japan opened hostilities against the United States and Britain with attacks against territories belonging to these countries across Asia and the Pacific. Near-simultaneous strikes were undertaken against the US at- Hawaii, the Philippines, Guam and Wake Island, while the British were attacked at Hong Kong and Kota Bahru in Malaya. The Japanese intention was to fight what amounted to a limited war to secure access to strategic raw materials in the Netherlands East Indies (present-day Indonesia) by destroying European and American military power and political influence in the region.

The decision to mount such a campaign had been taken by Tokyo the previous September, in the face of continuing American resolve to enforce economic sanctions to thwart Japan's expansion. The Japanese saw no possibility of peace without losing face, a commodity of vital importance in the bid to replace the Europeans in the area they planned to dominate. The Army was deeply committed in China, where it had suffered a million casualties; there could be no thought of a withdrawal from there. The Navy had scarcely two years' supply of oil fuel at even peacetime usage rates. The northern winter was fast approaching and Japanese strength, relative to that of the Americans, was ebbing. And so, at an Imperial Conference on 6 September, the die was cast to go to war despite its attendant risks, if negotiations had not made satisfactory progress by mid-October.

This decision was made in spite of a warning by the Chief of the Naval General Staff, Admiral Osami Nagano, that:

> if they [the Americans] should aim for a quick war leading to an early decision, send their principal naval units and challenge us to an immediate war, this would be the very thing we would hope for. However, even if our empire should win a decisive naval victory, we will not thereby be able

1

to bring the war to a conclusion. We can anticipate that the Americans will attempt to prolong the war, utilising her impregnable position, her superior industrial power and her abundant resources. Our empire does not have the means to take the offensive, overcome the enemy and make them give up their will to fight.[1]

Nagano was not the only senior naval officer who was unable to visualise how a war with America could be won. A year earlier Admiral Isoroku Yamamoto, Commander-in-Chief of the Combined Fleets, had told the Prime Minister at the time, Prince Konoye, that 'if I am told to fight regardless of the consequences, I shall run wild considerably for the first six months or a year but I have utterly no confidence in the second and third years'.[2] Even after the sinking of the modern battleship HMS *Prince of Wales* and the old battle cruiser HMS *Repulse* off Malaya in the first days of the war, Yamamoto told a member of his staff that their success could not possibly continue for more than a year.[3]

Yamamoto, who had spent some years in the US, had a great respect for American strength. In April 1939 he told the boys of the middle school which he once attended that:

It is a mistake to regard the Americans as luxury loving and weak. I can tell you that Americans are full of the spirit of justice, fight and adventure and their thinking is very advanced and scientific. Do not forget that American industry is much more developed than ours and, unlike us, they have all the oil they want. Japan cannot beat America; therefore she should not fight America.[4]

When, in September 1940, the Navy had to decide whether or not to support the signing of the Tri-Partite Pact with Germany and Italy, the majority of senior officers saw the choice as lying between remaining an equal partner with the Army in shaping Japan's destiny or losing influence and risking a great internal upheaval instigated by the Army. They chose the former even though Yamamoto, at a meeting of senior officers, told them that the pact would make war with America inevitable.[5]

Having committed themselves to a policy which they saw would lead to war, the Navy wanted to fight a short victorious war, such as those against China (1894–95) and Russia (1904–05), not a war of attrition against an antagonist whom the Navy believed Japan could never beat.[6] From the outset, therefore, the Japanese Navy's intention, once they had secured their sources of raw materials and established a perimeter to defend them, was to negotiate a settlement. A necessary step to negotiations was a decisive victory at sea; they knew that without it they stood no chance. The attack on the US Pacific Fleet base at Pearl Harbor represented to some, notably Yamamoto as its chief architect, a missed opportunity for that decisive battle.

By April 1942 the Japanese had achieved, at negligible cost, all that they had scheduled for the first phase of the war. A perimeter had been established which ran from Singapore through the Netherlands East Indies, northern New Guinea and the northern Solomon Islands to the Marshall Islands. All opposition had been eliminated, with the exception of the garrison of American and Filipino troops holding out on the Bataan peninsula. Apart from a French puppet regime in Indo-China, all western influence had been removed from eastern Asia.

On 16 April an Imperial Navy directive established the aim of a second phase as being to expand Japan's Pacific perimeter by capturing Port Moresby (May), the Aleutians (June), Midway (June) and Fiji, Samoa and New Caledonia (July). The Japanese Navy intended to stay on the offensive. By moving into the central Pacific they hoped to entice the Americans into the decisive battle which was still seen as a necessary step to the negotiating table. They were supremely confident, and did not expect the Americans to be able to mount an offensive within the time frame of their second phase—or, indeed, before mid-1943. Admiral Yamamoto was making good his promise to run wild but, as one naval officer was later to write:

> In the spring of 1942 the cherry blossoms, at their fullest bloom, seemed like a symbol of continuing victory for the Japanese Navy; but Japan's wind of misfortune was making up and would soon begin to blow.[7]

The move by sea to Port Moresby was halted by the battle of the Coral Sea, and the capture of Midway was prevented by the battle of that name in early June. These defeats—particularly the loss at Midway of four of their six fleet carriers, together with a significant proportion of their trained naval aircrew—caused the Japanese to postpone the moves against Fiji, Samoa and New Caledonia on 11 June and later to cancel them.[8]

The first real acknowledgment of the abandonment of the planned offensive was the Japanese decision to consolidate their position by strengthening their hold on the Solomons while continuing the assault on Port Moresby. The islands were seen as being necessary for the defence of their outer perimeter and it was planned to establish a number of air bases there, notably on Guadalcanal and Buka. Work on an airfield on Guadalcanal was begun in late June and scheduled for completion by early August.

The Japanese perceived that the balance of power had been tilted in favour of the United States. Their best chance of a decisive naval action now lay in the south-west Pacific where they could deploy land-based naval aircraft on island airfields to back up their remaining carriers. On 14 July they formed the Eighth Fleet, known operationally as the Outer South Seas Force, under the command of Vice-Admiral Gunichi Mikawa, whose task was to defend the area south of the equator and east of 141 East. This area had previously been the responsibility of the Fourth Fleet based on Truk, which had been planning to:

- Seize Port Moresby by advancing overland from Buna. The initial landing at Buna was planned for 20 July.
- Establish air bases in New Guinea and the Solomons. Sites had already been selected at Buna and at Lunga Point on Guadalcanal and work had already been started on the latter. An emergency airfield was being established on Buka Island.
- Establish a seaplane base on Tulagi. Work had commenced on this facility on 8 July and in the meantime a seaplane unit had been stationed there.

On its formation, Eighth Fleet assumed responsibility for those tasks.[9]

The Japanese regarded the Buna operation as being urgently important. Under the terms of an Army–Navy agreement, the Army had no responsibility for the defence of the Solomons and were devoting their entire effort in the area to the Port Moresby thrust to pre-empt its use by the Allies as a base from which to threaten Rabaul. The Solomons campaign was very much a naval matter and this had the great advantage to the Japanese of single service involvement.

While by mid-1942 the Japanese interest in the Solomons was almost entirely driven by their need to defend their perimeter, the American interest was the reverse. They saw the Solomons as a launching point for their attack on that perimeter, and as a first step on the road to Rabaul and so on to the Philippines and Tokyo. It had not always been so. Prior to Pearl Harbor, faced with the probability of one day having to fight Japan, the Americans had developed war plans which called for amphibious operations against the Japanese-held Caroline and Marshall Islands as soon as war broke out. But the successful Japanese pre-emptive strike against Pearl Harbor caused the postponement of such operations and forced the Americans onto the defensive.

Out of a conference in December 1941–January 1942 between US President Roosevelt and Britain's Prime Minister Winston Churchill came a policy to 'beat Germany first'.[10] Consequently it was expected that no real counteroffensive in the Pacific could be undertaken before 1944 at the earliest. It was, however, accepted that 'points of vantage from which an offensive against Japan can eventually be developed must be secured'.[11] The Americans saw the islands of the south-west Pacific as such vantage points.

As early as 18 February 1942, three days after the fall of Singapore, Admiral Ernest King, Commander-in-Chief of the US Fleet and therefore a member of the Joint Chiefs of Staff, had written to General George Marshall, his army opposite number, stressing the need to garrison the New Hebrides. In particular, he regarded the security of Efate Island as being of the greatest importance.

On 2 March King was already writing of an advance to the north-west. In a memo to the President three days later, he wrote that, 'Given the naval forces, the air units and the amphibious troops, we can drive from the New Hebrides into the Solomons'. In the same document he summarised the general plan for operations in the Pacific: hold Hawaii; support Australasia; drive northwards from New Hebrides.

King felt that 'no fighter ever won his fight by covering up—by merely fending off the other fellow's blows'. He was in a hurry to assume the offensive.[12] He found an ally in Churchill who, in a cable to Roosevelt dated 5 March, urged the President to develop forces which 'can attack a Japanese-held base or island and beat the life out of the garrison'. Churchill felt that once the capability to do that was developed, all the Japanese islands would become vulnerable and their resources would be stretched to strengthen their perimeter. He thought that a start could be made in 1942.[13]

The Americans made the first real step towards the establishment in the southern Pacific of the kind of force that Churchill had envisaged when Major General A. Archer Vandegrift received orders in May 1942 to move his 1st Marine Division from the east coast of the United States to New Zealand, to serve as the landing force of the recently established South Pacific Amphibious Force. Other troop movements prior to May had established garrisons in the islands that lay along the route to Australia, particularly in Fiji, Samoa and New Caledonia.

At the time Vandegrift was told that he had at least six months in New Zealand in which to assemble and train his division before it would receive its first commitment; the initial moves were planned on that basis.[14] Stores and heavy equipment were loaded into ships without any thought that these might have to be unloaded onto a beach in a combat area. In other words, they were administratively rather than combat loaded.

Any planning for an amphibious operation then supposed the use of no more than a battalion or, at the most, a regiment in a raid. The point was that the Americans did not envisage being able, with the forces then available to them, to escort an amphibious force to a target area, land it and support it for a long period in the face of the Japanese naval capability, notably that provided by the six-ship carrier strike force. In the first six months of the war this force had struck at places as far apart as Pearl Harbor, Darwin and Colombo—thus demonstrating a devastating ability to move over long distances quickly, and to concentrate overwhelming power in a small area.

The loss of two-thirds of Japan's large carrier strength at the Battle of Midway enabled the Americans to think in terms of an early start to their counterattack by assaulting an area and holding it against Japanese naval opposition. In other words, it was at last possible to plan realistically to begin the counterattack, using as the spearhead the 1st Marine Division which at that time was the only amphibiously trained division in the Pacific.

But even before Midway, General Douglas MacArthur, Commander of the South West Pacific Area (SWPA), believed that the Japanese had overextended themselves and were gambling on quick victories before the Allies could recover. He urged that the Allies should concentrate against them for a decisive blow. After Midway he proposed aiming that blow at Rabaul. He asked for the transfer to his command of two of the four fleet carriers remaining in the US Navy, and for the only Marine division. The Joint Chiefs of Staff felt that such an operation was beyond American resources in the Pacific at the time.[15] King was also against the proposal because it would have placed major fleet units under army control.

King made the case for a more gradual approach. On 25 June he proposed to Marshall the mounting of an offensive on 1 August against Tulagi in the southern Solomons, using the 1st Marine Division which was then in the process of moving to New Zealand from the United States. Although Marshall was in favour of the proposal, he wanted MacArthur to command the operation. As most of the resources would have had to be provided from Admiral Chester Nimitz's Pacific Command, King was adamant that the operation had to be under naval command and, in the end, his view prevailed.[16]

As Nimitz stated later, the Americans felt that the Japanese would be unable to further extend their gains by a seaborne advance and that the Americans now had the means to recapture Tulagi. King must have felt very confident that he would get his way because on the same day that he made his proposal to Marshall, he directed the Commander of the South Pacific Area, Vice-Admiral Robert Ghormley, to confer with MacArthur about an amphibious operation, to be launched on 1 August against Tulagi, using the 1st Marine Division.[17]

The American counterattack was about to get under way many months earlier than the Japanese had thought possible, and before they had been able to consolidate their defensive positions in the area. Both sides were being drawn inexorably into a showdown.

2

The Allies plan to strike back

On 2 July the American Joint Chiefs of Staff reached a decision to launch an attack on the Solomons and directed that 'offensive operations be undertaken with the ultimate objective of seizing and occupying the New Britain–New Guinea–New Ireland area'.[1] King had made his point over command and Nimitz was told to take charge of the first phase of these operations: the seizure and occupation of the Santa Cruz Islands, Tulagi and adjacent positions in the Solomon Islands. This task was codenamed Pestilence and the operation to take Tulagi was called Watchtower.

To enable Nimitz to exercise command in the Tulagi area, an adjustment had to be made to the boundaries of the areas for which Nimitz and MacArthur were responsible. When the Pacific and South West Pacific Areas were established in April 1942, the Solomon Islands lay entirely within MacArthur's command. The boundary between the two areas was accordingly moved west to 159 degrees East so that Tulagi lay just within Nimitz's area. This situation was to have an adverse effect on the conduct of Watchtower's operations because responsibility for all operations in the north-western approaches to Tulagi, through the northern Solomon Islands and in the Bismarck Archipelago, remained the responsibility of MacArthur, whose forces were already deeply involved in the defence of New Guinea against a growing Japanese threat.

In their directive, the Chiefs of Staff instructed Nimitz to designate the task force commander for the operation. King, however, tied Nimitz's hands in that selection by telling him that he assumed that he would make Ghormley the commander of the task force undertaking the capture of Tulagi. Aged 57, Ghormley had graduated from the US Naval Academy in 1906. In the intervening 36 years, his experience in command at sea had been limited to a destroyer in the early 1920s and the battleship USS *Nevada*

7

in 1935. He had not served in the Pacific for 30 years; he had been promoted to rear admiral in October 1938, but he had yet to fly his flag at sea.

Instead, Ghormley had spent two years in Washington, for a time as Vice Chief of Naval Operations, followed by a period in London where he arrived on 15 August 1940 as the Blitz was starting. He was originally sent there with a team of three to hold disussions at staff level within the Admiralty on how the US Navy could assist Britain under Roosevelt's existing policy of 'all aid short of war', and on cooperation with the Royal Navy if and when America entered the war.[2] When he left London almost two years later, his staff numbered more than 40 and his activities had expanded until he was, *de facto*, head of an American naval mission. He was actually initiating the close cooperation that exists to this day between the two navies and as such deserves a niche in history. He was kept informed of developments in the Pacific so that he could pass the information on to the Admiralty.

In a narrative dated January 1943,[3] Ghormley told how a committee, headed jointly by Admiral Sir Sidney Bailey and himself, met daily to produce a report which became known as the Bailey Committee Report and which was completed in November 1940. As a member of the USN team he subsequently attended the secret staff talks held in Washington between representatives of America, Britain and Canada in January 1941. The result was an agreement known as ABC-1 which formed the basis for future Anglo-American cooperation. Churchill gave Ghormley the credit for the development of a detailed plan for co-operation in the Atlantic. It is apparent that Ghormley sometimes acted as a go-between between Prime Minister and President in the period before Pearl Harbor.

Ghormley was liked and respected in London, and this was mirrored in the opinion of the ship's company of the battleship HMS *Rodney* who remembered him as 'a charming and interesting officer and gentleman' when he had taken passage in that ship across the Atlantic from Halifax.[4] He was recalled in mid-April 1942 at short notice, and it was not until he arrived in Washington that he was told by King that he was to command the South Pacific Area. King warned him that his would be a difficult task and that he, King, did not have the tools necessary to carry it out in a proper manner. King also warned Ghormley of his hope to start an offensive in the Fall of 1942—that is, about November.

In his narrative, Ghormley made no mention of his reaction to this assignment but it must have surprised him. He had had no experience in the exercising of command as a flag officer, had no recent experience in the Pacific region and was not even current with recent developments in America. It was clearly not a case of 'horses for courses'. His expertise lay with the war in Europe against Germany, and most—if not all—of his thinking since 1940 must have been related to Anglo-American cooperation.

Though Ghormley no doubt felt flattered by such an appointment, he

The Allies plan to strike back

Vice-Admiral R. L. Ghormley, Commander of the South Pacific Area, was placed in overall command of the seizure of key parts of the southern Solomon Islands from the Japanese. An officer of comparatively limited sea experience, the expectation that he could command such an important undertaking at the same time as remaining an area commander epitomised the unrealistic arrangements which characterised planning for Operation Watchtower. (US National Archives neg. 80–G–12864–A)

must have wondered, when there were others who were better qualified, why he had been chosen to command of all places the area from which the counterattack against Japan would be launched. He would have been aware that two of his contemporaries, Vice-Admiral Bill Halsey and Rear Admiral Frank Jack Fletcher, had had considerable experience in the war in the Pacific as carrier task force commanders. He must also have known that Admiral William Pye, who had been in command of the Pacific Fleet battleships at the time of Pearl Harbor, was then underemployed as Commander of the Support Force which was built around the remnants of the Battle Fleet then operating off the west coast. Pye had acted for a while as Commander-in-Chief Pacific Fleet after the dismissal of Admiral Kimmel, shortly after the attack on Pearl Harbor and before the appointment of Nimitz to that position.

Why was Ghormley moved from London, where he had made—and was making—what can only be described as a unique contribution to Anglo-American cooperation, to an area of activity where there were others better qualified? Nimitz had actually nominated Pye for command of the South Pacific but King had rejected this idea. Ghormley's appointment would appear to defy a rational explanation and therefore it is possible that King had an irrational purpose. The explanation could perhaps lie in Ghormley's close association with the Admiralty and other British authorities at a time when King was making strenuous efforts to convince the President to counterattack in the Pacific. Was King's purpose to get rid of what could possibly develop into an embarrassing link between the Prime Minister and the President?

But such a scenario, while explaining his removal from London, does not explain his appointment to the South Pacific Area. It also ignores

9

Churchill's opinion, first expressed in a paper written on 20 December 1941 while *en route* to Washington and which he later discussed with the Americans, that 'it was of the utmost importance that the enemy should not acquire large gains cheaply; that he should be compelled to nourish his conquests and be kept extended—and kept burning his resources'. Churchill felt that the Japanese should be fought whenever there was a fair chance of success, and that it would be unwise to discourage the Americans from doing anything on a large scale in the Pacific. He took for granted that the Americans were firm in their declared intention of defeating Germany first and therefore that there was no real danger that they would permit an undue share of their resources to be committed to the Pacific to the detriment of British requirements.[5] His confidence was not always shared by his Chiefs of Staff, perhaps because they were aware of King's preference for the Pacific War and had to deal with his outbursts in committee.

Another reason for Ghormley's precipitate removal from London may have been that it was necessary to find useful employment for Admiral Harold Stark, whom King had displaced as Chief of Naval Operations in the middle of March. Ghormley would then have become available for reappointment. Admiral William Leahy, who was Chief of Staff to Roosevelt from mid-1941, suggests as much in his autobiography when he mentions Ghormley's removal from London at the same time as Stark's replacement by King.[6] As Ghormley was well thought of by the President, and as Roosevelt at that time was taking a personal interest in the appointments of American senior officers, particularly naval officers, it is not unlikely that he was appointed to command the recently formed South Pacific Area at the President's insistence.

Be that as it may, Ghormley could have had no doubts about King's expectations of him and of the need for urgent action. King told him that he wanted him to be on his way to Auckland, New Zealand, in a week. Ghormley won a reprieve of an additional week with the plea that it would take more than seven days to discuss his directives, to get a feel for the task that he was being given and assemble a staff. He left Washington on 1 May with instructions to set up his headquarters in Auckland.

During his fortnight in Washington, Ghormley began the struggle for adequate logistic support which was to dominate his thinking for the next six months. He formed the opinion, while in the capital, that the logistic planners had no concept of the size and geography of his command or that it took twice as much shipping to maintain forces in the southern Pacific as it did to maintain similar forces in Europe. This, incidentally, was a powerful reason—in those days of desperate shipping shortages—for beating Germany first. MacArthur was experiencing the same problem and he solved it by hanging in his office, for the benefit of visitors, an outline map of the United States superimposed on a map of the central and southern Pacific. It apparently never failed to impress.

Ghormley's next seven weeks were spent familiarising himself with his area and in discussions with those who would handle his logistic requirements in San Francisco, with Nimitz and his staff in Pearl Harbor, with the New Zealand Government and Chiefs of Staff, and with the uncooperative French authorities in Noumea. He finally assumed the responsibilities of Commander South Pacific Area on 19 June, by which time he could have been in no doubt about the difficulties which lay ahead.

While Ghormley had been moving from Washington to Auckland, the Japanese moves to consolidate their position in the south-west Pacific received a setback in the Coral Sea. This battle prevented them from making an amphibious assault on Port Moresby, and the balance of power in the Pacific changed dramatically with the Battle of Midway. The Japanese strike capability had been destroyed, at least for some months, so that it was feasible for the Allies—with the forces then available—to launch an immediate amphibious operation against the Japanese perimeter. King was in a hurry to counterattack. The result was that within a week of his arrival in Auckland, Ghormley was told to prepare to launch the attack in five weeks that only two months before he had been told was a possibility for the Fall!

King, when he informed Nimitz on 2 July that he assumed that Ghormley would command the Watchtower Expeditionary Force, also told him that Ghormley 'should command in person in [the] operating area'.[7] Command is the function of directing, coordinating and controlling, and King did not qualify 'command' with any limiting adjectives. But neither had Nimitz when, on 27 June, he told King that Ghormley would be placed in full command of the operation. Thus both King and Nimitz envisaged the comparatively inexperienced Ghormley taking command of the Expeditionary Force while at the same time remaining an area commander.

It should have been obvious to both, and particularly to Nimitz who was closer to the problem, that Ghormley was in no position to plan and oversee the conduct of an operation of the extent and complexity of Watchtower. They could not have had any understanding of the difficulties that he was already facing in organising his command and in establishing a logistic base for future operations. Furthermore, Ghormley's very considerable diplomatic skills were being tested to the full in handling the sometimes diverse requirements of the French in Noumea, the New Zealand Government in Wellington and MacArthur in Melbourne.

During Ghormley's visit to Pearl Harbor on his way to Auckland, he had discussed with Nimitz the subject of his command of any Pacific Fleet task forces assigned to the South Pacific. The matter became the subject of a directive to Ghormley issued on 12 May, which instructed him that Nimitz would continue to assign task force commanders their missions in broad terms so that they would not be inhibited from using their initiative in the execution of those missions. He told Ghormley that the instructions he issued those task force commanders would ordinarily require little amplification by Ghormley. However, Nimitz qualified that statement by telling him that he expected him to interfere if circumstances changed, or unforeseen situations arose.[8]

Nimitz's intention was obviously to protect the initiative of his task force commanders, but in so doing he almost certainly inhibited his sub-area commander from exercising any control of the carrier task forces that he was to be sent for Watchtower and from interfering tactically. Yet on 25 June, just a little more than six weeks later, Nimitz was to tell King that Ghormley would be placed in full command of Watchtower. Precisely when Nimitz realised the extent of the hole that he had dug for himself is uncertain, but in a letter dated 9 July to Ghormley he resolved the problem by designating him as the task force commander and limiting the scope of his command, instructing him to 'exercise strategic command in person in the operating area which is interpreted initially to be the New Caledonia–New Hebrides area'.

Ghormley's reaction to what Rear Admiral Kelly Turner's biographer, Vice-Admiral Dyer, called 'fuzzy command directives'[9] was to:

- Form the task forces allocated to him into an Expeditionary Force (Task Force 61) and place it under the command of Fletcher.
- Assign his South Pacific Amphibious Force, commanded by Turner, to the Expeditionary Force.
- Move his headquarters on 1 August from Auckland to Noumea, into the operating area.

Ghormley had been given only limited authority to interfere with a force's mission and even less to interfere tactically. In the circumstances he could not have seen himself as an operational authority, and this would help explain his subsequent poor showing in Watchtower.

The selection of the officer to command the Expeditionary Force was automatic. Ghormley had no alternative other than to select him from among those task force commanders whose forces had been assigned to him for the operation, and this had to be the senior officer present. Of those senior officers normally available in the Pacific, Halsey would have been chosen because he was the senior of the carrier task group commanders since his promotion to rear admiral in 1938. Though he had not been present at either Coral Sea or Midway he had been responsible for a number of the minor carrier strike operations carried out since Pearl Harbor, and for launching the Doolittle raid on Tokyo. Unfortunately, he had succumbed to a severe attack of dermatitis before Midway and had been sent back to hospital on the mainland; he was still unfit in July. Ghormley therefore had to designate Fletcher as the commander of the Expeditionary Force.

Fletcher was 57 and, like Ghormley, had graduated from Annapolis in 1906, a year after Nimitz. He had been awarded America's highest decoration for bravery, the Congressional Medal of Honor, as a result of his gallantry under fire and for his work in extricating over 350 refugees from the port of Vera Cruz during operations in Mexico in 1914. His promotion to rear admiral in 1939 came after considerable experience at sea, principally in battleships including USS *New Mexico* which he commanded in 1936–37; he had also served in destroyers and commanded several. Fletcher was no stranger to the Pacific, having spent a total of eight years in the Asiatic Fleet—the last two in the early 1930s as Chief of Staff to the Commander-in-Chief in the ill-fated USS *Houston*.

Fletcher had been active at sea in the Pacific since before the attack on Pearl Harbor and had not always been successful. His first operation against the Japanese was a bid to resupply Wake Island after their initial attack had been repulsed on 11 December. Had he not spent ten hours on 22 December refuelling his task force, including four destroyers whose tanks were 75 per cent full, the carrier *Saratoga* would have been in a good position to strike the second Japanese landing force the next day while it was assaulting the island. The result was that Fletcher was over 400 miles away from Wake when, after a gallant resistance, the garrison was overwhelmed.[10] Paul Dull was to write that the Japanese invasion force had been inferior in every respect to that which the Americans could have mustered, and therefore the island had been lost because of timidity and caution.[11]

Under Fletcher's command, Task Force 17 took part in raids on the Marshall and Gilbert Islands in early February and later that month moved into the South Pacific. In early May, he was the senior officer in a two-carrier task force consisting of USS *Yorktown* and USS *Lexington* which played the major role in the Battle of the Coral Sea. Before that action King had expressed to Nimitz, at a meeting in San Francisco on 25 April, that he held doubts as to the suitability of Fletcher for high command because he felt that Fletcher lacked aggression. A month later, King was again unimpressed by Fletcher's conduct, feeling that he should have launched a surface strike on the Japanese during the night of 7–8 May, when the opposing carrier forces had got close enough for Japanese aircraft to join the American landing circuits. Nimitz supported Fletcher and recommended him for promotion and award of the Distinguished Service Medal, but King would not hear of it.

Immediately before the Battle of Midway, Halsey being unfit, Nimitz realised that King still had a poor opinion of Fletcher. He would have to convince King of Fletcher's suitability if the latter were to retain his task force and command the American forces in the approaching battle. Nimitz therefore decided on an interview to reassure himself that Fletcher was suitable for command of the forces involved. He sent for Fletcher as soon as *Yorktown* returned to Pearl Harbor from the Coral Sea and commenced to review with him his wartime record.

Fletcher was apparently exhausted after his long period at sea, but it was not long before he realised that Nimitz's questioning amounted to an inquisition into his conduct of operations in the Coral Sea.[12] According to Nimitz's biographer, both men became embarrassed; Fletcher became tongue-tied and was unable to continue. Pleading the necessity to consult his records, he asked for, and was granted, an adjournment until the following morning.

When the interview was resumed, Fletcher completed his report to Nimitz, who then asked him to put it in writing. This Fletcher did, apparently producing 'a full and manly account of his stewardship of Task Force 17'. Nimitz was impressed and forwarded it to King on 29 May under cover of his own letter, which reported that he had finally had an opportunity to discuss with Fletcher his operations in the Coral Sea area and to clear up what appeared to be lack of aggressive tactics of his force. He had also discussed with Fletcher the opportunities for the use of surface forces in night attacks. He reported that both those matters had been explained to his satisfaction.

Nimitz considered that Fletcher's caution at the Coral Sea had been due partly to the lack of sufficiently reliable combat intelligence upon which to base operations, to the necessity for replenishment of fuel and provisions and to the need for the replacement of defective leak-proof tanks in his fighter planes. He ended by telling King that he hoped and believed that he (King) would 'agree, after reading the enclosed letter, that Fletcher did a fine job and exercised superior judgement during his recent cruise in the Coral Sea. He is an excellent seagoing, fighting naval officer and I wish to

Vice-Admiral F. J. Fletcher, shown here in September 1942, was appointed to lead the allied expeditionary force involved in Operation Watchtower. He had a deeply flawed record of command at sea despite being a holder of the Congressional Medal of Honor. Complacent, timid and excessively cautious, his part in previous operations in the Pacific—including Wake Island, the Coral Sea and Midway—had not resolved his superiors' doubts as to whether he was a competent tactician. His action in deserting the Marines landed at Guadalcanal by the precipitate and unwarranted early withdrawal of his covering carriers went uncensured. It was only after Fletcher ineptly allowed his flagship, the carrier Saratoga, *to be torpedoed just three weeks after the Savo debacle—sailing at a leisurely thirteen knots in waters where at least ten enemy submarines had earlier been reported as operating—that action was finally taken to remove him to shore duty. (US National Archives neg. 80–G–14193)*

retain him as a task force commander for the future'.[13] In the face of such an endorsement King had no alternative but to agree.

Nimitz had decided to recommend the retention of Fletcher as the task force commander on the best information available to him, the majority of which was provided by Fletcher himself. But one wonders whether he would have been quite so confident in Fletcher's leadership qualities if the views of informed officers under that admiral had been available to him. Among such critics was Lieutenant (JG) Forrest Biard.[14] A 1936 graduate from Annapolis, Biard was an intelligence specialist, a Japanese linguist and the officer in charge of the radio intelligence team attached to Fletcher's staff in *Yorktown* for her entire deployment in the South Pacific—that is, from mid-February to mid-May, a total of 83 days. The team consisted of Biard and two sailors, both of whom were also linguists and trained to read Japanese morse. Before joining *Yorktown*, Biard was instructed to give Fletcher and his staff every assistance short of revealing—even to the admiral himself—the extent of the operations of the radio intelligence organisation or its very existence.[15]

From Biard's personal account, it is clear that his relationship with Fletcher was far from being a happy one. It was not long before Biard felt that in order to achieve any credibility with his admiral, he had to reveal that the intelligence he was passing to him was from a highly secret and therefore sensitive source. Fletcher's reaction was not that of an intelligent man, let alone the commander of a carrier task force on whom so much depended. At a lunch with his entire staff, and while the mess attendants were present, he called on Biard to tell the gathering all about the communication intelligence organisation and its code-breaking activities. Biard quite properly refused to do so, in spite of a direct order.

Matters came to a head, so far as Baird was concerned, when the Battle of the Coral Sea was approaching its climax on 7 May. By that time, the Australian Task Force 44, consisting of the RAN cruisers *Australia* (wearing the flag of Rear Admiral J.G. Crace) and *Hobart*, and USS *Chicago*, with three American destroyers, had been detached to the west with the aim of preventing the Japanese force bound for Port Moresby from entering the Coral Sea through Jomard Passage. In *Yorktown*, Biard's team was providing intelligence on the activities of Japanese carrier-based aircraft as his two sailors listened in to transmissions between those aircraft and their parent carriers. He became aware at 0900 that day that the Japanese had located the fleet tanker USS *Neosho* and her escort, the destroyer USS *Sims*, about 180 miles to the east and that they were searching for the American carriers.

An hour earlier an American search aircraft had sighted a Japanese force about 225 miles to the north which was reported to comprise two carriers and four cruisers. Believing that he was about to win the jackpot, Fletcher launched all available aircraft. At much the same time he turned over tactical command to Rear Admiral Fitch in *Lexington*.

By mid-morning Biard had deduced that Crace's force had been located, that the opposition consisted of the two large carriers *Shokaku* and *Zuikaku*, that they were to the east and that they were about to strike *Neosho* and *Sims*. Nothing could be done to help the threatened ships, as all combat aircraft not required for the air defence of *Yorktown* and *Lexington* were engaged in striking the Japanese force to the north. Until the return of his strike aircraft, Fletcher had to maintain absolute radio silence and hope that the weather front that was shielding him from the Japanese searches would continue to do so.

Biard continued to intercept Japanese messages which confirmed his earlier deductions and showed that the Japanese force was closing on them from the east. Debriefing of the search aircraft crew who made the earlier sighting revealed that the pilot had made a mistake in coding his message; in fact, he had seen only two cruisers and two destroyers. Fletcher was beside himself with fury, believing that the initiative had passed to the Japanese and that as a result his force would be annihilated by the still undetected enemy carriers. He made no attempt to keep this gloomy and morale-destroying belief to himself as he berated the unfortunate pilot in front of those on the flag bridge.[16]

Fletcher's luck held. By 1400 the aircraft had returned after sinking the light carrier *Shoho*, had been refuelled and rearmed, and were ranged ready for take-off. The Japanese had still not detected him and had instead launched their strike against *Neosho*, believing her to be a carrier. Biard by then was sure that the Japanese were close, were actively seeking the Americans and, on several occasions, he told Fletcher so. Fletcher gave him to understand that he was waiting for instructions from Fitch in *Lexington* who was the officer in tactical command and that it was too late to launch a strike that day. When pushed further, Fletcher exclaimed 'Young man, you do not understand. I am going to attack them tomorrow.' To which Biard replied 'But Admiral, they are going to attack you today'.

Indeed the Japanese did their best to do so. An hour or so later and only about a hundred miles to the east, Vice-Admiral Takagi launched a search and strike mission against the Americans. Though they did not succeed in finding them, their aircraft were detected by American radar and intercepted. Several were shot down and the remainder aborted their mission. So close were the forces at that time that several Japanese aircraft mistakenly joined the Americans' landing circuits. Fletcher was heard by Biard to say that he had not expected the Japanese to be so aggressive! Later it transpired that Fitch was waiting for instructions from Fletcher.

The sending of Crace's task force more than 250 miles to the west to cover the entrance into the Coral Sea through Jomard Passage has been the subject of criticism by some historians. Fletcher had placed almost a quarter of his entire force of ships outside the range at which carrier-borne fighters could provide them with air cover, yet well within range of Japanese aircraft operating from Rabaul and while enemy carriers were known to be operating in the vicinity.

Biard casts a possible new light on Fletcher's decision to detach Crace. He tells how the Chief of Staff, when telling him of the deployment early on the morning of 7 May, explained that Fletcher wanted Crace out of the area in which the battle would take place because 'he doesn't want to hand out medals to Britishers and Australians. The medals he will give out after the battle is fought he wants to go to Americans only.' The story approaches the unbelievable but, seen in the context of Fletcher's conduct throughout that period, it has a measure of credibility.

In the event, Crace's force was heavily and accurately attacked by torpedo and high-level bombers and only effective anti-aircraft fire and skilful ship handling saved his ships from damage or worse. As the Japanese were withdrawing, the force was again bombed, this time inaccurately and by American Flying Fortresses out of Townsville. After the attacks, Crace asked Fletcher for air cover and was told to seek it from Port Moresby some 400 miles to the west.

The rest is history. The next day both sides found their opponents and each made damaging attacks on the other. The Americans lost *Lexington*, and *Yorktown* suffered damage sufficient to warrant her return to Pearl Harbor where she was repaired in three days and sailed in time to take part in the Battle of Midway. The Japanese suffered severe damage to one fleet carrier, *Shokaku*, which kept her out of action for three months. The remaining carrier, *Zuikaku*, remained unscathed, but the Japanese had lost so many aircraft and trained pilots that they were unable to provide a complement of aircraft for her in time for Midway.

Biard's account of Fletcher's conduct of operations in the South Pacific prior to and during the Coral Sea action differs in several places from all accounts published save that of Rear Admiral Edwin Layton, Nimitz's combat intelligence officer. It reveals a Fletcher who many suspected existed but of whom there had been little hard evidence. There can be no doubt that Biard irritated Fletcher or that Biard disliked him intensely, and this should be taken into account when considering Biard's opinions. But also to be taken into account is that Biard was a highly intelligent and gifted intelligence officer, as well as being a professional naval officer; he had a successful naval career for many years after he left Fletcher's staff, achieving the rank of captain. While his language may be coloured by his personal feelings, it is most unlikely that his version of Fletcher's conduct is totally a figment of his imagination. Certainly Layton, who knew both the officers concerned, gave credibility to much of Biard's account when he included it in his *And I Was There*. In some US circles, however, Biard's account is regarded as that of a brilliant but opinionated junior officer somewhat lacking in tact. Because of his position and function in the flagship, he was not necessarily fully aware of all the factors and information which shaped Fletcher's actions.

Biard summed up Fletcher as being neither sharp nor perspicacious and as being humourless, uninformed and to a certain extent uninformable. Professionally, he considered him to be antiquated to the extent that he was approaching senility. It was his belief that anyone who talked to Fletcher for ten minutes could hardly help realising that this officer certainly should never have made the rank of captain. Nimitz's high regard for Fletcher's performance in the Battle of the Coral Sea was based on a report which Biard believed was purposely untruthful, and which contained inaccuracies and lies which varied from the small to the quite gross.

After his interview with Nimitz, Fletcher departed from Pearl Harbor in *Yorktown* as Commander Task Force 17, escorted by two cruisers and six destroyers, to take part in the Battle of Midway. Task Force 16, commanded by Rear Admiral Raymond Spruance, with the carriers *Enterprise* and *Hornet* and six cruisers and eleven destroyers, was already in position north of Midway Island to foil the expected Japanese attack on that island. Upon his arrival in the area, Fletcher assumed overall command of both task forces so that the opening moves of the Battle of Midway were fought under his command.

On the morning of 4 June, apart from ordering Task Force 16 to attack the Japanese carriers then known to be to the south-west, Fletcher allowed Spruance freedom of action while conducting his own task force's operations against them. The difference in the conduct of the two task forces is striking. Spruance immediately launched every available strike aircraft but Fletcher launched only half of *Yorktown*'s, preferring to keep a reserve available in case there were more than four enemy carriers in the area. Nonetheless, the outcome was that the dive-bombers of both forces succeeded in destroying three of the four Japanese fleet carriers before *Yorktown* was disabled by aircraft from the surviving Japanese carrier. Fletcher then turned over tactical command to Spruance and shifted his flag to the heavy cruiser *Astoria*. One of the results of the battle was that Fletcher was at last promoted to vice-admiral. He was also awarded the Distinguished Service Medal for commanding his task force with 'marked skill and resourcefulness', an award that was well earned as Fletcher had sewn the seeds of victory for Spruance to harvest.

One would have thought that Fletcher's participation in a victory of such magnitude would have laid to rest any doubts that Nimitz had regarding his junior's capacity. This was not so, though, because before the assault on Tulagi and Guadalcanal Nimitz expressed regret that Halsey had not been available to command the Expeditionary Force. There was therefore an ambivalence in Nimitz's attitude to Fletcher, and—strangely—this remained even after the latter's quite disastrous performance during Operation Watchtower. It was King who ultimately removed Fletcher from command at sea, against the recommendation of Nimitz. This did not occur, however, until after the torpedoing of Fletcher's flagship *Saratoga* on 31 August, in circumstances which finally convinced King, at least, that Fletcher was a poor tactician.

Saratoga's task force was operating to the south-east of Guadalcanal in an area where three days earlier Allied intelligence had estimated that at least ten Japanese submarines were operating. Rather than move his operating area, Fletcher maintained his position and soon after dawn, when the task force was almost inviting submarine attack by proceeding at a leisurely thirteen knots, *Saratoga* was torpedoed. Damage to the carrier's turbo-electric machinery immobilised her for three months but casualties were limited to thirteen wounded—among them Fletcher, who suffered a lacerated forehead. *Saratoga*'s records show that he was discharged to duty, but on return to harbour Nimitz sent him on leave for a rest.[17] Fletcher then requested a return to sea duty, which Nimitz recommended be approved, but King had had enough and ordered Fletcher to remain ashore and to command the Seattle Naval District.

Fletcher's overall performance between December 1941 and August 1942 justifies the opinion that as a leader he was badly flawed. He fits the description of the senior American naval officers in the Pacific Fleet given by a British naval observer in early 1942, who thought that a defensive spirit, caution and general complacency dominated their strategic planning and that they were unable to make up for a lack of realistic operational experience by their vision. He believed that their greatest weakness was the age of flag officers and ships' commanding officers (see Endnote 26 to Chapter 23). The performance of Fletcher's staff as described by Biard would also seem to justify the comment that staffs were mediocre and lacked ability for original thought.[18] However, future events were to prove that the same observer was equally justified in writing that the offensive spirit among junior officers and the sailors was active and determined, and moreover that the standard of technical ability was high. Not for nothing is the war at sea in the Pacific sometimes described as 'the Lieutenant Commanders' War'.

Those who would defend Fletcher's performance as the commander of the Expeditionary Force for Watchtower hasten to point out that, at the time he was not only the commander of the task group formed round *Saratoga* but also the commander of the Pacific Fleet's Striking Forces, which at that time comprised four task forces, each with a carrier.

As the commander of the Pacific Fleet's Striking Force he was in much the same position as Admiral Jellicoe had been in the British Grand Fleet in the First World War. Jellicoe was described by Churchill as the only man who could lose that war in an afternoon. Fletcher had command of the only four surviving fleet carriers in the US Navy, three of which were with him at Guadalcanal. Because no additional carriers could be expected for about nine months, and because the Japanese still possessed two fleet carriers (with two more about to come into service, apart from a number of smaller but effective carriers), damage to or the loss of any of the existing American carriers without a corresponding Japanese casualty could have materially altered the balance of power in the Pacific.[19]

Fletcher had been instructed by Nimitz prior to Midway that he was to be governed by the principle of calculated risks. He interpreted this to mean that his carriers should avoid attack by a superior force without a good prospect of inflicting greater damage on the enemy.[20] He believed that no damage he could inflict on Japanese land or air forces in the Guadalcanal area could outweigh the loss of or even damage to his carriers. He was therefore preoccupied with their safety to the extent that he had originally intended to withdraw them after two days in the area. As will be seen later, it was only with considerable reluctance that he agreed to remain for three days, even though Turner advised him that it would take at least five days to complete unloading.

In retrospect it would seem that, quite apart from his personal qualities, Fletcher's responsibility as commander of the Pacific Fleet's Striking Forces made him an unsuitable choice as commander of the Expeditionary Force. It might well be that King appreciated this when he instructed Nimitz that Ghormley himself should exercise tactical command. Such a move would not have surprised Fletcher, who expected Ghormley to join him in *Saratoga*.[21]

3

The Expeditionary Force and its commanders

Fletcher's Expeditionary Force was made up of the South Pacific Amphibious Force (23 ships carrying the American 1st Marine Division, plus its escort of six heavy cruisers, two light cruisers, fifteen modern fleet destroyers and five old 'four-stack' destroyers converted for the minesweeping role) and three supporting carrier task forces built round the aircraft carriers *Saratoga*, *Enterprise* and *Wasp*. The latter ships carried between them 99 fighters, 100 dive-bombers, and 40 torpedo bombers which also provided the reconnaissance capability. The carriers' escorts included the modern fast battleship *North Carolina*, recently transferred from the Atlantic, four heavy cruisers, one light cruiser and sixteen destroyers. The total was a fleet of 77 ships.

Of the three aircraft carriers, only *Wasp* could operate her aircraft at night. Like *North Carolina*, she had transferred from the North Atlantic where she had operated for a time with the British Home Fleet. Whereas the aircraft squadrons of *Saratoga* and *Enterprise* had been reformed after the Battle of Midway, *Wasp*'s had remained virtually intact during her service in the Atlantic and Mediterranean. All her pilots were completely qualified for night operations, an invaluable asset which was wasted during Watchtower.

Fletcher formed his Expeditionary Force into two separate task forces. Task Force 61 comprised the three carrier groups and included the Air Support Force. Task Force 62 was made up of the Amphibious Force of transports, store ships and minesweepers, with its escort of cruisers and destroyers.

Rear Admiral Leigh Noyes, who commanded *Wasp*'s carrier group, was designated by Fletcher as commander of the Air Support Force. Noyes was another graduate from Annapolis in 1906 and until Fletcher was promoted

21

to vice-admiral he was senior to him. He had commanded several destroyers in the late 1920s and the light cruiser USS *Richmond* in 1934–35 in the Pacific, before undergoing flight training to fit him for the command of *Lexington* in 1937–38. Promoted to rear admiral in July 1939 he had assumed command of Task Force 18 in July 1942, flying his flag in *Wasp*. Watchtower was his first operation as a task force commander and his first experience of command as a flag officer.

Fletcher remained in *Saratoga* as commander of a carrier group, Task Force 11, within the Air Support Force. By so doing he placed himself in a position where he was unable to oversee properly the activities for which the Expeditionary Force had been formed: the capture of Tulagi and Guadalcanal. There is no record of any consideration being given to Fletcher transferring his flag to another ship such as one of the four heavy cruisers in the Amphibious Force, none of which wore an admiral's flag. Had this been done he would then have been free to place himself where he could best exercise his command function.

The third carrier task force was commanded by Rear Admiral Thomas Kinkaid, the junior of the three carrier admirals. Kinkaid had graduated from Annapolis in 1908, two years later than Ghormley, Fletcher, McCain and Noyes. An ordnance engineer, he had enjoyed a distinguished career as a gunnery specialist, held destroyer commands, and was captain of the heavy cruiser USS *Indianapolis* in 1937–38. Promoted to rear admiral in November 1941 he commanded the cruisers that supported Fletcher's carriers at the Battle of the Coral Sea before moving on to command Task Force 16, flying his flag in *Enterprise*.

The Amphibious Force was commanded by Rear Admiral Kelly Turner, who had graduated from Annapolis in 1908 with Kinkaid. His career was spent in the world of battleship gunnery until he qualified as a pilot in 1927, at the age of 42. He had commanded the Asiatic Fleet air squadrons and the tender USS *Jason* in 1928–29, during which time he obtained considerable experience in aerial reconnaissance, and had served as Executive Officer of *Saratoga* in 1933–34. Declared unfit for flying solo in 1937, he turned down the opportunity of commanding an aircraft carrier in 1938 and instead commanded the heavy cruiser *Astoria* in the Pacific for two years immediately before the Second World War. During the latter part of his time in *Astoria*, the cruiser division to which *Astoria* belonged had been commanded by Fletcher.

In October 1940 Turner was moved to Washington as head of the War Plans Division in the Office of the Chief of Naval Operations (CNO) in the rank of captain. When he took part in joint discussions with members of the British Mission in Washington in January 1941, which Ghormley had also attended, he was told to wear a rear admiral's uniform to add to his status as a member of the USN's delegation and soon afterwards was promoted to that rank. Sir John Slessor, a member of the British delegation, later described him as:

> A very able and forcible officer whose influence in the Navy Department was perhaps more powerful than his position warranted. In 1940 he could be 'ornary as hell' and was rather liable to start from the assumption that he was right and everyone else were either fools or knaves. Nevertheless he was a splendid chap, a doughty champion of what he believed to be right, and he had an endearing trick, at the height of an argument when he was being as difficult as he could be, of suddenly laughing at himself and coming to meet our point of view.[1]

For the next eighteen months or so Turner played a prominent part in the preparations for the war which everyone in Washington realised was inevitable. He was dynamic, capable and intelligent and, as so often happens with those possessing such traits, soon found himself in conflict with his associates in CNO's Office—notably the Operations Division (then known as Ships' Movements) and the Intelligence Division—as he sought to exert his influence. Major General Vandegrift, the commander of the 1st Marine Division which was to form the landing force for Watchtower, was later to describe him thus: 'A lanky chap who wore steel-rimmed glasses, he resembled an erudite schoolmaster whose didactic manner proved irritating to some people'.[2] It was also to irritate Vandegrift when Turner sought to dominate him and to interfere in matters which Vandegrift felt were his responsibility.

Turner's disagreement with naval intelligence was to have a profound effect on the history of his country and of the Second World War. The terms of reference of the Office of Naval Intelligence (ONI), headed by the Director of Naval Intelligence (DNI), included the provision that it was to be responsible for the collection of all relevant information concerning foreign countries, especially that which affected naval and maritime matters. Particular attention was to be paid to the strength, disposition and probable intentions of possible enemy naval forces.[3] Thus USN instructions provided for DNI to estimate an enemy's (or possible enemy's) intentions and for the plans and operations divisions to decide on the courses of action to be followed.

In early February 1941 ONI promulgated an assessment that the Japanese would move into Indo-China.[4] This had been made on the evidence of Japanese dispositions and their capability to make such a move. Soon after this assessment was circulated, the authority for ONI to issue assessments of enemy or possible enemy intentions was withdrawn. In future they were to be the responsibility of the War Plans Division.

The catalyst for the change of policy was the promulgation by the War Plans Division, without reference to ONI, of an assessment that the Japanese were about to move into Manchuria. DNI protested at what he considered to be an infringement of ONI's responsibility but he lost the argument to the extent that the Chief of Naval Operations, Admiral Stark, decreed that, in the interests of coordination within his office, the War Plans Division would in future be responsible for the coordination of the preparation of assessments and for their promulgation. If ONI had always provided all pertinent information, and if the War Plans Division had always consulted ONI before promulgation of an evaluation of an enemy intention, this reversal of a well-tried policy would not have been disastrous. But consultation between the two staff divisions did not always occur, particularly in matters relating to the assessment of Japanese intentions.[5]

Turner was convinced that the Japanese would move north against Russia and this opinion was strenghtened when Germany invaded Russia in June 1941. He was sure that Russia would quickly collapse and that the Japanese would take advantage of the situation to seize Manchuria and the Russian Maritime Provinces. He strongly disagreed with ONI's opinion that the Japanese intended a move south, and disregarded their assessment—notwithstanding that it was based on a great deal of hard intelligence—that the Japanese had not reinforced their Kwantung Army which was deployed defensively rather than offensively, that they were very heavily committed in China, and that naval deployments were in line with a southerly move. Turner saw Japan acting in concert with Germany, whereas ONI believed that the Japanese would do whatever was best for themselves, taking advantage of any situation which increased their chances of success.

In May 1941, when DNI annotated a paper with the remark that 'In my view the Japanese will jump and pretty soon', Turner added his own view that 'I don't think that the Japs are going to jump now or ever'.[6] And in early July, Turner foretold that the Japanese would probably move against Manchuria later that month.[7] There was apparently a breakdown in communications between the two divisions when ONI received no prior warning that sanctions were to be imposed on Japan on 26 July, even though the message promulgating the imposition of sanctions assessed (correctly) that no immediate Japanese military response was expected.[8] And so it went on.

It was not only in Washington that naval staff opinion as to Japanese intentions was divided. In Hawaii the staff officer responsible for war plans was advising Admiral Kimmel, then Commander-in-Chief Pacific Fleet, that the Japanese were not going to attack. This view was supported by Rear Admiral Pye, commanding the Pacific Fleet's battleships, who at a conference on the eve of the Pearl Harbor debacle was to say, in response to Layton's assessment that the Japanese would not move south while leaving American forces on their flank: 'The Japanese won't attack us. We're too strong and powerful.'[9]

The result of these differences of opinion was that naval warnings regarding the threat from Japan were muted at a time when all naval authorities in the Pacific should have received firm guidance, if not instructions, on the actions to be taken in the face of the growing number of indications that the Japanese intended a move to the south which might well include action against American interests. An example of this was the failure by CNO's office to give any guidance on the actions to be taken on 3 December when it was known that Japanese consulates and diplomatic posts in Hong Kong, Singapore, Batavia, Manila, Washington and London had been instructed to destroy, immediately, all important confidential and secret documents and most of their codes.[10] It is indicative of the mood in Stark's office that the Head of the Far East Desk in ONI was absent in London from 25 August to 11 October 1942.[11]

To all intents and purposes the office of CNO was controlled by a triumvirate of Stark, Ingersoll (Vice Chief of Naval Operations), and Turner. Turner was the ideas man, and the heads of divisions responsible for ships' movements, communications and intelligence were often not consulted in regard to matters within their bailiwicks. For example, on 27 November 1941, a message to the commanders of the Pacific and Asiatic fleets advised them that there were indications that the Japanese were about to mount an amphibious expedition against the Kra Isthmus or Thailand or the Philippines within the next few days. They were directed to regard the message as a warning of war and to take appropriate defensive measures. DNI was not informed of this message until 1 December.

There is, therefore, a great deal of evidence that Turner was at least partly to blame for the state of mind of senior American naval officers which inhibited them from 'thinking the unthinkable' and from taking active steps to prevent what ultimately happened at Pearl Harbor; like avoiding the concentration of ships in harbour and aircraft on the ground, and increasing air patrol activity so that the island of Oahu was given effective all-round cover.

Eventually, Turner's uncompromising manner with his associates led to his dismissal from Washington, for he fell out with a man who was later to demonstrate a genius for getting on with people of different backgrounds who held contrary views to his own—Dwight D. Eisenhower.[12] Eisenhower and Turner were then respectively the army and navy senior planners on the Joint Planning Staff. In that body a basic disagreement existed between Army and Navy in the first half of 1942 over whether or not the holding of Australia was vital to the interests of the United States.

King made clear his views on the subject on 2 March, when he wrote to Marshall to say that:

> The scheme or concept of operations is not only to protect the lines of communication with Australia but in so doing to set up strong points from which a step by step general advance can be made through the New Hebrides, Solomons and Bismarck Archipelago. It is expected that such a step by step general advance will draw Japanese forces to oppose it thus

relieving pressure on other parts of the Pacific and that the operation itself will be good cover for the communications with Australia.[13]

It seems that Turner, in committee, put King's view forward in a forceful manner.

Eisenhower, no doubt arguing the views of his chief, Marshall, was very much an advocate of the 'beat Germany first policy' which had become the keystone of Anglo-American cooperation. He took the position that the holding of Australia was in the 'highly desirable' rather than in the 'essential' category, and that operations in the Pacific should not be allowed to impede the American build-up against Germany and Italy. The inference was that the Army was prepared to give further ground in the Pacific which was anathema to Turner.

Eventually, Eisenhower complained to Marshall that Turner was being unreasonable and that he could not work with him. King originally opposed any proposal to have Turner removed from the Joint Planning Staff but had to give way in May when Marshall approached Roosevelt for support. Although the President was in sympathy with the Navy's position, he told King to move Turner. As a result Turner became available for a command which was to be challenging and rewarding and which allowed him to exercise his dynamism and other talents to the full. He had no cause to regret his precipitate removal from Washington.

Turner's envisaged progress to his new command in the South Pacific was in marked contrast to that of Ghormley. Detached from his duty in Washington on 12 June, he drove across America with an allowance of ten days' travelling time and ten days' leave. He arrived in San Francisco a fortnight later. On 29 June, however, his itinerary suffered a major change when he met three officers who had been appointed to his new staff. They carried with them instructions from King to begin, at once, the preparation for an amphibious operation.[14]

Like Ghormley before him, Turner had left Washington before the full effect of the victory at Midway on the ability of the Americans to launch their counterattack had been realised. What in late May had been but a gleam in King's eyes had, by mid-June, become a practical proposition. Turner and his three staff officers quickly prepared an outline for what was to become Operation Pestilence, of which the capture of Tulagi (to be known as Watchtower) was a part. They were able to present it in person on 3–4 July in San Francisco to both King and Nimitz, who were conferring in that city. The plan was approved.

No time had been lost between the Joint Chiefs of Staff approval of Pestilence on 2 July and the acceptance of an outline plan for its execution. In retrospect it was remarkable that planning could be completed, forces assembled from places as far afield as San Diego and Melbourne and upwards of 20 000 Marines landed in the target area just five weeks later.

Nothing like it was to be seen again until the Falklands War 40 years later, when the British assembled a naval force and landed 8000 troops some 7000 miles away within seven weeks of the requirement arising. Many of the lessons learnt in Watchtower were put to good use in the Falklands campaign which, like its predecessor, demonstrated the flexibility and power of a maritime capability.

The outline plan called for the capture of Tulagi, the occupation of an airfield or airfield site on Guadalcanal, the occupation of Funafati in the Ellice Islands (now Tuvalu) as a patrol plane base and, surprisingly, the establishment of an aircraft warning service on outlying islands including San Cristobal, Malaita, Santa Isabel, New Georgia and Choiseul. The Americans were unaware at that time that the Australians had foreseen the latter requirement and already had an efficient warning system in place. The outline envisaged concentrating the Expeditionary Force in the Fiji Islands area on about 22 July, spending a week in training and rehearsals, and arriving off Tulagi on 7 August. No objection was raised by either King or Nimitz to that schedule.

While *en route* to Wellington Turner spent another four days in Pearl Harbor conferring with Nimitz and his staff and with Fletcher and Kinkaid. Noyes, the prospective commander of the carriers providing air support for the landings, was not present as he was *en route* from San Diego to the South Pacific with *Wasp*, the battleship *North Carolina* and the remainder of Task Force 18 covering the movement of the Second Marine Regiment. By that time the construction of an airfield on Guadalcanal by the Japanese had been confirmed, so that an assault on Guadalcanal became a firm requirement. Pressure mounted to advance the operation by a week.

While at Pearl Harbor Turner was offered the services of a radio intelligence unit for use in his flagship—a team similar to Biard's unit which had served the Americans so well in the Coral Sea. He refused the offer apparently because radio facilities were already inadequate for his purposes, and the radio receivers necesary for listening to Japanese radio traffic could not have been made available. However, with the judicious allocation of radio duties among the several heavy cruisers, the team could have been accommodated within the Amphibious Force. In view of Turner's behaviour in Washington vis-a-vis the naval intelligence organisation, it is more likely that he saw no useful purpose for the team. Certainly Layton, who was Nimitz's combat intelligence officer and who would have been in involved in making the offer, held that view.[15]

The Chiefs of Staff directive provided for the attachment to South Pacific Command from the South West Pacific Command of the necessary naval reinforcements. As a result Task Force 44, which had been active in the Coral Sea battle and based on Brisbane since May, was transferred to Ghormley and thereafter formed part of the Amphibious Force under the command of Turner. It was then under the command of Rear Admiral Victor Crutchley, who had relieved Crace on 13 June.

Aged 48, Crutchley was eight years younger than Turner and five years younger than most of the captains of the American heavy cruisers which he commanded. He had graduated from the Royal Naval College at Dartmouth in 1910. During the first three and a half years of the First World War he served in the battleship HMS *Centurion*, a unit of the Second Battle Squadron at Jutland, where he impressed his various captains as being a fine seaman with a bright future. In March 1918 he joined—as First Lieutenant—the old cruiser *Brilliant*, then fitting out for an attempt on the night of 22–23 April to block the ports of Zeebrugge and Ostend, which lay at the entrances to the canal to Bruges which the Germans were using as a major submarine base.

The operation to block Zeebrugge with three ships was a success, but that against Ostend failed because the Germans had shifted, that evening, a vital navigational buoy in the entrance. Crutchley was navigating for this second expedition, and, when he could not find the buoy, made his approach to the harbour by dead reckoning. It was unfortunate that while doing so, he sighted the buoy and adjusted his approach to take into account the positional information which the buoy should have provided. *Brilliant* promptly ran hard and fast aground, as did her consort *Thetis*, and both ships had to be blown up where they lay. They had hoped to be hidden by a smokescreen as they approached the port, but an offshore wind blew the smoke away. As a result the two ships were heavily pounded by shore batteries. Crutchley was lucky to survive, and for his efforts was awarded the Distinguished Service Cross.[16]

It was decided to have another go at Ostend as soon as possible, and the old armoured cruiser *Vindictive*—already badly damaged in the successful mission against Zeebrugge—was chosen as the blockship. Crutchley readily volunteered for this second attempt, which took place on the night of 9–10 May, and worked tirelessly as *Vindictive*'s First Lieutenant to prepare the ship for her new task. The actual operation saw him provide an outstanding display of bravery under fire. After his commanding officer had been killed and the second-in-command severely wounded, Crutchley took over and did his utmost to manoeuvre the ship into an effective position. After charges were blown, sinking the cruiser between piers in the harbour, he made a thorough torchlight search for survivors of the crew—the whole time under very heavy enemy fire—before himself joining the motor launch which moved in to take off the ship's company.

When the commander of the rescue vessel collapsed from wounds he had received, Crutchley took command here too (the second-in-command having been killed). The launch was full of wounded and very badly damaged by shellfire, with flooding forward. Still showing 'indomitable energy', he organised the unwounded to commence bailing with buckets and tried shifting weight aft in a losing battle to keep afloat. When picked up by HMS *Warwick* the launch was in a sinking condition, with its forecastle nearly awash. For his actions Crutchley was awarded the Victoria Cross, Britain's highest award for gallantry, the citation for which remarked that: 'The bearing of this very gallant officer and fine seaman throughout these operations off the Belgian coast was altogether admirable and an inspiring example to all thrown into contact with him'.[17]

The mind boggles at the thought of anyone moving round the upper deck under heavy fire, which included that of machine-guns, at night holding a torch! It was, as they say, a very good VC.

After the war Crutchley served in the Royal Yacht *Victoria and Albert* and in cruisers and battleships until, in August 1930 in the rank of commander, he was loaned to the then New Zealand Division of the Royal Navy (now the Royal New Zealand Navy) as executive officer of HMS *Diomede*, the flagship of the Division. During the next three years he was to visit many of the islands of the southern Pacific which were later to become well known as a result of operations in the war. When his captain became ill, Crutchley assumed command of the ship and remained in command when he was promoted to captain.[18]

Crutchley was to show courage of a different kind soon after he took command of the battleship HMS *Warspite* in June 1937. The ship had just completed an extensive modernisation and was due to join the Mediterranean Fleet as flagship. An element of the ship's company became disaffected because of the additional work and the curtailment of weekend leave which was necessary to prepare the ship in time to meet her program in the Mediterranean. The extent of the disaffection was not realised by Crutchley and his senior officers and, when matters came to a head on the day of commissioning, they became the subject of a Board of Enquiry which resulted in three officers, including the executive officer, being removed from *Warspite*.

Disagreeing with the Board's recommendation, Crutchley represented the matter to the Commander-in-Chief Portsmouth but without success. Called upon to submit a confidential report on his Executive Officer, he then recommended him for immediate promotion to Captain—thus effectively bypassing the Commander-in-Chief, the formidable Admiral the Earl of Cork and Orrery, because the report was sent to the Admiralty! The officer concerned later distinguished himself at the Battle of the River Plate and was eventually promoted to rear admiral, thus vindicating Crutchley's high opinion of him.

Crutchley remained in command of *Warspite* for no less than three years, during which time he was Flag Captain to Admiral Sir Dudley Pound and Admiral Sir Andrew Cunningham—neither of whom suffered fools gladly and who went on to serve as First Sea Lords during the war, Cunningham first having achieved fame as Commander-in-Chief Mediterranean. In April

1940 Crutchley took *Warspite* up Narvik Fiord in Norway where the ship played a major part in the sinking of eight German destroyers, her aircraft also sinking a submarine. He then received his first job ashore, although it did not take him out of the firing line because he was the Commodore in charge of Devonport Naval Barracks throughout the heavy bombing attacks which almost razed the Plymouth area during the Blitz.

Having been promoted to rear admiral, Crutchley was lent to the Royal Australian Navy and assumed command of Task Force 44 in Brisbane on 13 June 1942. Ten days later he took the Task Force—which included, for the first time, four heavy cruisers (*Australia*, *Canberra*, *Chicago* and *Salt Lake City*) as well as the light cruiser *Hobart* and three destroyers—on a sweep of the Coral Sea to within 150 miles of the Louisiade Archipelago, to the east of New Guinea. While in the central Coral Sea, a report was received of a possible Japanese supply ship about 150 miles south of Tagula Island. Cruiser aircraft were used to search towards the ship's reported position but nothing was seen.[19]

This was Crutchley's first experience in Australian waters of cooperation between air force reconnaissance aircraft and ships, and he was not impressed. He had received no information of shore-based air searches on which to base his own search effort and no evaluation of the contact. He reported the need for an authority to coordinate aircraft operations over the sea and better liaison with the air force. He had in mind the kind of organisation to which he had become accustomed when in command of *Warspite* in the North Sea and Norwegian waters.

Admiral Leary, MacArthur's naval commander, in a letter dated 5 July acknowledged that more information should have been provided, promised to do better next time and in the same letter warned Crutchley of an offensive operation with a tentative date of 1 August. Crutchley was to pursue the subject of joint operations whenever the opportunity arose, but unfortunately made no immediate impact on Allied Air Forces Headquarters, which paid little attention to air–sea cooperation in its planning for Watchtower.

Although the sweep had been unproductive, it had provided Crutchley with the opportunity to exercise his ships and to develop a tactical doctrine. A further week was spent in exercising off Brisbane in early July, during which surface and anti-aircraft firings and air defence exercises were conducted as well as a number of night encounter exercises which included the firing of starshell.[20] No doubt further training was envisaged, but on 13 July Task Force 44 sailed from Brisbane to take part in Watchtower and transferred to Ghormley's control.

MacArthur's naval component made one other contribution to the Allied forces taking part in Watchtower when the submarines *S-44* and *S-38* were committed to patrols in the New Britain area. They departed from Brisbane on 24 July and 28 July respectively bound for their patrol areas where they

The heavy cruiser Australia, *photographed at Guadalcanal. As a result of a major modernisation completed in 1939,* Australia *had a combined gunnery control position and director in her Director Control Tower, which was a great advantage over the arrangement in* Canberra *where these remained separate.* (A. Zammit)

Canberra, Australia*'s sister ship of the County class, pictured in Sydney Harbour before the war. She had been scheduled for modernisation in 1938, but delays in completing* Australia *and the outbreak of war led to cancellation* (A. Zammit)

were to remain under the command of MacArthur. Both boats had originally formed part of Admiral Hart's Asiatic Fleet, based in Manila Bay at Cavite, and had carried out several patrols since the attack on Pearl Harbor. They were old, badly in need of proper maintenance, small and uncomfortable. Their time in Brisbane after their previous patrols was cut short to meet the requirements of Watchtower, to the extent that the crew of *S-38* had forgone their leave to get their boat ready for their next patrol. The efforts of both crews were to be amply rewarded.[21]

4

The air reconnaissance problem

Ghormley did not assign any of his shore-based or water-based reconnaissance aircraft to the Expeditionary Force. Instead he formed a single task force—Task Force 63—from all such aircraft in the South Pacific Area (SOPAC), under the command of Rear Admiral John S. McCain. McCain was instructed to support the Expeditionary Force and to arrange with the Commander of South West Pacific Area (SWPA) for the coordination of aerial reconnaissance in support of that force.[1] The establishment of Task Force 63 as an entity separate from the Expeditionary Force meant that Fletcher had no shore-based or water-based aircraft under his immediate operational control.

McCain 'celebrated' his 58th birthday on 9 August 1942, the day of the Battle of Savo. Like Fletcher, Noyes and Ghormley, he had graduated from Annapolis in 1906 and had a relatively undistinguished career until qualifying as a pilot in 1936, after which he went on to command the carrier *Ranger* for two years in 1937–39. On promotion to rear admiral in January 1941, he assumed command of the naval reconnaissance aircraft based on the west coast of America. He became commander of all aircraft attached to the South Pacific Area in May 1942, soon after that area was established.

The Chiefs of Staff directive had provided for the transfer of land-based aircraft from the Allied Air Forces (AAF) Command within SWPA to reinforce McCain's command. But this did not happen, apparently to the mutual satisfaction of the two area commanders. As a result, all South West Pacific aircraft acting in support of Watchtower remained under the control of Headquarters AAF, Brisbane, even when airborne.

Within the AAF Command, operations in north-east Australia and in New Guinea were the responsibility of the Royal Australian Air Force's North Eastern Area Command with its headquarters at Area Combined

Headquarters (ACH) in Townsville. That command was, and had been for some considerable time, fully extended in fighting the war in New Guinea with inadequate resources. It was facing the probability of an assault on Milne Bay and an intensification of the threat to Port Moresby from across the Owen Stanley Range. The need to provide aircraft to support another area of operations must have been most unwelcome, particularly as the aircraft to be provided all had a strike and transport capability.

Operational requirements aside, the need for SWPA aircraft to take part in Watchtower could not have come at a more inopportune moment for MacArthur's airmen. Following his appointment in March as Allied Air Commander under MacArthur, Lieutenant General George H. Brett had decided to amalgamate the RAAF and American air elements in Australia. This had resulted in a period of administrative turmoil affecting all levels of the two services involved. As part of Brett's attempt to organise a joint Allied air staff, several staff divisions of RAAF Headquarters in Melbourne were in the process of moving across to Headquarters AAF. The latter headquarters itself moved to Brisbane from Melbourne on 20 July.

General Brett, disliked if not actually distrusted by MacArthur, was about to be relieved by Major General George C. Kenney on 4 August.[2] MacArthur was losing no opportunity to criticise his air forces. At his first meeting with his new air commander he told him that 'they couldn't bomb, their staff work was poor and their commanders knew nothing of leadership'. MacArthur also told Kenney that he considered that his aviators were antagonistic to his headquarters and that he was beginning to doubt their loyalty.[3]

Significantly, with Watchtower just a few days away, Kenney was told that his most urgent task was to gain control of the air over New Guinea. In view of MacArthur's responsibilities for the defence of Australia, this was not unreasonable but MacArthur was taking no chances that undue support would be given to what was, to him, an 'out of area' operation, to the detriment of operations in his own South West Pacific Area.

The boundary between SWPA and SOPAC, set at 159 East, lay no more than 35 miles west of Guadalcanal. Thus Rabaul, which was the source of any land-based air threat and the most likely source of any surface threat to the Expeditionary Force, lay outside Ghormley's area—as did the greater part of the north-western approaches to Guadalcanal. Ghormley had to rely on the cooperation of MacArthur to ensure his security from that direction, and he therefore directed McCain to arrange for the coordination of air searches to cover his north-western approaches.[4]

It was agreed between the two commands that SWPA aircraft would only search as far as 158 East and that SOPAC aircraft could encroach to the west of that meridian to a distance of 120 miles if required. In the event, B-17s from Espiritu Santo in the New Hebrides searching the passage between the Solomon Islands, which became known in the months that followed as the Slot, did not cover beyond 158 East. Furthermore, bad weather prevented B-17s from Noumea searching the area to the west of Tulagi on the crucial days of 7–8 August.[5]

To search the Solomons Sea and the northern Solomon Islands as far south as New Georgia, five Lockheed Hudson aircraft of No. 32 Squadron of the RAAF were moved on 5 August from their base on Horn Island to Fall River, an airstrip at the western end of Milne Bay.[6] Their search area was designated Area B. Three B-17 aircraft, operating from Port Moresby, were to reconnoitre the Bismarck Archipelago area and adjacent seas.[7]

Agreement was also reached for the interdiction of enemy facilities, though 'interdiction' was perhaps too strong a word to describe the scale of attack which SWPA was capable of delivering—all they were capable of was harassment. Only 21 B-17 sorties were flown against the Rabaul airfields in the two attacks made in the period 3–10 August, backed up by four Catalina sorties. Rabaul was not within range of the medium bomber force operating from Port Moresby, so it concentrated on the Japanese ground activities on the New Guinea coast. Aircraft of this force flew a total of 48 sorties against Lae and Salamaua in the same period, thereby serving MacArthur's purposes but adding almost nothing to the effort against Japanese supply lines to the Solomons.

The Captain of *Australia*, H.B. Farncomb, was later scathingly critical of the results achieved by this meagre effort when he wrote that:

> our first day's experience did not inspire us with much confidence in the efficiency of the 'interdiction', for not only did a large force of high level bombers and fighters from Rabaul, 600 miles away, manage to get at us, but a team of dive bombers, quite unexpectedly, did so as well. The second day's attack by 40 T.B.'s [torpedo bombers] and H.L.B.'s [high level bombers] subsequently confirmed our opinions on the value of this inter- diction; and we were glad indeed that we had U.S. naval aircraft co-operating directly with us.[8]

This was a jaundiced view but understandable in the circumstances. An Australian radio broadcast that the airmen were achieving wonders in support of the Guadalcanal operation was greeted with 'a certain amount of sarcastic comment' in *Australia*.[9]

As well as meeting McCain's request for surveillance of the Bismarck Archipelago and Solomons Sea, MacArthur's headquarters also provided for aircraft to be prepared to strike naval targets found within the search areas which threatened operations.[10] If sightings were made by SWPA aircraft, it was not envisaged, however, that ACH Townsville would initiate action to strike them until requested to do so by a SOPAC authority. The postwar analysis of the Savo battle undertaken by the US War College was critical of the directive to 'be prepared to strike'—rather than an unequivocal directive 'to strike'. Even if communications between aircraft, their bases and SOPAC bases had been satisfactory, there would have been delays in initiating strikes by South West Pacific aircraft. As it was, the Japanese force passed southward on 8 August and northward on 9 August with impunity, although they were within 600 miles of Port Moresby for twelve hours on each day and were sighted by Hudson aircraft on both occasions.[11]

As the aircraft were to remain under the command of North Eastern Command, the arrangements—as noted earlier—fell short of the requirement of the US Joint Chiefs of Staff that land-based air support was to be attached to the South Pacific Command.[12] Cooperation between SWPA aircraft and the forces off Guadalcanal did not extend to air–ground communications. Headquarters AAF directed that all signals originated in the North Eastern Area and addressed to SOPAC forces were to be routed via AAF in Brisbane. Only if urgency demanded could the air bases at Townsville and Port Moresby communicate direct with SOPAC air bases and task forces. There was no provision at all for SWPA reconnaissance aircraft to communicate direct with ships and aircraft of the Expeditionary Force. This was yet another seed for disaster.

AAF instructions to Townsville included an order that special precautions were necessary to preserve secrecy. The 'need to know' rule for information to be restricted to those ooperations and communications officers who required it for the proper execution of their duties was emphasised in a personal signal from General Brett.[13] As a result, neither the reconnaissance aircraft nor the base from which they operated was told of the reason for the searches being flown. Aircrew believed that they were flying in defence of New Guinea.[14]

Brett's instruction showed a total lack of understanding of the problem which any aircrew or intelligence staff faced when deciding what was actually urgent. Nothing he did or did not do to earn the displeasure of MacArthur could have justified that displeasure more than that message to North Eastern Command. How were aircrew and operations and communications personnel to determine the urgency of a report when they were unaware of its relevance to operations then in progress? In the event, sightings were made by RAAF aircraft which, in the context of the previous experience of those concerned, were of a routine nature but which, in the context of the Guadalcanal operations, were really of crucial importance.

Of the five Hudson crews deployed on 5 August from Horn Island (located off the northern tip of the Australian mainland) to Fall River, three were fresh out of the operational training pipeline. The detachment leader was Flight Lieutenant Lloyd Milne, an officer of very considerable experience to whom the sight of Japanese ships in waters adjacent to New Guinea and the Solomons was not new. He had been a member of the RAAF's No. 24 Squadron in Rabaul which was decimated when the Japanese took the town in January 1942. The remaining crews of the detachment were loaned from No. 6 Squadron, then in the process of relieving No. 32 Squadron.

Typical of those crews was that of Sergeant William Stutt. With him were three other sergeants: Wilbur Courtis (navigator), Eric Geddes (radio operator) and John Bell (gunner). All four had just completed their operational training, during which they had flown together as a crew for just over 30 hours. Late in July they were loaned to No. 32 Squadron, then based at Horn Island. Their first operation was a photographic mission from Port Moresby over nearby Yule Island on 4 August.

The next day they moved to Fall River to carry out a reconnaissance of Buka Island, off Bougainville. Their briefing for that mission was typical of many subsequent operations. The navigator remembers being handed maps and a series of coordinates as they stepped from their plane on arrival at Fall River and told to sweep the area between Milne Bay and Buka Island. To this day Courtis wonders if there could not have been better ways to brief a raw crew, just out of training and about to make their first flight into enemy-held territory.[15]

That first operational flight was also an introduction to things to come, for it was curtailed by bad weather over the Solomons—wild, thick, black, storm clouds. On return to base they were met by an American meteorological officer who asked them about the weather they had encountered. On being told, he said that a storm had passed over Cairns some three days previously and that he had expected that it would finish up near the Solomons. This encounter brought home to Courtis the lack of weather information that would be available to him in future flights, and focused his mind on the need for accuracy in making his half-hourly in-flight record of weather conditions. The probability of having to fly in cloud over Bougainville was not made any more enticing by the incomplete and inaccurate maps of the area, which warned that islands could lie miles from their charted position and that the height of mountains could be out by thousands of feet.

Stutt's crew had left Port Moresby without knowing the purpose of their deployment to Fall River or that their stay there was to be an extended one, so that they had with them only the clothes in which they stood. As they were wearing shorts and short-sleeved shirts, they had no protection at all against the malaria-carrying anopheles mosquito which was eventually to cause more casualties than the Japanese. Even their commanding officer, Wing Commander Deryck Kingwell, who remained at Horn Island, had not been told of the impending operations in the southern Solomons, so that two days later he was to ask Townsville about the expected duration of their deployment.[16]

Fall River was found to be a single strip of Marston steel matting, 5000 feet long by 80 feet wide; which floated on mud that oozed and splashed its way up through the matting every time an aircraft touched down. The strip was usually surrounded by a sea of mud, vines and coconut trees. All aircraft had to be manhandled as there were no tractors. Fuel was provided from drums which also had to be moved by manpower, and aircraft were refuelled with a hand pump. Water in the fuel was always a problem. The cloud base was seldom more than one thousand feet and it rained every night. There were no homing aids and no radar until mid-August, early warning of incoming raids being provided by coastwatchers especially placed for that purpose on the surrounding islands.[17] Initially, accommodation was six to a tent and of such a standard that at least one Hudson crew preferred to sleep in their aircraft. Later, native huts were built as dormitories.

The site had been chosen for an airfield just eight weeks earlier, on 11 June, and codenamed Fall River. US Army engineers from the 96th Regiment commenced clearing the selected area of coconut palms on 29 June. Headquarters AAF was in a hurry and ordered the RAAF's No. 76 Squadron with P-40 Kittyhawks to move to Fall River by 20 July. Fortunately, the Senior Air Staff Officer to the Air Officer Commanding North Eastern Area, Group Captain Bill Garing, decided to see for himself what progress had been made. Garing flew a Tiger Moth from Port Moresby to Fall River, landing at dusk on 19 July. His was the first aircraft to use the strip, of which only 300 feet had been matted. Working all night the engineers increased this to 500 feet, enabling him to take off next morning for his return to Port Moresby.[18]

As a result of the visit, ACH Townsville was told that the airfield could not be ready for at least another five days.[19] In the event, 76 Squadron's Kittyhawks arrived on 25 July, landing on a strip which by then had been surfaced with matting for 5000 feet, as planned. A second Kittyhawk squadron (No. 75 Squadron, RAAF) was deployed there five days later, followed by the five Hudsons on 5 August.[20]

The commanding officers of the two fighter squadrons shared the load of running the airfield, since there was no centralised base staff. Intelligence matters were handled by specialist air intelligence officers of both units, none of whom were accustomed to maritime reporting. Their reports of enemy shipping—including warship sightings—were addressed to Townsville in a format known as Form White, which had been introduced into RAAF Command as recently as 4 August and which was one of a family of forms developed by RAF Coastal Command for the exchange of intelligence.[21]

Point-to-point communications with Port Moresby and Townsville were provided by an RAAF signals unit but, early in August, the preferred route for signal traffic was via the Army signals network to Port Moresby and thence to Townsville. There being no base maintenance staff, any maintenance and repairs were carried out by the fighter squadrons' personnel. The Hudson detachment took with them only one maintainer, an armourer, who was accidentally killed on 16 August.[22] Such then was the base environment in which the Hudsons operated and from which Stutt and his crew flew on 21 of the 27 days that they remained there. It was hardly conducive to providing the reconnaissance effort on which so much would depend.

Air reconnaissance in the South Pacific Area was controlled from McCain's flagship, the seaplane tender USS *Curtiss* anchored in Segond Channel south of Espiritu Santo. To ensure that a Japanese carrier force could not approach the Guadalcanal area unseen from the direction of Truk or the Marshall Islands, McCain deployed the seaplane tender USS *McFarland* to Ndeni on Santa Cruz Island on 5 August. The seaplane tender USS *Mackinac* was also sent to Maramasike Estuary to the south-east of Malaita, arriving on 7 August. With *Curtiss*, these ships between them operated up to 20 PBY Catalina amphibious aircraft; these were used to patrol the Solomons, in an arc between north-west and north-east of Tulagi as far as the equator.[23]

B-17 aircraft of the 11th Bombardment Group of the US Army Air Corps, based on Espiritu Santo and Noumea, were given the task of watching the north-western and western approaches to Tulagi. Those from Espiritu Santo were to search through the Solomons as far as New Georgia, some 200 miles from Tulagi, while those from Noumea covered to the west of the southern Solomons.[24]

The Catalinas' searches were in an area which was relatively uncluttered by islands and were timed so that aircraft reached the outer limit of their sectors at sunset. They then employed radar on their return legs to provide warning of any attempt by a carrier force to take advantage of darkness to reach a position from which to launch attacks against the Allied forces off Guadalcanal.[25]

Such a tactic was not available to aircraft searching the island-dotted north-western approaches. Because of the limitations of their radar,[26] they could only search by day. As they were limited to searching to a depth of about 200 miles from Tulagi, they were ineffective against an enemy force coming from the north-west and making use of darkness for their approach to the Allied forces off Guadalcanal and Tulagi. This situation was exacerbated by the timing of the B-17 searches. On D-Day, 7 August, for example, aircraft were instructed to be abreast Tulagi by sunrise on their outward legs. They therefore reached their furthest position out by 0915. No further search of the immediate north-western approaches was conducted by McCain's aircraft during the day. A ten-knot steamer at the edge of the B-17 search at 1000 that morning could have reached Tulagi by dawn the next day.

The three carriers of the Air Support Force carried, between them, a total of 40 torpedo bomber/reconnaissance aircraft. These represented a significant organic reconnaissance capability available to the Expeditionary Force for searching to a depth in excess of 350 miles. One of the tasks

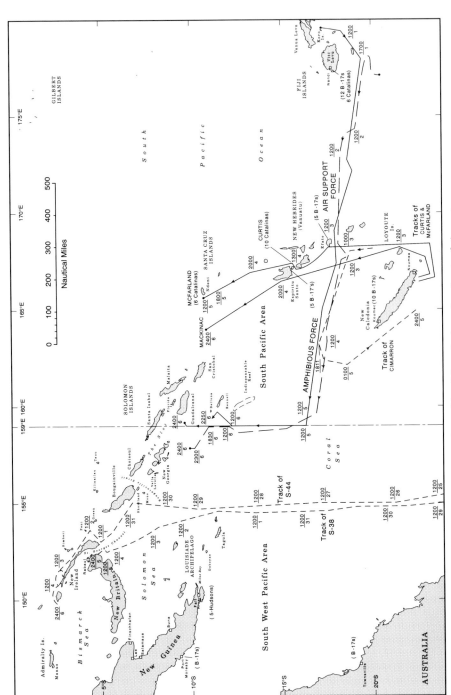

Movements of Allied naval forces and the positioning of land-based aircraft prior to 6 August

assigned to the Air Support Force was to 'make air searches as seem advisable or as ordered'.[27] It had not been assigned a specific task within a total Allied reconnaissance effort. Turner was assured by Fletcher, in the presence of McCain, that if he were informed by McCain that his aircraft had not been able to complete all the scheduled searches then he, Fletcher, would organise afternoon searches by carrier-borne aircraft to a depth of 200 miles. It was therefore up to McCain to inform Fletcher of any shortfall in his daily searches as he became aware of them. This was a practical proposition only in the case of the B-17s' searches, for the Catalina patrols were all scheduled to be completed after dark, but no doubt Turner was satisfied, at least initially, as his main concern was the security of his north-western approaches.[28]

Searches by SOPAC aircraft, or those planned as a stopgap by Fletcher, were therefore inherently inadequate to protect the assault area off Tulagi–Guadalcanal against high-speed or even moderate-speed penetration at night by a surface striking force. Only an effective search by SWPA aircraft operating from Fall River could ensure such protection.

41

5

A feeling of superiority

As the time for action approached, the Allies were aware of Japanese plans to consolidate their hold on the Bismarck Archipelago–Solomon Islands area and of their intention to reinforce their forces in the area. They had noted a movement of aircraft from the Netherlands East Indies and Marshall Islands to New Britain and estimated that there were about 60 fighters, 60 bombers and 30 reconnaissance aircraft available to the Japanese in the area. In addition to the airfields on New Britain, the Allies believed that airfields had been established on Buka Island, immediately to the north of Bougainville Island, and at Kieta, about halfway down the east coast of that island. There was uncertainty about the state of the airfield on Guadalcanal.

Included in the total number of Japanese aircraft available were approximately eight water-based reconnaissance aircraft and a similar number of float-fitted Zero fighters which were operating out of Tulagi. As a result Ghormley and MacArthur believed that surprise was improbable.[1]

In his tentative operation plan dated 22 July, Turner estimated that at that time there were four heavy cruisers, three light cruisers, twelve destroyers and eight submarines that could intervene in the Guadalcanal area operation.[2] The threat had increased to eleven cruisers, thirteen destroyers and fifteen submarines when the final operation order was promulgated a week or so later.[3] The presence of Cruiser Division Six (CRUDIV 6) of four heavy cruisers, led by Rear Admiral Goto in *Aoba*, had been confirmed as long ago as 10 July. It was also known that the heavy cruiser *Chokai* was in the Bismarck Archipelago as the Eighth Fleet commander's flagship and that he had moved his flag ashore in Rabaul.

Of more concern to Turner and Crutchley, particularly the latter as the Screening Force Commander, was the estimate that there were about fifteen submarines in the Bismarck Archipelago–Solomons area. There had also

42

been reports of small submarines and a mother ship in the Tulagi–Guadalcanal area on 25 and 27 July, and of a possible increase in midget submarine activity in the vicinity of Rabaul.

The Americans did not expect to receive timely warning of Japanese movements from their interception and decoding of enemy signal traffic because there was, at that time, a delay of about a week between interception and recovery of information from any particular message. In so far as signal intelligence was concerned, reliance had to be placed on traffic analysis to detect the movement of naval reinforcements towards Guadalcanal. This was an uncertain method, since such intelligence could be denied to the Allies if those units being moved maintained radio silence—as had happened during the movement of the Japanese carrier force towards Pearl Harbor.

The overall expectations of enemy activity against the Expeditionary Force was that air attacks were likely, and that the level of the submarine threat was high. It was not expected that attacks by an enemy surface force would be made by day, in view of the presence of the carrier support group. No opinion was expressed as to the likelihood of an attack on the assault area by night, but the screening forces were disposed so that an enemy surface force should not be able to approach the transport anchorages without being intercepted.

In the years before Pearl Harbor, information on the capability of the Japanese to fight at night had been, to all intents and purposes, non-existent. In February 1935 Captain J.G.P. Vivian, the British Naval Attaché in Tokyo, on instructions from the Director of Naval Intelligence, had made a long and comprehensive report on the Japanese Navy in which he reported that any attempt to estimate their efficiency was hampered by a complete ignorance of the number and types of weapon-training exercises carried out by the fleet, and by the refusal of senior officers to discuss tactics. He noted that unless sea conditions were such that the ships would suffer structural damage, surface, sub-surface and aircraft exercises were never cancelled on account of bad weather. This said a great deal for the realism of their training.[4]

Vivian also mentioned that great stress was laid on the importance of submarines and aircraft, but he was unaware that Japanese tactical doctrine was based on the assumption that they would be numerically inferior to any enemy and that a night encounter was therefore preferable. To that end they concentrated on developing the ability to fight at night at longer ranges than other navies thought were possible. They developed optical equipment, notably binoculars with 20 cm lenses, and selected personnel to use them. These men, as Petty Officers, then became 'Masters of Lookout'.[5] They trained day and night and developed the ability to accurately estimate range. No comparable specialist group existed in the British or American navies.

To enable guns to open fire outside the range at which starshell could provide enough illumination for purposes of range-taking and target identification, believed to be 18 000 yards, cooperation between surface forces and the aircraft carried in battleships and heavy cruisers was developed to the extent that aircraft could be catapulted at night to drop flares in order to illuminate the target. These aircraft had an endurance of nine hours or more, allowing them to remain aloft for the remainder of the night and land after dawn. In the event that radio silence was in force, they were provided with a rendezvous before launch. At that time both the Americans and British virtually ceased cruiser aircraft operations at dusk.

As their ability to sight an enemy at night exceeded the range of their 21-inch torpedo, the Japanese set about developing a long-range torpedo. In this they were remarkably successful, so that by the beginning of the war the majority of their cruisers and destroyers were equipped with a 24-inch torpedo having a maximum range of more than 21 miles at 36 knots, and twelve miles at 49 knots. In comparison, the 21-inch torpedoes carried by *Canberra* at Savo had a range of only five miles at 40 knots and seven miles at 35 knots.[6] The Americans were at an even greater disadvantage vis-a-vis the Japanese, in that their heavy cruisers did not carry torpedoes and those carried in the destroyers were limited to about two miles at 48 knots and four-and-a-half miles at 32 knots.[7]

Japanese tactical doctrine, based on the above developments, called for torpedoes to be fired at maximum visibility range and even—if the opportunity occurred—on a radio direction finder's bearing. Gunfire was to be used only as the torpedoes were about to reach the target, the aim being to surprise the enemy. This was a sophisticated doctrine and a deadly one, so far as the Allies were concerned, because they were in total ignorance of it. Until radar was put to proper use, there was no answer to it.

Concealment of their ability to fight at night and their intention to do so whenever possible was a major success for the Japanese, and was only achieved by adherence to a strict security policy. The British, even at the outbreak of the war, apparently had no inkling of it. Vivian's successor in Tokyo, Captain R.B. Rawlings, included a comment in his annual report for 1936 that:

> No information whatever regarding the weapon training of the Navy can be obtained. No mention of this subject, beyond vague references to full calibre firings, is ever made in the press and no Japanese naval officer would dream of referring to it, even indirectly.[8]

With the notable exception of the details of the Yamato class battleships, the attachés in Tokyo managed to keep abreast of the building, refitting and modernisation program until 1939. Naval Intelligence generally continued to obtain some details of Japanese ships from the occasional patrol in Japanese waters by submarines, through photography from merchant ships plying their trade in Japanese waters and, in Chinese waters, by observation of Japanese operations. But virtually no intelligence was obtained about

Japanese tactical thought, nor indeed of anything else the Japanese particularly wanted to keep secret—such as the size and armament of the Yamato class battleships, the performance of the advanced Zero fighter and the performance and fitting of the 24-inch fast long-range torpedo.

In so far as British efforts were involved, intelligence from within Japan virtually dried up in 1939. The naval attachés of like-minded countries such as Britain and the United States pooled their information, but Japanese treatment of attachés from all countries was even-handed. Even the German attaché suffered the same restrictions as his colleagues, at least until 1941. Japanese security was greatly assisted by the imposition of censorship on the outbreak of hostilities in China in the middle of 1937 and by the cessation of courtesy visits by foreign warships in the previous year. Internal movement of foreigners within Japan was also controlled.

As war in Europe became imminent the British naval intelligence effort was concentrated on Germany and Italy, though a small Japan section was maintained in London. To make up in part for the loss of coverage, the activities of the Far East Combined Bureau (FECB)—first in Hong Kong and later in Singapore—were increased. When the head of the Far East Desk in ONI, Captain McCollum, visited London in August 1941, he found that, while the organisation for making use of intelligence was more highly developed there, in general the Americans were better off than the British so far as information on Japanese naval aspects was concerned.[9] As a result of what they saw in London, the Americans were to reorganise and strengthen Nimitz's intelligence staff.

Biard, in his personal account of his experiences with Fletcher in the Coral Sea, wrote of the period that he was in Tokyo as an Assistant Naval Attaché. He recalled that the American Embassy received many trustworthy reports that Japanese surface forces were stressing their training in night fighting. This information does not appear to have been promulgated, as Fletcher does not seem to have been aware of it. He made no move to counter the threat of a Japanese surface attack after dusk on 7 May when he was aware that the two forces were not far apart. Furthermore, neither Nimitz or King criticised him for what they surely would have regarded as a dangerous oversight had they had an inkling of the Japanese capability. So far as King was concerned, the reverse was actually true, for he was of the opinion that Fletcher should have sought a night action.

The evidence of a total lack of knowledge of Japanese capability is strengthened by various reports of the Battle of the Java Sea in March 1942, when the loss of the two Dutch cruisers (*Java* and *De Ruyter*) was put down to either mines or submarine torpedoes. These ships had, in fact, been torpedoed by the heavy cruisers *Haguro* and *Nachi* at a range of seven miles, well beyond the maximum torpedo range then thought possible. The weekly report published by the Admiralty's Naval Intelligence Directorate on 27 March 1942 went so far as to state that, though the ships were probably sunk by torpedoes, they could not have been fired from the Japanese cruisers.

Yet the Americans ought not to have been surprised by the performance of the 24-inch torpedo. In 1938 or 1939 the Office of Naval Intelligence had received, from what they considered to be an impeccable source, a report that the Japanese had developed a 24-inch torpedo with a range of five miles at a speed of 45 knots, and that it carried a warhead of some 1200 pounds (544 kilograms). This information understated the true performance of the new weapon but still clearly indicated that it was a considerable advance on the American 21-inch torpedo.

The American Naval Intelligence Manual stipulated that the evaluation of technical matter was entirely the function of technical bureaux, not ONI. The report was therefore sent to the Bureau of Ordnance for evaluation. Here the yardstick for judging the credibility of such information seems to have been the capability of American technology to develop a similar item. In other words: if it could not be done in America, it could not be done.[10]

On this occasion the Bureau of Ordnance rejected the practicability of such a torpedo for at least two reasons:

- no useful purpose would be served by increasing the explosive power of the warhead from the then-common 800 pounds (363 kilograms) to 1200 pounds, as its length would entail the centre of burst being further aft so that it would not have an effect materially different from current warheads.
- no torpedo could travel at such a speed over that range.

So far as the second objection was concerned, if the Japanese torpedoes had been powered by a combination of alcohol and steam (like American ones) the Bureau might well have been correct. But it apparently overlooked the possibility that the Japanese might have improved on developmental work with enriched air torpedoes carried out by the British in the 1920s. *Canberra* had been equipped with such torpedoes on her completion in 1928, but these were discarded when it was established that the risk of handling and storing the highly inflammable enriched air in a ship was too great. Known as the Mark VII, the British 21-inch torpedoes were credited with a range of eight miles at 33 knots.[11] In 1924, the Royal Navy had also developed the 24.5-inch Mark 1 enriched air torpedo which carried a 742 pound (337 kilogram) warhead and had a range of seven-and-a-half miles at 35 knots (ten miles at 30 knots). These were installed in the battleships *Rodney* and *Nelson*, where they were fitted for firing from submerged tubes; in 1941 *Rodney* fired twelve at the German battleship *Bismarck*, without success.[12]

The failure of the Allies to accept the possibility that the Japanese would develop a long-range torpedo was not unique, as a similar instance involved the assessment of the Zero fighter. After one of these aircraft crashed in

China, it was examined and the type was assessed as having a range of 1500 miles. Notwithstanding that it was known that the aircraft had been escorting bombers on missions which involved flying 1500 miles, the Bureau of Aeronautics said that such a range was impossible. The report was withdrawn.[13]

The naval intelligence community would have been wise to have taken to heart a warning sounded by Vivian in 1935. Then he had said that while he had no knowledge of the weapon efficiency of Japan's fleet, and while it was true that he had to strain his imagination to the utmost to believe that the Japanese could spring a technical surprise of any importance, he nevertheless thought that the possibility that they could do so should not be overlooked.

The British Admiralty not only had no knowledge of the long-range torpedo, but they were completely ignorant of the development of a night-fighting capability which far exceeded the Royal Navy's even before 1939. In February 1942 the opinion of Admiral Sir Geoffrey Layton, then the British Commander-in-Chief Eastern Fleet, was published, to the effect that:

> evidence is accumulating which seems to confirm the pre-war impression that Japanese ships do not take kindly to night fighting. They do not usually succeed in seeing before being seen and are very liable to confusion, rash use of search lights and opening fire on their own side. It seems therefore that we should exploit this to the utmost and our policy should be to seek night actions by every means.[14]

Nothing would have suited the Japanese better!

This information seems to have been based on one night action off Endau in Malaya in which HMAS *Vampire* and HMS *Thanet*, two small destroyers, engaged one Japanese light cruiser and four destroyers. *Thanet* was sunk and, as *Vampire* retired behind her own smokescreen, she observed the Japanese shooting at each other. One swallow does not make a summer, and on this occasion the Japanese seem to have behaved with an unusual lack of discipline. The message was dangerously misleading but it was not until after the Battle of Savo that the Admiralty cancelled the advice which it contained.

What is surprising is that Layton should have made the observation attributed to him. As Commander-in-Chief China for the year or so before the attack on Pearl Harbor, he was one of a small group of senior RN officers who held a high opinion of Japanese fighting qualities. According to his secretary (Captain Doig) writing in 1979, he expected them to fight with fanatical determination and to carefully laid plans. He thought that their ships would be good and likely to be formidable and trained for any operations that they had in mind.[15]

Another of similar mind was Layton's predecessor on the China Station, Admiral Sir Frederick Dreyer, who in 1935 had made the last official visit to Japan before the war by a senior British officer. In all, he visited Japan four times in his three years in the East, and had witnessed flying operations and target practice. In 1939 he wrote to the Admiralty urging that the Japanese should not be taken lightly and that 'we must be ready for sudden and simultaneous blows'.[16]

There seem to have been no such cautions from senior American officers. These, by and large, had a feeling of technical as well as mental superiority, though they had enjoyed less of an opportunity to observe the Japanese at sea. A significant number despised the Japanese, and felt confident of the outcome—in any circumstances—of any battle with them.[17]

The difference in awareness of Japanese capabilities, such as it was, was probably partly due to the size of the respective naval forces in the Far East. Whereas in 1939 the British kept four heavy cruisers, an aircraft carrier, fifteen destroyers and escort vessels and fifteen submarines east of Singapore, the American Asiatic Fleet was made up of a heavy cruiser, a light cruiser, a squadron of destroyers and about six submarines.[18] The British also had the benefit of a residual master–pupil relationship between the RN and the Imperial Japanese Navy, stemming from their association as a result of the naval treaty between their two countries which had lapsed in 1921, only half a naval career previously.

6
The communications setting

The problems which Americans and Australians would experience during Watchtower as a result of inadequate intelligence were attributable, in the main, to a successful Japanese national security policy. But the Allies' difficulties with communications were very much of their own making. It was later said of the various communications plans for Watchtower that the problem lay with trying to cope with a complicated situation with inadequate facilities.[1] A member of the Board of Admiralty in London put it another way when he wrote, after examining a report on the Battle of Savo, that the possible cause for the disaster was the use of a number of task forces, all of which were independent and had communications with known inefficiencies.[2] While other factors—the need for haste, the lack of planning cohesion and the lack of experience—undoubtedly also played a part, the fundamental problem of communications deserves examination.

Reliable communications were—and indeed still are—a fundamental requirement for the success of any operation. If these fail, it is axiomatic that the conduct of that operation will become difficult, if not impossible. As Rear Admiral Spruance, Chief of Staff to Nimitz, put it: 'The history of war furnishes many examples of the disastrous results which may result from such failures [of communications]'.[3]

Both the British and the Americans had developed, over many years, networks of long-range communications that were based on the establishment of major naval radio stations in each naval command area. In the southern Pacific, the transmitter requirements of MacArthur's naval forces were met by Belconnen naval radio station situated just outside Canberra. Nimitz's forces relied on a similar station at Pearl Harbor.

Because of the distances involved, the frequencies used in those networks were in the medium and high frequency bands. Although the reception of messages transmitted in the medium band was limited to a distance of about 500 miles from the transmitting station, those transmitted on high frequency could be heard worldwide because they bounced off the iono-sphere, the height at which this reflection occurred varying in direct proportion to the frequency and according to the time of day and season of the year. Thus reception of a particular frequency in that band, outside the limited range of the ground wave, was confined to annular areas ringing the transmitter in which the reflected waves returned to earth. The distance between successive rings was known as the skip distance.

Each naval radio station transmitted on a number of frequencies, to ensure reception throughout its area. Knowing their position and taking into account the other variables of time and date, ships were able to choose the best frequency on which to listen to a particular station. They were not obliged to acknowledge receipt of any message unless specifically instructed to do so, so that ships could receive instructions and information without breaking radio silence.

To enable ships to pass messages to the shore from anywhere in their area, the area radio stations maintained watch on a number of other frequencies so that ships were able to choose the most suitable frequency for passing their messages ashore. Thus it was that long-range naval communications avoided the pitfalls of 'skip distance' and achieved a very high degree of reliability.

High and medium frequencies were also used for direct communications between headquarters and ships and aircraft. Because the area in which they would be used was limited, the number of frequencies allocated for inter-task force and intra-task force use was small, and reliability of communications depended very much on the frequencies chosen. A feature of Watchtower's communications was the difficulty experienced by Ghormley, based in Noumea, in receiving messages transmitted to his headquarters from task force commanders in the Guadalcanal area, although they—using the same frequency—were usually in communication with each other. However, inter-task force communications were, on the whole, less reliable than area broadcast or ship–shore communications.

The various communication plans for Watchtower followed the well-established naval practice of setting up radio nets within each task force to enable the task force commanders to exercise command within their forces. The task force commanders were also linked by a common frequency. Other information nets were set up to allow intelligence to be passed quickly between bases, ships and command authorities. These frequencies were common to both command areas.

Within MacArthur's area, a number of medium and high frequencies were allocated for use by reconnaissance aircraft and it was usual for aircraft to be briefed to use a particular frequency with another as an alternative. These frequencies, which were contained in a discrete AAF communication plan, were not common with those used by McCain's aircraft and were unknown to ships who had not worked with Task Force 44—that is, with the Australian cruisers and *Chicago*.[4]

To provide for the rapid dissemination of information related to Watch-tower operations and intelligence, Ghormley made provision in his communication plan for a net for communications between those bases in both areas which could launch long-range reconnaisance sorties and heavy bomber strikes. In the South Pacific Area these bases included Espiritu Santo, Efate and Noumea, and in the South West Pacific Area, Townsville and Port Moresby.[5]

Ghormley envisaged that this net would be used in a manner similar to the inter-force or Task Force Common nets used within the naval task forces. However, AAF instructed RAAF bases to use it only for urgent traffic, thus effectively inhibiting its use by Townsville and Port Moresby. RAAF bases were told to use the normal administrative channels so that all messages were to be passed back to AAF Headquarters in Brisbane, which would then pass them on to other authorities.[6]

Sighting reports which originated in SWPA and were not recognised as being of an urgent nature could only reach naval surface units under Ghormley's command via the fleet broadcast schedules. These were main-tained by the naval radio station in Canberra for Australian ships, and by the Pearl Harbor naval radio station for American ships.

Reconnaissance of the Solomons and the Bismarck Archipelago prior to Watchtower had revealed a certain amount of inter-island shipping, and the sighting of Japanese warships had not been uncommon. Although standard operating instructions for reconnaissance aircraft in SWPA stipulated that any aircraft making contact at sea was to report and remain in the vicinity of the contact until recalled or forced to retire,[7] these instructions had been ignored in the past. This was partly because emphasis was placed on building up a picture of Japanese activity throughout the area, but also partly because no strike aircraft were usually available to follow up any contact. All this had changed with the advent of Watchtower, though the aircrew and intel-ligence staff at Fall River were unaware of it.

The communications plans had one major and, as it turned out, fatal flaw. The only way that a report of the sighting of an enemy ship from an aircraft operating in SWPA could reach the Air Support Force or the Amphibious Force was via Port Moresby or Townsville, or by one of the two major naval radio stations. There was no provision for the ships to receive the message direct from the aircraft.

For short-range tactical traffic within naval forces, the Americans had adopted a VHF voice radio equipment known as TBS. This set was not fitted in the Australian ships or in *Chicago*. Thus, within Crutchley's screening group, *Vincennes*, *Quincy* and *Astoria* were manoeuvred and exchanged tactical information by TBS, but *Australia*, *Canberra* and

51

Chicago used directional flashing lights. The latter method was fast and did not suffer from the problems caused by the constant and often ill-disciplined use of TBS. On the other hand, it required a high degree of skill and practice, particularly at night when the power of the lights was very much reduced and their directionability greatly increased. American ships joining Task Force 44 before its deployment to the Solomons initially found difficulty with the system, so that some time was required to bring them up to a satisfactory standard.

The Australian-based Task Force 44 had recently changed from using British signal books to the use of the American books. As there were many significant differences between the two systems, the American and Australian ships exchanged signalmen to facilitate the changeover. As a result *Canberra* at Savo carried three American signalmen. These days, when Australian ships frequently operate with Americans using NATO-based publications, it is difficult to appreciate the limitations that being comparative strangers to each other's methods placed on ships off Guadalcanal. But the problems were real nonetheless, and were to have an important bearing on Crutchley's use of the heavy cruisers.

Measured against the size of the land, sea and air forces being provided by the Americans, the Australian contribution to Watchtower would have been almost insignificant if it had not been for the service provided by the Australian coastwatching organisation in the Solomon Islands. Halsey was later to remark of that organisation that 'The intelligence signalled from Bougainville by Read and Mason [two individual coastwatchers] had saved Guadalcanal and Guadalcanal had saved the South Pacific'.[8] Halsey was not noted for moderation in expressing his views—he was, after all, known as 'Bull' Halsey—but there are very few who would argue with his opinion regarding the important part played by the coastwatchers in the capture and successful holding of Guadalcanal. Throughout the Solomons campaign, the early warning of the approach of enemy aircraft and of shipping movements down the Slot enabled the Americans to make the best use of their slender resources by positioning themselves to counter those moves.

The coastwatching organisation was by no means new; it had been active in the Bismarck Archipelago, the Solomons and adjacent islands for many years. Nonetheless, when planning for Watchtower got under way, the existence of such a service in the future area of operations came as news to many American commanders. Among those pleasantly surprised was Vandegrift, whose 1st Marine Division was to play such a key part in the coming operation. Turner was also unaware of it. The outline plan for Watchtower which he presented to Nimitz and King in San Francisco included proposals for the establishment of posts in the Solomons to provide early warning of any enemy approach to Tulagi.

A scheme to employ residents and officials living in the sparsely populated north of Australia had been conceived as far back as 1919, when the District Naval Officer in Western Australia suggested enlisting selected civilians living on the coast into a voluntary organisation to watch for unusual or hostile activities in time of war. When the suggestion reached Navy Office in Melbourne it was approved and enlarged to include Papua, New Guinea and the Solomon Islands.[9]

The organisation received the enthusiastic support of various government bodies throughout the mainland and the islands, and as a result it prospered. Its members came from many walks of life and included policemen, postmasters, missionaries, airline pilots and, in the islands, planters and district officers—all of whom were selected, unpaid volunteers. They were trained in the use of a simple code for use in reporting. When war broke out in September 1939, 800 coastwatchers had been trained and were in position, controlled by representatives of the Director of Naval Intelligence in Brisbane, Port Moresby, Darwin and Fremantle.[10]

The biggest problem encountered was that of communications, particularly in the far north of the mainland and in the islands where there was no alternative to radio. Some used their own sets and several organisations allowed their networks to be used, but few radios were crystal controlled so that communications were not reliable.

In the first three months of the war, 40 reports of unidentified ships were received from coastwatchers in Papua, New Guinea and the Solomons and in almost every case communication delays prevented effective follow-up action. As a result, in December 1939, the Director of Naval Intelligence proposed the establishment of a discrete radio frequency for use by all coastwatchers in Papua, New Guinea, Torres Strait and the Solomons. He also proposed that the navy meet any costs involved in modifying existing radios, and that those coastwatchers without suitable sets be provided with a robust crystal-controlled tele-radio then under development.[11] Within a month the proposal had been approved at an initial cost of £6600 and an annual cost for maintenance of £2250. Seldom had public money been better spent.[12]

By early August 1942 coastwatchers were in position in the north and in the south of Bougainville, in the south of New Georgia, in the south of Santa Isabel, on San Cristobal and in the western, central and eastern parts of Guadalcanal and Malaita. They included a district commissioner on Malaita, a district officer, an ex-Merchant Marine purser/business executive and a plantation manager on Guadalcanal, district officers on San Cristobal and on New Georgia, and an assistant district officer and a plantation manager on Bougainville. To provide them with some protective status in the event of capture they were all given a military rank.

Backing up the individual coastwatchers was a communications organisation based on Malaita, where a controlling station was established to pass on their messages to Vila in the New Hebrides, and then on to the naval radio stations in Canberra and Pearl Harbor for transmission to the

South Pacific. Alternative links were provided with Port Moresby, Townsville and Vanikoro, the latter being used as a relay station in the event that
the link between Malaita and Vila was unsatisfactory.[13] Coastwatchers in the
Ellice, Gilbert, Phoenix and Tonga Islands each had their controlling stations, which in turn reported to Suva, Efate and Samoa; these, in their turn,
passed on messages to Auckland for retransmission on the Canberra and
Pearl Harbor broadcasts.[14]

7

New urgency to the timetable

When the US Chiefs of Staff first directed that Watchtower should be launched on 1 August, the date was of no particular significance. What King and, later, the Chiefs of Staff wanted was to commence a counterattack before the Japanese could resume their offensive in the southern Pacific. With the arrival of the 1st Marine Division in the area and the destruction of the Japanese carrier striking force at Midway they had the means to do so.

The Marines, however, were far from ready for action. The Division had never operated as a complete formation and its commander, Vandegrift, had not met many of his senior officers. Having assumed command of the Division in North Carolina in late March, he had been required almost immediately to detach one of his three regiments for garrison duties in Samoa—a reduction not immediately made good.[1]

On 1 May the Division had been ordered to move to Wellington and was still in the process of doing so on 1 July. Vandegrift had been assured that he would have six months in New Zealand to bring his troops to a satisfactory state for operations. There was, therefore, no thought of imminent combat and, as a result, all store ships were commercially rather than combat loaded to save shipping space. Before the Division could be deployed, all stores and equipment would have to be unloaded, sorted and then reloaded.

One regiment departed from Norfolk, Virginia, in the middle of May. Preceded across the Pacific by its depot stores, the unit was routed through the Panama Canal and arrived in Wellington on 14 June. A second regiment was moved by train to the US west coast and thence by sea to Wellington, but was not due there until 11 July. The third regiment, replacing that sent earlier to Samoa, would soon embark in San Diego but could not reach the

South Pacific area by 1 August. Sundry other units, which together with the three regiments made up a reinforced division, were scattered over the Pacific—among them a Defence Regiment in Hawaii and a Raider Battalion in Noumea.

When Vandegrift arrived in New Zealand with his first regiment, he quickly discovered that he had problems other than those associated with the move. He had expected to find the unloading of his supply ships completed but the Wellington dock labour force had not worked in accordance with the Marines' unloading schedule, which did not provide for the hours of meal and tea breaks that the wharf labourers regarded as their right. Moreover, the Marines had anticipated that the task would be an all-weather operation, but the labourers would not work in the rain. The end result was that unloading was well behind schedule.[2]

Faced with the need to house a large number of troops (and with more on the way) and realising that the ships were urgently needed elsewhere, quite apart from the fact that there was a war to be won, Vandegrift cut the Gordian knot. Having arrived in the morning, he had his Marines working in the ships that afternoon. The labour force was outraged but the New Zealand Government was secretly delighted! Vandegrift recorded in his autobiography that the Prime Minister, Mr Peter Fraser, congratulated him (off the record since he did not want to lose his job at the head of a Labour ministry) for getting the unloading done so expeditiously.[3]

The general was to find that the wharfside attitude was not mirrored by the rest of the community, and that his requirements for a camp were soon met. The speed at which construction took place was exemplified by the establishment of the US Naval Hospital near Mount Hobson in which the wounded from the Battle of Savo would later be accommodated. It was built on a hockey pitch in a fortnight.

Vandegrift was soon well organised and looking forward to a long training period in hospitable New Zealand when, on 26 June, he received a summons from Ghormley to pay him a visit as soon as possible. After a flight up to Auckland he was surprised to find Ghormley, whom he remembered from Washington as being an intelligent, quiet and most gracious person, harassed and almost brusque. Their conversation started with Ghormley remarking that he had had some most disconcerting news and handing him a top secret communication from King. This was the message, sent a week before the Joint Chiefs of Staff had approved the operation, which warned of King's intention to launch an assault on Tulagi and adjacent areas using the 1st Marine Division. D-Day was provisionally set for 1 August, barely five weeks away.

Vandegrift found it difficult to believe the contents of the message in his hand. Until that moment he had been contemplating the not unpleasing prospect of a prolonged training period in New Zealand which his division badly needed. Instead, he was faced with having to gather his division together from all over the Pacific and launch it against the Japanese—all in just over a month. He and his inexperienced troops were to make the first opposed amphibious assault since British and French forces landed at Gallipoli almost 26 years previously. That precedent did not augur well for the Marines! Ghormley looked at him and said 'Well?', and from that moment preparations for Watchtower moved into high gear.[4]

As the two senior officers discussed the problems that had to be overcome if King's schedule was to be met, one thing was immediately apparent. A landing on 1 August was out of the question. The troops were spread over 'hell's half acre' and the ships were not loaded for an assault landing. If there was one lesson that had been learnt from Gallipoli it was that the loading of stores and equipment for an amphibious assault had to be very carefully planned, to make sure that what was required first was loaded last and that unessential items were not loaded at all.

Quite apart from the problem of combat-loading the ships already in Wellington was the need to unload and combat load the ships bringing the 5th Marine Regiment, due on 11 July. These were carrying the divisional artillery, tanks, amphibious tractors and engineering equipment and had also been commercially loaded to make best use of available space. The details of what each ship carried were not known.[5]

Combat-loading provided for the ready availability of items when needed, and required the repackaging of stores and equipment in a manner suitable for unloading onto the beaches. It was uneconomical in the use of space. Because of this, and because there was insufficient shipping available, a number of critical decisions had to be made—not the least of which being to reduce the amount of ammunition carried by a third.

The marines were fortunate in having a large flat area known as Aotea Quay available to them for the sorting out and repackaging, and they needed every square foot of it. The time to unload and reload aside, allowance also had to be made for the usual rehearsal of the operation. This was necessary to test the practicality of the various support plans for shore bombardment, air support and communications, and for the loading of the landing craft and their passage to the beaches. Always desirable, such a rehearsal was essential with the 1st Marine Division about to embark on its first operation, in view of its state of training and the need to allow the various staffs (which had been separated during the planning period) to iron out any problems.

The proposed rehearsal area was in the Fiji Islands. This meant that, irrespective of any time spent rehearsing, at least eleven days was required for the passage from Wellington to Fiji and on to Tulagi. If rehearsals were limited to four days, a D-Day of 1 August required the Marines to depart from Wellington within a week of the 5th Regiment's arrival. That was clearly impracticable; the operation would have to be delayed.

Ghormley had doubts, not only whether 1 August was feasible, but

whether the operation—even if delayed—could be successful. He told Vandegrift that, although they should press on and do the best they could to
meet King's schedule, he would discuss the operation and its timing with
MacArthur when he met him in Melbourne on 7 July.[6] When Ghormley duly
flew to Melbourne for his discussions with MacArthur and the SWPA staff,
he found that the General shared his pessimistic views. MacArthur's worry
was that he lacked the air power to neutralise the Japanese bases in the
Bismarck Archipelago, and in any case he questioned the soundness of the
strategic concept.

In one respect MacArthur showed remarkable prescience of coming
events when he expressed his concern whether carriers, threatened by the
presence of any hostile naval forces, would be able to provide fighter support
for a transport area. His attitude was in marked contrast to that of a month
or so previously, when he sought to move on Rabaul with a Marine division
and two aircraft carriers, a change which did not go unnoticed in Washington. Following their meeting, the two commanders sent a message to the
Joint Chiefs of Staff expressing their gravest doubts that the operation could
be carried out successfully. They recommended the indefinite postponement
of Watchtower, suggesting instead an infiltration process through the New
Hebrides and Santa Cruz Islands.[7]

The Chiefs of Staff replied on 10 July that the disadvantage was fully
appreciated of undertaking the operation before adequate forces and equipment could be made available to ensure a continuous offensive towards
Rabaul. Nonetheless, they felt that it was 'necessary to stop without delay
the enemy's southward advance that would be effected by his firm establishment at Tulagi'. It was a momentous decision and probably deserves to
be ranked among the great decisions of the Pacific War.[8]

What had strengthened the Chiefs' determination to go ahead with
Watchtower was the realisation that there was no time to lose if the Japanese
were to be prevented from establishing a major air base from which they
could threaten American lines of communication with Australia. The Japanese had initially landed on Tulagi on 2 May with the intention of setting
up a seaplane and flying boat base, but subsequently decided to establish a
facility for land-based aircraft. It was 28 May before they crossed to
Guadalcanal (and then only to obtain meat and native labour), but by 19
June work had begun on an airfield near Lunga Point.

Progress of construction of the new base was closely monitored and
reported by the three coastwatchers on the island: Clemens to the east of
Lunga, Rhoades to the west and Macfarlan to the south. Macfarlan's cook
boy worked on the airfield, while Rhoades sent friendly natives to work
there. The extent of Japanese activities was confirmed by a photo reconnaissance aircraft on 4 July, so that the seriousness of the situation—not
previously appreciated fully in Washington or Brisbane, despite the best
efforts of the coastwatchers—was now there for all to see.

Apparently the two commanders were not at first told of the increased urgency of the situation. The day after the decision was made by the Chiefs of Staff, MacArthur's naval commander, Vice-Admiral Herbert Leary, wrote to Crutchley to alert him in advance that his task force was to be made available to Ghormley: 'I am sorry that things are in such an involved state but for some reason unknown to us the operation is being rushed and no details have yet been worked out'.[9]

In their message to MacArthur and Ghormley, the Chiefs undertook to send additional ships, troops and aircraft and asked Ghormley whether, with the promised reinforcements (to include 26 B-17 aircraft), he would now have sufficient forces to undertake Watchtower. Ghormley replied that he could undertake the operation, providing MacArthur was given the means to interdict hostile air activities in New Britain, New Guinea and in the northern Solomons area. He emphasised that the basic problem confronting the assault force would be the protection of surface ships against land-based aircraft during the approach, landing and unloading phases. As a result, MacArthur's B-17 force was reinforced and Watchtower planning proceeded apace.

But Ghormley still considered that the projected D-day of 1 August was impractical. He sought and obtained a delay of six days to 7 August, but with this approval came a warning from the Chiefs of Staff that there could be no further deferments. Once the Japanese were able to bring the airfield they were constructing on Guadalcanal into operation, the Allies would find it very difficult to establish bases in the Santa Cruz Islands and in the New Hebrides.[10] King was, however, not completely satisfied that the date of 7 August would pre-empt the Japanese use of their airfield. On 28 July he told Ghormley that it was of the utmost importance that D-Day not be further delayed, and if possible it should be brought forward. This proved to be impracticable so that 7 August remained a firm date for D-Day.

The race for the airfield was a near-run thing, as the Japanese intended to commence operating from the airfield on 12 August. It was not to have been merely an airstrip, like Fall River, but a major facility capable of supporting a large number of aircraft.

On 16 July Ghormley promulgated his operation plan which made provision for Pestilence to be accomplished in three phases. The first phase comprised rehearsals of the Tulagi–Guadalcanal attack, to be conducted in the Fiji Islands commencing on about 27 July. The second provided for the capture and occupation of Tulagi and adjacent positions, including an adjoining portion of Guadalcanal suitable for the construction of landing fields (Operation Watchtower), while the final phase was the occupation of Ndeni in the Santa Cruz Islands.[11]

MacArthur and Ghormley were not the only senior officers to be uneasy about Watchtower. On 17 July Nimitz informed King that, in his opinion, it would be unsafe to assume that the Japanese would not attempt to retake the area and that, if insufficient forces were assigned, the Marines might not be able to hold on. Fletcher also added his voice to those who doubted the practicability of the operation before he sailed in *Saratoga* to take command of the Expeditionary Force.

If ever an operation warranted careful and detailed planning at the centre it was Watchtower. Instead, the situation which confronted Ghormley, Fletcher, McCain and other senior officers was a planner's nightmare. They were geographically widely separated, had very little time and lacked experience in the type of operation for which they were planning. Ghormley was in Auckland, Vandegrift in Wellington, Fletcher at sea in the central Pacific in *Saratoga*, McCain in Noumea and Noyes *en route* from the US west coast in *Wasp*. Turner reached Wellington to take up his command less than a week before the Amphibious Force sailed for Fiji. Furthermore, they had to rely on the co-operation of forces operating under another command to cover the enemy's most likely direction of approach and interdict its sources of supply. This cooperation was of fundamental importance to the success of Watchtower yet little attention was given to it, particularly by Allied Air Forces.

Throughout July, ships of the Expeditionary Force were moving across the Pacific towards a rendezvous in the Fiji Islands which was set for 26 July. Of the 77 ships involved, fifteen sailed direct from San Diego and 28 from Australian and New Zealand ports on the other side of the Pacific. One of the carrier task forces which included the aircraft carrier *Wasp* and the battleship *North Carolina* had departed from Norfolk, Virginia, early the previous month. Most made it to the rendezvous on time, but two transports with the 3rd Defence Battalion on board, having left San Diego on 8 July, found the planned speed of advance too much for them; these missed making the rendezvous and the rehearsal, and joined as late as 3 August—just four days before D-Day.

Canberra leaving Wellington, New Zealand, on 22 July 1942 to take part in the operations off Guadalcanal which would prove to be her last. (US National Archives neg. 80–G–1345A)

The loading of the fourteen transports and supply ships in Wellington had just been completed in time for their departure on 22 July. The Marines had worked round the clock in eight-hour shifts, in almost continuous rain. One battalion commander was later to describe the loading period as a seemingly endless nightmare:

> Drenched men wrestled with rain soaked cartons of clothing, food, medicines, cigarettes and chocolate bars. The cheap cardboard containers containing Navy rations and Marine Corps supplies disintegrated; one officer remembers walking a hundred yards through a swamp of sodden cornflakes dotted with mushed Hershey bars, smashed cigar boxes, odd shoes and stained soggy bundles of socks.[12]

Vandegrift, in an understatement typical of that southern gentleman, called the lack of time and port facilities, the terrible weather, inadequate packaging and uncooperative labour an 'unparalleled logistical problem'. Ordinary Marines had other words for it all. In the end they completed the job, but were limited by lack of shipping space to taking with them only items actually required to live and fight. Comforts were limited to razor blades, soap, tobacco and matches.

8

Preliminary moves

The Amphibious Force sailed from Wellington late in the afternoon of 22 July, at which time it comprised fifteen transports and supply ships of all shapes and sizes. Turner's flagship, USS *McCawley*, was ill-equipped for her role as a command ship—particularly in the vital area of radio communications. Long-range communications had to be handled by two transmitters and five receivers, and short-range tactical communications by one TBS set of the type widely fitted in the American fleet but not in the RAN cruisers or in *Chicago*. Though the TBS radio was of robust construction and generally reliable, *McCawley*'s installation was never satisfactory and had a working range of not much more than five miles. In the operation area Turner was forced to send some messages to other ships by boat for onward transmission by radio to ships out of visual communications range. Contact with Marine units was maintained using their portable radio sets.[1]

The Marines were escorted by the Australian cruisers *Australia*, *Canberra* and *Hobart* and the American cruisers *Salt Lake City* and *Chicago* (the latter having been working with the Australian ships since the beginning of February). These ships had left Brisbane on 14 July with the American destroyers of Destroyer Squadron Four (DESRON 4) (*Ralph Talbot*, *Patterson* and *Jarvis*), to rendezvous with Turner's Amphibious Force east of New Zealand five days later. Some confusion obviously still existed, at least in MacArthur's headquarters, over the date when Vandegrift's Marines would be finished loading. Two days out of Brisbane, the task force was ordered into Wellington where it was joined by the remaining six ships of DESRON 4: *Selfridge*, *Blue*, *Henley*, *Helm*, *Bagley* and *Mugford*.

During the crossing of the Tasman, that sea had lived up to its reputation for bad weather so that a program of exercises, including gunnery firings, was severely curtailed. Of all the ships present this was to affect *Canberra*

The Type 271 surface warning radar had been installed in Canberra *during a three-month refit in Sydney just prior to her sailing to take part in Operation Watchtower. The low power transmitted by this relatively primitive equipment—the first centimetric radar produced in the world—required the aerials to be mounted immediately above a six-foot-square un-airconditioned 'office' which was bolted onto a platform above and abaft the Director. This example of the 271, the last survivor of the many hundreds produced, was photographed on HMS* Dryad *at Fareham, in Hampshire, England.* (Author)

most, as she had just completed a three-month refit in Sydney during which a surface warning radar was fitted. Known as a Type 271 and built around the recently developed cavity magnetron, it was the first centimetric radar set seen in Australia though it had been in service with the Royal Navy and Royal Canadian Navy in the Atlantic for some time.

The feasibilty of such a device had been established in Britain in November 1940 and by the end of March 1941 the first 271 set had been produced. After sea trials were successfully completed, the equipment was rushed into production. Within six months 39 sets were at sea and making a valuable contribution to the winning of the Battle of the Atlantic, primarily through their use in anti-submarine warfare. The Royal Navy had already given attention to the use of less sophisticated radar sets to provide tactical information, and for gunnery and torpedo control. Considerable success attended those efforts, notably in the hunt for the *Bismarck* in May 1941 when the cruiser HMS *Suffolk*, a sister ship of *Canberra*, shadowed the German battleship for 30 hours in poor visibility. Because the advent of the 271 enabled the detection of surface craft at longer ranges, it was quickly integrated into plotting and weapon control systems. In February 1942 the destroyer HMS *Campbell* used information from her 271 for torpedo control in an abortive attack on the German battleships *Gneisenau* and *Scharnhorst* in the English Channel.

The performance and use of warning radar at Savo has often been judged against these developments on the other side of the world. In Australia at this time, though, the use of radar at sea was a 'black art' and no expertise existed on how to make use of the information that it could provide. There was little knowledge, for example, of its use in navigation or for plotting the movements of ships, both friendly and enemy, to provide a better tactical picture than could be provided with the naked eye. At that time its value in surface warfare was generally thought to be the provision of information for the gunnery control systems.[2] Officers returning from service or training with the Royal Navy were slowly indoctrinating their associates in its wider tactical uses, but this was a gradual process which had scarcely begun in June 1942.

As late as 1943 the Prime Minister and Minister for Defence, Mr John Curtin, was to express an opinion that 'radar would not last' and censured a member of the Naval Board, Commodore H.A. Showers, for sending two RAN lieutenants to England to undergo an intensive training course in the technicalities of radar. Showers, who had just joined the Naval Board, was unaware of a government instruction that no permanent officers were to be sent abroad for such a course as it was believed that they lacked the intelligence and education to cope. Throughout that period Curtin rather quaintly referred to radar as 'that RDF apparatus'![3]

The acknowledged expert in *Canberra*—and for a while in the port of Sydney—was David Medley, who had obtained a Master's degree in physics in 1941 at Sydney University. During 1941 he was working with the Department of Munitions in designing and building optical equipment for the Army. He was a radio 'ham' in his spare time, so he was quick to answer a call by the Navy for scientists to become involved in their RDF, or as it was later to be called, radar program. His first task for the Navy was to plan the installation of two radar sets in *Canberra*: the Type 271, and a short-range air warning set known as Type A290. During this period he found and corrected a design fault in the aerial of the latter.

Late in 1941 Medley was commissioned in the Royal Australian Naval Volunteer Reserve as a sub-lieutenant and, after a short (and, to him, useless and frustrating) officers' indoctrination course, he joined *Canberra* with instructions to assist Garden Island Dockyard personnel in fitting the two radars. His seniors on board had other ideas for him and put him to work learning to become a seaman or executive officer, there being no concept of what later became known as a special branch officer with duties limited to a specialist qualification.

Medley found his situation intolerable, as he was unable to contribute to the task of fitting the radars and complained to the newly joined Executive Officer, Commander John Walsh. Walsh, who had had limited experience with radar when in command of the destroyer HMAS *Vampire* in the Mediterranean, saw Medley's point of view and told him to work with the gunnery officer. He stopped any further attempts to make a seaman of Medley.

From then on, Medley's efforts were concentrated on getting the two sets to work and to integrating them into the ship's gunnery department.

Neither the torpedo officer nor the navigating officer evinced any interest in putting them to use in solving some of their problems. Whereas today courses would have been held to familiarise officers with the use of the new equipment and their capabilities and limitations, in May 1942 there was no knowledge in Sydney on which to base such a course. Literally, the only person who would possibly have been able to devise such a course was Medley—a Master of Physics with less than six months' naval service and no sea experience, and who was already fully employed.

Canberra had had a quiet war, having been employed as an escort for troop convoys to the Middle East and, more recently, New Guinea and Singapore. During these missions there had been no contact with an enemy. The cruiser had spent long and lonely months on anti-raider patrol off the east Australian coast and in the Indian Ocean, steaming a total of well over a quarter of a million miles. The only excitement there had been the sinking of two German supply ships, *Coburg* and *Ketty Brovig,* in March 1941.[4] Whenever target facilities were available advantage had been taken of them for gunnery practice, but such opportunities had been few and far between. While many of the ship's key personnel remained on board, efficiency had suffered through numerous changes of officers and men, giving rise to a belief on board that she was being used as a training ship for the very large number of new men then entering the rapidly expanding Australian Navy. The ship's company had been embarrassed to be idle in Sydney when Singapore fell, when HMAS *Perth* had been lost in the Java Sea, and when her fellow cruisers had taken part in the Battle of the Coral Sea in early May.

Towards the end of the refit, there had been a feeling in the ship that the quiet life could not last and morale had been boosted by the appointment of a number of officers with recent war experience. The key member of the new command team was to be Captain Frank Getting,[5] who was well known in the Navy if only for his prowess as a boxer. He was coming to the ship after a spell ashore as Deputy Chief of the Naval Staff. Getting, who would join in June, was no stranger to *Canberra*, having served as her Executive Officer for three years in the period immediately before the war. His detailed knowledge of the ship and her systems was to occasionally embarrass his recently joined team.

In more normal times *Canberra*'s refit would have been followed by a lengthy working-up period, but those were not normal times. The Japanese carrier striking force was intact and the enemy's intention to move on Port Moresby, despite its recent setback in the Coral Sea, was obvious. Little time could be allowed to bring the ship back to an acceptable standard of efficiency—just two days off Sydney carrying out 8-inch day and night firings, and a week in the inclement weather environment of Melbourne which had severely curtailed anti-aircraft firings.[6]

When *Canberra* left Sydney for her all-too-brief shakedown in the

Captain F. E. Getting, commanding officer of HMAS Canberra *at Savo Island, pictured in younger days when he was well known in Australian naval circles as a boxer. He had lost none of his fighting spirit by 1942, and the circumstances of his ship's destruction in action does not warrant the relegation which his name has subsequently suffered.* (AWM neg. 106675)

Melbourne area, the A290 air warning radar was functioning to the best of its limited capability but the 271 remained mute because of the lack of a cavity magnetron without which it could not transmit. Many years later Medley was to describe his reception of this vital (and, at that time, highly classified) piece of equipment in the following terms:

> With some ceremony I was handed two magnetrons and asked to sign a paper which said in effect that I understood that I was to protect these units with my life if necessary to stop them falling into the hands of the enemy. In this context I kept a box containing two sticks of gelignite in the 271 antenna enclosure just for this purpose. I remember a Chief Petty Officer from the gunnery department thinking I was nuts when I requested this but eventually he understood and gave me a crash course in demolition. Those were indeed desperate times!

The ship was back in Sydney at the end of May, lying at a buoy in Sydney Cove under a brilliant full moon on the night that a raid by Japanese midget submarines helped focus the minds of all on board on the task that lay ahead. After joining Task Force 44 in the Queensland area, several gunnery practices had been carried out notwithstanding that these were limited by a shortage of target facilities north of Sydney. While the majority of key gunnery personnel had remained unchanged and all the gunnery systems were performing well, there remained a feeling that *Canberra* was far from being in a satisfactory state of fighting efficiency when she arrived in Wellington even though every effort had been made, using her own resources, to improve that.

In one important respect *Canberra* was totally unready for operations and would have benefited from at least a week at sea working with a consort or two. This would have provided an opportunity to resolve problems associated with the use of the 271, including the integration of information obtained from it into the gunnery and torpedo control systems and the display of this information on a tactical plot.

Type 271 was not fitted with a display which gave a plan view of the set's contacts.[7] The only display was a cathode-ray tube of about six inches (fifteen centimetres) diameter on which echoes appeared as spikes along a green trace. Ranges were read off against a paper strip stuck to the tube. Bearings were obtained by observing the direction in which the aerial was pointing at the moment of contact, and read off from a pointer driven mechanically by the handwheel used by the radar operator to rotate the aerial (located immediately above the transmitter and housed in a lantern-like structure). Bearings were reported relative to the ship's head as there was no gyro compass in the radar hut, which was situated above and abaft the gunnery control position. The classification and identification of contacts depended very much on a dialogue with bridge personnel. In *Canberra* this was complicated by the need to pass messages through the compartment in which was fitted the A290, as there was no direct phone between the bridge and the 271.

As can be seen, the proper use of all the information which the 271 set could provide required a great deal of skill and experience—if only for the sorting out of the confusion caused by the many side, or false, echoes which resulted from what was a primitive aerial system. There was little time to develop that skill, and much of what time there was available was lost when the fitting of the cavity magnetron was delayed until just before the ship left Brisbane for Wellington. During that passage the set was only available for calibration and tuning, so that the opportunity to develop its tactical use did not occur. *Canberra* was fitted with the answer to the Japanese night fighting capability but had no real idea of how to make the best tactical use of it.[8]

Australia and *Hobart* were in a worked-up state, notwithstanding the fact that they had both recently suffered from some changes in personnel. They had both seen considerable active service—not only in the Coral Sea, but (in the case of *Australia*) in the Atlantic, particularly off Dakar, and (in *Hobart*'s case) in the Red, Mediterranean and Java seas. *Chicago* was short of gunnery practice, not having fired her 8-inch guns since Pearl Harbor—indeed, not since October 1941—but she was well versed in the tactical doctrine of the task force, having been a member of it since February.

The capability of the destroyers was still a matter of conjecture. Generally speaking, these had been joining piecemeal since the middle of May and had spent little time with the task force. A feature of their design which caused some comment in *Canberra* was their covered bridges, because of possible effects on the ability to keep an effective visual lookout. Their substantial anti-aircraft armament was admired, as was their torpedo armament of sixteen tubes. The opportunities for these ships to carry out gunnery practices had been few, as they had been detached frequently on escort duties, and none of them had been able to carry out a torpedo firing for some considerable time. They were all fitted with the radio set TBS.

During the passage to the Fijis, Turner and Crutchley exchanged a number of messages setting up the command structure of the Amphibious Force for the operation. The exchange began with Turner asking Crutchley to act as his second-in-command. Crutchley at first declined, pointing out that Rear Admiral Scott would also be available and suggested that, as an American, he would be more suitable. But Turner insisted and duly appointed Crutchley as his deputy. On 23 July, in advance of receipt of Fletcher's operation order, Turner told Crutchley that he was to command the screening group, with responsibility for the protection of the amphibious force on the passage to Tulagi and of the assault area during the landings.

Turner then suggested that Crutchley should shift his flag from *Australia* to *Chicago* in order to take advantage of the latter's better air warning radar. Crutchley demurred, on the grounds that his Chief of Staff was also Captain of *Australia*. He also felt that he could exercise whatever control of the fighter defence of the area was necessary by listening in to the messages between *Chicago* and the fighters she was controlling and signalling any necessary instructions to *Chicago*. In retrospect Turner's suggestion was impractical, as it would have meant moving Crutchley from an operating environment with which he was thoroughly familiar into one in which almost the only common ground would have been the language. Even today, with so much common equipment and operating procedures, it would be a difficult change. This time Turner accepted Crutchley's advice.

The passage to the rendezvous was uneventful, and so it was that at 1400 on 26 July contact was made with the remainder of the Expeditionary Force as the various groups from Pearl Harbor, San Diego, Tonga, Samoa and New Caledonia hove into sight. The Amphibious Force was reinforced by five more transports, four destroyer transports and five destroyer minesweepers. At the same time *Salt Lake City* left Crutchley's command and joined *Wasp*'s carrier task force.

The afternoon was fine and bright, the sea smooth with a long low swell. There were few in *Canberra* who did not avail themselves of the opportunity to witness a display of sea power such as had not been seen before in the South Pacific and to see, at first hand, ships which up until then had only been names to them. If there had been a vote among the onlookers for the ship that caused the most comment it would have been awarded to *North Carolina*, the first of the American fast battleships to be completed and considered by many to be the most beautiful ship of that type ever built.

There was a certain amount of confusion to start with, particularly among the transports joining the Amphibious Force. Perhaps understandably, they seemed reluctant to leave the protection of *North Carolina* which had escorted them from Tonga. But eventually the various task forces and task groups sorted themselves out and course was shaped for the island of Koro, lying 75 miles north-east of Suva and the scene for the rehearsals which were due to start the next day.

Before the various task forces dispersed to make their separate ways to the rehearsal area, a meeting took place in *Saratoga* the importance of which it is almost impossible to exaggerate. Chaired by Fletcher (the Expeditionary Force Commander), those attending included the commanders of all the South Pacific elements which together made up the forces employed on Watchtower and their senior staff officers: Turner (the Amphibious Force Commander), Vandegrift (Landing Force Commander), Noyes (Air Support Force Commander) and Kinkaid (commander of *Enterprise*'s carrier task group), McCain (commander of all land-based and water-based air support) and Colonel Saunders, USAF (the commander, under McCain, of all Army Air Corps aircraft). Crutchley, as a group commander, was not invited.

Also missing was Ghormley, the officer who had been instructed by Nimitz to take strategic command, in person, within the operating area. Instead of attending himself, Ghormley sent his Chief of Staff, the recently promoted Rear Admiral Dan Callaghan, and his Staff Communications Officer to represent him. He was later to explain that he was unable to spare the time for travel,[9] but others believed that he was busy in Noumea attending to the many vexing details that should more properly have been left to his staff.[10]

Whatever the reason, later events were to show that his priorities were wrong. He had missed his only chance of being able to set his imprint on the conduct of Watchtower and to provide the cohesion that the Expeditionary Force lacked. This absence of cohesion, which was at the root of many of the problems which were to occur later, was due partly to the unavoidable dispersion of the various elements during the planning stage and partly to the haste with which the operation had to be carried out. They were, after all, planning what was—even by today's standards—a most complex operation, and one for which there was no precedent in the history of warfare. Not only were all arms of the American services involved but also two of an ally whose ways were comparatively strange to them.

Despite Ghormley's absence, the meeting should have been invaluable in allowing the task force commanders to obtain a view of the overall picture, to take part in a general discussion of the problems that each command was having, and go at least some way towards refining their plans so that all bits of the Watchtower mosaic fitted. Instead of this, the meeting was a stormy affair, being described by Turner's Chief of Staff, Captain Thomas Peyton, as one long bitter argument between Fletcher and Turner. He was amazed and disturbed by the way the two admirals talked to each other.[11] Had Ghormley been present, and in retrospect there can be no doubt that he should have been, the meeting probably would have been conducted in a manner more befitting the occasion.

The conference opened badly. Fletcher seemed to Vandegrift to be both nervous and tired, and to the general's surprise appeared also to lack knowledge or interest in the forthcoming operation. Fletcher quickly let his audience know that he, the officer now responsible for the conduct of affairs, had no confidence in its success.[12] They answered his arbitrary objections as best they could, but made little impression. It could have been said of Fletcher that his mind was made up and he did not want to be confused with facts.

Turner's biographer, Dyer, presents two versions of this unfortunate meeting: Peyton's and Kinkaid's. The latter called it animated rather than stormy, but Peyton's account confirms the recollections of Vandegrift in describing how Turner heatedly backed his plea that the carriers should remain for a period longer than the two days planned by Fletcher. Vandegrift recalled that Fletcher made many arbitrary objections, forcibly expressed, to aspects of the plan.[13] Regarding the expedition as a brainchild of Turner's, Fletcher felt that the planners of Watchtower had had no real fighting experience, that the operation had been too hurriedly devised and that the logistic arrangements were inadequate. He was also critical of the lack of training.

Fletcher was 'fighting the problem', though there were more than a few grains of truth in what he said. What almost defies belief is that he should have said it at that time and in that company. At the end of the meeting he suddenly interrupted Turner to ask him how long it would take to land the troops, to which Turner replied that it would take five days. In fact, the retirement plan which was contained in Turner's operation plan (but was not issued until 30 July) tentatively planned for all transports to leave the Guadalcanal area on the evening of the 8th and for the supply ships to leave two days later. In the meeting, therefore, Turner was taking a conservative view of the time required. Fletcher then announced that he was going to leave the area in two days, and that if the landings could not be completed in that time then they should not be undertaken. He cited as his reasons the danger of air attacks to his carriers and shortage of fuel.[14]

Vandegrift was aghast at the prospect of operating without the benefit of air support while in the process of unloading, and before his troops were established ashore. He said so, and tried to explain that Watchtower was not a ships' landing force manoeuvre of the type frequently exercised in the Caribbean but a major operation to gain a permanent position in strength on enemy-held territory—even planning to complete it in five days was taking a risk. Fletcher curtly announced that he would stay until the third day and then closed the meeting.

Kinkaid was the only other member of the meeting to agree with

Fletcher's decision, so that it is not surprising that his view of the proceedings differed from Vandegrift's. In addition to thinking that the meeting was animated rather than stormy, Kinkaid considered that Turner asked for a lot of things, much of which he did not get because they were impossible.[15] Turner was eventually to say of the decision that it represented the judgment of the most experienced battle commander in the USN and therefore he had had to live with it. Immediately after the conference, however, he evidently held a very different view, being heard to exclaim to Fletcher: 'You son of a bitch, if you do that you are yellow'.[16] On this evidence it would seem that the meeting had been a good deal more than animated.

As Ghormley's representative, Callaghan took notes of the proceedings, of which no formal record was kept.[17] He made no mention of any problems at the meeting, merely noting Fletcher's proposal to withdraw after two days. On his return to Noumea he informed Ghormley, who investigated the possibilities of flying fighters into Guadalcanal when the airfield was serviceable. Ghormley eventually suggested to Fletcher, after stating his requirement for continuous fighter cover for the Guadalcanal–Tulagi area, that one or two squadrons of fighters be flown into Guadalcanal before the carriers withdrew (assuming the airfield would be ready). The carrier squadrons would then be exchanged with belly tank-fitted fighters from Marine squadrons from Efate, staging through the small ferry carrier USS *Long Island*. This idea came to naught at the time but the method of providing fighters and other aircraft to Guadalcanal by staging them through a carrier became a standard practice later in the year, being the only way to supply the island with single-engined aircraft. Apart from that suggestion, Ghormley does not appear to have put any pressure on Fletcher to change his mind and did not protest when Fletcher subsequently withdrew his carriers after only two days of operations.

The meeting duly broke up and those who had attended went back to their ships or were taken into Suva by destroyer. They could not have been happy with what they had observed, and if they were confident of victory it could only have been because of a feeling of superiority over the Japanese—a feeling that was to lead some into a fatal state of complacency.

Turner and Vandegrift had had a bad day, and things were not to get any better as the rehearsals proceeded and two practice assaults were carried out on Koro Island. They found that the choice of beaches on Koro did not allow many of the landing craft to beach because of coral outcrops, so that only a third of the troops embarked were actually put ashore. The boats themselves proved to be mechanically unreliable, naval gunfire support was inaccurate, and the carriers' pilots showed the need for a lot more practice.

But there was a positive side. Procedures for loading troops and stores into the landing craft were revised, the defective engines removed from them and either replaced or repaired, and the communication plans for the landing parties also refined. Boats' coxswains learnt a great deal about handling their craft in a seaway and those organising the movement of boats between ship and beach realised the need for flexibility in schedules, leading to the development of the 'boat pool' concept. Many of the troops who had been cooped up in the transports for periods varying between one week to a month also benefited from the physical exercise they received.

The lessons learned were put into practice. Turner and Vandegrift consoled themselves with the thought that things could only get better, and of course they did. It may not have seemed so on 31 July when the last boats were hoisted and everything made ready for departure, but the time spent off Koro was time well spent.

9

Planning of night dispositions

While the rehearsals were being conducted, the various staffs were putting the finishing touches to their orders and plans for operations which were less than ten days away. Among the staffs so employed was Crutchley's which, having been given a draft copy of Turner's operation plan on 26 July, prepared the orders for the conduct of the Screening Force in time for Crutchley to obtain Turner's approval of them on 29 July.

Before setting course for the Solomons, Turner held a lengthy meeting in *Australia* attended by Crutchley and Vandegrift and his group commanders, at which he went over his operational plan and Vandegrift explained his for the beach assaults. The plans called for the Amphibious Force to split into two groups. The first, Group Yoke, would assault the Tulagi area to obtain the use of Tulagi Harbour and to knock out the centre of Japanese strength in the area, believed to number about 1850 men. The second, Group X-ray, would put their troops ashore three miles east of Lunga Point on Guadalcanal to secure the airfield area. The latter landing was expected to be opposed by approximately 5000 Japanese, of whom a substantial portion would be engineering personnel engaged in airfield construction.[1]

Group Yoke, comprising four transports and the four destroyers converted to carry troops and landing craft, was to land a raider battalion and a defence battalion on Tulagi, a parachute battalion on nearby Gavutu, and a Marine infantry battalion on the larger island of Florida adjacent to Tulagi, the total being a little less than 4000 troops. Group X-ray, made up of the remaining transports and the store ships, was to put ashore the greater part of two Marine regiments and supporting troops totalling approximately 11 000 men. Initially, the ships were to anchor about four miles off the beach in deep water, to reduce the risk from mines, but were to move to within a mile of the beach after the five minesweeping destroyers had swept the

73

landing area. The transports would thus occupy two anchorages about sixteen miles apart.

The cruisers and destroyers were split into a screening group under Crutchley, and two fire support groups (one for each of the beachheads). Crutchley's command consisted of the three Australian cruisers and *Chicago* and the nine destroyers of DESRON 4. Its function was to protect both anchorages against submarine, air and surface attack. For air defence he was allocated two carrier-borne fighter squadrons which were to be controlled by *Chicago*. Anti-submarine air patrols were to be provided by the cruisers' aircraft. The light cruiser *San Juan* and the destroyers *Monssen* and *Buchanan* were to provide fire support for the Tulagi beachheads while *Vincennes*, *Quincy* and *Astoria*, with the destroyers *Hull*, *Dewey*, *Ellet* and *Wilson* were to support the assault on Guadalcanal.

Turner's operation plan specifically stated that in the event of air attack the fire support groups were to operate under the direction of Crutchley, but made no provision for the concentration of those groups with Crutchley's screening group in the event of a surface attack either by day or night. Provision was only made for them to support Crutchley in such circumstances.

From the allocation of ships to the various task groups, Turner could not, at that stage, have envisaged that *Vincennes*, *Quincy* and *Astoria* would join Crutchley's command in the assault area. It is hardly surprising, then, that during the rehearsals no provision was made for tactical exercises to be carried out between the Australian and American heavy cruisers to enable them to work together in company.

Crutchley, however, clearly intended to use all warships in the vicinity for the defence of the anchorages at night because, when he submitted his plans to Turner on 29 July for the conduct of operations of the screening group, he included the three heavy cruisers and *San Juan* (with their destroyers) in his command. Turner agreed with the proposal, but it was by then too late for him to reorganise the rehearsal schedule and refuelling program to provide for tactical exercises in which all six heavy cruisers could take part.

Crutchley accordingly issued his 'Special Instructions to Screening Group and Vessels temporarily assigned' before the Expeditionary Force left Koro.[2] These provided for the use at night of all six heavy cruisers, along with *Hobart*, *San Juan* and fifteen destroyers, and made no provision for the possibility that *Quincy* and four destroyers might be detached on D-Day to escort the Ndeni occupation force. Though the reduction by one in the number of heavy cruisers would probably not, by itself, have altered Crutchley's decision to split his cruiser force, the loss of four destroyers from the anti-submarine screen protecting the anchorages would have required a drastic rethink of the use of his destroyers, which may in turn have influenced the disposition of his cruisers. The possible loss of the ships from his night dispositions must have been a source of anxiety to him.

The document, which shows every sign of the haste with which it was prepared, has been the subject of a great deal of American criticism. For example, Ghormley felt that, though it may have been adequate for a British force, it lacked sufficient detail for the Americans in that it 'did not reflect clearly the Commander's scheme of manoeuvre or battle plan to meet the approach of an enemy force'. In the pamphlet 'Battle Experience—Bulletin No. 2: Solomon Islands Actions, August and September 1942', issued in late 1942 in the name of King as Commander-in-Chief US Fleet, it was also said that, though the order covered a number of assumed situations after arrival in the assault area, it did not cover the situation that actually occurred—that is, the arrival of an undetected enemy force. This criticism was repeated in the analysis made by the US Naval War College in 1950, even though King's critical comment had been specifically answered by Admiral Hepburn in his informal enquiry into the loss of *Canberra*, *Vincennes*, *Quincy* and *Astoria* carried out at King's request.

Hepburn found that he could not give much weight to the criticism that no special battle plan was prescribed for night action. There were too many imponderables which included the range at which the enemy was sighted, the relative bearing on which it was sighted, its course and speed at the moment of making contact and the visibility. Only one plan of action was practicable, namely to bring the armament into action as quickly as possible and to remain between the enemy and the transport areas, or at least to destroy the enemy before it could open fire on the transports.[3]

One of Crutchley's problems in drawing up any plan of action for the Americans to follow was that at that time, unlike the Royal Navy, they had no tactical doctrine common to all squadrons, fleets or task forces.[4] When an American task force was formed, as on this occasion, the task force commander was expected to write a book instructing commanding officers how to act in a variety of situations.

Crace, Crutchley's predecessor as Rear Admiral Commanding the Australian Squadron and Commander Task Force 44, had initiated the development of such a book for Task Force 44 and it was in use before Watchtower. Ghormley clearly thought that Crutchley should have done that for Watchtower and it may have been that Turner appreciated the problem when he originally planned to keep the two groups of heavy cruisers apart. Certainly Turner saw problems in operating with ships other than American, for he had first asked that only US ships be placed under his command for Watchtower.

Not until a year later, August 1943, was a book (Pac 10) published which obviated the need for every task force commander in the Pacific to write a special book of tactical instructions. The book came into use throughout the Navy in April 1944, when it was rewritten and named USF

V.A.C. Crutchley, an officer on loan from the Royal Navy, was Rear Admiral Commanding Australian Squadron from June 1942. Placed in charge of arrangements to provide a protective sceen for the troop transports involved in the landings at Guadalcanal, he was blamed by some American critics for the disaster which befell the ships of his force. Subsequent investigations showed, however, that his dispositions were not the cause of the Allies' defeat at Savo. In 1943 the Commander-in-Chief of the US Navy, Admiral E. J. King, commended his and Turner's performance in the Solomons campaign, declaring that they were 'in no way inefficient, much less at fault, in executing their parts of the operation'. The same could not be said of others.
(W. Crutchley)

10A. The lack, prewar, of a central operational authority was also felt in the matter of staff procedures. Although the Naval War College had developed procedures and organisations which were designed to be used throughout the service, many senior officers before 1942—when taking over a major command, such as the Battle Fleet—organised and ran their staffs in a highly individualistic manner.

In preparing his plan, Crutchley had to provide for the defence of two anchorages in an area to which there were three entrances. The entrances most likely to be used by an approaching enemy were those which lay between Guadalcanal and Savo, and between Savo and Florida. They were effectively seven and ten miles wide respectively. The third entrance—lying between Florida and Guadalcanal, to the east of the anchorages—was seemingly much wider, but was full of navigational hazards which made it unsuitable for all except light craft such as destroyers or PT boats, particularly at night.

Crutchley did not expect a surface attack by day, in view of the overwhelming local air superiority of the Americans, but he nonetheless made provision for the heavy cruisers of the screening group to form into two groups, one or both of which could be deployed against the enemy depending on the size and composition of the attacking force. Each group was to contain three heavy cruisers led by *Australia* and *Vincennes*, the destroyers of Destroyer Squadron Four being split between them. Because of the extensive aerial reconnaissance, he expected sufficient warning to be able to fight outside the sound. In the event that both groups were deployed he did not intend to concentrate the heavy cruisers, and instructed that the *Vincennes* group should act independently of *Australia*'s group while providing mutual support. He made provision for the remainder of the screening group to protect the anchorages.

Planning for the protection of the anchorages by night, Crutchley's first decision was whether or not to rely on early warning of an enemy's approach being obtained from aerial reconnaissance. If he could rely on such warning, the cruisers could either leave the assault areas (which were submarine probability areas) and seek the comparative safety of open waters or remain close to the transports protected by a destroyer screen common to both forces. Either would have reduced considerably the submarine threat to the cruisers, but experience had taught Crutchley and his staff that aerial reconnaissance was not infallible. He therefore decided to keep his cruisers and destroyers under way by night, clear of the transports and disposed between the anchorages and any likely threat.

The possibility of placing a heavy cruiser patrol outside Savo was considered but discounted, because of the possibility that an enemy—having succeeded in approaching Savo from the north-west—might also succeed in working his way round the cruisers and enter the sound unopposed. In the light of what we now know of the Japanese ability to see without being seen this was a prudent decision.

The only sure way of preventing an enemy approaching the transport area unopposed was to place the cruisers inside the sound. Crutchley's plan called for each of the entrances to be covered by a group of cruisers, the channels either side of Savo each being guarded by three heavy cruisers and the eastern entrance by the two light cruisers. To keep them out of each other's way, he divided the sound into three areas and allocated a cruiser group to each area. The chosen dividing lines were geographically obvious, one being a line to the south-east from the unmistakable bulk of Savo Island down the centre of the sound; the other line joining the two anchorages, which would be obvious at night as the ships used their cargo-handling lights while unloading. The light cruisers were to remain to the east of this latter line, while *Australia*, *Canberra* and *Chicago* were to patrol south of the line drawn from Savo and *Vincennes*, *Quincy* and *Astoria* were to stay to the north of it.

Crutchley had the option of keeping his heavy cruisers together and patrolling across the sound inside Savo but he discarded the idea for a number of reasons. The first undoubtedly was that an enemy force using the Guadalcanal side of the passage between Savo and Guadalcanal would not have been detected by *Canberra*'s centimetric radar from the north-eastern end of the patrol line, even assuming a detection range of twelve miles. Similarly, an enemy force staying on the Florida side of the other passage past Savo would not have been detected from the south-western end. Furthermore, an enemy approaching Savo Island with the intention of

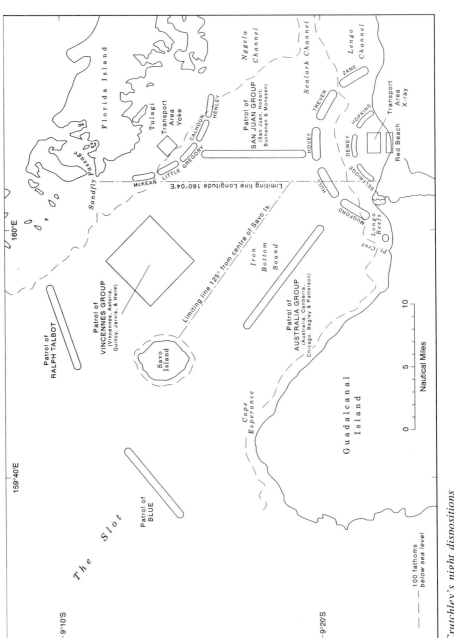

Crutchley's night dispositions

passing close to it would have been shielded from *Canberra*'s radar by the island itself for a very considerable portion of the cruisers' patrol line.

Crutchley had to weigh up the risk of an enemy force's unopposed approach to the transports against the possible advantage of concentration. He already held the view that a group of more than four cruisers would be an awkward force to handle at night, so he was predisposed in favour of splitting his forces from the start.[5] In this case, his preference was reinforced by the difficulties he saw in controlling that particular group of cruisers. As the Japanese were to demonstrate, night fighting was an art which could only be mastered by a great deal of practice in all conditions of light and weather by ships which habitually worked together. As will be shown later, Crutchley's opponent, Mikawa, shared his views regarding the difficulty of handling a heterogeneous group of ships at night—this in spite of a common doctrine and much practice of that doctrine.

Crutchley had three ships which were partly trained in a single doctrine, had worked together at night for some time and carried out a number of night encounter exercises in the previous three months. The other three were complete strangers to him, and if they had a night-fighting doctrine he was unaware of it; but at least they belonged to the same navy.

The situation was exacerbated by the difference in the primary method of tactically communicating within each group. *Australia*, *Canberra* and *Chicago* had been operating together for some time at night using low-powered small directional signal lamps and were at ease with the system. When the American destroyers joined his task force, they initially had difficulty with it and there was no reason to suppose that experience with the larger ships would be any different. They had come to rely on the TBS voice radio.

After examining the problems that would arise from operating the heavy cruisers as a single unit, Crutchley rejected the idea. Not only was there a considerable risk that the Japanese might be able to approach the transports unopposed but also, in his opinion, concentration was impractical. For those reasons he decided to split his forces, blocking one entrance with the ships he knew he could command and leaving *Vincennes*, *Quincy* and *Astoria* to look after the other.

Turner agreed with Crutchley's decision to divide his heavy cruiser force, both at the time and some years later. When asked to comment by the Deputy Chief of Naval Operations (Administration), Rear Admiral Charles Welborn, on remarks made by Morison in *The Struggle for Guadalcanal*, he gave his reasons which were generally similar to Crutchley's.[6]

Analysing the various options for positioning the heavy cruisers, Turner concluded that, given sufficient warning, a concentrated group inside Savo had a chance of intercepting a Japanese force passing south of that island, but that there was little chance of an interception before they could attack the transports off Tulagi if they passed north of Savo—even if warning was given of their approach. He concluded that the only way that interception could be assured was to split the cruisers and position them so as to guard both entrances. He, like Crutchley, emphasised that the purpose of the defending forces was the protection of both of the anchorages.

Turner also thought that effective tactical control of a long column of high-speed ships would have been very difficult, particularly when they had not trained together. He quoted the experiences of the Americans in three night battles in the Solomons to prove his point: Rear Admiral Scott at the Battle of Cape Esperance in October; Rear Admiral Callaghan at the Battle of Guadalcanal in November; and Rear Admiral Wright in the Battle of Tassafaronga, also in November. In the last-mentioned battle no less than four of five heavy cruisers steaming in line ahead had been torpedoed at a cost to the Japanese of one destroyer.

In his remarks, Turner revealed that there had been a considerable body of opinion in the USN before the war which favoured the use, in night action, of two or three separated groups rather than a single concentrated and therefore unwieldy force. This opinion had evolved from the results of many night exercises. This view was, however, not universally held because, in the pamphlet 'Battle Experience—Bulletin No. 2' referred to earlier, the sweeping statement was made that 'the fallacy of dividing defending forces was as old as war'; according to this, the cruisers should have been kept concentrated. At the time that opinion was published, the Hepburn Inquiry had not been undertaken and neither Turner nor Crutchley had received an opportunity to explain their reasons for splitting the heavy cruiser force.

It is noteworthy that King, in commenting on the Hepburn Report in September 1943, did not take issue with the acceptance of Crutchley's positioning of the heavy cruisers, despite the categoric statement of the pamphlet issued earlier in his name. Perhaps this was because he had taken the lesson of Tassafaronga to heart.

To extend the distances from the anchorages at which an enemy force aiming to attack them could be detected, Crutchley decided to place destroyer pickets to seaward of the heavy cruisers. He initially considered placing one in the channel either side of Savo but decided that they would give insufficicient warning. They clearly had to patrol outside Savo. The questions then arose as to how many destroyers, and how far outside. If they were placed too far to the north-west, an enemy force would be able to outflank them by using the passages between Florida and Santa Isabel, or between Guadalcanal and the Russell Islands, unless a large number of pickets were used.[7]

In the end it was the number of destroyers available which determined the issue. The three cruiser groups required anti-submarine protection and this would entail the use of six destroyers, two to each group. Crutchley considered, in view of intelligence reports of the movement of submarines towards Tulagi and Guadalcanal, that an anti-submarine screen of destroyers was required for each group of transports. The minimum requirement here was for three off Tulagi and four off Lunga Point, these being in addition to the four destroyer transports and four of the five minesweepers that had an anti-submarine capability and would be available for screening duties when not employed elsewhere.

Crutchley therefore decided to use only two destroyers for picket duty. He stationed the destroyer *Blue* seven miles to seaward of the southern entrance to the sound to patrol a line six miles long, oriented approximately north-east/south-west across the expected·line of approach through the Solomon Islands. The destroyer *Ralph Talbot* was instructed to carry out a similar patrol to seaward of the northern entrance. There was a gap of eight miles between the two patrol lines. *Blue* would approach to within seven miles of the Guadalcanal coast and *Ralph Talbot* within five miles of islands off Florida.

Crutchley chose those two ships for picket duty after the commander of Destroyer Squadron Four told him that, of the nine ships in his squadron, *Blue* and *Ralph Talbot* had consistently obtained the best results with their search radar. He advised Crutchley that the reliable detection range against a large ship would be six miles. Crutchley accepted what was the best advice available to him and considered that, as the patrol lines lay astride the track of any force seeking to pass either to the north or south of Savo, the chances of detection were excellent.

The patrols were by no means watertight and could have been avoided by an enemy force aware of their position. A single enemy ship tracking so as to pass through the centre of the gap between the patrols had a good (67 per cent) chance of avoiding detection, as did a single enemy force approaching close to the Florida coast. It was possible to achieve an undetected approach by hugging the coast of Guadalcanal. An enemy force of five ships in line ahead at high speed had less chance of avoiding detection, so that such a force approaching through the centre of the gap between the pickets had an even chance of avoiding detection. But in those days, before the use of radar for navigational purposes, the most likely route for an enemy force approaching the sound at night in the visibility which prevailed in that area would have been through the centre of one of the channels either side of Savo. Crutchley's patrols covered such an approach and this was exactly what Mikawa planned.

The argument regarding the number of pickets is one in which the chances of an enemy avoiding the aerial reconnaissance, and the two pickets too, had to be measured against the risk incurred by reducing the number of destroyers employed on anti-submarine screening duty inside the sound. Crutchley was aware of the considerable aerial reconnaissance effort which would be made to cover the approaches to Guadalcanal from the north-west, and had no reason to think that it would fail in its purpose. Yet his previous experience had made him cautious in placing complete reliance on it. The positioning of the pickets was in the nature of an insurance against an event which reason told him would probably not happen, but which he felt just possibly might.

Crutchley's night dispositions would have been altered after the departure of the Ndeni Occupation Force which was tentatively planned for the night of D-Day. This force, which was embarked in four transports and one supply ship, was to be escorted by *Quincy* and four destroyers. The dispositions would have had to have been changed again with the departure of the remaining eight transports escorted by *Vincennes, Astoria, San Juan*, two destroyers and the destroyer minesweepers tentatively set for the day after D-day.[8] The Australian cruisers and *Chicago*, with DESRON 4, were to stay with the five remaining store ships until they had completed unloading, when all would depart for Noumea on the fourth day after D-day. In the meantime bombs, aircraft fuel and lubricating oil would have been off-loaded from two ships scheduled to arrive on the day after D-day.

There was considerable intelligence of Japanese submarine activity in the Bismarck Archipelago and Solomon Islands, and in the New Caledonia area. There was therefore a real threat of submarine attack in the sound. If Crutchley had a low possibility of an undetected approach by surface forces on the one hand, on the other he faced a high probability of submarine attack in inshore waters where the odds would be in favour of the enemy. His judgment on 28 July was that the defence of the anchorages against submarine attack had priority, and with that there would seem to be no argument. Whether or not that judgment was still valid on the evening of 8 August is another matter which will be examined later.

During the last two days of the rehearsals, the cruisers and destroyers of the Amphibious Force fuelled from the American fleet tankers, *Platte* and *Kanawha*. These were large fast ships built especially for the supply of fuel to warships under way. Each ship carried 12 000 tons of oil fuel and was manned by an American naval crew and commanded by a naval officer of captain's rank. They were commissioned American ships and in that respect were different from anything *Canberra* and her captain had previously encountered. In the Indian Ocean *Canberra* had usually fuelled at anchor or, if under way, astern of relatively small, slow tankers manned by the merchant service.

Canberra was ordered to fuel from *Platte* at dawn on 28 July and the operation began with an argument between the two captains as to who was in charge of the operation and how they should go about it. In the end the American convinced Getting that *Canberra* should conform to the tanker's movements and that he should maintain his position alongside *Platte* rather than vice versa. This was a standard procedure in the USN, and had been for the three years since 1939 when much of the American doctrine for replenishment at sea had been developed as a result of trials conducted by the then recently promoted Rear Admiral Nimitz.

Canberra's fuelling was therefore quite an event and provided yet another example of the difficulties the two navies were experiencing in operating together. Twenty-five years later the author was often to take his ship alongside *Platte* during exercises in the China Sea for fuel. The procedures *Canberra* had found strange were by then routine, though the challenge of maintaining a ship within 150 feet (50 metres) of another while steaming at fifteen or more knots remained.

At sunset on the last day of July, the Amphibious Force formed up as a complete unit for the first time and set course at thirteen knots for Tulagi and Guadalcanal, following a route that was a dogleg south of the New Hebrides thence north to the Solomons passing to the west of Guadalcanal. The formation adopted was a circular one with the transports and store ships in the centre and the cruisers grouped ahead and astern of them, so as to provide a defence against aircraft attack. The whole was surrounded by a circle of seventeen destroyers providing not only a defence against submarine attack, but a further measure of anti-aircraft support. The three carriers and their escorts remained just over the horizon so as to be able to provide fighter defence if needed.

In anticipation of problems with oil fuel, the opportunity was taken to detach *Hobart*, six destroyers and the five destroyer minesweepers to obtain fuel in Vila Harbour as the force passed close to the south of Efate Island, but none was available in the port as the expected tanker had not arrived. The ships therefore rejoined and later fuelled from the fleet tanker *Cimarron*, after that oiler had topped up *Saratoga* and some destroyers in the carrier groups.[9] The problem of obtaining fuel was never far from the various commanders' minds and particularly that of Fletcher. The needs of the very short-ranged destroyer minesweepers and destroyer transports was a source of concern to them and their peace of mind was not eased with the loss of the services of the British Royal Fleet auxiliary *Bishopdale* which was damaged by a mine off Noumea.

The complement of the Amphibious Force was completed on the afternoon of the 3rd when the two transports joined that had not succeeded in making the rendezvous in Fiji. They brought with them a number of recently graduated officers from Annapolis. To the surprise of many, the entire Amphibious Force stopped on the afternoon of 5 August so that those young gentlemen could be transferred with their baggage to their new ships. There was a feeling of unease in *Canberra* as the ship rolled gently in the swell and this feeling must have been common throughout the force. The relief many felt was obvious when the ships got under way again. It was surely an unwise exercise and Fletcher saw fit to caution Turner lest he do it again.

For the first five days of the passage the weather was excellent and visibility generally good. The prospect of avoiding detection by the long-range flying boats operating out of Tulagi appeared slim but as the forces turned north towards the Solomons, the weather became overcast and dull and remained that way until the evening of the 6th. The Japanese were prevented by their local weather from any searches on 5 August, and the next day three Kawanishi flying boats got airborne from Tulagi but within an hour aborted their sorties because of low visibility and a cloud base of less than 100 feet.[10]

The submarine *S-44* arrived off the port of Kavieng in the north of New Ireland on the morning of 4 August. Plenty of targets were seen but none could be caught, so the patrol was moved to the southern end of Steffan Strait between New Hanover and New Britain. *S-44* arrived in her new station on the morning of 7 August, just too late to meet some very big game in the shape of the Japanese Cruiser Division Six, but luck was to change a few days later. The second submarine, *S-38*, arrived in the entrance to St George's Channel, between New Britain and New Ireland, at sunrise on 6 August.[11]

On 5 August, as the Expeditionary Force made its way north toward Guadalcanal, McCain's reconnaissance aircraft began operations in support. B-17s flew searches once a day from New Caledonia and Espiritu Santo to cover the Solomon Islands and the area to the west as far as New Georgia, while Catalinas, based on seaplane tenders, searched the sea areas to the north and east of Guadalcanal. During the forenoon of 6 August, *Chicago*'s radar detected an aircraft approaching. It was probably one of the three B-17 reconnaissance aircraft which flew from New Caledonia that morning to search to the west of Guadalcanal but no chances could be taken. All ships went to action stations and stayed at a high state of readiness for action for the remainder of that day; in the event they were to stay in that condition until 10 August, after the withdrawal of the surviving ships from Guadalcanal.

There was an important difference between the Australian and American cruisers' higher conditions of readiness for action. Although the British first degree of readiness and the American condition one both entailed instant readiness, the British second degree of readiness required all positions to be fully manned and the American condition two did not.[12] In *Canberra*, for example, personnel were at or near their action stations, but only half the guns and gunnery control positions were in an alert state. Personnel in the other positions were relaxed, perhaps sleeping or eating near their action stations, and with a small number away washing, getting some fresh air or obeying calls of nature.

Engineering personnel were rotated between their machinery spaces and damage control parties where they too could relax. They, in effect, had two action stations, as the machinery spaces and damage control parties were fully manned in the second degree. *Canberra* was following procedures that had been developed in the Royal Navy since the beginning of the war some three years previous. The call to action stations could be obeyed within seconds, as only a very small number of officers actually had to change their stations.

Condition two in the American ships was similar, in that it required half the armament and control positions to be manned and alert. There was, however, a very significant difference in that those off watch could sleep in their cabins or in their accommodation spaces which could be some distance away from their general quarters stations. Some had condition two stations which differed from their general quarters positions. The result was a considerable hubbub in a ship which lasted several minutes as men moved to general quarters.

Crutchley had discussed the states of readiness with Rear Admiral Scott, who was flying his flag in *San Juan*, during the meeting held in *Australia* on 31 July. It was because of what Scott told him that, after he instructed the escorting ships on 6 August to assume the first degree of readiness, he did not order a relaxation to the second degree at any time while the ships were off Guadalcanal. To have done so would have reduced the American ships to what was, in his view, an unacceptable state of readiness. Instead, he signalled to all ships that when they were in the first degree of readiness they could send small numbers away from their quarters to eat. In effect, he was introducing the Americans to the British second degree of readiness.

10

Watchtower launched

At 0130 on the morning of D-day the first contact with Guadalcanal was made when *Henley*'s radar detected the high land at the western end of the island at a range of nineteen miles. The Amphibious Force had already split into its two groups in preparation for the final approach to their objectives. Visibility had steadily improved after dark, so that when the moon rose at 0224 the invaders were able to navigate confidently towards their anchorages. Group Yoke, the Tulagi assault force, steered so as to pass to the north of Savo Island while Group X-ray, bound for Guadalcanal, passed to the south.[1]

As they approached the passages into the sound, hands were sent to action stations in the expectation that the Japanese would have patrols guarding the approaches into the sound. Nothing was seen and people relaxed a little, though still watchful for any sign of enemy activity. As *Canberra*, following *San Juan*, shepherded Group Yoke towards Tulagi, those on *Canberra*'s bridge were inclined to whisper in case they disturbed the sleeping enemy. Dawn broke and the smoke from cooking fires could be seen ashore, but there was still no sign of enemy activity.

Then, at 0615, when the leading transports were less than five miles from their anchorage, the peace on board *Canberra* was shattered as her aircraft was started up on the catapult and launched for an anti-submarine patrol. Ashore, the peace was disturbed by the arrival of a squadron of fighters and a squadron of dive-bombers from the carriers 70 miles to the south-west. The fighters strafed and destroyed, without loss to themselves, seven Japanese flying boats and nine seaplane fighters before they could take off, while the eighteen dive-bombers dropped their 1000-pound (454 kilogram) bombs on the Marines' first objective, the northern half of the island.

Canberra *under way off Tulagi during the landings on 7–8 August. She is flying battle ensigns in addition to the white ensign at the gaff. American transports and landing craft are in the background.* (US National Archives neg. 80–G–13485)

As the aircraft attacked, *San Juan* and two destroyers opened fire on selected targets ashore. During the bombardment, *San Juan* and some of the destroyers sighted what they took to be a periscope and the latter carried out several depth charge attacks, with no visible results. The incident was a reminder of the intelligence reports which told of submarine activity in the area.

The transports of Group Yoke steamed on to anchor at 0637 and prepared for the landings which were due to commence at 0800. On the southern side of the sound, Group X-ray had a similarly uneventful passage to its anchorage off Lunga Point, arriving at 0650. H-Hour for the landings there was set for 0910.

For the naval forces protecting Group Yoke the rest of the day was almost an anticlimax, as the Japanese made no attempt to disrupt the landings in the Tulagi area by air attack, but for the Marines it was an entirely different matter. The first landing occurred a few minutes before H-hour, not on Tulagi, but on nearby Florida Island opposite Tulagi, in order to seize a position from which the approach of landing craft to Gavutu later in the morning could be covered. The landing was unopposed.[2]

Precisely at 0800 the 1st Raider Battalion landed on Blue Beach on Tulagi. Finding a way through or over the coral provided more of a challenge than did the Japanese, for once again the landing was unopposed. But the Japanese more than made up for their lack of opposition later in the day, and the Marines made slow progress as they moved against enemy positions at the southern and higher end of the island. At dusk, having been reinforced by an infantry battalion, the Marines established a line for the night which was savagely attacked four times during darkness. The next day the Japanese retreated into caves which, after much hard fighting, were sealed so that by late afternoon the capture of Tulagi had been completed at a cost to the Marines of 155 casualties.

In the meantime, at midday on D-Day the Marine Parachute Battalion,

The scene in Tulagi Harbour on D-Day, 7 August 1942, looking south-east over Tanambogo and Gavutu; Tulagi itself is out of view to the right. The causeway linking the two islands can be seen beneath the righthand edge of the smoke pall. Various arms of Florida Island are visible at the top left of the picture and in the distance. While Tulagi fell to US Marines by the afternoon of that first day, Tanambogo and Gavutu were the scene of bitter fighting with heavy American casualties—some of them accidentally caused by dive-bombers from the US carriers during 8 August. (US National Archives neg 80–G–11899)

under cover of gunfire support from a destroyer, assaulted the tiny island of Gavutu which prewar had been the headquarters of Lever Brothers in the Solomons. This time the landing was bitterly opposed from enemy positions in well-protected dugouts and caves. With a great deal of difficulty the parachutists succeeded in establishing themselves on the island, but reducing the Japanese strong points one by one was a long process. An assault on the nearby island of Tanambogo, connected to Gavutu by a causeway, was beaten back with heavy losses. As on Tulagi, the Japanese vigorously counterattacked during the night.

Vandegrift was not satisfied that he had the strength necessary to overcome Japanese resistance on Gavutu and Tanambogo. That evening he asked Turner to release one of the two battalions being held in reserve for use on Gavutu. Turner released both battalions, one of which landed on Gavutu early the next morning and enabled the Marines to renew their attacks; by midday nearly all oppposition there had been overcome. As these two battalions were the core of the Ndeni Occupation Force, the detachment of that force was postponed.[3] The retirement plan was already out of gear

88

USS San Juan *pictured off Norfolk, Virginia, in June 1942. On 7 August she made a spectacular sight as she sailed in close to Tanambogo and fired rapid broadsides against Japanese dug in on the island.* (US National Archives neg. 19–N–31525)

and Crutchley's Screening Group would remain at full strength throughout the night.

The Japanese on Tanambogo continued to hold out with the result that personnel on deck in nearby cruisers and destroyers had ringside seats as six dive-bombers attacked the tiny island in the middle of the afternoon. The attack was worse than useless, as several bombs fell among the Marines on Gavutu and killed several of them.[4] *San Juan* then closed on the island and for five minutes gave an awesome display of naval firepower, as she unleashed rapid salvos against the island using her full broadside of fourteen 5-inch guns. As the ship was using full flash cordite there were times when she seemed to be enveloped in flame.

San Juan's act was followed by a repeat performance by dive-bombers with only slightly better results than before. This time Tanambogo was hit, but then so was Gavutu with further Marine casualties. After that second experience, the Marines on Gavutu decided that they would forgo carrier air support for the remainder of the day.

The destroyer *Buchanan* then closed to within a few hundred yards of Tanambogo and, like *San Juan* before her, for five minutes fired full flash rapid salvos into the island. This apparently had the desired effect because a few minutes later a Marine company was able to land. It was to be another day, however, before all Japanese opposition on the two small islands had been overcome.

Vandegrift was later to describe the assaults on Gavutu and Tanambogo as 'a storming operation, unremitting and relentless, decided by the extermination of one or another of the adversaries engaged'.[5] It was to be followed by many more similar experiences for the United States Marine Corps, culminating in the capture of Iwo Jima in an operation which cost the Marines 5300 dead.

Across the sound on Guadalcanal, the experiences of the landing force from Group X-ray were very different. The initial landing by two battalions was preceded by a bombardment by *Australia*, *Vincennes*, *Quincy* and *Astoria* and four destroyers. The landing was unopposed and as the day wore on it became clear that the enemy had 'gone bush', leaving behind them a large amount of stores and the materials to build a first-class air base—all of which the Americans were to put to good use, particularly an ice-making machine and large quantities of beer. The inventory of captured material also included generators, nine road rollers, over a hundred trucks and a large quantity of aviation fuel in underground storages.[6] The Marines were impressed with the quality of much of the captured material. Some of it, particularly the medical stores and equipment, was better than that of the Marines and was put to immediate use. The biggest prize was an airfield which could be ready for use within four days.

Having started the day keyed up to a high pitch of excitement in expectation of action against the enemy, the ships' companies of Crutchley's Screening Group had begun to relax when, at 1120, the first indication was received that the Japanese did not intend to give up their foothold in the southern Solomons without a fight. The coastwatcher in the south of Bougainville, Lieutenant Paul Mason RANVR, had sighted a strong force of enemy bombers heading towards Guadalcanal, and immediately passed the information to his controlling radio station.[7]

Within 25 minutes, ships off Guadalcanal had received the message via the Canberra and Pearl Harbor naval radio stations and news of an impending attack was broadcast to ships' companies. The broadcast in *Canberra* ended with an order for hands to proceed to dinner, this being a meal of cornish pasties washed down with tea, which was distributed throughout the ship while personnel remained at their action stations.[8]

Thus warned, at 1325 a force of 27 twin-engined bombers and 18 Zero fighters were intercepted by the defending fighters fifteen miles west of Savo Island. The fighters and anti-aircraft fire between them shot down three bombers and two fighters. No less than 21 bombers and two fighters were damaged at a cost to the Americans of nine fighters.[9] The attack was made on the transports of Group X-ray from a height of about 10 000 feet, all aircraft dropping their bombs simultaneously on a signal from the leading

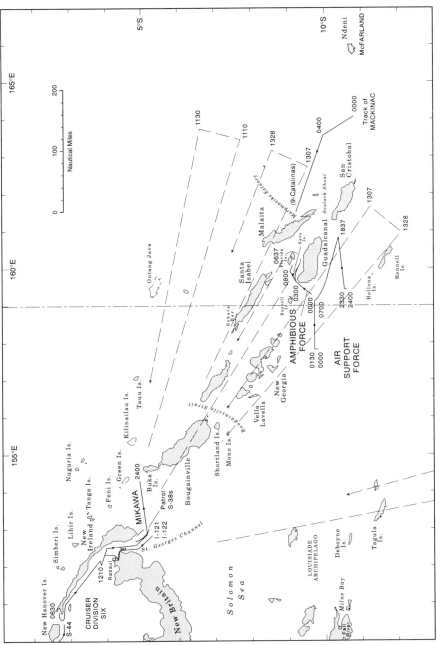

Allied and Japanese naval movements and Japanese air searches on D-Day

aircraft. This method of attack had been very accurate in the Coral Sea when *Australia* was straddled by a pattern of bombs, several falling close enough to the ship to deluge personnel with water thrown up by the explosions. At Guadalcanal, though, the Japanese did not even come close, as all bombs fell in open water to the north-west of the transports.

There was no warning of the next attack, which was carried out by sixteen dive-bombers of a type normally operated from carriers. These aircraft made a split-level attack, with the result that only those at the lower level were intercepted; fortunately, these attackers did no damage but lost six of their number. Those at the higher level went on to bomb the screen around Group X-ray but, surprisingly, made no attempt to attack the transports at anchor nearby. The only damage caused was to the destroyer *Mugford*, which was hit aft by a 250-pound (113 kilogram) bomb. This caused loss of life and put out of action the aft two 5-inch guns, but the ship was still able to carry on with her screening duties—albeit with a reduced anti-aircraft capability.[10] The two attacks had cost the Japanese a total of eleven aircraft, but the Americans lost ten fighters and the Zero lost none of its reputation as a fighter superior to the Grumman F-4 Wildcat.

Noyes correctly evaluated the carrier-type dive-bombers as having come from Rabaul and been routed through Kieta or Buka. Because of the prevailing south-easterly wind, his carriers had moved during the day from a position at dawn which was about 40 miles south-west of the western end of Guadalcanal to a position at dusk 25 miles south of the eastern end of the island. He intended to move back during the night to the north-west, and to resume flying the next day to the south-west of Guadalcanal.[11]

The Expeditionary Force Commander, however, had other ideas. Fletcher assumed that the use of the carrier-type aircraft indicated the presence of a carrier to the west of Guadalcanal. He therefore overruled his Air Support Commander and instructed him to commence the next day's operations 110 miles further east.[12] By so doing he may have decreased the threat from a possible single carrier to his three carriers, but he also reduced the chances of finding and striking it to remove a potent threat not only to his carriers but to the Amphibious Force too.

Fletcher was effectively placing the force he was there to protect and support between himself and Rabaul, the main enemy base, and he ensured the aircraft searches planned for the next day could serve only to provide security for his own force. They would do almost nothing to back up the reconnaissance effort provided by McCain's B-17s in covering the most likely approach of any Japanese force to Guadalcanal—that is, down the passage which lay through the centre of the Solomons, later known as the Slot. There could be no clearer demonstration of Fletcher's obsession with the safety of his carriers. He had decreased the risk to them but increased the vulnerability of the Amphibious Force. It is difficult to fathom his reasoning except in the context of 'calculated risk', but where was 'the superior force'?

During the day Nimitz warned the ships off Guadalcanal that enemy submarines were on the move to attack the Expeditionary Force. MacArthur also warned that an enemy submarine had been heard during the afternoon transmitting on its radio about 120 miles south-east of Tulagi. This latter report seemed to confirm the submarine sightings made at much the same time by aircraft on two separate occasions, the position given on each being close to Tawara'o Island, a small islet to the east of Guadalcanal. One report was of a surfaced submarine and, in retrospect, both sightings were probably of reefs in that vicinity. In making their plans for the next day, though, Turner and Crutchley could not afford to ignore the possibility that a submarine was attempting to enter the sound from the east, through either Lengo or Sealark Channels.

At dusk ships moved to their patrol and screening stations for the night, which passed uneventfully. The nature of the patrols of the three cruiser groups had been left to the senior officers of each group. Crutchley chose for *Australia*'s group a patrol line running parallel to the Guadalcanal coast and lying just to the eastward of the passage between Savo and Guadalcanal. Course was reversed to starboard every hour without signal, the patrol speed being twelve knots. The two destroyers were stationed on each bow and did not change sides when course was reversed—that is, *Patterson* always remained on the Guadalcanal side of the formation and *Bagley* on the Tulagi side. Thus the hiatus which inevitably follows any alteration of course within a formation was reduced to a minumum, and the bridge of *Canberra* was a very quiet place.

As the senior officer of the group which his ship led, Captain Riefkohl of *Vincennes* chose to carry out a box patrol in the centre of the passage between Savo and Florida, and just inside the sound. The sides of the patrol box were five miles long and were traversed at a speed of only ten knots. *Vincennes* thus altered course every 30 minutes and the destroyers, to maintain station on their respective bows of the formation, spent much of their time changing station. The hiatus in the formation which followed each alteration of course was considerable and prolonged. Another distraction on the bridges of the American ships was the almost ceaseless chatter on the TBS. Scott in *San Juan* conducted his patrol in the same manner as Crutchley, orienting his patrol line north and south between the two anchorages.

As D-Day drew to a close, the Allies had every reason to feel satisfied with the progress made. The Marines were ashore on Guadalcanal in strength, and although progress towards the airfield had been slow—due principally to the difficulties unfit troops had in penetrating a rainforest—there was little doubt that this would be occupied on the morrow. The only visible cloud on the horizon was the slowness with which the ships were being unloaded, due to congestion on the beaches. It soon became clear that the manpower allocated for unloading was inadequate, but troops could not yet be spared from their primary task of establishing themselves ashore.[13]

On the northern side of the sound, there still remained a lot of hard fighting to be done before all resistance had been overcome. A reserve battalion would need to be committed there, but a successful issue did not seem in doubt. Unloading of the ships had still to begin, however, due to the level of resistance experienced. It must have become clear to Turner during the afternoon—even before Vandegrift asked for reinforcements for an attack on Gavutu—that the Ndeni Occupation Force was not going to be able to depart that night, and that the retirement plan would have to be amended.

The anti-submarine defence of the anchorages had been boosted by the release, earlier than expected, of the minesweeping destroyers from their minesweeping tasks. No mines had been found, so that the transports had been able to move closer to their beaches to facilitate unloading.

There was, however, another cloud on the horizon which went unrecognised as the harbinger of disaster that it was. Just before midnight a signal was received from MacArthur's headquarters advising that, at an unspecified time during the day, B-17s had sighted six unidentified ships in St George's Channel heading south-east. The message also advised that, just before midday, a total of four cruisers and one destroyer had been seen off Rabaul on a westerly course.[14]

The signal from MacArthur's headquarters provided no other information. Its recipients off Guadalcanal were, therefore, left to decide for themselves whether the first report was of warships and, if so, whether the reports referred to the same group of ships. They were also left to assess for themselves whether the enemy ships sighted were any threat to the Guadalcanal area. No doubt intelligence officers throughout the force advised their superiors to wait and see. The Japanese were known to be reinforcing New Guinea. Might not the forces sighted be involved in those troop movements? If they were heading towards Guadalcanal, they still had to pass a submarine patrol and through an area patrolled by long-range reconnaissance aircraft. If they were heading for the Expeditionary Force, they would no doubt be seen again and reported.

During the afternoon, Turner realised that the searches provided by the B-17s based on Espiritu Santo could not guarantee him adequate warning of the approach of surface forces from the north-west—the direction of greatest threat. He saw that an enemy force could still be north of New Georgia at dusk and approach Guadalcanal under the cover of darkness. He was not happy to leave the task of searching north-west of New Georgia in the hands of aircraft with which he could not communicate, and which were provided by another area commander. He therefore asked McCain to extend the searches of his Catalinas to the west so that they would search the area between New Georgia and Rabaul. He acknowledged that the aircraft would have to 'poach' in MacArthur's area, but he believed that a morning search of that area was necessary to ensure his force adequate security.[15]

In conversations in 1960 with his biographer, Vice-Admiral Dyer, Turner expressed the opinion that, if McCain had fully appreciated the problem that an undetected Japanese approach would pose to the forces off Guadalcanal, he would have instituted searches that were 'more airtight'. Turner also felt that McCain should have instituted late afternoon searches through the island chain. He wanted Dyer to thoroughly research 'the air reconnaissance matter' and to present the results to him, but Turner died before this could be done.[16]

If Turner had any other concern about the coverage achieved by McCain's aircraft during the day, he had to wait until almost 0200 the next morning for the report from McCain which informed him that bad weather had prevented reconnaissance to the west and south-west of Guadalcanal. The carrier force flew no searches that afternoon, either of their own volition or in response to any request from McCain. If Fletcher's phantom carrier had been to the west of Guadalcanal, it would have remained unmolested.

At daybreak, the patrolling cruisers resumed their duties of the previous day. *Canberra* and *Chicago* patrolled near the transports off Tulagi, while *Australia* and *Hobart* operated near those off Lunga Point. The destroyers either rejoined their fire support groups or joined the anti-submarine screens off each of the anchorages. Ashore, the Marines were preparing to clear Tanambogo of the enemy and launch an attack on Gavutu. Unloading had still not got under way on Tulagi, while that on Guadalcanal had been suspended during the night because of congestion on the beaches. The tentative plan to withdraw the transports, escorted by all the warships except for Crutchley's Task Force 44, was looking increasingly optimistic.

Crutchley was aware that the withdrawal plans were in a state of flux and that the operation was behind schedule. He therefore sought clarification of the situation from Turner in a message that read: 'As second in command, when you have time, could I have rough outline of present situation and future intentions'.[17]

Following this message, which was sent by flashing light to *McCawley* at 0911, Crutchley's Operations Officer, Commander Gatacre, paid a short visit to Turner's flagship between 0945 and 1030. No record of his purpose has survived; indeed, the only mention of the visit having taken place is in *Australia*'s Deck Log.[18] Gatacre was obviously on his admiral's business as he used the admiral's barge, but the purpose is unlikely to have been connected with Crutchley's request for information regarding Turner's future plans. This had been taken care of in the signal sent just a few minutes before Gatacre left *Australia*.

The most likely reason for the visit is that Gatacre (and Crutchley) was seeking Turner's views or those of his staff on the submarine threat. Since

0700 two radio reports of submarines being in the vicinity had been received, and as a result Turner had given Crutchley fresh instructions regarding the use of cruiser aircraft on anti-submarine patrol. If this was so then it is yet another indication that the submarine threat loomed large in Crutchley's thinking that day. In such circumstances it is most unlikely that he would have given any consideration to increasing the number of destroyers on patrol to seaward of Savo the following night. Such an increase could only have been made at the expense of the anti-submarine protection of the cruisers and transports.

In response to the apparently increasing submarine threat, the destroyer minesweepers were employed in patrolling the western end of the Lengo and Sealark channels and all available cruiser aircraft (which sometimes totalled as many as six) were engaged on anti-submarine patrols. The perceived threat from submarines intensified at midday, when Nimitz signalled that a number of Japanese submarines were *en route* to the Florida Island area. These were apparently in addition to those reported the previous day as being on the move to Tulagi. Apprehension peaked when Turner informed all ships just after midday that there was a possibility that one or more submarines were in the transport area.

Submarine threat aside, Crutchley's request for information on Turner's future intentions was to have an effect which no one could have foreseen. It would appear from the text that Crutchley was asking for nothing more than a signalled situation report while seeking to be informed of what Turner had in mind for a revised withdrawal program. He was responsible for the defence of the anchorages, and therefore it was important for him to know as far in advance as possible which forces he would have available to him to carry out the task and what he would be required to defend. He was to wait all day for a reply.

For a while during that morning, concern over the increasing (but as yet unrealised) submarine threat was obscured by the reappearance of another threat which distracted the attention of all those afloat in the sound. At 1018 Canberra naval radio station broadcast a message from the coastwatcher, Lieutenant W.J. 'Jack' Read RANVR, that 40 large twin-engined aircraft had passed him 36 minutes earlier, heading south-east. Read's station was in northern Bougainville, overlooking Buka Passage, and that morning he had been resiting his radio when the enemy flew over him.[19] Read did not see all the aircraft, as the total was actually 23 twin-engined torpedo bombers (Bettys) and four carrier-type aircraft with an escort of 37 fighters.

Soon after the receipt of Read's message, all the transports were told to get under way and manoeuvred in two groups between Florida and Tulagi awaiting the attack.[20] At 1120 *Chicago*'s radar detected the incoming raid, but it was not until midday that what were obviously torpedo bombers were sighted approaching from the east over the tip of Florida Island. Flying at

Japanese Navy 'Betty' bombers fly in at very low level to drop torpedoes against Allied ships off Guadalcanal, at midday on 8 August 1942. Despite the impressive sight these aircraft presented, the results achieved by the enemy were meagre and cost them eighteen of the 23 Bettys in the attacking force. (US National Archives neg. 90–G–17066)

This photograph, taken from Australia, *shows a Japanese bomber about to crash after taking gun-fire from the RAN cruiser. (A. Zammit)*

between 20 and 40 feet, these swept in a gaggle past *Canberra* and Group Yoke, strafing ships as they went. Only one minor casualty was caused by this fire: a sailor near *Canberra*'s bridge who suffered concussion when his steel helmet was knocked off his head by a machine-gun bullet.

The attackers flew on to launch their torpedoes against Group X-ray but suffered considerable damage as they did so, for the anti-aircraft fire was both spectacular and highly successful. Observers in *Australia*, *Chicago* and *Hobart*, who had seen the same 25th Air Flotilla in action during the Battle of the Coral Sea, considered that the range at which torpedoes were dropped this time was too long, thereby allowing the transports and other ships to turn away to avoid them. The only hit registered was on the destroyer *Jarvis*, which was severely damaged but remained afloat. One of the aircraft crashed into the transport *George F. Elliot*, causing that ship to catch fire and eventually become a total loss.

Crutchley described the scene in the following terms:

> A magnificent curtain of bursting high explosive was put up and enemy aircraft were everywhere crashing in flames. Torpedoes were dropped mostly at long range but many of the aircraft continued to fly in towards the formation to strafe personnel.[21]

At the other end of the naval pecking order, the author was later to enter in his Midshipman's Journal that:

> As the bombers cleared the land they swooped down close to the water. It was then that it was realised that they were torpedo bombers flying in three V-formations with Zero fighters protecting them. They spread out and selected their targets. *Canberra* opened fire as they came down close to the water. They passed down our port side out of range of the Oerlikons but the port four-inch had an excellent target. We fired an eight-inch barrage but results were not seen. Two bombers sheered out of line and headed towards our bow. We turned away at the same time opening fire with Oerlikons. We succeeded in bringing down one if not both of them.

Almost at the same time as the torpedo bombers attacked, other Japanese aircraft carried out an unsuccessful medium-level bombing attack. The 25th Air Flotilla had learnt nothing from their previous experience in attacking heavily armed warships during the Battle of the Coral Sea. Once again they had all approached from the same direction instead of several directions simultaneously, thus making it easier to evade their torpedoes and facilitating their own destruction. In all, no less than eighteen Bettys and two fighters were destroyed, the majority by intense anti-aircraft fire which included 8-inch fire from most of the heavy cruisers present.

The guns had had a most successful shoot but where had the fighters been? In *Canberra* someone was heard to mutter 'Just like the Air Force; never there when you want them'. It transpired that only three of the more

The American destroyer Jarvis *dead in the water after being hit by a Japanese torpedo.* (J. Langrell)

than 80 fighters available in the carriers, which were twenty minutes' flying time away, had been over Tulagi at the moment of attack—in spite of the more than 90 minutes' warning that Read had given of the enemy's approach.[22]

The reason is difficult, even now, to understand. The basic cause was Fletcher's obsession with the possibility that a Japanese carrier was operating in the Coral Sea. He had instructed Noyes, the Air Support Force's commander, to carry out a search towards Rabaul on the morning of 8 August. Noyes had allocated the search to *Wasp*, with instructions to employ twelve aircraft. To enable any carrier located by the search to be attacked without delay, and to facilitate the reinforcement of fighters airborne in the event of an attack on his carriers, he ordered *Saratoga* to maintain her air group in a state of instant readiness on deck until midday, when *Wasp* was to take over that responsibility. This effffectively reduced by a third the carrier air effort available to support the Marines and provide for the fighter defence of the anchorages.

When Read's message that 40 twin-engined aircraft were on their way was received, ten fighters were airborne over Tulagi and seventeen over the carriers. This was half of the total fighter complement of *Wasp* and *Enterprise*, sixteen remaining in *Wasp* and about ten in *Enterprise*. Eight fighters were scrambled from *Wasp* before the morning search aircraft started landing on, and these had joined those over the carriers even though seven of the fighters over Tulagi were due to return to *Wasp* at about midday.

The Force Fighter Control Officer in *Enterprise* had been concerned all

Contrary to the image of havoc created by this picture, the enemy air attack caused the loss of just one allied ship: the US transport George F. Elliot *(seen burning at left) which was set on fire amidships after a Japanese aircraft crashed into her. The other two plumes of smoke are from bombers downed in the sea.* (NHC neg. NH69114)

morning at the paucity of fighter cover. Twice, at 0758 and 0946, he asked for approval for *Saratoga* to keep a carrier aircraft patrol (CAP) airborne. Noyes refused permission each time, on the grounds that *Saratoga* must remain at immediate notice to launch a strike against the suspected carrier or to send up fighters to reinforce those already airborne if the carriers were attacked. If she had maintained a CAP airborne, *Saratoga* would not have been able to launch a strike during the period that fighters were being recovered and the flight deck reorganised.

Those were the days before the development of the 'angled deck'. Whereas carriers today can launch and receive aircraft at the same time because of that angled deck, in 1942 this was not possible. An aircraft would land, be brought to a halt by an arrester wire stretched across the flight deck to catch the aircraft's tail hook, and then taxied forward into a deck park of aircraft. When all aircraft had landed, those in the deck park had to be either struck down by a lift into the hangar or moved aft and readied for take-off—a lengthy process.

When word was received in *Enterprise* of the aircraft over Buka, the Force Fighter Control Officer once again, at 1050, asked for approval to launch *Saratoga*'s fighters. His plan was to have all available fighters airborne, half over Tulagi and half over the carriers, from 1100. Noyes was waiting for the results of the morning search and, when the last aircraft returned to *Wasp*, his flagship, at 1025, he must have been made aware very quickly that nothing had been sighted. Yet it was not until 1105 that he originated a message releasing *Saratoga*'s fighters for use against the incoming raid. It was to be 1135 before *Saratoga* received that message, which was made visually from *Enterprise*.

Saratoga commenced launching 27 fighters six minutes later. The first eight were led by their squadron commander who was later to state that, after being launched and forming up the remainder of his two flights, he climbed to 16 000 feet to get above the weather. He arrived in time to see the anti-aircraft bursts still in the air, but no enemy aircraft were in sight. During the following twenty minutes he was joined by the remainder of *Saratoga*'s fighters. The Air Support Force had plainly failed to provide, from resources which were available, an adequate fighter defence of the Amphibious Force that morning—notwithstanding the extensive warning period given by Read. For that, Captain Ramsey of *Saratoga* must be held accountable.

The previous evening, *Saratoga*'s Air Group Commander had returned from the last mission of the day over Tulagi with a specific request from Turner for a bombing mission against Tanambogo, in support of a dawn attack on that island. *Saratoga* was unable to obtain approval for this mission from Noyes, because of the need to maintain radio silence and because *Wasp* was outside visual signalling range of *Saratoga*. On his own initiative, therefore, Captain Ramsey of *Saratoga* launched 31 aircraft at sunrise and planned to recover them at about 1030. This was half the carrier's entire strike force and with it were the Air Group Commander and three out of four squadron commanders. Ramsey must surely have realised that once he started to recover the Tanambogo strike, he would be unable to scramble fighters and the remaining strike aircraft for some time, and that therefore he would be unable to comply during that period with any order to launch his air group.

The extent to which confusion prevailed in the Air Support Force that morning can be gauged from an examination of the following log of events, which has been compiled from records in the archives of the Naval War College:[23]

0605 *Saratoga* commenced launching 27 strike aircraft for dawn raid on Tanambogo, an action which was contrary to Noyes's instructions promulgated by signal the previous afternoon.

0702 *Saratoga* launched four fighters also in contravention of previous orders.

0758 Kinkaid (in *Enterprise*) passed to Noyes (in *Wasp*) a request from the Force Fighter Control Officer, for *Saratoga* to launch eight fighters as a CAP at 0830 and again at 1030.

0820 Noyes refused permission for *Saratoga* to launch fighters, explaining that that carrier must be ready to launch a strike or fighters in case of an attack and directed Kinkaid's attention to his instructions of the previous afternoon.

0925 Noyes politely told Ramsey in *Saratoga* that he did not appear to be obeying orders, repeated those orders and directed that any further requests for action which conflicted with those orders be referred to him.

0946 *Saratoga* told Noyes that *Enterprise* had requested the launch of eight fighters and requested advice.

0952 *Saratoga* launched eight fighters.

0959 *Saratoga* recovered the four fighters which had been launched at 0702.

1003 *Enterprise* launched fighters, three of which joined seven from *Wasp* as a CAP over Tulagi.

1007 *Saratoga* commenced recovering Tanambogo strike aircraft.

1015 Noyes refused request from *Saratoga* to launch fighters and repeated his instructions regarding being ready to launch in the event of an attack.

1023 *Saratoga* recovered her eight fighters.

1024 *Wasp* completed recovery of her search aircraft.

1043 *Wasp* launched eight fighters for CAP over the carriers, making a total CAP of 25.

1048 *Saratoga* completed recovering Tanambogo strike.

1050 Kinkaid reported intercepting Read's message and suggested to both Fletcher and Noyes that all *Saratoga*'s and half of *Wasp*'s fighters be stationed over Tulagi and the remaining fighters from *Enterprise* and *Wasp* be kept over the carriers.

1058 *Wasp* reported to Noyes (presumably by telephone or voice pipe) that the morning search had seen no carrier.

1105 Noyes originated a message to *Saratoga* authorising the use of her fighters against the impending bombing attack. Possibly because *Saratoga* was not initially within visual signalling distance of *Wasp*, *Saratoga* did not receive this message until 1135. (This may have saved Ramsey some embarrassment as *Saratoga*'s flight deck would not have been ready for a launch until about that time.)

1130 CAP over Tulagi reduced to three aircraft by departure of the seven *Wasp* fighters because of a lack of fuel.

1141 *Saratoga* commenced flying off her fighters.

1200 Japanese aircraft attacked the Amphibious Force which was defended by three fighters.

In the circumstances, it must be assumed from his actions that Captain Ramsey was convinced that an enemy carrier was not in the vicinity. That he should have been able to flout Noyes's instructions under the very nose of Fletcher and his staff almost defies belief. As a result of this episode, Noyes was criticised for losing control of his air operations during a critical period. He could and should have replaced *Wasp*'s fighters as they returned from Tulagi with some of those 25 already over the carriers, replacing them in turn with some of *Saratoga*'s fighters who would have been at altitude over the carriers soon after 1100. That neither he nor Fletcher took any action to ensure that there was an adequate fighter defence over the transports, at a time when attack was expected, is further proof that neither of them fully accepted their responsibilities for the air defence of the entire Expeditionary Force.[24]

Another harbinger of disaster went unrecognised when, at 0739 on the 8th, a report was received from MacArthur's headquarters that a submarine had sighted two destroyers and three larger unknown ships proceeding at dusk the previous evening through St George's Channel at high speed on a south-easterly course.[25] This was a report from *S-38* and seems to have attracted very little attention, probably because it was already twelve hours old. The sighting was also close to a major enemy base where considerable traffic was only to be expected, as evidenced by the sighting of a destroyer and two merchant ships by *S-38* earlier that day. If the ships were bound for the Guadalcanal area, it would have been expected that the considerable air reconnaissance scheduled for that day would relocate them.

As the day wore on, the intelligence picture for the waters between Rabaul and Buka became confused when reports were received from various aircraft of a two-funnelled cruiser of 8000 tons; two merchant ships; a two-funnelled destroyer; a light cruiser in company with a destroyer, a small escort and an 8000-ton merchant ship; and a corvette with a 6000-ton merchant ship. The subjects of these sightings were steering courses all round the compass. Immediately to the south of Bougainville, three escorts and a merchant ship were seen near the Shortland Islands.[26] The tendency among intelligence officers must still have been to wait and see. In the evening ACH Townsville issued an analysis of the situation which assessed that the shipping and aircraft movements observed indicated the possibility that the occupation in strength of Bougainville and Buka was under way, and that Kieta airfield would be activated. The fog of war was descending over the area.[27]

11
Precipitate withdrawal of the carriers

In the sound, the afternoon passed without any further air attacks or submarine alarms. There was, however, an air-raid warning which, though it proved to be a false alarm, unfortunately caused unloading to be interrupted yet again as the ships got under way and moved from their anchorages.

Fletcher's anxiety over the threat of attack from shore-based aircraft was heightened by the raid at midday, particularly when he learnt from *Enterprise* that pilots intercepting the raiders were of the opinion that some twin-engined aircraft were carrying torpedoes. He sought verification of this from Noyes and 25 minutes later asked him if he agreed that the carriers should be withdrawn, because of the possibility of torpedo bomber attack and a reduction in fighter strength. In the same message he asked Noyes whether he agreed that, if the carriers remained in the area for the next day, they should remain to the south-east of Guadalcanal. Fletcher was certainly not in an aggressive mood that afternoon, even though there had been no sign of a Japanese carrier—in spite of his best efforts to find one—and the midday raid had been decimated by anti-aircraft fire and a very small number of fighters.

Noyes replied within an hour, and within another hour Fletcher made his decision to recommend withdrawal. During that time the latter made no attempt to obtain from Turner an update of the report, made the previous evening, of the situation ashore. From that report Fletcher knew that all the troops were ashore on Guadalcanal and that only light opposition had been encountered, that the eastern end of Tulagi and Tanambogo were still in enemy hands, and that in the course of two air raids only one ship, *Mugford*, had been damaged. He also knew that Turner had been forced to commit his reserves, and that therefore the occupation of Ndeni had been postponed.

104

From his own observations of the employment of his aircraft by the Marines, he probably knew that fighting had continued during the day on Gavutu and Tanambogo. He must surely have appreciated that there was every possibility that the Marines would require air support the next day, yet made no attempt to find out what that requirement might be.

Fletcher also knew that Turner's retirement plan had been disorganised by the need to delay the detachment of the force to occupy Ndeni. He could not have failed to consider the possibility that air attacks and the unexpected delays in capturing Tulagi and adjacent islands had delayed unloading. Regardless of whether he thought that unloading had gone to plan, he knew that unloading of the heavy equipment was expected to take four days (in fact, Turner had told him at the *Saratoga* conference that it would take five). Even if unloading had proceeded at a pace which left the transports free to depart early on 9 August, withdrawal would still leave the five supply ships and Crutchley's Task Force 44 to face the expected heavy air attacks without the benefit of fighter defence.

Turner would then have been faced with the decision whether to accept for Task Force 44 and the supply ships the role of a tethered goat, with all the attendant risks, or to withdraw and deprive the Marines of their equipment—including what was necessary to complete the airfield. It is no defence of Fletcher to claim that his withdrawal did not prevent the airfield being ready for operations on the evening of 10 August, because at the time he made his decision to leave he had not been informed by Turner of the capture of sufficient construction machinery and material to enable the airstrip to be completed. When he finally made up his mind at 1807 to recommend to Ghormley the withdrawal of his carriers, he therefore did so in ignorance of the current situation ashore.

Fletcher's decision was taken with callous disregard for the damage which could be inflicted by an enemy force, which he himself was not prepared to face, on an Amphibious Force which lacked fighter defence. In the euphemistic words of the Naval War College Analysis:

> the fact that such a precipitous [*sic*] departure might seriously jeopardise the success of the entire operation at Tulagi–Guadalcanal, for which he was responsible as Commander Expeditionary Force, and might prevent the inauguration of Task Two [of Pestilence] which the Joint Chiefs had indicated a desire to expedite, does not appear to have been given the serious consideration it deserved.[1]

Fletcher's message to Ghormley was short and to the point:

> Total fighter strength reduced from ninety nine to seventy eight. In view of large numbers of enemy torpedo and bomber planes in area recommend immediate withdrawal of carriers. Request you send tankers immediately to rendezvous decided by you as fuel running low.[2]

This signal made no mention of the situation ashore or of unloading delays, thus depriving Ghormley of the ability to make an assessment of the effect that the carriers' withdrawal would have on the success of the operation.

Being unaware of the situation in the sound and of the fuel situation in the Air Support Force, Ghormley felt he had no option other than to accept the advice of the man on the spot. He had already demonstrated, by his absence from the *Saratoga* meeting, an unwillingness to interfere in what he clearly regarded as Fletcher's show, and he had been given no reason to doubt Fletcher's judgment. Perhaps if he had possessed an inkling of the problems Turner and Vandegrift were having, and had known that all the transports would be in the sound for at least another day, he might have asked for further information. But, in the absence of any reason to question the judgment of the man on the spot, he approved the immediate withdrawal of the carriers at 2241.

When making his first report on the Battle of Savo to Nimitz on the morning of 10 August, Ghormley did not mention that Fletcher had recommended withdrawal on the grounds that he had inadequate fighter aircraft to meet the threat from enemy air attacks. Instead, he informed Nimitz that Fletcher was withdrawing because of a shortage of fuel. Probably because of Ghormley's message and the fact that Fletcher himself—when writing to Hanson Baldwin of *Time* magazine in July 1946—gave the shortage of fuel as the sole reason for his action, argument on the question of Fletcher's withdrawal has since centred on the fuel issue.

At least two investigations into the fuel situation of the Air Support Force on 8 August have found that there was no real shortage. The Naval War College Analysis found that the destroyers of *Saratoga*'s task group were, on average, 75 per cent full. Those of the other two task groups were not so well off, averaging 43 per cent. The cruisers were better than 50 per cent full, and *Enterprise*—the carrier that was worst off—had fuel for another three days of flying operations. The fuel state of the battleship *North Carolina* was not analysed, but it would have been an admirable milch cow in an emergency—as indeed would *Saratoga*, which had been topped up with fuel as recently as 3 August. The analysis concluded its study of this whole aspect with the remark that the facts seemed to indicate that, while fuel in the command was diminishing daily, it was not at that time so critically low as to force retirement from the area.[3] Dyer, in his biography of Turner (published in 1969), was of a similar opinion.

Fletcher, who had always shown concern for the fuel state of his various commands since Pearl Harbor, would have been personally aware of the fuel state of his force and known it not to have been critical. As neither he nor Noyes had mentioned fuel in their exchange of messages, it would seem that he was merely taking a seamanlike precaution in seeking to refuel his ships as soon as possible when he asked for a rendezvous with the tankers. Written four years later, his letter to Baldwin can only be seen as an attempt to justify his desertion of Turner, in that shortage of fuel was a more seemly reason for his unquestionably questionable behaviour than concern over possible enemy action.

Fletcher's withdrawal message not only misrepresented the fuel situation, and was inadequate in that it gave Ghormley no information on which to assess the risks being run by the carriers if they stayed against the likely effect on operations if they were withdrawn. It was also inaccurate in its statement of the number of fighters available and did not take into account the heavy losses which the Japanese had suffered in their strikes against the Amphibious Force. Furthermore, it made no mention of the fact that Fletcher had so far apparently avoided detection.

Added to all its other deficiencies, Fletcher's message had stated that the total of serviceable fighters remaining was 78; it was, in fact, 83—four more than had been available at the Battle of Midway. If the experience of the Amphibious Force was any example then there was every prospect of defeating any torpedo-bombing attack, particularly in view of the warning being obtained from the coastwatchers. That morning, even though full advantage of the coastwatchers' warning had not been taken, just three fighters and the ships' anti-aircraft fire had broken up a determined attack by approximately 25 enemy aircraft. Just two hours after that attack, Fletcher himself sent a message to Noyes summarising operations since their arrival in the area, in which he noted that no serious damage had been sustained from air attacks; this same message also commented on the fact that 'over 30 to 40 enemy planes' had been accounted for, while American plane losses had been light in comparison.[4]

The conclusion is inescapable that fuel was not Fletcher's prime concern. As he had shown earlier, when he moved the carrier operating area so that the Amphibious Force was between the carriers and Rabaul, he regarded the preservation of his carriers as more important than the responsibilities he held as the commander of the Expeditionary Force for the protection of the Amphibious Force and for the support of the Marines. Evidently he thought so little of the possible effect of his withdrawal on the operations that he failed to even ask Turner for his opinion, a courtesy he had at least extended to Noyes. Perhaps this was because he knew what Turner's view would be, having already had that made perfectly clear to him at the *Saratoga* meeting! Fletcher made up his mind to withdraw and, as had happened at the *Saratoga* conference, he did not want to be confused with facts.

If Fletcher had held a genuine concern about the fuel aspect, while remaining mindful of the safety of the Amphibious Force and the needs of the Marines ashore, there was an easy and obvious remedy: to withdraw one carrier group at a time in order to refuel. As aircraft types were common to all carriers, he could have transferred aircraft from the fuelling carrier to the other two so as to reinforce their fighter defence in the operating area.

On the evening of 8 August, when the carriers completed flying for the day, they were about 60 miles east of their planned dawn position if they were to continue their operations next day in support of the Marines. But without waiting for a reply from Ghormley, Fletcher set a course to the south-east away from Guadalcanal at 15 knots. He had decided, willy-nilly, to quit and this is exactly what he did, losing no time in putting as many miles as possible between his carriers and Rabaul. As Vandegrift wrote, 'this was the [*Saratoga*] conference relived except that Fletcher was running away twelve hours earlier than he had already threatened during our unpleasant meeting'.[5]

As Fletcher deserted them, the cruisers and their screening destroyers began moving out to their patrol stations. The sun was setting, and the tension eased a little as the threat of air attack disappeared. In *Canberra* men were allowed to leave their action stations in small groups for washing and to change clothes. A sign of a return to more normal times was the gathering on the quarterdeck of a small group of officers to enjoy the twilight and to chat about the day's events. Elsewhere this reduction in tension lasted only a brief time. After Fletcher's message to Ghormley was intercepted in *McCawley*, all Turner's plans for retirement were now in the melting pot and he had a very difficult and potentially most unpleasant decision to make.

In *Canberra*, too, the idle chat on the quarterdeck was interrupted when a seaman brought another message from the bridge for the Executive Officer. It was then too dark to read it without the help of a torch, which was provided by the Damage Control Officer. Those present had no means of knowing that that message was the final harbinger of disaster that was soon to overcome the ship and its company. The reader and the torch bearer were both to have a most unpleasant and painful night.

During the afternoon, Turner had himself seen that unloading from the transports off Guadalcanal was going well—so well in fact that, on the strength of his own observations, he sent a signal warning the transports to be ready to depart next morning. It was not long, however, before he became vaguely aware that unloading had scarcely begun onto the Tulagi beach-heads. If that were confirmed then the retirement of the transports would have to be deferred.

Turner knew that very little of the heavy equipment had been landed from the supply ships, and most certainly their unloading could not be completed by the time the carriers departed on schedule at the end of the following day. That extra day of air cover which Fletcher had so reluctantly undertaken to give was definitely going to be needed. He was probably beginning to worry about completing the unloading of the supply ships without fighter support, once the escorting force had been reduced to only the Australian cruisers, *Chicago*, and the eight remaining ships of DESRON 4. He was at dinner when Fletcher's notice of withdrawal arrived. It induced what Griffith has described as 'One of the bursts of colorful profanity for which he was justly celebrated'.⁶ He was not, after all, to have that extra day's air support!

Very shortly afterwards Turner received the same message that was being read by torchlight on *Canberra*'s quarterdeck. General MacArthur's naval headquarters was reporting that, at 1025 that morning, a Hudson had sighted three cruisers, three destroyers and two seaplane tenders or gunboats off Kieta, in central Bougainville, travelling on a south-easterly course at a speed of fifteen knots. Turner and his staff would have quickly discarded the possibility that the reported force contained two gunboats, as this type would not have been tactically compatible with the other six warships. They would have assumed that the two seaplane tenders which had previously been reported as being in the Bismarck Archipelago area were present in the group. This being so, it was a logical step to conclude that the purpose of the combatant ships was to escort the seaplane tenders to an anchorage from which they would operate aircraft against his amphibious force.

After a look at a chart, Turner decided that the most likely place from which they would operate would be Rekata Bay, on the northern tip of Santa Isabel Island and 130 miles north-west of Savo. He knew that the Japanese had a small base there, if only because it had come to his notice that morning when an aircraft from *Wasp* had shot down a twin-floated seaplane near it. His perception of his tactical position must have changed drastically within the space of a few minutes. He was now faced with the probability of Japanese torpedo bomber attacks from as close as 130 miles, as well as from Rabaul, so that the severity and frequency of air attacks would be increased at a time when he could no longer count on a fighter defence. Whereas previously he may have thought of sticking it out for a couple of days by relying on ships' anti-aircraft gunfire to defend his force, that was probably no longer a practical proposition.

But the alternative to remaining was to desert the Marines before unloading had been completed, and before they were properly established ashore. This was a step which Turner must have found difficult to contemplate, since the Marines were the US Navy's army and a feeling of mutual trust had been engendered over the years; to leave early would be a betrayal of that trust. On the other hand, to stay would be to risk the only transport force in the Pacific, and one on which future operations against the Japanese would depend.

If he decided to leave, Turner had to ensure that sufficient food and ammunition had been unloaded to meet the Marines' short-term needs. The only person who could assess that was Vandegrift, who was not immediately available as he had moved his headquarters ashore. Turner also needed to meet with his screen commander, Crutchley, to discuss the possibility of staying in the sound for a day or so without a fighter defence, and the changing tactical situation in view of the appearance of a Japanese force to

The commander of the Amphibious Force, Rear Admiral R. K. Turner (left), with Major General A. A. Vandegrift, Commander of the 1st Marine Division, on the flag bridge of USS McCawley. *Dynamic, capable and intelligent, Turner was also described by Vandegrift as resembling 'an erudite schoolmaster whose didactic manner proved irritating to some people', including him. The decision by Turner to call a meeting with Vandegrift and Crutchley late on the night of 8 August had entirely unforeseen consequences, through causing the absence of the commander of the naval screen and his flagship* Australia *at what proved to be a crucial juncture.* (US National Archives neg. 80–CF–112–4–63)

the north-west. Turner therefore called both Vandegrift and Crutchley to a meeting in *McCawley*. Crutchley received the summons by radio at about 2035 but Vandegrift proved difficult to find ashore, which delayed the meeting.[7]

Crutchley, who had been hoping for a situation report and notification of future plans all day as a result of his signal sent early that morning, was not surprised to receive the summons. He knew of Fletcher's withdrawal because *Australia* was listening to the Pearl Harbor radio broadcast; and he had received, an hour or so earlier, the report of the sighting of the Japanese force off Kieta that morning. He was aware, therefore, that the tactical situation had changed for the worse, and there could have been little thought of querying the call to *McCawley*.

Before Turner's summons was received, Crutchley, his Chief Staff Officer, Captain Farncomb, and Staff Officer Operations, Commander

Gatacre, discussed the implications of the Hudson's sighting. They were all aware of the scheduled reconnaissance flights planned for the day, and of Turner's request for an additional search. There had been no report of a failure to carry out (or a curtailment of) any search, and there had been no report of a second sighting. They therefore thought it unlikely that the Japanese force had continued to head for Guadalcanal but, because all three had had experiences during the war which inhibited them from relying on the results of aerial reconnaissance, they did not completely rule out that possibility.

Crutchley and his staff did not, however, expect the Japanese to attack, because of the reported presence of two seaplane tenders. The composition of the force as reported was not that of a raiding force, but a force whose purpose was to set up a seaplane operating base from which to strike the Guadalcanal area by air. A look at *Janes' Fighting Ships* would have shown them that each tender was capable of operating more than 20 seaplanes, so that the setting up of a base for that purpose was not an unrealistic concept. Their feeling was that a group of three cruisers and three destoyers—being markedly inferior to the Allied naval presence in the sound—would be unlikely to mount a raid, though such a possibility was not completely discounted. If a raid were attempted, though, they were confident that the picket destroyers would provide warning of the enemy approach, and that the three heavy cruisers and two destroyers patrolling each side of Savo would be able to deal with them on an equal basis. They were, of course, unaware of the Japanese expertise in night fighting.

In *Canberra*, Getting's appreciation was that although enemy surface craft were frequently seen off Bougainville, the size of the reported force was abnormal and indicative of preparations by the enemy to establish a base closer to Guadalcanal and Tulagi, from which frequent air attacks on the Amphibious Force could be mounted. His Navigating Officer, Lieutenant Commander Mesley, recognised that the cruisers and destroyers could, if they wished, arrive any time after midnight.[8] This view was remarkably similar to that held by Riefkohl in *Vincennes*, who thought that the destination was Faisi,[9] and by MacArthur's headquarters which believed the base would be established in the Shortland Islands.[10]

When summoning Crutchley to *McCawley*, Turner told him that he would send a boat to collect him when he arrived in the vicinity of *McCawley*. There was, therefore, no doubt in his mind that Crutchley would use *Australia* for his journey of about twelve miles into the anchorage. The alternative vehicle was a destroyer, but that would have involved delays and reduced the screen for *Australia*, *Canberra* and *Chicago* to one.

At 2055 *Australia* left the patrol and headed inshore. Bode in *Chicago* was told by flashing light to take charge of the patrol and that *Australia* might or might not be back by dawn. As *Australia* increased speed, *Chicago* pulled out from astern of *Canberra* and began overtaking to assume the lead. As *Chicago* came abeam, the two captains had a conversation by megaphone and decided that less disruption would be caused when *Australia* rejoined if *Chicago* remained astern of *Canberra*; Bode accordingly dropped back. That seemingly unimportant conversation was to seal the fate of both men.

Riefkohl of *Vincennes* was always to maintain that he was unaware that Crutchley and *Australia* had left the southern patrol, or that in consequence he was now the senior officer among the heavy cruisers. Some American authors have subsequently criticised Crutchley for this apparent failure to inform Riefkohl of his movements. Years later, Gatacre was to answer such criticism by pointing out that, as *Australia* neared the anti-submarine screen protecting the transports, Crutchley sent a message by radio to inform Commander Destroyer Squadron Four (COMDESRON 4) in *Selfridge*, the screen commander, that he was approaching. In fact, according to Gatacre, a signal to *Vincennes* had been considered but not sent precisely because this message to *Selfridge* was transmitted by radio on a frequency common to all ships. Both the message from Turner summoning Crutchley to *McCawley* and Crutchley's message to the screen commander that he was approaching the transports would therefore have been received in *Vincennes*. In Gatacre's opinion, Riefkohl should have been informed of the admiral's movements by his radio office.

That ships would use messages other than those addressed specifically to them to gain information was expected throughout the Royal and Royal Australian Navies, in order to reduce signal traffic. This was not the case in the American Navy—at least, not in *Vincennes* evidently—though there is later evidence that Riefkohl did know of Crutchley's absence.[11] Whether or not Riefkohl knew was ultimately of little consequence, as it had no real bearing on Riefkohl's handling of the situation which developed. The matter is, however, indicative of the problems and misunderstandings that differences in doctrine were causing.

Locating *McCawley* was to prove difficult, so that it was not until 2230 that Crutchley eventually reached that ship. Vandegrift had not yet arrived for the meeting, so Crutchley took the opportunity to discuss with Turner the implications of the sighting of the Japanese force that morning. Both admirals agreed that the composition of the force was not that of a surface strike force; they also noted the absence of any further sighting report, which they took as indicating that the force had not continued towards Guadalcanal. Turner told Crutchley of his belief that the Japanese were heading for Rekata Bay with the intention of setting up a seaplane base from which to mount air attacks on the force, adding that he had requested McCain to raid the bay early the next morning. There was therefore a large measure of agreement with the view adopted by MacArthur's headquarters concerning the purpose of the Japanese force. Nevertheless, Turner went over the disposition of the pickets and cruisers with Crutchley, before agreeing that these arrangements should be effective in preventing any enemy force reaching the transports.[12]

In the Naval War College Analysis both admirals were later criticised for having given too much weight to the enemy's presumed intention and not enough to actual enemy capability. Such criticism itself does not give sufficient weight to the misleading impact of the reported presence of seaplane tenders, and in any case is not in accordance with the facts which show that the admirals did not ignore the threat. They had each separately re-examined the screening force dispositions and arrived at the conclusion that these were adequate to deal with the expected level of threat.[13]

Turner and Crutchley had no reason to doubt the report which in effect said that there were three cruisers and three destroyers present, plus two ships which did not look like cruisers or destroyers. Their best guess was that these were seaplane tenders rather than gunboats, but whatever they were it was reasonable to assume that they were not combatants. The question which both men addressed was, therefore, whether a force of three cruisers and three destroyers constituted a surface striking force of sufficient strength to carry out a raid on the anchorage, considering the relative strengths of the opposing forces. Either of the groups of heavy cruisers which barred any approach to the transports was sufficient to deal with an attack on that scale, particularly as the support of the other similar group was only minutes away. Viewed on this basis, there was no need to change the dispositions and concentrate the cruisers.

Even if Crutchley's staff in *Australia* had carried out a full staff appreciation in accordance with the dictates of a naval staff college, an attack on the transports would not have emerged as 'the enemy's most probable course of action'. In those circumstances there was no reason to sacrifice the security of the transport force against submarine attack in order to concentrate, especially if the existing dispositions already established to ensure the protection of the transports were adequate to meet the assessed threat. Had the threat level been raised to that posed by eight ships, five of which were heavy cruisers, this would have represented an entirely different 'ball game'—one which, without doubt, would have been played very differently.

In retrospect, either admiral (but more properly Turner) having seen the need to review the night dispositions should have provided the forces off Guadalcanal with a situation report in which enemy intelligence was summarised and a threat assessment given for the next 24 hours. In the absence of such a signal, each ship's captain made his own assessment of the position. These varied greatly from ship to ship but agreed on one thing: with the possible exception of *Chicago*, all appreciated that an enemy force could be in their vicinity during the night. Yet, of those who took part in the battle and rendered post-action reports, only one took positive precautions against the possibility of an unannounced Japanese arrival.

113

Commander Frank Walker of *Patterson* wrote in his Night Order Book that it was possible that enemy surface ships would arrive that night. He accordingly ordered that all torpedo tubes were to be armed with their primers and held in readiness for firing, and that from midnight the forward sets of torpedo tubes and their telephones to the bridge were to be manned.[14] He himself remained on the bridge throughout the night. It is ironic that Walker, having prepared his ship to use torpedoes at short notice, was actually presented with the opportunity—but failed to do so because the noise of his own guns drowned his order to fire![15] The Fates were indeed unkind that night; nothing went right.

In *Canberra* no enemy attack was expected before dawn, while in *Chicago* the Japanese were not expected before 1100 the next morning. No measures were apparently taken to alert the ship's company of *Quincy*, as the Gunnery Officer was later to say that he did not expect to encounter the enemy that night. In *Vincennes* Riefkohl appreciated that if the enemy had not been destroyed by carrier aircraft they could arrive after 0200, but although he alerted key personnel he did nothing to increase his ships' state of readiness for action at short notice. Only half the boilers were connected in at least *Astoria* and *Bagley*, so that full speed was not immediately available. In the destroyer *Ralph Talbot* all hands were warned of the possibility of an attack that night, but in *Blue* no warning was given. In *Hobart* knowledge of the enemy sighting off Kieta was restricted by the Captain to the extent that even the Gunnery Officer was not aware of it.

At 2315 Vandegrift arrived in *McCawley* and the meeting got under way. Turner told him over a cup of coffee of the sighting of the Japanese force that morning and his opinion that this was bound for Rekata Bay. He then showed Vandegrift Fletcher's message, told him of his proposal to withdraw the next morning and asked both Crutchley and Vandegrift for their views. They agreed that, considering the scale of air attacks which were expected, the transports and supply ships should be withdrawn because of the lack of a fighter defence. But Vandegrift voiced his concern that an early withdrawal would leave the Marines short of ammunition, food and other stores required for the immediate future.[16]

The discussion then centred on whether or not the ships could remain for another day, or whether the Marines could exist on what they already had ashore plus what could be landed that night. It was finally agreed that the ships should withdraw at dawn the next morning provided that essential items, to be specified by Vandegrift, could be got ashore during the remaining hours of darkness. Vandegrift was reasonably satisfied with the stores situation on Guadalcanal but had no information of that on Tulagi, so Turner offered him the use of the destroyer minesweeper USS *Southard* to take him there to personally ascertain what was required.

The meeting broke up just after midnight. Vandegrift accepted a lift in Crutchley's barge to *Southard*, but great difficulty was experienced in finding that ship due to a heavy rain squall. As a result Crutchley did not succeed in returning to *Australia* until 0115. When the two commanders parted, Crutchley showed that he was not at ease with the decision to leave that morning when he said, 'Vandegrift, I don't know if I can blame Turner for what he is doing'.[17]

Crutchley had grown up in a navy with a long history of supporting the army ashore and which prided itself in its determination to support them no matter what the cost. The example set by the Royal Navy in evacuating the army from Norway, Dunkirk, Greece and Crete, and the support provided for the army in Tobruk in the face of overwhelming enemy air superiority and at considerable cost, must have given Crutchley food for thought at that moment. Was he right to acquiesce in what amounted to the desertion of the Marines in the face of what had so far been an ineffectual enemy air offensive?

The one Japanese torpedo-bombing raid had been dealt with most successfully, at the essentially insignificant cost of one transport destroyed and a destroyer seriously damaged but salvageable. The one medium bomber raid had been no more effective than the many Italian air attacks experienced by Allied ships in the Mediterranean, almost as a matter of routine. The dive-bombing attack had been misdirected and—in spite of the element of surprise—had achieved just one hit with a small bomb on a destroyer which was still able to perform all its functions, albeit with a reduced gunnery capability. Why had he not spoken out against Turner's decision to withdraw?

These were the days before Americans and Britons had got used to a free exchange of ideas or operating as part of an integrated force. They were still at the 'honeymoon' stage of their relationship. For instance, Crutchley was prefacing his messages with such phrases as 'when you have time could I', 'until you leave please do so and so' and 'please keep one plane on patrol'. Turner was behaving in much the same way. In his own service environment Crutchley would have been much firmer, with 'request rough outline of present situation', 'until you leave, maintain one aircraft etc.' and 'maintain one plane on patrol'.

In addition to the above factor, Crutchley would have been mindful of the fact that in the present situation he was commanding only a small part of the Amphibious Force, and that the assets which would be put at risk if they stayed were predominantly American. He was taking part in an operation conceived and planned by the United States Navy in pursuance of American plans for the prosecution of the war. While no one ever accused Crutchley of being a rubber stamp on other people's ideas, undoubtedly he was inhibited in the present situation from expressing a view at variance with those of the piper who had to call the tune. And at the back of his mind there probably was a feeling that he had a responsibility to his Australian masters to see that he preserved their ships by not taking

115

unnecessary risks. It would be surprising therefore if he had not thought, 'if that's the way they want to play it, then so be it!' His apparent ambivalence, as demonstrated by his remark to Vandegrift, is understandable in the circumstances and not to his discredit.

Would Crutchley have changed Turner's mind if he had spoken against the decision? That must remain a matter of conjecture, of course, but it appears unlikely in view of Turner's confidence in his own ability, as evidenced by his insistence in retaining command of the Marine landing force even after Vandegrift had established his own headquarters ashore and Turner's conduct in Washington as the senior naval planner. Speculation along these various lines is, in any event, irrelevant because—even as the decision was being made—events were taking place to the north-west which would ultimately destroy any possibility of a worthwhile anti-aircraft defence of the transports and supply ships being provided by the ships of the screening group.

Crutchley was tired. In fact, at the meeting on *McCawley* Turner had thought that he appeared to be exhausted, a view shared by Vandegrift, who put Turner in the same category; Turner may even have advised Crutchley to get some rest. His tiredness was no doubt heightened by the thought that he would have to function efficiently throughout the day just starting as the commander of the forces required to defend the anchorages against the heavy air attacks which were thought sure to develop. He had not slept in a bunk for three nights, preferring to doze in a deck chair on the lower bridge of his flagship.

There were still four hours to daylight as *Australia* got under way. Crutchley could have rejoined the patrol group within an hour, but was later to write that:

> I decided not to rejoin my night patrol group for the short time that remained before 0500 when units would resume screening stations round the transports, and accordingly I ordered *Australia* to patrol in the vicinity of Squadron 'X'.[18]

But only an hour before, Turner and he had reviewed the situation and assessed that there *was* a possibilty—albeit slight—that the Japanese might attack during what remained of the night. The course of action he chose was therefore that of a tired man who badly needed rest and whose perception had been blunted by fatigue.

There is doubt whether Crutchley informed Turner that he was not resuming patrol. The analysis found that he did not and there is no record of any message having been sent. On the other hand, Turner's recollection in 1946 was that he had received a message from Crutchley at 0130 that *Australia* would remain near the transports.

While Crutchley's barge was searching for *Southard*, Turner gave effect to the decision of the meeting and informed all ships that the force would commence withdrawing at 0630 that morning. Transports and store ships were told to give priority to the landing of food, ammunition and aviation fuel in the time remaining before departure. Any landing craft that could not be hoisted in time were to be left behind with their crews. The message was sent at 0118.

Vandegrift met Brigadier General Rupertus, commander of the assault on Tulagi and adjacent islands, on board the transport USS *Neville*. Rupertus reported that Gavutu had not yet been captured. It did not take long to establish that very little had been landed but that sufficient food and ammunition could be unloaded by morning to keep the Tulagi force going for a few days. Vandegrift re-embarked in *Southard* and set out to return to *McCawley*.

One other matter was probably discussed by Turner and Crutchley in *McCawley* before Vandegrift arrived: namely, the damage to the destroyer *Jarvis* and what to do about it. As this ship was a unit of Task Force 44, her fate was of more than passing interest to Crutchley. *Jarvis* had been torpedoed forward of the bridge on the starboard side and suffered very considerable damage extending from keel to upper deck. Initially she had been towed by the destroyer *Dewey* towards Guadalcanal, but had been able to complete the move under her own steam at about seven knots and had anchored in shallow water. Turner sent a working party from *McCawley* to render whatever assistance they could.

While *Jarvis* was moving towards Guadalcanal, the commander of DESRON 4, Captain Flynn, inspected the damage and recommended to Turner that the ship proceed alone to Sydney for repairs. Turner disagreed, believing the damage was too great for such a long passage to be undertaken. He told Flynn that he would send *Jarvis* to Efate escorted by a destroyer minesweeper, and during the afternoon ordered the Captain of *Jarvis* or his Executive Officer to report to him in *McCawley*. In accordance with these instructions, the Executive Officer, Lieutenant Ray, reported to him at 1830.

After discussing the *Jarvis*'s condition with Ray, Turner ordered him to inform his captain that *Jarvis* was to proceed to Efate escorted by a destroyer minesweeper, departing via the eastern entrance to the sound after the minesweeper had completed fuelling at about 2200. He also directed that *Jarvis* was to proceed via sheltered waters, and as close to land as possible, so that she could be beached if necessary. Ray was told that a confirmatory message would be sent by a visual signal. The message was duly sent by flashing light soon after 2000, but conditions were not good during its transmission so that there was some doubt as to whether *Jarvis* had received all of it. Boats being at a premium, it was not until 2200 that one was available to take an officer to the destroyer to deliver the message by hand. Two hours later the boat returned to *McCawley* without having found *Jarvis*. In the meantime *McCawley*'s working party had returned to their ship,

117

having been ordered to leave *Jarvis* at 2130 as the destroyer was about to get under way.

Due to delays in fuelling the minesweepers, it was not until about 2330 that USS *Hovey* was ordered to escort *Jarvis* to Efate but, in spite of searching until sunrise, was unable to find her. *Jarvis* was not seen again by American eyes until she was sighted by *Blue* close inshore off Cape Esperance at approximately 0330, steering to the south-west and making about eight knots.

In comments made in August 1950, Turner expressed the opinion that *Jarvis* had departed the anchorage at 2200 and had proceeded west out of the sound bound for Sydney. Even if the benefit of the doubt is given to *Jarvis* and it is accepted that she did not receive the visual message, there can be no reasonable doubt that Ray would have given Turner's message to his captain. Turner therefore concluded that the Captain of *Jarvis* had decided to proceed to Sydney regardless of his orders to head for Efate. Turner also found it incredible that the Captain of *Jarvis* should have taken his badly damaged ship, unheralded and without radio, through an area known to be patrolled by a group of heavy cruisers in such visibility.[19]

At the end of the second day, a statement of the situation seen through Allied eyes would have shown that the gains included the virtual elimination of Japanese forces ashore, the destruction of a significant proportion of the Japanese air forces known to be in the Bismarck Archipelago, and the capture of an airfield almost ready for use. But these gains were being put at risk because of the inability, due to Fletcher's withdrawal, to properly establish the Marines ashore.

12
Japanese reactions

Although the Japanese Eighth Fleet had been formed on 14 July, it was not until 30 July that its commander, Vice-Admiral Gunichi Mikawa, arrived in Rabaul. In the meantime his Operations Officer, Captain Toshikazu Ohmae, carried out a reconnaissance of the forward areas to see for himself the state of the Japanese bases there and for briefings on the current situation. While the US Marines were loading their transports in Wellington, Ohmae attended briefings in Truk, headquarters of the Fourth Fleet, where he was told of plans for the capture of Port Moresby by proceeding overland from Buna and the establishment of airfields in eastern New Guinea and the Solomons. Fourth Fleet staff officers considered there was little chance that American aircraft carriers would carry out strikes in the area, and they were confident that the Allies were incapable of mounting a large scale counterattack.[1]

From Truk, Ohmae flew on to Rabaul on 20 July. He was not happy with what he found, for there was a clear lack of aggressiveness or cooperation between those responsible for surface and air operations, the Eighth Base Force and the 25th Air Flotilla respectively. The latter formation had been in Rabaul for some time, having taken part in the air attacks on Crace's task force during the Battle of the Coral Sea. The flotilla was due to be replaced by another, and Ohmae put their lackadaisical attitude down to their anticipation of relief. The air of complacency which Ohmae thought he detected appeared to extend throughout the Rabaul headquarters, and it was made clear to him that the new Eighth Fleet organisation was not welcome. From staff officers of the 25th Air Flotilla he nonetheless learnt that the airfield on Guadalcanal would be ready to operate 60 aircraft by early August, and many more by the end of that month.

After two days in Rabaul, Ohmae returned to Truk to await the arrival of Mikawa in his flagship, the heavy cruiser *Chokai*. This ship duly arrived

The heavy cruiser Chokai *at anchor in Kagoshima Harbour on 12 April 1939. As Vice-Admiral Gunichi Mikawa's flagship, she led the surprise raid into Iron Bottom Sound on 8–9 August 1942 which resulted in a humiliating defeat of allied naval forces covering amphibious operations on Guadalcanal and Tulagi.* (IWM neg. MH6207)

from Hashirajima on 25 July for a two-day visit. Notwithstanding Mikawa's view that the Allies could not mount a full-scale counteroffensive before 1943,[2] an entry in the Eighth Fleet War Diary for 23 July reveals that the admiral had noted the frequent aerial reconnaissances of Guadalcanal being carried out by the Allies and the fact that they had assembled a considerable number of aircraft in the New Hebrides area. He therefore appreciated that they planned to act against Guadalcanal before the airfield could be brought into use, although presumably he envisaged an American blockade of the island rather than an amphibious assault.

Because of his assessment of Allied intentions, Mikawa thought that Cruiser Division Six of *Aoba, Kako, Kinugasa* and *Furutaka* should remain with the Eighth Fleet, rather than being withdrawn to Truk as was then planned. During the meetings held between the staffs of the Fourth and Eighth Fleets, the latter voiced Mikawa's concern at the possibility of an American attack on the Solomons. They were told that, as new boys, they did not understand the situation and they apparently accepted that dictum! Mikawa was indeed a new boy in that area, but there was no flag officer who had had more experience at sea since Pearl Harbor than he. One of the criticisms levelled at senior Japanese naval officers was that they spent too

Vice-Admiral Gunichi Mikawa, commanding the Japanese Eighth Fleet, was to give the Allies off Guadalcanal a stunning display of Japanese naval professionalism and in particular his ships' proficiency at night fighting. (US Naval Historical Centre neg. NH 63697, courtesy Samuel Eliot Morison.)

much time ashore, but this could not be said of Mikawa since he had been at sea for much of the previous decade. After three years in Europe up to 1931—as a member of the Japanese delegation at the League of Nations in 1928–29 and the London Naval Limitation Conference of 1929–30, then as Naval Attaché in Paris (his second tour of duty in that city, as he had been assistant attaché there for two years immediately following the First World War)—he had spent only two periods ashore after his return to Japan. Between 1932 and 1934 he had been the Chief of Instructors at the Eta Jima Naval Academy, and following his promotion to rear admiral he had served in the navy's Tokyo headquarters in 1938–39.

Having served at sea continuously since 1939, Mikawa had assumed command of the four fast battleships of Battleship Division Three in September 1941. These ships were the Japanese Navy's only capital ships that could keep up with their aircraft carriers, until the commissioning of the 70 000-ton *Yamato* and *Musashi*. For that reason the division supported the six carriers of the striking force which attacked Pearl Harbor. After the attack, Mikawa had urged Vice-Admiral Chuichi Nagumo to launch a second strike as soon as possible but, as is now well known, such advice was ignored.

Subsequently, Mikawa remained in command of the support force accompanying the carriers during the capture of the Bismarck Archipelago and Java, the bombing of Darwin, and the move into the Bay of Bengal to strike Colombo and Trincomalee. He accompanied Yamamoto when he took the Combined Fleet to sea to support the capture of Midway. As a result of the Battle of Midway, and the overwhelming of the heavy cruisers HMS

121

Dorsetshire and HMS *Cornwall* off Ceylon by accurate dive-bombing, he was convinced that surface ships stood no chance against attack by carrier-borne aircraft unless supported themselves by fighters.

Mikawa had graduated from the Eta Jima Naval Academy in 1910, having been placed third in his class of 149. Aged about 51, he was more of a contemporary of Crutchley's than his American opponents. He was described by Ohmae as a gentle, softly spoken man, and an intelligent naval officer of broad experience who was recognised for his judgment and courage. The Naval War College Analysis described him as a competent commander of naval forces—active, quick and clear-thinking, and possessed of considerable initiative.[3]

The War College, however, also branded Mikawa as a man lacking resolution when faced with an air threat. This was hardly fair comment, since the same view was not taken of Fletcher, who deserted the Amphibious Force for that reason, or Turner, whose premature departure from the sound left the Marines in a very precarious position. Fletcher had the advantage of a fighter defence, and Turner had—at least initially—a large number of ships with a proven anti-aircraft capability. Mikawa's cruisers, except for *Chokai*, had an indifferent anti-aircraft defence, being less than that of *Dorsetshire* and *Cornwall*. Moreover Mikawa, more than most Japanese senior officers, was aware of the total lack of new heavy cruisers in the construction pipeline, as he had been the director of the Japanese naval build-up in 1938–39.

Chokai finally arrived in Rabaul on 30 July and Mikawa lost no time in getting to work. The next day, knowing nothing of the approach of the Allied expeditionary force (which had sailed that same day from Fiji), he discussed the situation in New Guinea with the Seventeenth Army. The next few days were subsequently spent in planning a move against Allied facilities in Milne Bay, as a prelude to a sea-borne assault on Port Moresby in mid-August to support the advance over the Owen Stanleys. This operation became the Eighth Fleet's primary mission, and units of the Eighth Fleet—other than the heavy cruisers—were to be engaged in supporting the army's move to Buna.[4] A heavy air attack by shore-based naval aircraft on the Fall River airfield was scheduled for the morning of 7 August.[5]

On 5 August the Imperial General Headquarters Special Duty Group (radio intelligence) suggested that there was a possibility of enemy operations in the Eighth Fleet's area. Mikawa estimated that such operations would be confined to a carrier task force strike against the Japanese supply route to Buna; the recent stepping up of air raids on Tulagi and Guadalcanal was seen as being diversionary.[6] He was misled to some degree by an erroneous report that a powerful American force, which included three carriers and a number of cruisers, had sailed from Hawaii on 2 August. Mikawa expected this force would attack in his area, but it could not be in a position to do so for some time.[7]

Nevertheless, Mikawa successfully pursued his recommendation that Cruiser Division Six remain in the area, based on Kavieng as a support force for the Outer South Seas Force.[8] Mikawa intended that all his heavy cruisers be based there, rather than Rabaul, so as to be beyond the range of B-17 aircraft operating from Port Moresby. So, after transferring his headquarters ashore on 30 July, he dispatched his flagship to Kavieng.

The Japanese were apparently unworried when, on 6 August, all native labour employed on the construction of the airfield on Guadalcanal took to the bush[9]—even though reconnaissance aircraft from Rabaul were prevented from searching the Solomons area by bad weather on both 5 and 6 August. The same weather shielded the approaching Allied force from detection by flying boats based on Tulagi.[10] The situation changed with dramatic suddenness when the first reports were received from Tulagi of the Allied landings at dawn on 7 August. Though the Japanese were not to know it, they had lost the strategic initiative and were never to regain it.

Mikawa's reaction to the news of the presence of Allied forces off Tulagi was swift and positive. By 0730 he had decided 'to put the fleet into immediate action to destroy the enemy'.[11] Even as *Canberra* was escorting the invasion transports into Tulagi, *Chokai* and the four heavy cruisers of Cruiser Division Six were weighing anchor and departing Silver Sound in western New Ireland. *Chokai*, *Aoba* and *Kako* were proceeding for Manus Island and *Kinugasa* and *Furutaka* for Rabaul. They had apparently been undergoing a weapon training period because *Kako*'s War Diary recorded that on 6 August this ship had completed training on her main armament and topped up with ammunition and supplies; her torpedo tubes had been examined and she was fully prepared for battle. The difference between the readiness of the Japanese cruisers and their opposite numbers in the Allied Amphibious Force is striking.

At 0652 the Japanese ships had all just entered the Bismarck Sea through Steffen Strait when they intercepted Tulagi's initial report of the sighting of the Allied force. Anticipating Mikawa's instructions which followed shortly afterwards, the force concentrated and headed for Rabaul at high speed.[12] They were met by the destroyer *Yunagi* with instructions for *Chokai* to enter Simpson Harbour while Cruiser Division Six remained outside, using their own aircraft for anti-submarine protection. During the afternoon they watched some B-17s pass overhead to bomb the Rabaul airfields as part of MacArthur's interdiction support plan for Watchtower. They were no doubt apprehensive when the aircraft were first sighted, not knowing that targets such as themselves would only be attacked by prior arrangement with McCain.

Mikawa's first requirement as Commander of the Outer South Seas Force was to ascertain the strength of the invading force and later, when it became clear that carriers were providing air support, to find the carriers. In addition, therefore, to the two early morning routine flying boat patrols

The Japanese heavy cruiser Furutaka, *pictured here during speed trials in June 1939, was very similar in appearance to* Aoba, Kako, *and* Kinugasa—*the other ships comprising Cruiser Division Six under the flag of Rear Admiral Arimoto Goto. With Mikawa's flagship* Chokai, *these four formed the backbone of the Japanese force which fought the night surface action off Savo Island.* (IWM neg. MH6199)

flown to search to the north and north-east of the Solomons, three land-based reconnaissance aircraft took off at 0900: two to reconnoitre the lower Solomons and one to search west of the islands. Bad weather interfered with the searches near Tulagi, so that sightings were limited to the Allied shipping in the Tulagi–Guadalcanal area. The carriers were not seen although the sector allocated to one of the land planes covered the carriers' operating area. A fourth land plane took off soon after midday to reconnoitre the sound and report the results of the two air attacks which were made later in the day.[13]

The result of this considerable reconnaissance effort was that, by 1530, the Japanese command assessed that there were three heavy cruisers, several destroyers and about thirteen transports off Tulagi, and that there were several destroyers and 27 transports off the airfield on Guadalcanal. A large number of aircraft had been sighted over the beachheads so that the Japanese knew that there were carriers in the vicinity even though none had been sighted. They knew that the Allies were there in strength and that this was no raiding party.[14]

In the meantime, the Japanese had carried out two air strikes on the forces off Guadalcanal. The first, involving 27 bombers and 18 fighters, had taken off at 0900—at the same time as the reconnaissance aircraft, and scarcely more than two hours after the alarm had been raised. These aircraft had been standing ready for the scheduled major raid on Fall River but were diverted; it was these that carried out the unsuccessful medium-level pattern bombing attack on the transports off the landing beaches at 1325, and they lost five aircraft. Because the aircraft were already bombed up when their mission was changed, use had not been made of the preferred and more accurate weapon: the torpedo. This was fortunate for the transports, as they had remained at anchor and therefore would have been very vulnerable to a torpedo attack. The second wave of sixteen carrier-type dive-bombers was airborne at 1045. After staging through Buka, they had struck the destroyer screen off Guadalcanal at 1500, causing damage to *Mugford* for the loss of six aircraft.

While these events were in train, Mikawa had begun planning a surface strike against Allied shipping in the sound. He quickly settled on a night action, a decision which he explained after the war in the following terms:

> My choice of a night action was made because I had no air support on which to rely—and reliable air support was vital to anything but a night action. On the other hand I had complete confidence in my ships and knew that the Japanese navy's emphasis on night battle training and practice would ensure our chances of success in such an action even without air support.[15]

Mikawa originally intended to use only the five heavy cruisers, as such an homogeneously armed group would facilitate his tactical control of the battle. He was, however, persuaded by staff officers to include what he regarded as 'the rabble': the light cruisers *Tenryu* and *Yubari*, together with the destroyer *Yunagi*. He proposed to lead the force himself, as commander of the Eighth Fleet, since that very day he was to be relieved of his responsibility for the Outer South Seas Force by the commander of the Eleventh Air Fleet (who was moving from Tinian to do so). Such a move was in accordance with a Tokyo directive that, in the event of an enemy attack in either the Fourth Fleet or Eighth Fleet areas, the commander of the Eleventh Air Fleet would exercise tactical command of both fleets.

As a navigation specialist, Mikawa's first look at charts of the area between Rabaul and Guadalcanal gave him a lot to worry about, since it was incompletely surveyed by any standard. Soundings were few and far apart, and—as in the case of the air maps which were bothering Allied Hudson crews—the positions of many land features were known to be inaccurate. Mikawa's plan called for the use of high speed at night in such waters, so that he regarded the navigational hazards he was facing as seriously as he did the threat from carrier aircraft.[16] To reduce them, he planned to pass to the east of Choiseul and, possibly, Santa Isabel Islands.

Mikawa referred his proposal to carry out a surface strike to Tokyo for approval. The Chief of the Naval General Staff, Admiral Nagano, initially regarded the plan 'as dangerous and reckless' and would have vetoed it but for the strong support it received from his staff officers. He therefore reluctantly agreed to leave the decision to the man on the spot.[17] While awaiting word from Tokyo, Mikawa conferred with the Seventeenth Army staff which was then conducting operations in New Guinea and planning an assault in the Milne Bay area. The Army assured him that there would be no difficulty in driving out of Guadalcanal the expected relatively small numbers of American troops, but they were not prepared to send the only army division then available. Mikawa therefore organised a unit of 519 troops from his naval garrison resources, and embarked them in two transports[18] which sailed for Guadalcanal at 2300 that night escorted by the minelayer *Tsugaru*. This force was recalled at 1355 the next day, when it was twenty miles to the southward of Green Island, as it was clearly inadequate for its mission.[19]

Mikawa's initial moves were completed when he ordered the two submarines *I-121* and *I-122* out of Rabaul. These were instructed to join with the remaining submarines of Submarine Squadron Seven already at sea, and concentrate around Guadalcanal.[20] Having received his staff's intelligence summary at about 1530, Mikawa decided to proceed. He embarked in *Chokai*, which departed Rabaul an hour later in company with *Tenryu*, *Yubari* and *Yunagi*. Cruiser Division Six joined the flagship as the sun set and course was laid for Tulagi via Buka Island and east of Bougainville.

The next day, the entire reconnaissance force from Rabaul concentrated its efforts on locating the carriers. The first aircraft, a long-range flying boat, was airborne at 0540 to search to a depth of 700 miles. The course taken to the west of Guadalcanal should have brought this aircraft within visual distance of the carriers at about 1100, but it passed without seeing them. This probably occurred because, though surface visibility was unlimited, the aircraft was flying above partial cloud at 6000 feet. A second flying boat departed Rabaul an hour later, but its search track took it well to the east of the Solomons so that it also sighted nothing.

At 0700 three land planes took off to search a sector covering either side of the island chain as far south as San Cristobal, a mission carried out without success. A fourth land plane departed Rabaul at the same time tasked to reconnoitre the Tulagi–Guadalcanal area. Though at one time pursued by fighters, this aircraft remained in the area for about two hours. The need to dodge fighters obviously hampered the search as much as the cloud cover encountered because the aircraft only reported that there were ships near Tulagi, several destroyers mostly anchored off Guadalcanal, and that a number of fighters and bombers were airborne.[21]

By dawn Mikawa's cruiser force was 55 miles north-east of Kieta, on the east coast of Bougainville. His plan was to remain in that vicinity during the forenoon while three cruiser aircraft searched an area between north-east and south-east to a depth of 200 miles, to ensure that the American carriers were not operating in that area. A fourth aircraft was to reconnoitre the

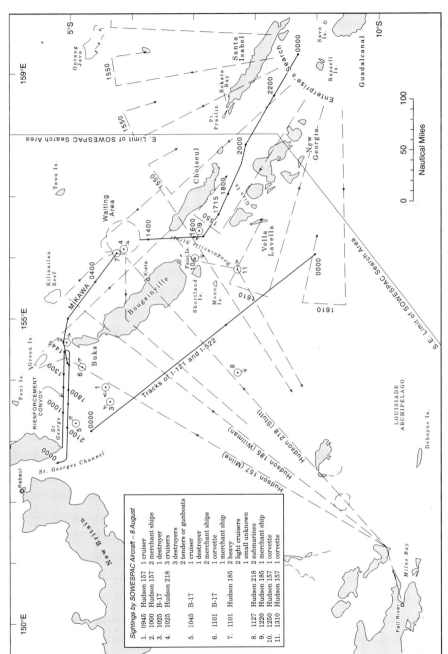

Sightings by SOWESPAC Aircraft — 8 August

1.	0945	Hudson 157	1 cruiser
2.	1000	Hudson 157	2 merchant ships
3.	1025	B-17	1 destroyer
4.	1025	Hudson 218	3 cruisers
			3 destroyers
			2 tenders or gunboats
5.	1045	B-17	1 cruiser
			1 destroyer
6.	1101	B-17	2 merchant ships
			1 corvette
7.	1101	Hudson 185	1 merchant ship
			2 heavy
			2 light cruisers
			1 small unknown
8.	1127	Hudson 218	2 submarines
9.	1220	Hudson 185	1 merchant ship
10.	1250	Hudson 157	1 corvette
11.	1310	Hudson 157	1 corvette

Searches and naval movements, N. Solomons—8 August

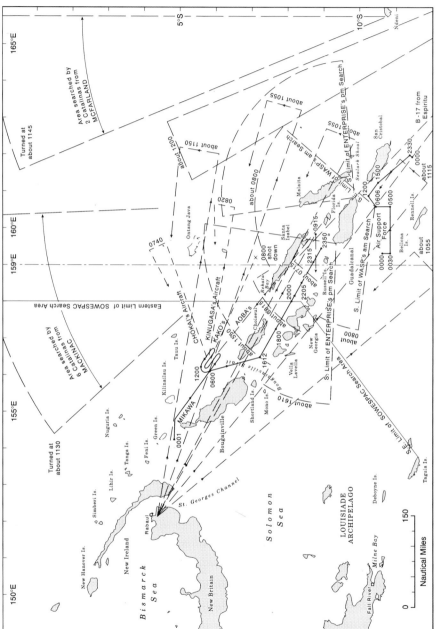

Searches and naval movements, S. Solomons—8 August

The Japanese light cruiser Tenryu, *which flew the flag of Rear Admiral Matsuyama at Savo. Mikawa included her in his striking force—as with the light cruiser* Yubari *and destroyer* Yunagi—*almost reluctantly, regarding these smaller ships as 'rabble' compared to his five powerful heavy cruisers.* (National Maritime Museum, London, neg. N6002)

Tulagi–Guadalcanal area.[22] If the carriers were operating closer to Guadal-canal, as he thought more likely, his position would be outside their aircrafts' search radius. He was very conscious of the need to achieve surprise, so that an additional reason for 'hovering' off Kieta was to conceal his intentions from any reconnaisance aircraft which sighted him during the forenoon.[23] He planned to start his dash towards Guadalcanal at midday.

Chokai, Kinugasa and *Kako* each launched an aircraft soon after dawn, to search 250 miles to the eastward. *Aoba* launched one aircraft for the reconnaissance of Tulagi and Guadalcanal, then distant some 330 miles. *Aoba, Kinugasa* and *Kako* each launched a single-winged Jake, while *Chokai* employed an Alf. *Kako*'s aircraft was shot down near Rekata Bay later that morning by a reconnaissance aircraft from *Wasp*.[24] *Chokai*'s and *Kinugasa*'s aircraft returned by 1020 and were waiting to be recovered when *Aoba* sighted a Hudson to the south-west. Five minutes later the same aircraft was sighted by *Chokai*, at a distance reported as being almost nineteen miles (30 000 metres). The aircraft remained in sight for a further ten minutes before disappearing to the north-west towards Bougainville.[25]

Soon after the Hudson was sighted, Mikawa altered the course of his force to the north-east as if heading for Truk and slowed to fifteen knots. During the next hour he ordered two more turns in order to conceal his intentions from his enemy. He knew that he had been sighted, because an

The Japanese light cruiser Yubari, *pictured in pre-war days. Both she and the other light cruiser in Mikawa's force (*Tenryu*) justified their inclusion by each torpedoing an American cruiser at Savo—*Vincennes *in the case of* Yubari, *while* Tenryu *accounted for* Quincy. *(National Maritime Museum, London, neg. N6013)*

enemy report from the aircraft had been intercepted by *Chokai* which reported the sighting of three cruisers, three destroyers and two seaplane tenders or gunboats on a course of 120 at a speed of fifteen knots.[26]

Chokai and *Kinugasa* had just recovered their aircraft when, at 1103, the former sighted what was assumed to be the same Hudson approaching from the north-west and flying at about 2000 feet. The aircraft continued to close until within 8-inch gun range, when *Chokai* fired a six-gun salvo from her forward turrets. The aircraft turned away and *Chokai* lost sight of it on a bearing of 330 at 1113.[27]

Aoba's aircraft returned at midday and reported having sighted a battleship, four cruisers, seven destroyers, one ship resembling an aircraft carrier and fifteen transports off Guadalcanal; the cruisers and destroyers were stated to be conducting a roving patrol. Off Tulagi there were reported to be two heavy cruisers, twelve destroyers and three transports. The total of ships within the sound therefore made a total of one battleship, one possible light carrier, six cruisers, nineteen destroyers and eighteen transports.[28]

As had happened during the Coral Sea action, *Chicago* had been mistaken for a battleship, and one of the transports had been misreported as resembling a carrier. Despite this, Mikawa had been given what was, in the circumstances, a remarkably accurate description of the forces off the beachheads. He does not appear to have given much credence to the reported sighting of the carrier, probably because—in those days before the advent of the helicopter carrier—it was a most unlikely place for a carrier to be from the security point of view and because of the lack of sea room for launching and recovering aircraft.

Mikawa had intended to strike at 0100 but, assuming that the carriers supporting the operations were to the south or south-east of Guadalcanal, he assessed that he would have to delay his attack by an hour if he were to remain beyond the range of carrier aircraft until dusk. He had originally planned to pass to the east of Choiseul Island, as there was less navigational risk in that. But now, as he had been reported in a position and on a heading which would appear to be taking him east of Choiseul Island, he decided to divert to the south, to accept the additional navigational risks and pass through Bougainville Strait.[29] In so doing, he was the first of many to lead a Japanese force down what was later to become known as the Slot.

After *Aoba*'s aircraft had been recovered, Mikawa set course at 24 knots for Bougainville Strait which he entered just before 1600. Shortly afterwards *Aoba* launched an aircraft to carry out a reconnaissance of the sound at twilight, with instructions to fly to the Shortland Islands on completion of the mission.[30]

During the afternoon the cruisers had seen the survivors of the air attack on the Amphibious Force making their way back to Rabaul in twos and threes, obviously having been badly mauled. Mikawa was informed later that the attackers had reported the sinking of three cruisers, two destroyers and nine transports. The odds against him had apparently been reduced, but so had the attractiveness of the target; there were seemingly only nine transports remaining, and two of these were reported to be on fire. This misleading information may well have been a factor in the admiral's decision immediately after the battle to withdraw without attacking either transport anchorage.

The sea was calm and the visibility good—too good for their purpose. As the afternoon wore on the Japanese must have wondered why no action had been taken on the message that had accurately reported their position during the afternoon. They had not been attacked and indeed they had seen no more reconnaissance aircraft. There had been a few anxious moments when a mast was sighted fine on the starboard bow, but it was eventually identified as that of the flying boat tender *Akitsushima* on her way to establish a seaplane base at Gizo Island. As they approached their target area they could hear the chatter of pilots in the landing circuits of the carriers and were reassured by it. There was no indication that a strike was being readied.

Twilight came and went, without a report from *Aoba*'s aircraft to verify the number of ships remaining in the sound apart from one report that six ships were in flames. The significance of the aircraft's single report was that it apparently confirmed in part the extravagant damage claims arising from the midday torpedo bomber raid. No more reports were received, though the aircraft later landed safely in the Shortland Islands in accordance with instructions given before take-off.[31]

During the approach to Savo Island the cruiser force was in a disposition which had the heavy cruisers in line ahead, screened by the light cruisers on the port bow and *Yunagi* on the starboard bow. If any Allied destroyers were encountered, Mikawa's intention was to brush these off with the screen while the heavy cruisers continued their dash towards Savo. At midnight the force was formed into a single column, in the order: *Chokai, Aoba, Kako, Kinugasa, Furutaka, Tenryu, Yubari* and *Yunagi*. The ships were 1300 yards apart (bridge to bridge), so that the column was four and a half miles long. There was no finesse in this formation, ships being expected to follow the next ahead. Mikawa was taking no chances of confusion in his own force. To assist in the identification of friend from foe in the mêlée to come, each ship was told to fly a white pendant seven metres long from each yardarm.

Mikawa's plan of attack was to pass south of Savo Island and 'torpedo the enemy main force at Guadalcanal' and then to 'move toward the forward area at Tulagi and strike with torpedoes and gunfire, after which we will withdraw to the north of Savo Island'. At that time he had no intelligence of the two destroyers patrolling to seaward of Savo Island, or of the disposition of the heavy cruisers inside the sound, but was basing his plan solely on the information provided by *Aoba*'s morning reconnaissance.

Subject always to the Japanese cruiser force's night-fighting doctrine, which included the dictum that no ship was to open fire before the flagship had done so unless in an emergency, ships were told to act independently in choosing their own torpedo and gunnery targets.[32] Mikawa's final instruction was to jettison all inflammable items from the upper deck. This included depth charges and all light oil stored above the water line, as well as aircraft fuel. Accordingly, aircraft remaining on board were defuelled, thus removing a hazard that was ignored by the American cruisers—an oversight that was to cost them dearly.[33]

As twilight ended, Mikawa sent a message to his ships containing more than a Nelsonian whiff. As a number of his tutors at the Eta Jima Naval Academy had been English, and as the training of young officers at that academy had been closely modelled on that of the Royal Naval College at Dartmouth, this is hardly surprising:[34] 'In the finest spirit of the Imperial Navy we shall engage the enemy in night battle. Every man is expected to do his best.'[35]

The personnel in Mikawa's force did what was expected of them, and in the process gave the Allies a lesson in the art of night fighting they were never to forget and an exhibition of the Japanese mastery of that art which was never equalled.

Between 2300 and 2313, *Chokai, Aoba* and *Kako* each successfully catapulted an aircraft. None of the pilots had previously been catapulted at night, but the risk had to be taken as time did not permit stopping to hoist out the aircraft for a normal water take-off.[36] Led by Lieutenant Fumio Kiyose of *Chokai*, the aircraft had the role of reconnoitring the sound and providing illumination when ordered, before then proceeding to the Shortlands on completion of their mission. They were also to lay, *en route*, a flame float 30 miles north-west of Cape Esperance, which was to serve as a navigational marker on which the ships could make a landfall before setting course for the southern entrance to the sound. The float was duly sighted at 2335 and course adjusted. A few minutes later *Chokai* sighted, at a distance of about 60 miles, the loom of the fire still burning in the transport *George F. Elliot*.

13
Allied failures of detection

While the movement of Mikawa's striking force from the Rabaul area had not gone unobserved, reports of the sightings were to take a long time to reach the Expeditionary Force. News of the sightings by B-17s was not received until midnight, and *S-38*'s report was not passed on by MacArthur's headquarters until 0738 the following morning.[1]

Delays in passing on the B-17 reports can be attributed to the lack of knowledge within the AAF organisation of the operations proceeding in the Solomons. It is difficult, however, to understand why a submarine's report was delayed to such an extent, since the naval component of MacArthur's headquarters was well aware of Watchtower. *S-38* had sighted the Japanese almost at dark and at such close range that she had been unable to manoeuvre for a torpedo attack, which explains the incomplete nature of her sighting. The boat had surfaced to pass an enemy report as soon as it was safe to do so.[2]

During the day, the teams at Pearl Harbor listening to Japanese naval radio traffic intercepted messages ordering submarines to Guadalcanal[3] but did not glean from intercepts any intelligence regarding the movement of the striking force. Not only was Mikawa keeping radio silence, but the Americans' ability to read the Japanese encrypted operational traffic had been limited by a recent change in the Japanese code so that there was a time lag of a week or so between the interception of a message and its decryption.[4]

An entry in the War Diary of Nimitz's headquarters in Pearl Harbor for 7 August recorded the belief that planes from Rabaul and submarines ordered to the Guadalcanal area were the only effective outside opposition that the Expeditionary Force had to contend with at that time, though it was expected that aircraft reinforcements were on their way to Rabaul. The diary also noted that Mikawa had sent a lot of messages from Rabaul but that they were to units already known to be in the area. This increased activity was obviously related to the Allies' move into the Solomons but there was no means of deriving, from the increased traffic, what the Japanese intended.

In fact, the message that would have provided positive information on Mikawa's intentions had been intercepted but could not be deciphered until 23 August. Originated by Mikawa at 1000, it informed the commander of the Combined Fleet (Yamamoto) and the Naval General Staff in Tokyo—among others—that *Chokai*, in company with Cruiser Division 18 (*Tenryu* and *Yubari*) and *Yunagi*, would depart from Rabaul at 1500 and, after making a rendezvous with Cruiser Division Six, proceed to the Guadalcanal area. Their subsequent operations would depend on the results of aerial reconnaissance.[5]

On 8 August Nimitz's War Diary recorded that there was no new evidence of an aircraft carrier in the Solomons area although at least two seaplane tenders were present. All available submarines were *en route* to Guadalcanal and all available aircraft in the Bismarck Archipelago were being concentrated in the Rabaul–Buka Island area. There was no entry covering the activities of major surface ships but the general comment was made that the Japanese were relying entirely on aircraft and submarines, except for movements of Cruiser Divisions Six and Eighteen in the Bismarck Archipelago. The lack of any warning of the departure of the force from the vicinity of Rabaul is testimony to the effectiveness of Mikawa's policy of radio silence.

There was, however, one 'straw in the wind' which went unnoticed. Traffic analysis on 7 August showed that Mikawa had shifted his flag from ashore at Rabaul to an unidentified ship, and the information was included in a communications intelligence (Ultra) summary the next day. There was obviously some suspicion in Pearl Harbor that the ship was *Chokai*, but this could not be confirmed since no transmissions had been intercepted from that cruiser since May. *Chokai* was known, however, to be in the Bismarck area,[6] and an alert staff should have associated Mikawa's flag shift with the sightings of cruisers off Rabaul, in St George's Channel and off Kieta. This did not happen, though, perhaps because the highly classified nature of communications intelligence inhibited its use within Nimitz's operations and intelligence staffs, and its distribution to those of Ghormley and Fletcher. Turner, having refused the offer of a communications intelligence cell, would not have received the raw information.

The diary of MacArthur's naval component for the same two days makes little mention of operations in the Solomons, apart from recording the reports referred to above and the fact that considerable air opposition was being encountered. Just before midnight on the 8th, however, as Mikawa was approaching Savo, MacArthur's headquarters issued a message summarising the latest intelligence on Japanese movements which informed Nimitz and all task force commanders in the South West Pacific and Pacific Areas that Mikawa had shifted his flag from ashore to *Chokai*. No inference was drawn from the information, which went unnoticed.[7] It was received in *Australia*, presumably while Crutchley was in *McCawley*.

McCain planned to search the approaches through the islands south of New Georgia on 8 August using two aircraft. These were to be abreast Tulagi at sunrise, which entailed them being at their furthest out points by 0915.[8] But weather, as on the previous day, interfered with the searches to the extent that one aircraft aborted its mission soon after take-off and the other turned back when still south-east of New Georgia. Even if these missions had been completed, though, they would have been no threat to Mikawa, who that morning remained 150 miles beyond the planned limit of the searches.

No provision had been made for an afternoon search and, though the morning searches had quite clearly failed to ensure that the north-western approaches were clear of the enemy, no impromptu searches were flown. Nor was Fletcher informed immediately of the inability of the B-17s to complete their searches.[9]

McCain's orders to his air bases and seaplane tenders included instructions for them to report the day's coverage of their assigned sectors after all searches had been completed. As on the previous day, he waited until all the reports had been received before sending a summary of the day's operations to the other task force commanders. Since the Catalina searches were completed well after dark, it was almost midnight before Turner became aware that the coverage of his north-western approaches had been incomplete. Mikawa was then barely 40 miles away and about to sight Savo Island. No mention was made of the additional search that Turner had requested the previous day.[10]

The War Diary of the seaplane tender *Mackinac* and McCain's headquarters contain no mention of that additional search, so that most historians have assumed that it was not undertaken. For example, the official history of the Royal Australian Navy states categorically that it was not carried out.[11] The Naval War College analysts, however, were less definite, and found that there was a measure of doubt as to whether or not the search was flown. They were influenced to a degree (but obviously not wholly convinced) by a statement in 1948 by McCain's Chief of Staff, Rear Admiral Gardner, who gave as his recollection that it had been carried out by two B-17s from Espiritu Santo.[12] Gardner's recall was suspect because the weather that day had already prevented an effective search by B-17s from Espiritu Santo. Moreover, any B-17 search from Espiritu Santo could not have covered the area requested by Turner, who had envisaged the use of Catalinas from Malaita.

Turner's own comment, made in 1950, was that his 'impression at the time' had been that a Catalina pilot had attempted the search but that he

136

had been turned back by the weather. This claim is suspect, too, as the message from McCain, to which he was referring, made no mention of either Catalinas or Malaita.[13] This was not the only occasion on which Turner's memory proved to be fallible.

In view of the terms in which the additional search was requested—namely, that Turner considered that the scheduled searches had been inadequate ('I consider a morning search by you is necessary for adequate cover')—failure by McCain to inform Turner that he had been unable to meet this requirement would have been inexcusable; to use Gatacre's remark made after the war, it would also have been incredible. This was a request that could not have been ignored, as even the most cursory re-examination of the search plans would have shown that it was justified.

The explanation of the apparent failure of McCain to comply with the request lies in the manner in which it was made and the fact that McCain's task force was not a member of Fletcher's Expeditionary Force. *McCawley*'s communications organisation was such that her two transmitters were tuned to the frequency of the radio net linking all ships in the Amphibious Force, including Crutchley's Screening Group, and to the net linking all the task force/task group commanders of the Expeditionary Force. Messages destined for others outside the Expeditionary Force, including Ghormley and Nimitz, were sent by TBS, flashing light, or even by hand to a ship (usually a cruiser) which had a transmitter set up to pass messages to Pearl Harbor naval radio station. These would reach their destination after being rebroadcast on the naval area broadcast.

Any message sent by *McCawley*, or any other ship for that matter, could be transmitted in one of two ways: direct to the addressee, in which case the addressee would have been required to break radio silence to acknowledge receipt; or broadcast blind, in which case no receipt was expected. *McCawley* chose to send Turner's request 'blind' to *Curtiss* on the task force commanders' net and accordingly was not concerned when an acknowledgment of receipt was not received. The message was sent twice to ensure receipt by any ship on that net.[14]

The problem arose because *Curtiss*—not being a member of the Expeditionary Force—was not listening, and at no time did the radio office in *McCawley* realise this! Had *McCawley* chosen to send the message direct to *Curtiss*, as might well have been done because *Curtiss* was not keeping radio silence, the absence of any acknowledgment of receipt may not necessarily have alerted *McCawley* to her error but it certainly would have led to the trying of the alternative route—that is, via Pearl Harbor.

Turner had, in effect, scored an 'own goal' because his communications staff had placed undue reliance on a method of communications which was inherently uncertain. Nimitz was to pinpoint the reason for this and other failures in communications between Turner, Ghormley and other task force commanders when he highlighted the lack of experienced communication officers. He regarded the correction of this—and other failures in communications during Watchtower—as being of the greatest urgency, and was only placated when his communications officer, Captain Redman, pointing out that the failures were due to poor advance planning and the organisational set-up, told him that a big improvement was expected. Nimitz's reply was a laconic, 'O.K. Noted'.[15]

The inadequacy of the coverage of the north-western approaches to Guadalcanal does not reflect well on the judgment of McCain. If the availability of aircraft for afternoon searches was a problem, then he should have availed himself of the arrangement made at the meeting in *Saratoga* on 26 July. Under this, 'it was specifically arranged by the Commanders of Task Forces 61, 62 and 63 that if the air scouting could not be made in any sector, Task Force 61 (the carrier groups) would fill in for short range scouting, both morning and afternoon, to protect against the approach of surface forces'.[16] The resources were there; all McCain had to do was ask for them. If Turner had known of the shortfall in McCain's output, he could have (and in view of his concern over aerial reconnaissance probably would have) asked for carrier aircraft searches to the limit of the aircrafts' range. But McCain precluded such an approach by not informing Turner of his problems with the weather until after dark.

The Air Support Force flew a morning and an afternoon search that day. *Wasp*'s morning search of twelve aircraft, designed to ensure that the American carriers were not threatened by a Japanese carrier, searched between west and north-east to a depth of 220 miles. They saw no shipping except for a small ship in the vicinity of Rekata Bay, which was strafed. Forty miles north of there, *Kako*'s twin-float seaplane was shot down.[17] These minor actions were to have a disproportionate effect on future events, as they drew attention to Rekata Bay where the Japanese were known to have a seaplane base.[18]

The afternoon search was flown by fourteen aircraft from *Enterprise* and searched an arc between west and east to a depth of approximately 200 miles from Savo. If Fletcher had not overruled Noyes and moved the carriers' operating area to the east, the aircraft would have searched as far as Bougainville and been in the vicinity of Bougainville Strait at 1600. A heavy price was to be paid for Fletcher's conflict of interests.[19]

14

Air Force scapegoats?

The search of the stretch of water between New Georgia and New Britain, through which Mikawa had to pass, was undertaken by three of the five RAAF Hudsons deployed to Fall River. These aircraft were scheduled to take off soon after 0700 and the navigators were given the coordinates of their searches by the detachment commander, Flight Lieutenant Milne, as they stood by their machines.

The crews were warned that there might be some American naval activity in the area, and that they might sight friendly ships. When the Hudsons took off, therefore, they were ignorant of the operations at Tulagi and Guadalcanal which had then been in progress for 24 hours, believing that their missions were related to the defence of Port Moresby. Moreover, they expected to see American rather that Japanese ships.[1]

The RAAF men were unaware that, with the initiation of Watchtower, the purpose of their reconnaissance had changed from intelligence-gathering in defence of New Guinea to ensuring that the Allied forces off Guadalcanal received timely warning of any movement of Japanese forces from the Rabaul area towards the southern Solomons. Lacking knowledge of their purpose, they had no means of judging the importance to the forces off Guadalcanal of anything they found.

The aircraft which made the first sighting was Hudson A16-218 flown by Sergeant Bill Stutt who, having passed over the centre of Bougainville, saw a group of eight ships at 1025 some 37 miles north-east of Kieta. Mikawa's cruiser force had been relocated and at that moment, with a little more than eight hours of daylight left, the chances of preventing Mikawa from striking at Guadalcanal should have been excellent. But some of the decisions already made by the Allies at command level were to increase his chances of success.

Expecting the ships to be friendly, Stutt had closed to within four miles of them before he realised that they were Japanese. A single-winged float plane was then sighted in the vicinity of one of the larger ships which he took to be a Zero fighter with floats. Not realizing that the aircraft—which was actually a cruiser-borne reconnaissance type—was waiting to land after completing a search to the east, and fearing that it might attempt an interception, Stutt retired to the north-west towards one of the few clouds in the area. He thought at the time that the aircraft had been catapulted for the purpose of engaging the Hudson, but in fact no additional Japanese aircraft were launched and no attempt made to intercept the intruder with aircraft already airborne.

The Hudson crew of four had a good look at all eight ships for some time—Stutt with the aid of binoculars. Lacking any ship recognition aids in the aircraft, the crew discussed what they had seen. The navigator thought that there were a number of cruisers and destroyers but there were two ships that looked rather different. Because a seaplane had been seen, there was a feeling that these might be some sort of 'back-up vessels' which carried seaplanes. Eventually they decided to report that they had seen three cruisers, three destroyers and two seaplane tenders or gunboats on a course of 125 degrees at fifteen knots. The intention in reporting 'two seaplane tenders or gunboats' was to indicate their uncertainty regarding two of the contacts, but this attempt went disastrously wrong.

The two types named were markedly different in size and operational characteristics. Generally speaking, gunboats were small, slow and operated in rivers or coastal waters. They were not, in today's jargon, 'air capable' and were not usually found in open waters in company with more conventional warships. There were four Japanese seaplane tenders, specially constructed for that role. Of cruiser size, they were flush-decked, approximately 570 feet in length, capable of 28 knots and carried up to 24 aircraft. The bridge structure and arrangement of the armament forward resembled that of a light cruiser. Two large gantries were fitted amidships to handle the aircraft. Seen from ahead they may not have been unlike cruisers, but from any other aspect they should have been unmistakable. While not normally operated in company with cruisers in a tactical sense, seaplane tenders possessed the mobility to do so, as evidenced by their eventual conversion to light aircraft carriers. This mobility gave the Japanese the capabilty to move quickly into an anchorage and almost immediately to operate aircraft in a strike or torpedo-bombing role with fighter defence.

The threat that this capability posed had a profound effect on the reaction of Allied naval commanders to news that a Japanese force, which possibly included two seaplane tenders, had been sighted in the northern Solomons. Because of the incompatibility of gunboats with the company and environment in which they had been reported, naval commanders without exception rejected the possibility of their presence and—on the

Chitose, a typical Japanese seaplane tender, shown during speed trials in Japan's Inland Sea in July 1938. At Savo, allied airmen managed to misreport a cruiser for a vessel of this type, a mistake which only inadequate ship recognition training could have allowed. (IWM neg. MH6497)

premise that if these were not gunboats they had to be seaplane tenders—accepted without question the proposition that two seaplane tenders had been sighted. This was not unreasonable in the circumstances, as two seaplane tenders were included in the estimated Japanese order of battle for the area which was included in the various operation orders and plans.

The method used to indicate inability to determine the type of two of the ships sighted was a measure of the RAAF crew's inexperience and poor training. Where doubt existed in such matters, communications doctrine required the use of the description 'unknown'. If the crew had described the two different-looking vessels as being of an unknown type, the message that reached the ships off Guadalcanal would have read 'Aircraft reports at 1025 three cruisers, three destroyers and two medium unknown etc.', which would probably have led the recipients to seriously consider the possibility that the reported force was a raiding party.

Quite apart from the problem with the identification of the two ships, there are other aspects of the report which are puzzling. *Yubari* and *Tenryu* were both about 3500 tons and were therefore very small light cruisers by Allied standards, being half the displacement of *Hobart*. It would be understandable then if these two ships had been taken for destroyers. But *Tenryu* was counted among the cruisers, for one of the cruisers was described in the subsequent Form White as having three short raked funnels, large superstructure and a raked bow—an accurate description of *Tenryu*. This being so, one of the heavy cruisers must have been counted among the

141

destroyers! It is also difficult to understand how only two of the remainder could be identified as cruisers when four were virtually identical (the Aoba class heavy cruisers) and the fifth (*Chokai*), though larger and more heavily armed, was similar in outline.

The problems which the crew of Hudson 218 experienced in identifying the composition of the Japanese force were by no means unique during the Second World War, but were common to both sides. Sometimes use was made of this difficulty by disguising ships to confuse the enemy. For example, *Bismarck* constructed a dummy funnel during her run towards the French coast, and a British fast minelayer operating in the Gulf of Lyon disguised herself as a French destroyer. Ship recognition from the air is notoriously difficult, even for experienced naval aircrew. For example, in the Indian Ocean in 1941 the light cruiser HMNZS *Leander* was reported as a German pocket battleship by an aircraft flying from *Canberra*, and during the hunt for *Bismarck* a squadron of carrier-borne naval torpedo bombers attacked, in poor visibility, the light cruiser HMS *Sheffield* after mistaking her for their German quarry.

What is remarkable about the episode under consideration here is that it occurred only three months after the attention of AAF Headquarters had been drawn to another potentially disastrous mistake in ship recognition by its aircrews. During the series of actions in the Coral Sea, a group comprising *Australia*, *Hobart* and *Chicago* screened by three destroyers, having survived a torpedo attack by approximately a dozen Japanese twin-engined aircraft and an extremely accurate high-level attack by nineteen similar aircraft, was subjected to an attack by three B-17 bombers operating out of Townsville. Fortunately they missed comprehensively. In a photograph taken from one of the aircraft soon after bomb release, *Australia*'s three funnels were unmistakable![2]

The admiral commanding the cruiser group, Rear Admiral Crace, complained in forthright terms to Admiral Leary who was MacArthur's naval commander. Leary replied that the US Army would do their best to ensure that there was no repetition, but the AAF commander, Lieutenant General Brett, refused to accept that any such incident had taken place. Ignoring the photographic evidence, he prohibited further discussion, with the result that nothing was done to improve the quality of ship recognition either in operational training or in the provision of recognition aids in aircraft and operation rooms.[3]

A report of the sighting of the Japanese force was transmitted several times by the radio operator in Hudson 218, Sergeant Geddes, but this message was not acknowledged by Fall River or any other Allied radio station. Stutt therefore decided to return to Fall River as quickly as possible. Delayed only by the need to make an unsuccessful bombing attack on two submarines west of Bougainville,[4] he landed at 1242 and was immediately taken by jeep to the operations hut and debriefed. In due course, Fall River's first Form White for the day reporting the ship and submarine sightings was prepared and transmitted to Townsville via Port Moresby. According to the Australian authors Denis and Peggy Warner, the message reporting Stutt's sighting took no less than an hour and 55 minutes to be cleared by Fall River radio.[5]

The debriefing officer, probably because he also had no ship recognition aids and was inexperienced in maritime matters, accepted the ambiguity of 'two seaplane tenders or gunboats'. A debriefing officer with experience would not have accepted such a report, recognising the seaplane tender/gunboat description to be a nonsense if only because of the difference in size between the two types. A more knowledgeable debriefer would have resolved the misleading nature of the report then and there.

For reasons that have never been explained satisfactorily, the Form White did not arrive on the duty staff officer's desk in the naval headquarters in Brisbane until soon after 1820, some five and a half hours after Stutt had landed and three and a half hours after it had been transmitted by Fall River. He quickly had it dispatched through the naval radio station in Canberra to Australian ships off Guadalcanal and to other interested authorities. Canberra radio also sent the message to Pearl Harbor radio for transmission to American ships.[6]

Again for reasons that have never been explained, the US official historian (Samuel Morison) sought to explain the delay in the passage of the report by repeating, as fact, an outrageous rumour regarding the behaviour of the Hudson crew. This calumny had it that the pilot of the aircraft did not attempt to make a report of his sighting by radio as soon as he saw the Japanese; that he had continued on his patrol after the sighting and not returned immediately to base; and that, after he had landed, he had tea before going to the operations hut to be debriefed.[7]

Since Savo, this story has been retold many times by various authors, notably Richard Newcomb, Brigadier General Samuel Griffith, Vice-Admiral George Dyer, Paul Dull and most recently, in 1982, by Rear Admiral Gatacre. For some years after Morison's book was published in 1951, the story went unchallenged until, in 1963, during compilation of the RAN official history, the crew of Hudson 218 was approached and the truth emerged. Even then, it was mistakenly held that the lack of a radio report was attributable to an equipment failure—a not unlikely reason in view of the lack of maintenance at Fall River and the failure of radios in two Hudsons the following day.

There can be no doubt whatever that Stutt returned to base immediately after he failed to receive an acknowledgment of his report from Fall River, as the aircraft's time of arrival back at Fall River was recorded in several documents. There is also at least one contemporaneous account of the aircraft's reception when it returned, and of the use of a jeep to take the crew to debriefing as soon as they had landed.

143

Corroboration of the transmission of an in-flight report eluded researchers until 1983, when Nancy Milne, wife of Flight Lieutenant Milne, was researching the part the Hudsons had played in the sighting of Mikawa's cruisers. She wrote to Commander Sadao Seno, a retired Japanese naval officer, to ask for his assistance in checking Japanese records relating to the sighting. Seno, who had been associated with Denis Warner in the writing of *Kamikaze: The Sacred Warriors 1944–45*, found—in *Chokai's* detailed action report—a record of the interception of a message from the Hudson which contained, verbatim, the report that Stutt had said was transmitted. It looked as if it was game and set to Stutt, though two questions remained to be resolved before the match could be awarded to him: why had not Fall River received the report; and why had the record of the intercept not been noticed by Morison and the War College analysts who had had access to all Japanese records after the War?

The answer to the first had lain unnoticed in the Signal Log of ACH Townsville until the middle of 1991. There it is recorded that Fall River radio station shut down between 1032 and approximately 1100 because of an air-raid alert. The answer to the second is almost bizarre. While no formal copies of *Chokai's* Action Report survived the war, an engineer officer had—quite improperly—kept a copy of that highly classified document and it was among his papers which he presented to the Japanese National Institute of Defence Studies in 1963. The Institute has since authenticated the copy.[8]

The facts relating to Stutt's conduct that morning would have been established during or soon after the war, had the activities of the RAAF Hudsons and the AAF Command been subjected to the same close scrutiny as those of the naval forces and the American aircraft flying in support of them. As it was, the terms of reference of the RAN's Board of Inquiry convened to investigate the loss of *Canberra* confined that inquiry to matters pertaining to the loss of the ship, and no evidence was heard which related to the conduct of Hudson searches, of AAF Headquarters or of RAAF Administration in North Eastern Command. Hepburn's informal investigation examined the extent of the searches made by RAAF, USN and US Army Air Corps shore-based and USN carrier-based aircraft, but made no finding as to their adequacy apart from establishing that there had been 'a lack of timely receipt of vital enemy contact information'.[9]

In an article entitled 'Scapegoat' published in the *Australian Magazine* on 1 August 1992, the Warners stated their belief that the crew of Hudson 218 had been made the scapegoats by Hepburn for the defeat at Savo. The word 'scapegoat' had first been used in January 1964 by Sergeant Geddes, the radio operator in Stutt's crew. In a bitter attack on Morison, he alleged that the US historian had 'searched for a scapegoat' to take the blame for Savo and had settled on Stutt and his crew as the culprits.[10] While there can be no doubt that Morison's criticism of that crew was almost completely unjustified and his comments untrue, the Warners' extension of the blame to include Hepburn is equally unjustified. They were replacing one injustice with another, thereby adding to the misinformation which is current about the Battle of Savo.

Hepburn, far from attributing blame for the Allies' defeat to the crew of the Hudson, found that it was the result of the surprise achieved by Mikawa. He was of the opinion that, of the five reasons why the Japanese were able to achieve that surprise, the failure in communications which resulted in the lack of a timely receipt of vital information ranked fourth in importance. He found that the reason for that delay had been unascertainable. He reported that he had endeavoured to determine whether a report had been made at the time of sighting, or on return to base, but had been unable to do so. Hepburn was certainly not the source of the rumour that was picked up by Samuel Morison some seven years later.

Had all gone according to plan, the error in identification would not have been critically important because Stutt's radioed enemy report could have been received in Fall River by about 1045. Communication channels had been set up that would have permitted the rapid passage of the report from Fall River via Port Moresby, and thence direct to McCain's headquarters and his major air bases. There was ample time to relocate Mikawa's force, verify its composition and position, and strike it with shore-based and carrier-based aircraft before dark. The carriers' response would have been particularly rapid because Fletcher, worried about the possible presence of a Japanese carrier, had kept *Saratoga*'s entire air group ready for a strike as soon as a target was found. Even if Mikawa had escaped serious damage, it is most unlikely that he would have continued with his mission in the face of a thoroughly aroused and numerically superior opposition. But everything did not go according to plan; in fact, nothing went according to plan.

That a message with a precedence of 'emergency' should have taken the best part of two hours to be cleared by the radio station in Fall River, and a further three hours or so to reach MacArthur's naval headquarters in Brisbane, is ample justification for labelling its handling by successive RAAF authorities as dilatory. The sense of urgency that led Stutt to hasten back to Fall River was completely lacking.

Port Moresby was in contact with every air base operating aircraft in support of Watchtower in both MacArthur's and Ghormley's areas by means of a radio net common to all. The requirement for using that net was that it should be used when urgency demanded. This, of course, called for a judgment as to what constituted 'urgent information'. Such a judgment was not made in the case of the Hudson's report, not only because of a lack of knowledge of Watchtower but also because of the lack of a naval liaison officer in the air base which was the hub of operations in New Guinea.

Port Moresby passed the message on to Townsville where it eventually reached Area Combined Headquarters. The time of receipt by Townsville radio of the report is not known, but at 1817 ACH Townsville originated a message passing Fall River's report to RAAF Command W/T Station Brisbane. Like Port Moresby, Townsville radio had the option of passing the report direct to SOPAC commanders using the common net, but again— like Port Moresby—had failed to realise its importance. In the meantime, the sun was sweeping relentlessly towards the western horizon and time was running out for 1000 Allied seamen.

The RAAF radio station at Brisbane received the report at 1820 and immediately passed it by a pneumatic tube to the nearby USN Communications Office in the headquarters of the naval component of MacArthur's command. The message was shown to the duty officer and within five minutes it had been passed by land-line to the RAN's radio station at Canberra. By 1837, that is twenty minutes after it had been originated in ACH Townsville, it had been transmitted on the area broadcast and passed to Pearl Harbor for rebroadcast to American ships and commands. Ghormley's headquarters received it at 1842.[11]

What should have taken minutes had taken over eight hours. The sun set over Guadalcanal that evening at 1816. Daylight had gone and with it the last chance of preventing Mikawa's assault on the Allied forces in Iron Bottom Sound. The Naval War College Analysis summed it all up with the following:

> Unfortunately the Allied Air Forces were dependant upon the communication facilities and personnel of the Royal Australian Air Force. The latter personnel had unhappily become complacent as a result of their inability to take offensive action prior to the influx of American Forces and were slow in responding to the demands of the situation.[12]

This is probably a fair comment, as there is evidence in the Signal Log of ACH Townsville that message-handling delays in RAAF communications did not only occur at Fall River. Ironically a message from AAF Headquarters in Brisbane, complaining of excessive message-handling delays, took nine hours on 8 August to reach Townsville! There can be no doubt that the reaction of RAAF personnel would have been very different had they known of the operations then under way.

The Japanese had watched Stutt's aircraft fly off towards Bougainville and, having lost sight of it at about 1035, recovered their aircraft. This evolution had scarcely been completed when, at 1103, *Chokai* sighted Hudson A16–185 flown by Flying Officer Mervyn Willman.[13] The Allies were being given a second chance and, if fate had been kind that day, Willman would have provided information which would have corrected the error made by his predecessor on the scene and shown Mikawa's force to be what it was—a surface striking force. But it was not to be.

When Willman sighted the Japanese, he—like Stutt before him—

assumed they were American. Carrying out the correct procedure for approaching a friendly force, he was at a height of 1000 feet and a distance which he estimated to be 1500 yards when *Chokai* opened fire, hitting the aircraft with splinters in three places. Willman withdrew but—unlike Stutt—continued with his mission, and an hour and twenty minutes later sighted a 2000-ton coal-burning merchant ship at the southern end of Bougainville Strait. He landed at Fall River at 1501.

The Japanese account of Willman's approach given by Captain Ohmae, then Operations Officer to Mikawa, told how the cruisers recovered their aircraft at 1045 and were stowing them when they sighted, in visibility that was 'too good' for their purposes, a Hudson flying quite low which they assumed was the first aircraft coming back for another look. This time it came close enough for *Chokai* to open fire with her three forward 8-inch turrets which caused the aircraft to turn away and to disappear into the distance. In the words of Sergeant John Davies, navigator of the aircraft, they bolted.

Soon after he landed, Willman told Courtis, Stutt's navigator, of his encounter with the Japanese. A fortnight or so later Courtis wrote of that meeting to a mutual friend in which he told how Willman had said that they had approached to within 1500 yards of the Japanese who 'threw every thing at him; he said that he didn't mind that so much but when the cook got out of the galley and threw the stove at him he thought it was a bit over the fence'. A copy of that letter has survived. Willman had obviously had a few bad moments, although it is doubtful that he got as close as 1500 yards since the Japanese did not open fire with their medium-range anti-aircraft guns which had a maximum effective range of about four miles.

This account of Willman's sighting of the Japanese is at variance with that of the Warners, who wrote that his Hudson passed over the ships and dropped two bombs in doing so.[14] Had Willman carried out such a bombing run, there can be no doubt that the Japanese would have fired more than one salvo of 8-inch at him as he approached. Davies, Willman's navigator, makes no mention of a bombing run in his notes. The story may have originated as the result of a comment by the Japanese correspondent Niwa Fumio to the effect that 'when the shell burst round the Hudson, the enemy flew away dropping something which made a column of water'. This may well have been caused by a shell burst, or by a dud hitting the water.[15]

Be that as it may, there can be no doubt that Willman got uncomfortably close to the Japanese after they had recovered their aircraft and as they were forming up to resume their passage to Guadalcanal. Visibility was so good that half an hour or so earlier Stutt had been sighted at nineteen miles, and he had had to fly toward Bougainville to find a cloud in which to hide. In those conditions, given that the Japanese must have been sighted several minutes before they opened fire, the crew of Hudson 185 had a prolonged and undisturbed opportunity to look around them. It would be surprising if all eight ships were not sighted. Willman decided to continue his patrol and attempted to send an enemy report but was told to maintain radio silence, apparently by Fall River radio. After landing, he was immediately debriefed and reported the sighting of six cruisers and two destroyers. The debriefing officer apparently refused to believe that he could have seen such a force and, despite what Willman later was to describe as 'a flaming row', reported in the subsequent Form White that Hudson 185 had seen two heavy cruisers, two light cruisers and one small unknown type. One of the cruisers was described as being similar to the Royal Navy's Southampton class.

Willman recorded his sighting and the damage to his aircraft in his logbook and got on with his war. After the war ended, he became a barrister in Sydney. According to his family, he never discussed his wartime experiences so that it came as a surprise to them when, as he was reading a book in the mid-1980s, he suddenly shouted angrily to no one in particular, 'It wasn't like that at all!' He was reading Denis and Peggy Warner's book on the kamikazes, which included a description of the part played by Stutt and his crew in the sighting and reporting of Mikawa's force.[16] No mention was made of the part played by any other aircraft.

After a visit to Melbourne he seemed much happier about the affair, probably as the result of a talk with his erstwhile detachment commander at Fall River, Lloyd Milne, and his wife Nancy. He told his family that it had all been fixed. Nancy Milne was researching the part played by the Hudsons that day and presumably she gave an undertaking to Willman to give a balanced account of the sighting of Mikawa. Willman made it clear to the Milnes that he did not intend to pursue the matter himself and left them a copy of the relevant page of his log book. Unfortunately Nancy Milne died before her work could be completed, so that it was to be exactly 50 years before the part he played was revealed in an article published in the US Naval Institute's magazine *Proceedings*.[17]

Willman, in August 1942, was of course unaware of the significance of what he had seen and could not have foreseen the calamitous consequences of his inability to convince his debriefer. It is tempting to blame that debriefing officer for the disaster which was to follow, but because of a decision taken in ACH Townsville some days previously to restrict the knowledge of Watchtower to that headquarters, this would be unfair. He could, however, be said to have been guilty of arrogance and indeed professional incompetence in not reporting what the captain of an aircraft said he had seen. He could have, and should have, passed on the report and included his own assessment of the reliability of that report.

His assessment would have been wrong but others further up the chain of command, who had knowledge of Watchtower and of the previous sightings of Mikawa by aircraft and submarine, could hardly have come to the same conclusion as he had. Had Willman's information reached the task forces off Guadalcanal during the evening, their commanders would have been in no doubt that Mikawa's purpose was to raid the amphibious area and acted accordingly. There would have been no debacle at Savo.

The report arising from Willman's sortie took even longer to reach the ships off Guadalcanal than Stutt's, as it was not received in *Australia* until about 2130 that night. To add insult to injury, Willman was reprimanded for breaking radio silence. Fall River was apparently not only unaware of the Guadalcanal operations but also of AAF instructions that radio silence was to be broken to report the enemy. If this was the case, then ACH Townsville's signal—made at 2228 that evening instructing Fall River to comply with a previous order regarding action on sighting the enemy—made sure that the same would not happen again. For those off Guadalcanal, though, it was a case of shutting the stable door after the donkey had escaped, as it was all too late. Irreparable damage had been done.

The third Hudson, A16-157 flown by the experienced Milne, did not sight the Japanese force but had an eventful sortie nonetheless. Fall River's third Form White for the day describes how he sighted and was fired on, on three separate occasions, by single Japanese warships. One of these was probably the minelaying cruiser *Tsugaru*, then escorting the convoy taking reinforcements to Guadalcanal and at that time north-east of Buka. South of the Shortland Islands Milne made an unsuccessful bombing attack on the destroyer *Oite* against heavy and accurate small-calibre anti-aircraft fire. *Oite* was on a search and rescue mission to pick up downed Japanese

The Japanese minelayer Tsugaru *engaged in trials off Yokosuka on 17 October 1941. On 8 August 1942 a RAAF Hudson located this ship north-east of Buka and reported her as a two-funnelled cruiser of 8000 tons, an example of the problems encountered by even experienced allied aircrew in identifying ships from the air.* (IWM neg. MH6504)

aircrew.[18] Milne also reconnoitred Green Island, the Shortlands, Faisi and Choiseul Bay before landing at 1600, having been airborne for almost nine hours.[19] Intelligence from Milne's flight reached the ships at 2316—some seven hours after he had landed. Time taken by the communications system to send intelligence to those for whom it was obtained had steadily deteriorated during the day.

15

The communications factor

Towards the end of the investigation which resulted in the Hepburn Report into the Savo disaster, Commander Donald Ramsey,[1] who had been assisting Hepburn, made a partial summary of some of the communication problems encountered on 8–9 August. Among the matters he addressed were the inordinate delays incurred in passing intelligence to those who needed it. Various survivors had vague recollections that the two sightings of Mikawa's force off Kieta were known in some of the ships before the reports sent out by MacArthur's naval headquarters in Brisbane had been received. One survivor stated that he thought the information had been picked up in a message from a coastwatcher, but Ramsey had been unable to verify that that was so.[2] Ramsey concluded that he was unable to definitely establish that the information had been received any earlier.

The survivors who suggested earlier receipt of the sighting reports were: Commander Irish, the Navigating Officer of *Chicago* (who had been interviewed in February 1943); Captain Greenman of *Astoria* (interviewed in March); Captain Riefkohl of *Vincennes* and Captain Bode of *Chicago* (both questioned by Hepburn in April); and Chief Radio Electrician Daniel of *Quincy,* who had submitted a letter to *Quincy*'s senior surviving officer giving the salient points of his opinions formed before, during and after the battle. Greenman, Riefkohl and Bode had also submitted reports of their ships' part in the battle in mid-August.

On completing his investigation, Hepburn agreed with his assistant and reported that, though he had questioned survivors of ships supposed to have received news of the contact during the afternoon, 'it had not been possible to adduce any reliable positive information on this subject'.[3] But the matter was far from settled, and those 'vague recollections' were to receive the attention of a number of authors in the fifty years which have elapsed since Savo.

The first to examine the possibility of an earlier reception was Morison, when he was collecting material for his book *The Struggle for Guadalcanal*. He received a copy, presumably from Turner, of the message sent through Pearl Harbor resulting from the Form White arising from Willman's sortie in Hudson 185. This was annotated in Turner's own handwriting with: 'Note made on Jan 10 we received a report direct from plane during p.m. as I remember. Can't find any record of it.'[4]

Morison, in considering whether to accept this as *prima facie* evidence that Turner had received a message direct from Hudson 185, probably quickly disregarded it. No other ship or shore station had received a similar message, even though Turner had told him on 16 May 1943 that 'he had some arrangement for guarding scouting plane circuit'. Morison knew *McCawley* was incapable of guarding the circuit because of inadequate communication facilities, so he would have expected to find a record somewhere—in all the evidence in the Hepburn Report and in the *Canberra* Board of Inquiry Report—that word of the sighting of two heavy and two light cruisers had been received by some other ship during the afternoon. But there was none, so Morison ignored Turner's note. It was not, after all, the only time that this officer's memory had been at fault.

After considering what Riefkohl and Greenman had told Hepburn, Morison concluded that both captains were referring to the report from the submarine *S-38* when they talked of the reception of a message in the morning. He estimated that they would have received that report at about 1000.[5] Along with the report of the sightings by B-17s received the previous evening, this would have fuelled any incipient rumours of possible Japanese retaliation which must have been legion in the ships at that time. The subject of retaliation was certainly discussed in *Canberra* from time to time.

Morison's book was published about the same time that Commodore Richard Bates of the US Naval War College completed his analysis of the Battle of Savo, and there is evidence in Morison's notes and in the college archives that there was a great deal of cross-pollination between the two authors. But Bates stuck to facts on this occasion, making no mention of any rumours of reports received before dusk.

In 1963 Richard Newcomb, in his book *Savo: The Incredible Naval Debacle off Guadalcanal*, repeated Morison's story of the conduct of the crew of Hudson 218 and included the statement that radio silence was not broken. He wrote that:

> Later they could not say for sure when they first knew it, but for certain the fleet knew by mid-afternoon that the Japs were coming. Maybe they only heard rumours of the Friday sightings and built them into a full-blown sea story, or maybe they really knew something. The records do not show

it but after all, records don't tell everything. There are too many men who knew something was in the wind for one to believe that they all made it up later.[6]

Newcomb does not appear to have examined the sources of those stories, and did not explain how anyone in the ships off Guadalcanal *could possibly* have known of the sighting off Kieta before the messages from Canberra and Pearl Harbor if Stutt had not broken radio silence! He certainly was not reflecting the evidence presented by the vast majority of those who submitted reports or were interviewed during one or other of the inquiries held after the battle. He may well have been airing the more convincing of the 'lower deck buzzes' or 'scuttlebutt' current at the time, which would not have died with the ships but gained strength as time went by and sailors—mourning friends and having little to do—swapped stories of recent events.

In an unpublished paper written in 1988, Captain Emile Bonnot USNR (Rtd) wrote that a Melbourne radio station had received Stutt's message but presumed that any action would be taken by Fall River and so did nothing.[7] The source of this story was not revealed. The fact is, however, that it was not possible for a radio station in the Melbourne area to have received a radio transmission from Hudson 218. The minimum frequency which could have been received in Melbourne from a tranmission made in the Solomons that morning was about 9000 khz.[8] This was well above the frequency used by the Hudsons, which is believed to have been 6700 khz.[9]

Bonnot wrote that the captains of *Vincennes* and *Astoria* probably knew of the sighting during the morning or afternoon, and that Crutchley also probably knew because he had written that he had the report during the day. This writer introduced a new dimension to the rumour, though, when he told how an assistant gunnery officer in the carrier *Enterprise* had seen the report in the early afternoon and calculated that the enemy could be expected around 0100. Bonnot also wrote that Lieutenant Commander Wight in *Canberra*, when he came off watch at sunset, had already seen the report. This is contrary to Wight's own statement and evidence given to the *Canberra* Board of Inquiry.[10]

The major assault on Hepburn's finding that it had not been possible to adduce any reliable positive information on this aspect was mounted by well-known Australian authors Denis and Peggy Warner. They had been interested in Savo for some time, for they had included a passage in their book *Kamikaze: The Sacred Warriors 1944–45* describing the battle. The connection between kamikazes and Savo was that the same Japanese officer, Captain Kami, planned both Mikawa's dash into the sound and that of the battleship *Yamato* and its escorts towards Okinawa in the closing stages of the Pacific War. The latter was a kamikaze mission on a grand scale, but Kami believed that the same audacity which had led to Mikawa's victory could enable a successful assault to be mounted on the American forces off Okinawa before *Yamato* was sunk, or at least see that ship beached to provide artillery support for the island's garrison. In the end, audacity could not prevail against repeated and heavy air attacks, and *Yamato* was disposed of less than halfway to her destination.[11]

The Warners apparently became convinced that both Turner and Crutchley were aware of the presence off Kieta of Mikawa's cruisers, well before Canberra and Pearl Harbor naval radio stations broadcast the message from MacArthur's headquarters at about 1830 on 8 August. Consequently, they believed that both admirals—together with Hepburn, Morison, Nimitz, King and others—had deliberately ignored supposedly 'irrefutable evidence' by presenting the cause of the Allied defeat as due to the surprise achieved by the Japanese force. Their arguments in support of that claim were woven into the fabric of their book *Disaster in the Pacific*, published by the US Naval Institute Press in Annapolis in August 1992.

The Warners set the scene for their denouement of the plot, allegedly developed by a somewhat nebulous group of naval officers, when they chose 'The Tangled Web' as the title for the chapter summarising their thesis of deceit. This phrase is, of course, drawn from the old saw:

> Oh what a tangled web we weave,
> When first we practise to deceive!

If their allegations were correct, then the Battle of Savo should be viewed in an entirely new light. But was their interpretation of events justified?

Turner's War Diary recorded that, at about 1800 on 8 August, he received a report that two destroyers, three cruisers and two gun-boats or seaplane tenders had been sighted at 1025.[12] Six months later, in answer to a questionnaire sent by Hepburn in advance of his interview in Noumea in early March, Turner wrote that he had received the report on the afternoon of the 8th—that is, that he had seen it between noon and evening,[13] the *Shorter Oxford Dictionary* defining 'afternoon' in that manner. 'Evening' is defined as being from about sunset to bedtime.

No transcript was made of the interview which followed. It would seem certain, however, that when running through the answers to his questionnaire with Turner, and knowing of the entry in the War Diary and of the time of the receipt of the message from Pearl Harbor, Hepburn clarified the matter. How else could one explain the inclusion in his report that it had been established that Turner and Crutchley did not receive the report of the sighting off Kieta until between 1800 and 1900.[14] This was not 'weasel wording': the lack of qualifying adjectives such as 'probably' shows that Hepburn was certain of what he wrote.

When reviewing Turner's statements, the Warners omitted mention of the War Diary entry—despite the fact that its contemporaneous nature meant that it merited serious consideration, and any discussion on whether or not

154

Turner knew of the sighting off Kieta earlier than dusk is simply incomplete without it. They wrote that 'Admiral Turner told Hepburn that he too had received the information during the afternoon . . . He made no mention of this, however, in his comment to Nimitz on the Hepburn Report.' If the War Diary entry is read in conjunction with this, though, it will be seen that Turner was, in fact, being consistent when, commenting to Nimitz on the Hepburn report, he wrote that 'it may be stated that the contact report received via NPM FOX [Pearl Harbor area broadcast] about 1820 presumably was received by all vessels of Task Force 62'.

The Warners went on to say that:

> Hepburn did not accept Turner's word for it. He noted: 'Admiral Turner's recollection was that [a report of] three cruisers, three destroyers, and three gunboats or seaplane tenders [*sic*], was received by him during the early afternoon, but no confirmation of this'.[15]

This statement is contrary to Hepburn's finding that he had established that Turner had received the report between 1800 and 1900 and not before.[16] Clearly, he had decided that Turner's recollection, given some six months after the event, was not entirely to be relied upon.

Perhaps the strongest rebuttal of the rumour that Turner somehow knew of Mikawa's presence off Kieta in ample time to have done something about it was provided by the Admiral himself in the 1960s, in his instructions to his biographer, Vice-Admiral George Dyer:

> I have been accused of being and doing many things but nobody before has ever accused me of sitting on my arse and doing nothing. If I had known of any 'approaching' Jap force I would have done something— maybe the wrong thing, but I would have done something. What they wrote is a g.d. distortion, and that is why I want you to be g.d. sure that you don't distort in what you write.
>
> What I failed to do was to assume that the g.d. pilots couldn't count and couldn't identify and wouldn't do their job and stick around and trail the Japs and send through a later report. And I failed to assume that McCain wouldn't keep me informed of what his pilots were or were not doing. And I failed to guess that despite the reported composition of the force, and the reported course, and the reported speed, the Japs were headed for me via a detour, just like we arrived at Guadalcanal via a detour.
>
> I wouldn't mind if they said that I was too damned dumb to have crystal-balled these things, but to write that I was told of an 'approaching force' and then didn't do anything, that's an unprintable, unprintable, unprintable lie.
>
> Nobody reported an 'approaching force' to me. They reported a force which could and did approach, but they reported another kind of a force headed another kind of way. It was a masterful failure of air reconnaissance and my fellow aviators.[17]

155

There can be no doubt that had he been alive today, Admiral Kelly Turner would have replied to the charges made by the Warners in a similar manner. He was a man with many faults, but lack of aggression was not one of them.

Criticism of Morison's judgment was inferred in the following passage:

When he was writing his account of the action, Morison also consulted Turner. In his papers, under the heading 'The Plane Sighting', the following passage appears: 'TOR August 8 1036 (2236 Love). Air sighting 0001Z/8 (1101 Love) position 05° 42S' 156° 05E' 2 CA, 2L, 1 smaller cruiser similar to *Southampton* class. Ships opened fire on plane at 0120Z/8 (1220L). . .'[18] Then in handwriting: 'This despatch annotated in Admiral Turner's hand: "Note made Jan 10. We received a report direct from plane during pm, as I remember. Can't find any record of it" '. In brackets, Morison added, 'He had some arrangement for guarding scouting plane's circuit so he told me on May 16, 1943'.

In other words Morison had reason to believe that Turner had received Stutt's report long before it was transmitted on the Fox and Bells schedules. Despite this, he preferred the version given in the Hepburn report . . . Even more curiously, he made no mention of Mikawa's intercept, an omission that has puzzled Japanese historians ever since especially as Mikawa and Ohmae went over the chapter before its publication and made 'sundry suggestions'. . .[19]

The message quoted by the Warners was derived not from any report by Stutt but from information in the Form White which had been transmitted by Fall River after the debriefing of Willman. It could not, therefore, have given Morison any reason to suppose that Turner was aware of Stutt's sighting before dusk. Furthermore, those notes gave no clue as to the time when Turner first heard of Stutt's sighting except that it was p.m.—that is, that it was after midday, at least an hour after the sighting was made. This precluded the possibility that he had heard it direct from an aircraft, a point Morison no doubt appreciated in reviewing his notes for his book. It must also have added to his doubts as to whether Turner's memory was reliable.

It is puzzling why the suggestion was made by the Warners that Morison was somehow remiss in not mentioning *Chokai*'s interception of Stutt's message when the authors were aware of the extraordinary story of how a copy of *Chokai*'s Action Report did not become available to Morison, or any other researcher, until late 1963.[20] Morison was by no means blameless for some of the misinformation that has been spread about Savo, but he cannot be criticised for failing to accept that Stutt's report had been received long before dusk.

With regard to Crutchley, the Warners, in the following passage from their book, assessed that he was 'less frank than Turner' when he was interrogated by Hepburn:

In his 'Report of Proceedings', written soon after the action, *he had referred to an afternoon sighting* of Mikawa's force. He failed to make any reference to this when Hepburn interrogated him. Hepburn's questions included the following: 'With respect to operations on D and D plus 1 day, what information did you have of enemy surface forces in the area? My information indicates one contact report on 8 August. This was from an allied plane who at 1127 [*sic*] sighted a force of eight ships on course 140 degrees near Choiseul Island, evidently the force with which you were later engaged. Is that correct? When did you receive this report?' Crutchley listed the Fox and Bells signals at 0717Z/8 and 0742Z/8, contradicting a statement in his 'Report of Proceedings' that he had received a report during the afternoon, a fact subsequently confirmed to the apparent satisfaction of the Australian Naval History Office.[21]

Crutchley's Report of Proceedings was a document of only 28 pages into which he squeezed an account of Watchtower's command organisation, the composition of the Expeditionary Force, the concept of operations, as well as events on a day-to-day basis beginning with the departure from the Fiji Islands and covering the Savo battle before concluding with the arrival in Noumea fourteen days later. In his final paragraph of the section covering the events of 8 August he described how, 'during the day', there had been a report of an enemy force east of Bougainville steering south-east. He had sought Turner's opinion as to their purpose and Turner had replied that he thought that they were bound for Rekata Bay, that they could expect two torpedo bomber attacks a day, and that he had asked for a full-scale bombing of the ships which he felt sure would be found in the bay.[22] The Warners have therefore misquoted Crutchley, who at no time mentioned having received a report during the afternoon. Their contention that 'Crutchley knew, although under interrogation by Hepburn he did not admit it',[23] is quite without foundation.

In the context of Crutchley's report, which Hepburn was to describe as by far the most complete and lucid report he saw during his investigation, the use of the phrase 'during the day' to describe the time of receipt for a message did not rule out its reception at dusk. It was not incompatible with his statement—included in a written answer to a questionnaire sent by Hepburn in preparation for his interrogation of Crutchley—that he had received the first report at 1817.[24] If there was 'a tangled web' then Crutchley had no part in the weaving of it.

Just what transpired between Crutchley and Hepburn when they talked on board *Australia* in Melbourne on 22 February 1943 is not known. Years later, however, in 1960, Crutchley was to recall how Hepburn and Ramsey had arrived on board for a meeting with Farncomb, Gatacre and himself 'breathing fire and slaughter' against them, and went away convinced that they were not such fools as he had been led to suppose.[25]

In Riefkohl's report of *Vincennes*'s part in the battle, he made the statement that he had received the report of Mikawa's presence off Kieta in the 'afternoon'—that is, sometime between noon and evening.[26] When he was interrogated by Hepburn on 3 April 1943 in Corpus Christi, he was asked for his reactions to the contact reports received during the day. He said that he had received two reports, the first at 1015 in the morning and the other at 7.30 or 8.00 at night.[27]

Because submarine *S-38*'s contact report had been received during the day, having been originated in Brisbane at 0736, the report which Riefkohl said he had received at 1015 was almost certainly this one. As *Vincennes* received only two signals during the day (and notice how Riefkohl used the word 'day'), then that received in the evening was the report of Stutt's contact with Mikawa's force. This was confirmed by the statement of Ensign Underwood, made five days after *Vincennes* was sunk. Underwood told how, when he had reported the completion of a radar repair to his captain at about 2030, Riefkohl had told him that he had received a message earlier in the evening that a force of three cruisers, four destroyers and two seaplane tenders were heading their way. Apparently Willman's sighting was not received in *Vincennes*, for it was not mentioned by Riefkohl or any other survivor from that ship.[28]

Riefkohl was to make two, possibly three, further statements on the time of receipt of Stutt's report. The first was to an audience in the Pentagon in January 1945, when he repeated that he had received the report 'during the afternoon'. The second was in a letter to Admiral Carpender in August 1946 in which he said that 'It was about 1930 when I got their reported 1200 position, which aroused my suspicions of their possible intentions.'[29] The possible third statement was reported by the Warners, who noted that Morison had recorded that Riefkohl had had a report at 1530 which included mention of two seaplane tenders.[30]

An examination of the first four statements on the subject of the receipt of enemy reports shows that there is no justification for stating that Riefkohl intercepted Stutt's signal, or that he was aware of its content before he received it from Pearl Harbor. The fifth confuses the issue because, although the information said to have been obtained from it could only have come from Stutt's report, it could not have been received from Stutt because of the time. The evidence of Ensign Underwood supports the acceptance of a time of receipt by Riefkohl of about 1930.

Yet the Warners concluded—possibly because they had overlooked the fact that *S-38*'s report was also received on 8 August—that the message received at 1015 was Stutt's and Riefkohl had been mistaken about the time of receipt. They considered that: 'Captain Riefkohl had no doubt whatsoever that the *Vincennes* had intercepted Stutt's signal long before it was trans-mitted on the Fox and Bells schedules'.[31] There seems to be no justification for such a categorical statement.

In his original report following the loss of *Astoria*, Greenman had stated that he had received a message 'during the day' reporting the sighting of three cruisers, three destroyers and a gunboat off Bougainville. He also said that he received no further information on that force.[32] When he was interviewed by Hepburn in Pearl Harbor in March 1943, Hepburn asked him if he had received a report of Stutt's sighting after informing him that, although it had not reached Fletcher or Turner until about sunset, some survivors had told him that they knew of the report during the day. Hepburn also said that he had been unable to find out how people knew or who sent the message.

Greenman told Hepburn that *he* knew it and that the report was made to him sometime after the air attack at midday by the torpedo bombers. He then went on to say that the report was made in the morning or sometime before the afternoon action. He had been told that it had been picked up by a coastwatcher near Bougainville, and that *Astoria* had intercepted the coastwatcher's report.[33]

In a report submitted soon after *Astoria*'s sinking, that ship's Communications Officer, Lieutenant Davidson, had stated that an urgent plain language message had been received from Pearl Harbor between 1800 and 2000 reporting three heavy cruisers and other ships in a given position on a course of 120 at 15 knots; that report, he asserted, had been the only one received of enemy ships in the Solomon Islands area before the battle. Davidson's report included a list of those frequencies being guarded by his radio organisation but this did not include any of the coastwatcher frequencies.[34]

In summary therefore, Greenman told Hepburn that he had received just one report of Mikawa's force during the day, in the morning, after midday, in the afternoon before 1500, from a coastwatcher on a frequency that was not being guarded in the ship! It is not altogether surprising that Ramsey thought that Greenman's evidence was inadequate to establish receipt of Stutt's report, particularly when the positive evidence of *Astoria*'s Communications Officer was taken into account.

In the face of that evidence, it is difficult to understand how the conclusion could have been reached that: 'Captain Greenman was no less emphatic that Mikawa's presence off Bougainville had been reported early enough in the day for the carriers to take action'.[35] There does not seem to be any record of him ever having said so, and for reasons that will be explained later there was no chance that he could have intercepted a coastwatcher's report—even if *Astoria* had been listening to a coastwatcher's frequency.

In his report on *Chicago*'s part in the battle dated 13 August, Bode confined himself to describing the events of the battle and made no mention of having received any intelligence of the enemy beforehand.[36] However, in a memorandum prepared for Hepburn on 3 April 1943 he reported that, at about 1700, he had received a message which he recalled as reporting the sighting of several destroyers and two other ships which may have been cruisers or carriers. After the navigating officer had plotted the position given, the executive officer had reported to him that the enemy could not reach them before 1000 or 1100 the next day.[37] Although Bode was present when Riefkohl told Hepburn that he had received a report at 1015, he volunteered no comment on the subject of intelligence. Ramsey could well have had Bode's evidence in mind when he described some survivors as having 'vague recollections'.

Commander Irish, Bode's navigating officer, was hardly less vague when he told Hepburn in Pearl Harbor early in February that he had received a report 'sometime in daylight' of the sighting of two small enemy detachments approaching by different routes from the north. He told the Admiral that his calculations had shown that, depending on their speed, they could arrive any time after midnight. He also told Hepburn that he could not recall exactly the source of the information.[38]

The Warners made no mention of the vagueness of both officers' evidence, confining their comment to reporting that: 'In their discussions with Admiral Hepburn, the *Chicago*'s Captain Bode and Commander Irish confirmed that reports of Mikawa's force had been received during daylight hours'.[39] They also inferred that Hepburn had deliberately ignored Bode's and Irish's evidence, but—taking into account all that they told him—it would seem that Hepburn had no choice other than to comment on its vagueness.

Of all the survivors who submitted reports on their experiences, only Chief Radio Electrician Daniel of *Quincy*, who was stationed in that ship's radio office, regarded the intelligence received as ample, timely and accurate. He was unique in that regard! In comments written on 19 August, he was of the opinion that the composition, position, course and speed of the Japanese was known at 1600. But he did not give the source of his information.[40]

Commander Heneberger, *Quincy*'s Gunnery Officer and senior surviving officer, was unaware that any message regarding the approach of an enemy force had been received in the ship, but after the battle heard that there had been one message to that effect.[41] Lieutenant Commander Andrew was also unaware of the receipt of an enemy report before the battle, but also heard later that one had been received in the evening from reconnaissance forces.[42] Both Heneberger and Andrew were critical of the security policy in *Quincy* which prevented such information being promulgated to the gunnery control positions. Clearly *Quincy* survivors, like those of *Vincennes* and *Astoria*, were unable to help Ramsey to establish whether a message had been received earlier than that transmitted from Canberra at dusk and retransmitted from Pearl Harbor.

The Warners mentioned that: 'Both the *Wasp* and the *Saratoga* were aware of Stutt's signal. According to Clark Lee, the *Wasp* considered sending a force to attack Mikawa and, for reasons that cannot be established, decided not to'.[43] The inference here is that, though both ships were aware of the presence of the Japanese off Kieta, the captain of *Wasp* had decided not to launch a strike against them. This statement is not credible for two reasons, the first being that Captain Forrest Sherman of *Wasp* did not seek approval to strike Mikawa's cruisers until after the first reports of the battle had been received in *Wasp*.[44] The second is the inaction of both Fletcher and Noyes, who were in *Saratoga* and *Wasp* respectively; if the ships knew, the flag officers embarked in them would have known also. Even if they had decided for some reason or other not to launch a strike, they had the opportunity—by extending *Enterprise*'s afternoon search—to investigate the possibility that seaplane tenders were approaching the carriers, yet they did not do so. In view of Fletcher's undeniable sensitivity to the threat of an aerial torpedo attack, it is inconceivable that he would not at least have sought further intelligence of the enemy force when he had both the means and the opportunity to do so.

Ramsey also had access to the statements of Australian survivors included in the report of the Board of Inquiry, convened in Sydney in August, to investigate the loss of *Canberra*. The Captain having died of wounds and the Gunnery Officer having been killed, the senior officers questioned on the intelligence received in the ship on 8 August were the Navigating Officer (Lieutenant Commander Mesley), the Torpedo Officer (Lieutenant Commander Plunkett-Cole) and the First Lieutenant and Intelligence Officer (Lieutenant Commander Wight).[45] The Executive Officer, Commander Walsh, having lost the use of an eye during the battle, was not able to appear before the Board until it had almost completed its deliberations. He was not interrogated on the matter of intelligence.

Mesley, in a statement made before the Board convened, was positive that a report of three cruisers, three destroyers with two possible seaplane tenders had been received at about 1900. In response to questioning by Board members, he said that there had been a total of three reports of enemy surface craft 'during the day', two of which had come from submarines after dark and the third from aircraft. This latter report must have been Stutt's, to which he had already referred in his written statement. It would seem that Mesley, like Crutchley and Riefkohl, was using 'day' in the sense of a 24-hour period rather than in the sense of the period between dawn and dusk.

Plunkett-Cole's preliminary report also said that there had been three reports, two from submarines and one from an aircraft. The reports had indicated the presence of a force of cruisers, destroyers and possible seaplane tenders or gunboats to the west of Buka Island. He realised that the ships could increase speed and arrive in the transport area before dawn. He subsequently told the Board that he had been on watch when the aircraft's report was received and that it was then dark. He also told them that he had previously heard of, but had not seen, two other reports but he gave no indication of their contents or time of receipt.

Wight told the Board that he had gone to the bridge at sunset and had taken part in a conference at which the report of the sighting of three cruisers, three destroyers and two seaplane tenders or gunboats was discussed. He mentioned that he had seen two earlier reports of substantially the same number of ships on various courses and up to 50 miles apart—which description fitted the reports from *S-38* and from the B-17s of sightings made the previous day.

There was, therefore, a degree of unanimity among those experienced officers from *Canberra* concerning the intelligence received on 8 August: namely, that there had been a total of three reports, one of which was received after sunset and which announced the sighting of cruisers, destroyers and possibly seaplane tenders. The disagreement lay in the source of the other two reports, but two of the officers thought that a submarine had initiated them and the third—Wight—inferred that, though one had been originated by a submarine, the other had resulted from a sighting by B-17s. There was no common ground regarding the time of receipt of those other two reports, except that no-one said that either had arrived during daylight.

The partial investigation into some communication problems undertaken by Commander Ramsey towards the end of Hepburn's inquiry left many questions unanswered. He did not, for example, adequately investigate whether 'organisationwise' it was possible for Stutt's report to reach the task forces in advance of the messages sent through Canberra and Pearl Harbor. Had he done so, Hepburn could have ignored that possibility.

Ramsey ascertained that a message containing intelligence of the results of Stutt's mission had been compiled in Fall River, after he had landed, and had been routed via ACH Townsville, RAAF Command W/T Station Brisbane, the US Naval Communications Office Brisbane and the Canberra naval radio station. He reported that the investigators had been unable to determine whether a report had been sent by radio while the aircraft was airborne.[46] It is now known that such a message was sent, and that this was intercepted by the Japanese who were close to the transmitter. It was not received in Fall River, because the radio station there was shut down during an air-raid alert.[47]

Had a RAAF radio station heard the aircraft, the message would have been relayed to ACH Townsville in accordance with instructions. From ACH it would have been passed to Brisbane, and so on to Canberra naval radio and to ships off Guadalcanal. This did not happen, so that the possibility of a RAAF station either at Port Moresby or on the mainland north of Brisbane having passed on Stutt's report can be ruled out.

Is it possible that a coastwatcher heard the Hudson's transmission and passed it on? Greenman had told Hepburn that this was how he believed he first heard of the sighting. For that to have happened, though, a coastwatcher would have needed to be listening on the same frequency as the transmission, which is believed to have been 6700 kcs.[48] This frequency had been allocated to the coastwatchers in the Gilbert, Ellice, Phoenix and Tonga Islands for passing reports to Suva between the hours of 1600 and 0500.[49] It was not a frequency in use in the Solomon Islands, and therefore would not have been guarded by any ship in the Expeditionary Force. Furthermore it was not in use, even in the islands adjacent to the Solomons, by day.

In any case, if by chance a coastwatcher in those adjacent islands had heard Stutt's transmission, he would have passed the message to his controlling station in Suva, who would have passed it to Auckland, who in turn would have passed it on to Pearl Harbor and/or Canberra for placing on their area broadcasts. As neither Canberra nor Pearl Harbor broadcast any information regarding Mikawa's force before dusk, no coastwatcher in the Gilbert, Ellice, Phoenix or Tonga groups could have been involved.

But what of the coastwatchers in the Solomon Islands? Their reporting frequency was 6765 kcs and all ships in the Expeditionary Force were aware of that, so that any of them could have set watch on the frequency and intercepted coastwatcher reports. It is, however, most unlikely that they did for the same reasons—explained below—which inhibited the cruisers from listening in to the Hudsons' frequency.

As *McCawley* was incapable of guarding the Solomon Islands coastwatcher frequency, known as the 'X' Frequency, Turner instructed *Australia* to set watch on it and to relay to him any messages received.[50] *Australia* heard no reports relayed from the Hudson that morning, but the system was working well because word of the torpedo bombers passing over Buka was received on the area broadcast from Canberra within 36 minutes of Read having sighted them, and on the previous day *Canberra* had received sufficient warning from a coastwatcher's message passed through Canberra to send the hands to dinner before the arrival of the Japanese aircraft. If only the Allied Air Forces' communications had produced the same result! The involvement of any coastwatcher in the passing of Stutt's report can therefore be ruled out.

There remains the possibility that a ship heard the transmission direct and, in considering that possibility, the circumstances of the moment should be borne in mind. As Ramsey noted, the communications organisation was complicated and available facilities were inadequate. Personnel were fully stretched meeting the requirements of the communication plan. They had been at a high degree of readiness for several days, in a climate that was enervating in the extreme, and could expect no relief for some time. In those circumstances it would have been entirely unreasonable to have employed men to guard any frequency which was not required—particularly as it was known that other arrangements existed for receiving reports from MacArthur's reconnaissance aircraft.

Farncomb of *Australia*, in a memo prepared on 21 February 1943 for Crutchley's meeting the next day in Melbourne with Hepburn, recorded that *Hobart* was guarding the SOPAC reconnaissance frequency for Crutchley, as there was no spare effort in his flagship. No arrangements were made to listen to the SWPA reconnaissance aircraft because their reports were rebroadcast by Canberra.[51]

McCawley certainly was not listening to the Hudsons. Her facilities were so limited that Turner had to resort to the use of other ships to pass even urgent operational traffic to Pearl Harbor. *Canberra*'s only spare receiver was moved from the wireless office to the bridge plotting office to listen to the fighter control net. *Astoria*'s Communications Officer told Hepburn that all that ship's communication positions were manned to listen to frequencies which did not include any aircraft reconnaissance frequency, save that used by her own aircraft. There is no reason to doubt that the other cruisers were in a similar situation.

In summary, the evidence to support a claim that Turner and Crutchley both knew, before dusk, that a Japanese force had been sighted off Bougainville on the morning of 8 August does not stand up to critical examination. Such a claim is discredited partly because it is based on the questionable recollections of Turner, partly because Crutchley is misquoted, partly because well-founded findings of Hepburn and Morison are ignored or peremptorily swept aside, and partly because selective use is made of passages from Hepburn's report to prove the thesis while those that do not are disregarded. On this issue, therefore, there are no grounds for challenging the competence, judgment and honesty of Turner, Crutchley, Hepburn, Morison and others.

16
The Japanese penetrate the sound undetected

At 2345 the aircraft from the Japanese cruisers passed close to *Ralph Talbot* without seeing her. That ship, however, saw one of the aircraft which was showing navigation lights and recognised it as a cruiser-borne reconnaissance type. The destroyer immediately broadcast a warning on TBS that an aircraft had been sighted heading east towards Savo Island but omitted to mention that it was believed to be of a type operated by cruisers.[1] This would not necessarily have indicated to those receiving the message that the aircraft was of enemy origin, as Japanese cruiser-borne aircraft were similar in many respects to those of the Americans. It might, however, have caused someone to link the appearance of an aircraft off Guadalcanal with the sighting of cruisers off Kieta earlier in the day. As it was, noone connected the two events.

Of the heavy cruisers, *Vincennes*, *Quincy* and *Astoria* received *Ralph Talbot*'s message on TBS—as did *Selfridge*, *Blue*, *Henley* and *Patterson*, to name just a few of the destroyers. The warning was not passed on to *McCawley*, however, so that Turner remained in ignorance of the strangers' presence. *Blue*, having heard the report, picked up the aircraft on radar over Savo Island and at 0015 reported the contact on the intra-force MF/HF Warning Net. This report was received in *Australia* but Crutchley was not told of it until the aircraft dropped its first flare at 0145, though he had returned to the ship half an hour earlier.[2]

Before Crutchley rejoined his flagship, the aircraft had been seen or heard by several ships including *Canberra*, *Vincennes* and *Quincy*. In *Canberra*, Wight was on watch and informed the captain of the aircraft's presence. Presumably because the previous night an American aircraft had flown over the ship without prior warning, before making a landing alongside a ship in Group X-ray, the possibility that this one was Japanese did not occur to him. The Executive Officer, Walsh, also saw the aircraft from his position in the after control. Reacting to his instinct for danger engendered by his experiences as captain of the destroyer HMAS *Vampire* in the Mediterranean from mid-1940 to mid-1941, he went forward to the bridge to discuss the sighting with those on watch. As he arrived, he heard Wight report the matter by voice pipe to the captain. Because everyone seemed satisfied he did not pursue the matter but, before he returned to his station, he walked round the ship. Still feeling uneasy he remained awake, keeping—in his own words—'a vague lookout'. As a result, he would actually see the torpedoes fired by *Chokai* approaching the ship.[3]

In *Vincennes*, the captain personally investigated the validity of the sighting and, having verified it, took no further action. He said later that he felt sure that, as *Selfridge* had acknowledged receipt of *Ralph Talbot*'s message and she was close to *McCawley*, Turner would also have received it. As he heard nothing from Turner, he assumed that the aircraft was friendly and had been carrying a message for Turner from the Air Support Force. When later interviewed by Hepburn, he was to say that he found it difficult to believe that an enemy aircraft would fly over the force at night with its lights on. He apparently gave no weight at all to the fact that *Ralph Talbot* had reported it heading east towards Savo Island, whereas during the day the carriers' aircraft had all approached from the south-east.[4]

Only in *Quincy* was a voice raised to proclaim that the aircraft must be hostile. Unfortunately it was that of a junior officer who was regarded by his seniors as being mildly hysterical.[5] Thus was the fourth and absolutely final harbinger of disaster ignored.

In many ways this final warning was the most blatant. The first had involved the sighting by B-17 aircraft of a force off a major enemy base and in an area where its presence need not have involved a move on the Allies at Guadalcanal. The second warning, from a submarine, was of a small high-speed force which was also in an area where the enemy could be expected to operate. As the location of this force lay on the route to the newly-established Japanese base at Buna, which they were known to be reinforcing, there were still no reasonable grounds for thinking it might be bound for Guadalcanal. The third warning, a bit further down the track, involved the presence of a force which had the capability to reach Guadalcanal that night but which was apparently an escort group. If the reported three cruisers and three destroyers did make a pass at the anchorages, the Allies were thought to be in sufficient strength to deal with them before they could do any damage.

Looking back, it is astonishing that no captain of any of the screening force's major ships linked the presence of the cruisers off Kieta that morning with the aircraft then overhead. Even Farncomb in *Australia*, well-known for his perspicacity, did not think the sighting of sufficient importance to inform Crutchley when the Admiral returned on board, thus depriving him of the last opportunity he was to get to ward off the approaching disaster.[6]

After passing Savo Island the Japanese flight leader, Kiyose, broke radio silence at 0023 to report the sighting of three heavy cruisers eight miles south-east of Savo Island. He broke silence again at 0030 to report about twenty ships using their lights in the Guadalcanal anchorage and three or four heavy cruisers or destroyers at the eastern end of the anchorage.[7] Mikawa must have been reassured by the news that the ships in the anchorage were using cargo lights, since this indicated an attack was not expected.

The Japanese risked nothing in breaking silence because there was no communications intelligence team in the Amphibious Force capable of intercepting their transmissions. It will be remembered that Turner had refused the services of such a team, offered by Nimitz's staff when he passed through Pearl Harbor on his way to Wellington.[8] It is tempting to think of what might have happened had the transmissions been intercepted. They could only have meant that a surface striking force was in the area and an attack was imminent. But the likelihood must be admitted that a team, unless larger than that in *Yorktown* at Coral Sea, would have ceased listening at times when Japanese signal traffic was not expected, such as after dark.[9]

After reporting the situation in the anchorage off Guadalcanal, Kiyose moved over western Guadalcanal and orbited above cloud. He returned to the anchorage at 0115 and waited below cloud at a height of about 2000 feet for orders to begin illuminating the area.

If Crutchley could have obtained that night a bird's-eye view of the scene to seaward of Savo Island at 0045, he would have been very satisfied with his positioning of *Blue* and *Ralph Talbot*. With Mikawa heading straight for the gap between Savo Island and Cape Esperance, *Blue* was very nearly on a collision course with *Chokai* and must surely see her. If *Blue* were disabled before an enemy report could be sent, the noise of her encounter with the Japanese would surely alert *Ralph Talbot*, *Chicago* and *Vincennes*. The badly damaged *Jarvis*'s presence in the passage south of Savo Island was a bonus, as she was effectively a back stop to *Blue* in the most unlikely event that the screening group had still not been alerted.

For Crutchley, it would have looked as though *Chicago* and *Canberra* would be given sufficient warning to position themselves across the enemy's line of advance, so as to engage the head of the long Japanese column as it advanced towards them through the gap south of Savo. Mikawa would then be faced with the choice of either withdrawing to seaward, holding course, or altering to port and away from the Guadalcanal shore to bring his cruisers' broadsides to bear while at the same time gaining sea room inside the sound. True, *Vincennes*, *Quincy* and *Astoria* were close to the northern limit of their box patrol, but they would still have more than enough time to race to the south and either support the other cruisers as Mikawa

167

forced his way into the sound or block any attempt he made to move into the middle of the sound.

Crutchley would have noted that the Japanese numbered eight ships. He may even have seen that he was opposed not by three cruisers and three destroyers, as reported from Brisbane, but by a force which included no less than seven cruisers and only one destroyer. This would have caused him to have some misgiving about the ability of *Chicago* and *Canberra* to deal effectively with the Japanese column without the support of *Australia*. Everything would depend on the northern group of cruisers getting into action as quickly as possible.

After some reflection, Crutchley might well have appreciated that the two light cruisers and the destroyer with Mikawa's force could be taken care of by his own destroyers. These smaller enemy ships, with a total of ten 5.5-inch and three 4.7-inch guns, were over three miles astern of the leading heavy cruiser. The four destroyers on his side between them could muster—in addition to 64 torpedoes—sixteen 5-inch guns, all having a much higher rate of fire than the Japanese could achieve. It was true that the five heavy cruisers, if allowed to concentrate their full broadsides on each of his heavy cruiser groups in turn, would enjoy a considerable advantage. But their column was over two and a half miles long and visibility so poor that *Chicago* and *Canberra* would have the opportunity to inflict severe damage on the head of the column before the tail could become effective. By which time, no doubt, the three other American cruisers would have entered the fray and if—as Crutchley no doubt would have expected—Mikawa turned to port, these would be in a good position to bring their full broadsides to bear while the Japanese advanced towards them. In other words Crutchley, from his lofty perch, would have enjoyed the prospect of Mikawa's 'T' being crossed, not once but twice.

Such a battle would require tight control by the commanders of each Allied group, particularly when attempting to cross the 'T'—a manoeuvre which even in peacetime exercises was difficult to achieve and hold for long enough to be effective. Luck would have to play a part but, then, luck had so far favoured the Expeditionary Force. Why should not the good fortune continue?

If he had worried about the ability of Riefkohl and Bode to cope in his absence, he would no doubt have reflected on the fact that both the Americans were men of considerable experience and, from their previous record, obviously competent. After all, had not *Chicago*'s Bode achieved, the previous year, what every naval officer then craved: command of a battleship. Only Pearl Harbor had robbed him of the chance to exploit the opportunities which command of *Oklahoma* had offered.

Crutchley probably would have felt relief at the thought that he had resisted any suggestion to concentrate his heavy cruisers when on patrol. As a result, each group was of manageable size, an important consideration in the battle he could envisage. Furthermore, as the cruisers were not concentrated, Riefkohl would not have to cope with the problems of controlling two ships which were not fitted with TBS radio in a situation that would have required a lot of manoeuvring.

What *Australia*'s part in the battle would be depended on when Crutchley would be able to rejoin her, but it would have been clear to him that his flagship could not rejoin *Chicago* before the battle commenced. There would no doubt be difficulty in sorting out friend from foe as the ship joined in what promised to be a mêlée, the like of which had not been seen since the destroyer action during the Battle of Matapan. However, the use of fighting lights fitted to all Allied ships for use in such a confused situation would have reduced the problem to manageable proportions. As soon as he was back on board, he would have to make up his mind what to do with *San Juan* and *Hobart* and the ten destroyers available to him. He might even have felt a twinge of envy at the thought of the opportunities being offered to Bode and Riefkohl which circumstances were denying him, at least in the early stages of the forthcoming battle.

If Mikawa had enjoyed a similar vantage point he could not have felt as confident as his opponent. Approaching the gap between Savo and Cape Esperance he might have noted that he would have the light in his favour, as a result of the loom provided by the ship burning in the shallows off Guadalcanal. This advantage would be increased by the illumination provided by the flares dropped from Kiyose's three aircraft, a procedure that had been frequently exercised in their training for such a moment. Countering this plus, however, was the probability that he would not achieve the surprise he had hoped for.

Thanks to his communications intelligence team, Mikawa knew that he had been reported by an Allied aircraft off Kieta some fifteen hours previously. He was therefore expecting to have to fight his way into the sound. Lacking fighter cover, everything depended on him being able to force his way into the sound without delay, wreak havoc on the ships in the anchorages and be well clear of the area by dawn.

Mikawa would have seen, however, that his preferred route south of Savo was blocked by two destroyers and that two heavy cruisers with two destroyers were advancing towards the gap between Savo and Cape Esperance. To engage them effectively he would have to turn to port once he made contact with them, in order to bring his full broadsides to bear, and the nearness of Savo Island was going to interfere with that manoeuvre. The enemy would have the advantage until he completed that turn. The heavy cruiser which seemed to be loitering off the Guadalcanal beachhead could move to reinforce the two approaching him at any time. If she did not move to join that southern group, she would still pose a threat to any ship which continued to approach the anchorage after the battle. And then there were the numerous destroyers still screening the anchorages.

Mikawa had chosen to advance into the sound in a long column because it reduced the chances of his force becoming disorganised. All his ships had to do was to follow their next ahead, and shoot at anything they saw after *Chokai* opened fire. But it made it difficult for him to concentrate his fire on any particular target, and made his force vulnerable to an enemy able to cross his 'T'—especially until he was clear of Savo Island. Even then, the northern group of Allied cruisers would be well placed to carry out that manoeuvre as he turned to port to engage the southern group. That northern group would benefit from any delay he experienced in overcoming the southern cruisers, so he would have planned to launch torpedoes as soon as he could against the latter in the hope of achieving some quick 'kills'. In doing this, though, he would have accepted that the chances of obtaining hits were considerably decreased by the narrowness of the targets as they steamed towards him.

Bearing in mind that the range at which torpedoes could be launched exceeded effective gun range, there can be little doubt that Mikawa would have preferred his enemies to be patrolling across his line of approach—that is, across the sound—thereby presenting the best possible torpedo target. He might even have preferred to see all the heavy cruisers concentrated for the same reason. He would have been confident that a column of cruisers would become disorganised as the torpedoes began to take their toll and ships began to take individual avoiding action.

But the realities of the situation at 0045 were very different. The Japanese knew from Kiyose that transports were still off Lunga Point but had no confirmation that the anchorage off Tulagi was still occupied. Kiyose had seen only the southern group of cruisers which was barring the way to the Lunga Point anchorage. Mikawa had no knowledge of the *Vincennes* group. He also did not know about the destroyers to seaward of Savo Island or of *San Juan* and *Hobart*, though Kiyose had told him that there might be as many as four heavy cruisers at the eastern end of the anchorage.

Mikawa may not have had the entire picture, and his lack of knowledge of the northern group was potentially dangerous to him, but he was much better off than his opponents who were totally ignorant of his approach. The initiative still lay with the Japanese and surprise was still a possibility. As far as the Allies were concerned, everything depended on the picket destroyers providing sufficient warning of the Japanese approach. This was essential to permit the two groups of heavy cruisers to deploy against a force entering by the southern entrance in such a manner that the Japanese could not concentrate on only one of them. The only potential advantage that—given adequate warning—the Allies had, was that Mikawa's disposition would permit them to concentrate on the leading ships before those in the rear could become effective.

Before returning to the real world and the events of that depressingly humid, still, dark night, it might be as well to dwell for a moment on the words of Captain Roskill, a noted naval historian and Captain of the light cruiser HMNZS *Leander*, which took part in operations in the Solomons the following year:

> The reader who feels strongly about the unreadiness of the ships, the failure of communications and the poor lookout maintained, should himself experience the strain of trying to remain alert for several consecutive nights after long and anxious days in the deadening and exhausting heat of the Solomons Islands' climate.[10]

Having informed his ships of the reported presence of three cruisers south of Savo Island and ordered them to be prepared to fire torpedoes, Mikawa continued his south-easterly dash towards the southern entrance to the sound. At about 0053 *Chokai* saw a destroyer fine on the starboard bow bearing 162 degrees, at a range which was estimated to be about 11 000 yards and closing on a north-easterly course.[11] The destroyer, which was *Blue*, showed no signs of seeing them.

To avoid being seen as *Blue* continued to close, at about 0059 Mikawa ordered an alteration of course to port of 40 degrees and a reduction in speed to 22 knots. This action was to reduce the visibility of the wakes of his ships, which was amplified by the phosphorescence normal in those latitudes on such a still night. By that time *Chokai* was using voice radio for manoeuvring and enemy reports, though the two light cruisers and *Yunagi* were unable to receive the frequency in use.[12] *Tenryu*, *Yubari* and *Yunagi*, unaware of the sighting of *Blue*, followed in the wake of Cruiser Division Six and *Chokai*. As *Blue* continued to close, the Japanese held their fire, the ships that were following *Chokai* waiting for her to open fire before they did.

Believing that the southern entrance was blocked to him, Mikawa decided to pass to the north of Savo Island and informed his ships accordingly. But, four minutes later, a destroyer was seen on the port bow moving away on a bearing of 059 at an estimated range of about 16 000 yards. This was *Ralph Talbot* in the vicinity of the south-western limit of her patrol line.[13] Once again the enemy destroyer showed no sign of having seen them.

Mikawa held his course until, very soon after sighting *Ralph Talbot* on his port bow, the destroyer now broad on his starboard bow and little more than a mile away, reversed course. Immediately he changed his mind, ordering *Chokai* to alter course back to the south-east and to resume the speed of 26 knots. He was through a gap in his enemy's patrol line which was then no more than nine miles wide. Unbelievably, no one seemed to know that they were there!

Three and a half miles astern of *Chokai*, *Tenryu* had sighted *Blue* at a range of about 7000 yards as the American was approaching *Chokai*. A little later *Tenryu* turned towards *Blue*, but as she did so the American ship turned away and *Tenryu* resumed her station.[14]

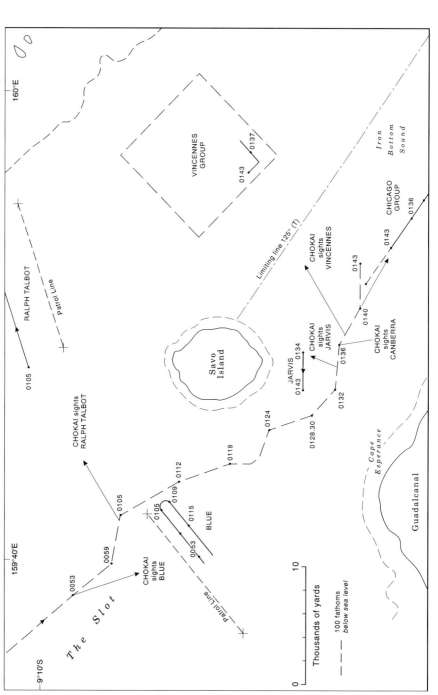

Mikawa's dash into Iron Bottom Sound

The above description of the penetration by the Japanese of the destroyers' patrol line is based entirely on Japanese records. The Naval War College Analysis gives a very different picture, one much more favourable to *Blue*.

According to the analysis, *Blue* was on a south-westerly course when sighted by *Chokai* and it was not until 0110 that the ship turned towards the Japanese column:

> At about 0053 she was sighted by the *Chokai* bearing 162(T) distant 8700 yards. However the *Blue* did not sight the *Chokai* which was closing her rapidly. At 0110 the *Blue* once again reversed course to 051(T). Between 0105 and 0120 her average distance from the *Chokai* was 13,000 yards.[15]

The significance of the average distance over that period is not apparent and tends to disguise the fact that, even if *Blue* were steering 231 when first sighted, her closest point of approach would have been about 7500 yards—half the reliable detection range expected of her radar and well within the assessed visibility for the night in that vicinity.

Regarding the sighting of *Ralph Talbot*, the analysis found that:

> At about 0103, he [Mikawa] sighted on bearing of 159(T) what he mistook to be another destroyer but what was evidently a two masted schooner. This schooner was probably the same ship which had been reported by an *Enterprise* plane on August 7th in a position north west of the Russell Islands since no other Japanese ships had been observed in the area.[16]

Apparently to justify Mikawa's turn back to the south-east on making his second sighting, the analysis also found that:

> It must have seemed to him [Mikawa] that this second destroyer [which the Analysis put on Mikawa's starboard bow, that is on the same bow as *Blue*] was part of a patrol across the entrance. He decided that he would gain no advantage by endeavouring to enter through the north channel which would also be patrolled. It would be wise to strike immediately. He also observed that both 'destroyers' (*Blue* and the schooner) were gradually withdrawing to the south west.

The analysts based their conclusion that *Ralph Talbot* could not have been seen on the grounds that when *Chokai* altered back to the south-east at 0105, some 19 000 yards separated her from the destroyer which was in the centre of her patrol line. Footnotes in the analysis show that *Ralph Talbot*'s position was based on information from her preliminary report submitted after the battle on 11 August.[17] But neither this ship's preliminary or final report provided any navigational information. The analysts ignored the Japanese report that whatever they saw was moving away from them, and paid no regard to the proven visual acuity of the Japanese. They also ignored Mikawa's statement in June 1949 to Lieutenant Pineau, who was then working with Morison, that both he and Ohmae had seen both *Blue* and *Ralph Talbot*.[18] For a number of reasons therefore the finding that no Japanese ship saw *Ralph Talbot* at that time was not justified.

Regarding other disagreements between the Japanese records and the Naval War College Analysis, the author experienced the same difficulties that had beset Hepburn and Ramsey when they were examining the movements of American ships during the battle—namely, the determination of the times at which events took place. Hepburn had written of the American records that:

> No indication is given as to the accuracy of the clock times reported and the times of the same events as noted on different ships are naturally subject to a considerable allowance for error. It is interesting to note the following in the report submitted by *Wilson*, 'The times in the above narrative are approximate, for the hands on the bridge clock fell off with our first salvo and it was not realised that the quartermaster was not making exact time records of the occurrences until sometime later'.[19]

Something similar must have happened to the Japanese time-keepers because it is not possible to correlate all their reports of the sighting of *Blue*. There is, however, general agreement in Japanese naval records, which is reflected in the War College Analysis, that it was about 0053 when *Blue* was first seen by Mikawa's ships, and that because she was closing on the starboard bow Mikawa eventually ordered an alteration of course to port and a decrease in speed, and decided to pass to the north of Savo. Japanese accounts also agree that it was the American ship's reversal of course which prompted Mikawa's decision to alter course back to starboard and to return to his original plan to pass south of Savo Island.[20]

The actions of Mikawa are therefore entirely consistent with what would be expected if he wished to escape detection by a destroyer closing on his starboard bow. The actions of *Tenryu* are also a strong indication that *Blue* was closing the Japanese, for she left the line by turning to starboard to close *Blue*. Had *Blue* been heading away from the Japanese, would the Commander of the Japanese 18th Cruiser Division, whose flag *Tenryu* was wearing, have turned to engage an unalerted destroyer that was clear of the Japanese and moving away when the aim of his commander was to achieve surprise? Clearly the answer is in the negative.

It is therefore surprising that the Naval War College Analysis of *Blue*'s movements found that *Blue* was moving away from the Japanese column when detected and that she remained on a southwesterly course until 0110. The analysis was based on a letter from the Captain of *Blue* written on 17 August in Noumea which listed the times at which *Blue* altered course whilst on patrol on 9 August. It, in turn, was based on an entry made in *Blue*'s pencil-written Deck Log for the period 1–23 August which apparently listed the courses steered during the middle watch. The information was furnished voluntarily to Turner and Crutchley to amplify the original report submitted on 12 August because it was thought to be of 'probable interest in the light of subsequent events'.[21]

The two versions are totally incompatible: one or the other may be right but certainly not both. Because Mikawa's and *Tenryu*'s movements support the Japanese account there can only be one conclusion and that is that, for a reason that cannot now be determined, the entry in *Blue*'s Deck Log was inaccurate. There can therefore be little doubt that *Blue* got a lot closer to *Chokai* than the War College analysts believed in 1951: perhaps not as close as Ohmae's assessment of 500 yards,[22] but certainly close enough for the Japanese to be able to look down on the destroyer and see men moving about on her deck.[23] Furthermore, the Captain of *Kako*, in reporting that *Blue*'s closest point of approach to him was less then three miles, effectively placed *Blue* within two miles of *Chokai*.[24]

What should be accepted, therefore, is that no one on watch in *Blue* saw, at a range of about a mile, a column of eight ships, five of which were about 10 000 tons, moving across the line of sight at high speed, and this on a night when *Chokai*'s lookouts could see a single destroyer, proceeding at 12 knots, at eight miles. The later comment by Gatacre that the Japanese would have had to collide with *Blue* that night to have made their presence known would seem to be justified.[25] *Blue*'s failure to see the Japanese is inexplicable and inexcusable.

Whatever the reason for the inaccuracies in *Blue*'s Deck Log which resulted in the second letter from *Blue* and the misinformation it contained, the effect was to put *Blue* in a much more satisfactory light than should have been the case. A side-effect was to facilitate criticism of Crutchley and to apportion some of the blame for what subsequently happened to his positioning of the pickets.

Whilst it is arguable that Crutchley reduced the chances of detection by over-estimating the assured detection range of the destroyers' radar and that more destroyers should have been placed on patrol, these arguments are irrelevant to the Battle of Savo though undoubtedly of academic interest in a tactical school or war college. Much has been made in various accounts of the battle that the proximity of land that night degraded the performance of the picket destroyers' radar. Such comments are not valid in the circumstances because land echoes would not have interfered with the detection of ships and aircraft at ranges that were less than those of the nearest land. *Blue* was rarely less than seven miles from land.

Mikawa continued to the south-east until, at 0132, when three miles south of Savo Island, course was altered to the east and all ships were ordered to attack. He was commencing his dash into the sound. At that point he must have felt confident of the outcome, since he was apparently opposed by only three heavy cruisers. At 0123, however, Kiyose sent a report which would have given Mikawa a great deal to worry about, had he seen it.

At that time, eight minutes after the aircraft had returned over the anchorage, Kiyose reported the sighting of a battleship and a carrier at the entrance to the sound. This report—obviously of *Chicago* (which had been mistaken for a battleship on a number of previous occasions) and *Canberra*—is another example of the difficulties which even experienced naval aircrew find in recognising ships from the air.

There was no reaction to Kiyose's report, which is surprising as the presence of a battleship in the sound would have materially altered the balance of forces. Mikawa would certainly have discussed its implications with his staff, particularly with Rear Admiral Shinzo Onishi, his Chief of Staff. Apparently the report went unnoticed on the flag-bridge because, in 1956, Onishi was to state that he did not see it until the ships were on their way back to Rabaul.[26] It may have been overlooked in the excitement of the moment, for tension must have been building up on *Chokai*'s bridge as they approached the passage south of Savo Island.

There had still been no reaction to the Japanese from their enemy, although they had been reported many hours before, and they had just passed two picket destroyers which gave no sign of having seen them although they had passed within a mile or so of one of them. Could it have been that they were being led into an ambush? If so, the most likely place would be in the comparatively confined waters of the passage into the sound.

Almost immediately after Mikawa ordered his force to attack, *Jarvis* was sighted on *Chokai*'s port bow at a range of about 3000 yards on a reciprocal course.[27] Once again Mikawa's nerve held and he did not open fire immediately on the destroyer, in spite of her being in an admirable position for launching a torpedo attack. His decision shows a measure of confidence that is remarkable, for he had no means of knowing that *Jarvis* was severely damaged, was limited to slow speed and had jettisoned her torpedoes in the interests of maintaining stability.

Even if he had known of her true state, Mikawa was taking a risk because *Jarvis* was still capable of inflicting damage by gunfire before being overwhelmed. She was far from being a spent force and, although lacking mobility, was capable of defending herself—as *Yunagi* was to find out. Later that day the destroyer gave a good account of itself when attacked and sunk by sixteen torpedo bombers and fifteen fighters from the Rabaul area. There were no survivors, but Japanese records show that before *Jarvis* sank she shot down two aircraft, caused another to make an emergency landing and damaged two more.

Mikawa must have been confident that his lookouts would spot any indication that *Jarvis* had seen him, such as a turn away and an increase in speed, in sufficient time for him to dispose of the destroyer before she could launch torpedoes. It was a brave decision which paid off. Though *Jarvis* passed within a mile down the entire Japanese line, eight warships making 26 knots in a column five miles long, she gave no sign at all of having seen them. An officer who watched her pass from the port wing of *Tenryu*'s bridge estimated the American destroyer's closest point of approach was less than 1100 yards. As he looked down on the ship he could see no one on her decks.[28] Once again, only such words as 'inexplicable' and 'inexcusable' can describe the performance of a unit of Destroyer Squadron Four.

Jarvis, and of course *Blue*, were not the only Allied ships that failed to keep a proper lookout that night. *Jarvis* must have passed quite close to *Canberra*, *Chicago* and *Bagley* on her way to the north-west towards Savo Island from the anchorage off Lunga Point, yet she was not seen by any of them. There was now nothing between the Japanese and *Canberra*. Each and every one of the early warning devices had failed, even the final trip wire that was *Jarvis*.

17

Canberra's ordeal

Inside the sound the sea was calm, the wind negligible and there was no moon. A feature of the night was the phosphorescence which made the wakes of ships glow white, and was later to facilitate the sighting of torpedo tracks. During the night visibility varied from 100 yards to ten miles. The visibility from *Canberra* to the north-west, as Mikawa approached, was about 4000 yards.[1] Between *Canberra* and Savo Island lay an intense black cloud bank which obscured the island from that ship's view, but to the south-east of Mikawa the visibility was excellent with light from the fires in the burning transport *George F. Elliot* reflected from the clouds.[2] The Japanese therefore had an advantage which was crucial. They could see the Allied ships against the loom cast by the burning transport, whereas they themselves were operating against the backdrop of a heavy black amorphous mass.

Chokai had just passed *Jarvis* when, at 0136 at a range of 12 500 yards, *Canberra* and *Chicago* were seen on a bearing of 120. Mikawa immediately ordered an alteration of course towards them.[3] *Canberra* was steering 310 so that *Chokai* was then 10 degrees on her port bow. As *Canberra*'s speed was twelve knots, the closing speed was greater than a mile every two minutes which allowed little time for second thoughts during the close-range encounter which was to follow.

Soon after they sighted *Canberra* and *Chicago*, the lookouts in *Chokai* saw the *Vincennes* group 60 degrees on the port bow at a range of about 18 000 yards. Thus for the first time Mikawa knew that he was opposed by two groups of cruisers. It was imperative for him to dispose of the two ships on his starboard bow as quickly as possible, so as to be able to concentrate on the second group. It also meant that he was not immediately able to force his way into the sound to tackle the transports which, in view

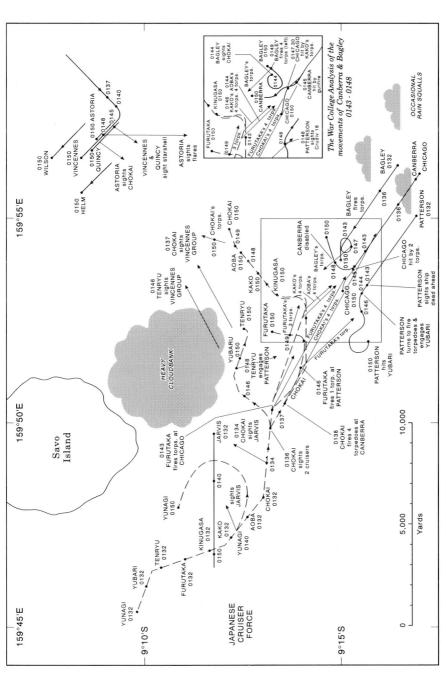

Battle of Savo Island: 0132–0150

of the information provided by Kiyose, he probably assumed were all off Guadalcanal. Crutchley, absent though he was, was dictating the course of the battle by his decision to split his heavy cruisers into two groups—a decision which was, in the end, to save the transports.

Two minutes after sighting *Canberra*, *Chokai* launched four torpedoes in an almost 'straight down the throat' shot from fine on *Canberra*'s port bow. As they were straight runners, it must have been realised that they did not have much chance of success if the ships maintained their heading. At 0140, or four minutes after sighting *Canberra*, *Chokai* led round to 090 to open gun arcs which would bring all five twin 8-inch turrets into action.

Overhead, Kiyose had been growing impatient. At 0124 he asked if he should drop his flares, and was told to wait. Finally, at 0142, his moment arrived and he was told to start illuminating.[4] The timing and positioning were wellnigh perfect, as the first flare burst to starboard of *Canberra* and beyond her—just as *Chokai*'s torpedoes were about to reach her after running for six minutes. At that moment five Japanese heavy cruisers were poised to open fire on *Canberra* at ranges between 9000 and 4500 yards. All that was needed before *Canberra* became the target for as many as 34 8-inch guns and others of lesser calibre was for *Chokai* to open fire, which she would do as soon as her torpedoes reached *Canberra*.

Almost as Kiyose was ordered to start illuminating, bridge personnel in *Canberra* heard an explosion off the starboard bow. One of *Chokai*'s torpedoes had exploded prematurely, a not uncommon fault in the Long Lance torpedo.[5] The senior officer on watch, known as the Principal Control Officer or PCO, was Lieutenant Commander Wight. He immediately summoned the Captain to the bridge by voice pipe. Very shortly after the explosion, a port lookout sighted a ship ahead but no one on the bridge was able to see it.

Getting had retired at midnight to his sea cabin, a deck below the bridge, and was dozing in a chair. He was on the bridge within seconds. At the same time the Officer of the Watch, Sub-Lieutenant Gregory, called the Navigating Officer, Lieutenant Commander Mesley, who was also asleep in his sea cabin; this officer was slightly delayed in reaching the bridge by the need to put on his shoes. Wight, seeing the wakes of three ships ahead against the blackness of Savo, ordered the action alarm to be sounded.

The speed at which the situation then developed is indicated by the experience of Mesley, who had been called immediately after the explosion was heard. As he left his cabin, he heard the action alarm ring. He was one deck below and a little abaft the bridge and reached it in time to hear the Captain order 'Hard to Starboard' and 'Full Ahead'. In the time that it took Mesley to reach the bridge, Wight—seeing three ships fine on the starboard bow—had alerted the armament with the order 'Alarm starboard; load, load, load!', indicated the direction of the enemy by means of the starboard enemy bearing indicator and, to bring the after turrets to bear, ordered the wheel to be put hard to port as the Captain arrived on the bridge.[6] As *Chokai*'s remaining torpedoes were observed passing down each side of the ship and before the order to turn to port had had any effect, the Captain reversed the wheel to starboard and gave the order for full speed. He had apparently realised at once that a turn to starboard was necessary if *Canberra* were to remain between the enemy and the transports.

Having given the wheel and engine orders, Getting turned to the Signal Yeoman of the Watch, Yeoman Johnson, and ordered him to report to *Chicago* the sighting of three cruisers. Johnson moved a few steps down from the bridge and aft to the starboard side of the torpedo control platform, so that he could see *Chicago* who was emerging from astern on to the starboard quarter as *Canberra* commenced swinging to starboard. Using a red signal lamp, he flashed a few 'N's, the alarm signal for 'enemy in sight', followed by 'three cruisers'. As he did so, he noticed that *Canberra* was on fire amidships.

Mesley, when he arrived on the bridge, took over the handling of the ship from Gregory. He had hardly had time to check the positions of the rudder and engine room telegraphs when he looked around him and saw at least two torpedo tracks approaching from the port side, apparently coming from the centre of three enemy ships which were on the port bow at a range which he estimated to be about 1500 yards. He at once moved to a nearby voice pipe and ordered the plotting office to send an enemy report of the sighting of three ships of an unknown type on a bearing of 300 degrees at a distance of one mile.

Returning to the centre of the bridge he noticed torpedo tracks on each side of the ship coming from abaft the beam and gave orders to stop the ship swinging so as to parallel them. Just at that moment there were two explosions to port and abaft him. The second killed the Gunnery Officer and mortally wounded the Captain. He noticed that *Canberra* was slowing down and had taken on a list of about ten degrees, when he received a report from the steering position that the ship would not answer her helm. He was horrified that the ship had been disabled without firing her 8-inch guns.

The Torpedo Officer, Lieutenant Commander Plunkett-Cole, arrived on the bridge immediately after the sighting of *Chokai*'s torpedoes and also saw three ships but by that time they were fine on the port bow. He moved quickly down to the torpedo control position on the port side immediately abaft the bridge and was setting up the torpedo sight when he was knocked down by an explosion behind him. A shell had wrecked the plotting office and prevented the passing of Mesley's enemy report. When he got to his feet he found that he was unable to fire his torpedoes. All electric power had been lost and he noticed that the ship was listing to starboard.

The Gunnery Officer, Lieutenant Commander Hole, had reached the bridge just ahead of Plunkett-Cole and as the *Chokai*'s torpedoes were seen.

He moved at once to the starboard enemy bearing indicator (EBI) and took over from Wight the task of controlling the main armament. Wight had apparently still been looking for a target about 20 degrees on the starboard bow, but by that time *Canberra* was swinging to starboard and the bearing of the enemy was drawing left. It seems likely that Wight had not made a switch on the EBI which stabilised the binoculars and compensated for the swing of the ship. Unable to find a target on the starboard bow, and no doubt appreciating that the enemy's bearing must be drawing left, Hole moved quickly to the port EBI and commenced searching. He had carried out two sweeps of the horizon without success[7] when he was killed by a shell which exploded on the port side of the bridge.

The six paragraphs immediately above take over three minutes to read aloud, which is about the time which elapsed from the first sighting of *Chokai* by the lookout to the loss of all power in *Canberra*. In that time, below decks, the ship's company had moved quickly to the action state. Damage control headquarters had received word from all sections of the ship that the various damage control parties were at the ready.[8] Ammunition supply and medical parties were standing by. In the boiler rooms all sprayers had been connected and the boilers were responding to the demands of the turbines for steam as experienced and well-trained personnel, under the watchful eyes of the engineer commander and his senior engineer, opened the throttles. The engines had achieved the revolutions for 26 knots when all steam suddenly disappeared.

Above decks all four 8-inch turrets were fully manned, the guns loaded, an operation which even in the worst circumstances could be achieved in less than 27 seconds, and all control personnel were at their stations. The turrets were moving in unison with the director as its crew sought a target. Torpedo tubes crews and searchlight control parties were standing by. In short, before power was lost, *Canberra* was ready in all respects to go about the business of engaging the enemy.

Only a few seconds more would have been necessary for what was an experienced command team to become effective. All key personnel, both officers and men, were specialists in their professions and men of considerable experience both in the navy and in the ship. Contrary to the Naval War College Analysis, an enemy report had been initiated—*Canberra* being the only one of the four heavy cruisers to attempt to do so. The Torpedo Officer was about to fire torpedoes, the searchlights were burning behind their shutters, the guns were loaded and the gun ready lamps burning in the gunnery control positions, and the ship was working up to full speed. All that was lacking was an aiming point before opening fire and a little more time because, just as power was lost, the director saw a cruiser on the port beam.

Chokai had opened fire as her torpedoes passed *Canberra* and had been followed by the other heavy cruisers as they sighted *Canberra* and *Chicago*.

Furutaka, the fifth ship in the Japanese line, had seen *Canberra* as *Chokai* opened fire and followed suit, firing four torpedoes as she did so. These all missed. Very soon afterwards *Furutaka* had a steering breakdown which caused her to leave the line and eventually to follow the light cruisers as they headed north. She took no further part in the action with *Canberra*.

Aoba opened fire at *Canberra* at about 0144, when the range was 4200 yards; her four torpedoes were those seen by Mesley approaching from the port side. *Chokai* was by that time heading north-east, away from *Canberra*, so that it is probable that the three cruisers seen by Mesley and Plunkett-Cole were *Aoba*, *Kako* and *Kinugasa*. Very soon after *Aoba* opened fire, *Kako* also began shooting with her 8-inch and 4.7-inch guns; she also fired four torpedoes, but soon ceased fire as she followed *Chokai* and *Aoba*. By that time *Canberra* was approaching an easterly heading so that *Kako*'s torpedoes, which Mesley also saw, overtook her passing down each side. It was at about that moment that *Canberra* lost all power.

Kinugasa, now the last in the line, had opened fire on *Canberra* as she went past at a range of about 2000 yards. As she followed *Kako* towards the *Vincennes* group, she fired a parting salvo of four torpedoes at the disabled ship. All missed and were not seen by anyone in *Canberra*.

In all, the Japanese had fired nineteen torpedoes at *Canberra* without a single hit being obtained on that ship. Getting's actions in turning hard to starboard and increasing to full speed had undoubtedly saved his ship from being hit by *Aoba*'s and *Kako*'s torpedoes, and also made her a difficult gunnery target despite the short range. Nevertheless, the effect of the Japanese cannonade had been devastating. Before Mikawa's raiders went on to the north-east in pursuit of other game, *Canberra* suffered at least 27 hits—all on the port side. She was on fire amidships and effectively left a drifting hulk.

Canberra's violent manoeuvring had had a most unsettling effect on the attempts of the gunnery control systems to acquire a target and was the greatest single reason for her failure to open fire. For example, as the ship swung to starboard the gunnery officer was forced to interrupt his search for a target, leave his position on the starboard side and cross to the port side of the bridge. Inexperience of the gunnery control personnel was not a factor, as all were specialists in gunnery with many years experience in that field behind them. Captain (later Vice-Admiral Sir) John Collins, a noted gunnery specialist, when reviewing the course of the battle at Navy Office, Melbourne, remarked that:

> Undoubtedly the task of getting the director and guns on to the target was complicated by the ship being under full wheel. This once again emphasises the disturbance to own ship's fighting efficiency caused by drastic alterations of course.[9]

But Captain Getting had had no alternative to turning to starboard and increasing speed. His aim was the protection of the anchorages and if he had restricted his manoeuvring to provide a better gun platform, he would have allowed the enemy to pass between him and the ships he was there to defend. The problem was exacerbated for *Canberra* by the hazy conditions and the inky black background which provided no reference point on which to base a visual search.[10]

To those on the bridge, the loss of power not only manifested itself in a gradual slowing down of the ship but also in the sudden absence of ship noises amid the frequent explosions and the crackling of flames as the aircraft and after superstructure caught fire. The whine of the boiler room fans and the vibration associated with a ship accelerating under the thrust of unsynchronised propellers suddenly ceased.

Down below, in the machinery spaces, the effect was even more dramatic. Whatever happened to destroy the steam-generating capability of all eight boilers killed every man in the boiler rooms. In the engine room, those who had been engaged in opening the throttles noticed that the steam pressures had collapsed. The lights went out as the dynamos suddenly stopped and the turbine-driven fans no longer forced air into the boiler rooms. Fifty years later Ordinary Seaman Warne was to recall hearing, from his action station in the after shell room situated above the propellers, the noise of the engines die and the shell room become 'enveloped in silence'.[11]

Throughout the ship the weak battery-powered emergency lighting came on. All turret machinery stopped, so that the turrets remained trained 120 degrees to port and, above the gunnery control position, the director—now trained by hand—was unable to follow the target that had fleetingly appeared in the director layer's sight. Damage control parties found that there was no water in the fire main. Those who knew of the diesel generators which were lying ashore in Sydney, waiting to be fitted at the next available opportunity, no doubt cursed those responsible for the decision not to fit them in the recently completed refit.

To understand the argument that developed as to how it was that *Canberra* could be brought so quickly to such a state of helplessness, it is necessary first to understand the ship's propulsion machinery layout and the method of generating steam. Oil was heated and vaporised before being pumped under pressure into the furnaces where it was combined with air, also under pressure. There were two ways in which air could be induced into a marine boiler to produce the forced draft necessary for efficient combustion. The first was to trunk air direct to the boiler faces. The second was to increase the air pressure in the boiler room by making it airtight and to raise the pressure within the boiler room by means of steam-driven fans situated outside the boiler room, in what were known as fan flats.

Of the above two methods, the latter was used in *Canberra*. Four boilers, two each side, were fitted in each of two boiler rooms separated only by a single bulkhead. Above each boiler room was a fan flat containing a number of turbine-driven fans. Air locks between each flat and its boiler room allowed access without loss of air pressure. A sudden loss of air pressure would cause the boiler fires to flash back into the boiler room with fatal results for personnel. A loss of oil pressure, though not as dramatic as loss of air, would still result in a loss of power as the fires subsided.

Aft of the boiler rooms, and separated from them by magazines and oil fuel tanks, were two engine rooms adjacent to each other—each with two sets of turbines. Two boilers supplied each engine. It was possible to cross-connect boilers and engines, but at Savo *Canberra*'s boilers were not cross-connected. The dynamos were similarly isolated from each other. The forward boiler room provided steam to the after engine room and the after boiler room to the forward engine room. Boilers to starboard in the boiler rooms supplied the starboard engines in the engine rooms. To cause an interruption in the supply of steam to all engines, two steam lines on each side of the ship would have to be damaged. For a loss of steam to be suffered simultaneously by all engines, damage to all four steam lines would also have to be simultaneous.

In *Canberra* that night, steam pressure did suddenly collapse and all power generation stopped. This therefore signified one of the following causes:

- the sudden stopping of all fuel supply pumps
- major damage to all four main steam lines
- catastrophic damage in both boiler rooms by the release of steam from one or more boilers simultaneously in each boiler room, which would kill all personnel and put out the fires
- a 'flash back' through loss of air pressure, caused by the destruction or at least the sudden stopping of all fans in both fan flats
- the sudden flooding of both boiler rooms because of torpedo damage.

The first report of the Board of Inquiry held in Sydney in August and September 1942 to inquire into the loss of *Canberra* concluded that it was improbable that a torpedo had caused the damage. The principal witness had been the Engineer Officer, Commander (E) McMahon. He was convinced that the ship had not been torpedoed and that therefore the damage must have been caused by shellfire.[12]

When the first report was considered by the Naval Board, board members were not satisfied that the question of why *Canberra* suddenly lost all steam had been properly investigated. The President of the Board of Inquiry, Rear Admiral Muirhead-Gould, was instructed to reconvene his Board to examine further whether the ship had been torpedoed. By the end of September a second report was submitted to the Naval Board which concluded that both boiler rooms were so damaged by shellfire that steam generation ceased and all machinery stopped. It found that *Canberra* had not been torpedoed because:

- There was no actual witness who could state that he saw or felt any explosion of such magnitude as might be expected from a torpedo exploding on the hull. There were many men in the engine room and other compartments below the water line, yet none of them had described anything like a severe underwater explosion.
- There was no evidence of any severe upward damage within the ship, such as decks buckling or the ship hogging or sagging, as might be expected from a torpedo explosion amidships.
- There was no sudden lurch, and the list was at first comparatively slight—5 to 7 degrees—and this was acquired gradually.
- There was no serious leakage of oil—in fact there was no sign of oil in the sea.

The Board of Inquiry reported that evidence had been found of at least one explosion in each boiler room, but that there was no indication that the total failure of steam in the four isolated units was caused by damage to the main steam lines or boilers. There was no evidence that all the fan engines had been damaged. The most likely cause of a total loss of steam was considered to be damage to all the oil fuel supply pumps, of which there were eight (grouped in pairs on the floor plates in the centre of each boiler room). The list of 7 degrees could have been caused by shells entering the port side and exiting below the water line on the starboard side, or by direct hits on the starboard side.[13]

The first report was sent to Crutchley by the Naval Board for his remarks. After reading it, he stated his belief that, though the absence of oil on the water would support the Board's finding, he found it difficult to believe that anything other than a torpedo would have caused the ship to list 7 degrees in such a short time. He also did not accept that shellfire alone would put all boilers out of action almost instantaneously.[14]

Muirhead-Gould was also beginning to have doubts. In a letter to the Naval Board in mid-September, before the second report had been submitted, he commented that he regarded the evidence that the ship may have been torpedoed as very conflicting. At the inquiry he had been convinced that *Canberra* had not been torpedoed. He was less sure after a conversation with the ship's Executive Officer, Commander Walsh, and after reading the statements of survivors who had not given evidence to his Board. He still thought, however, that the principal damage was done by shells in the boiler rooms or fan flats and that the list might have been caused by shell bursts on the starboard side.[15]

Walsh had given Muirhead-Gould an account of the movements of the Japanese which conflicted with what he had been told at the inquiry, and it apparently made him question whether *Canberra* had been hit on the starboard side before she was disabled. Hits on that side had been a mainstay in McMahon's explanation for the list to starboard, when he stoutly rejected the proposition that the damage had been caused by a torpedo—a rejection made on the grounds that he had not felt any shock of the magnitude which he expected from the explosion of a torpedo.

Walsh was not new to war, having taken part in the Battle of Calabria, the evacuations of troops from Greece and Crete and the Tobruk 'ferry' runs and had been subjected to high-level bombing and dive-bombing on many occasions. McMahon's war had been much quieter. From his position in the after control when the action started, Walsh was one of many who reported having heard or felt a particularly heavy thud among all the other thuds. In 1973 he was to tell Alan Payne, author of a history of *Canberra*, that he also saw a column of water which he hoped would assist with the fire fighting. At the inquiry, however, he had said that injury to his eyesight had prevented him from seeing much.

Walsh had not given evidence at the first session of the Board of Inquiry as he had been in hospital in Auckland recovering from a head wound which had rendered him blind in one eye. He was returned to Sydney earlier than the other seriously wounded survivors to give his evidence at the Board's second session and in later years was to complain of the reception he was given. He was convinced that *Canberra* had been torpedoed, but when he appeared before the Board he found that McMahon's views were by then so deeply entrenched in the minds of board members that, in his opinion, his views were not given the consideration which they merited.[16] After he had given his evidence he was not invited to be present for the remainder of the inquiry, though this courtesy was extended to McMahon who had been present for the greater part of both sessions of the inquiry.

Walsh's views may have been strengthened as a result of conversations he had with Lieutenant (S) Rose in hospital in Auckland. Rose had been in charge of an Oerlikon gun position on the starboard side above the forward boiler room. He had seen a 'terrific orange greenish flash' which came up from the forward boiler room's fan flat, about 20 feet from where he was standing. McMahon had mentioned Rose's story in his evidence to the first session, during a very long answer to a question asking for his opinion of the cause of the damage, but it was not specifically discussed. Rose was not asked to submit a written account of his experiences, and did not return to Sydney until after the inquiry had been concluded.[17]

A copy of the second report, together with all the reports of survivors, was sent to Crutchley by the Naval Board in mid-October. After studying the documents Crutchley found himself in total disagreement with the Board's opinion that the *Canberra* had not been torpedoed. He believed that it was notoriously difficult to gauge whether a ship had been torpedoed. Sometimes it was quite obvious, but on other occasions there was no more shock than a broadside of guns, depending on where the torpedo struck. His reading of the evidence, and of the accounts of survivors, revealed to him that there were many stories which described shocks quite likely to have been a torpedo explosion and which at the time were attributed to a torpedo hit. These witnesses had not always been called to give evidence.

Regarding the lack of distortion to the hull, he pointed out that the ship had been constructed with anti-torpedo bulges. Both the bulge abreast the boiler rooms and the air space inboard of the bulge would have absorbed some of the blast. As the boiler rooms were the best vented spaces in the ship, he felt that the air intakes and funnels would have absorbed any residual blast pressure. He told the Naval Board that he had had calculations carried out to determine the list to be expected from the flooding of the boiler rooms, the starboard bulge and the starboard wing compartment. The answer had been 7.6 degrees. And finally he knew that there was a very considerable space in the vicinity of the boiler rooms' bulkhead where no oil was carried, and that a hit near there would have been unlikely to have produced oil.

Crutchley did not accept the theory that the loss of oil fuel pressure was due to damage to the oil fuel pumps. It probably seemed to him to have been a desperate attempt by McMahon to sustain his argument that the damage had all been inflicted by shellfire. Crutchley wrote:

> they [the oil fuel pumps] were situated well down below the water line; the range was short and therefore the trajectory [of shells was] flat. Thus a short would be expected to ricochet immediately on striking the water and therefore hits below the water were very unlikely. It would be necessary for shells striking above the water line to be so deflected downwards as to put four separate pumps in two groups of two in two different compartments out of action simultaneously . . . On the other hand a torpedo in the vicinity of the bulkhead between the two boiler rooms could well flood both boiler rooms simultaneously thus accounting for all the trouble . . . While it would have been possible to cause a list of 7 degrees to starboard by shell fire in a comparatively short time, I think that in this case where nearly all the fire was from Port, it is extremely unlikely that the list could have been caused in the time by anything except a torpedo.[18]

In commenting on Crutchley's letter at Navy Office, Captains Collins and Dowling both agreed with him. Collins found difficulty in accepting that a 10 000-ton cruiser could take on a 7-degree list to starboard so rapidly as a result of gunfire from the port side and quoted the experience of the cruiser HMS *Trinidad*. In that ship, a cruiser of about 9000 tons, the shock of a torpedo explosion felt in the machinery control room, a compartment which was very close to the explosion, had given the impression that the ship had been hit by a shell.[19]

Dowling had been torpedoed in HMS *Naiad*, a Dido-class cruiser which was considerably smaller than *Canberra*. He had been standing on the upper deck and the ship had lurched in a manner similar to that which had been

This section of a model of Canberra *in the Australian War Memorial shows the starboard side amidships, where the damage occurred which crippled her during the opening moments of the Savo Island battle. Rear Admiral Crutchley rejected the finding of a naval Board of Inquiry that Japanese shellfire entering from the other side and exiting here below the waterline could have caused the list which the ship developed. Along with other senior Australian naval officers with war experience, he was convinced that the cruiser must have been torpedoed, but by whom?* (Author)

reported in *Canberra*. The ship's deck had not been distorted and there had been no fountain of water alongside from the explosion.

The matter was never resolved by the Naval Board but the *coup de grâce* to the anti-torpedoing lobby was given in 1973 during Alan Payne's research for his book, *HMAS Canberra*, when he received a letter from Able Seaman St George who had written one of the best of the survivors' accounts after the sinking. St George was remembered by other survivors as a 'bit of a character', especially for his impersonation of an officer's idiosyncrasy of wearing a monocle. Payne had written to St George, asking if he could amplify his original report as he had not been questioned by the Board of Inquiry.

In his account St George told how, just as *Blue* was approaching to take off the survivors from the port side of the forecastle, he had been sent over the side to disentangle the securing lines for the rafts which had been launched in preparation for abandoning ship. He described how he had swum down the starboard side and, as he was abreast the boiler rooms, he got 'a hell of a shock'. He had been looking for a hole, expecting to see damage from a torpedo about twelve feet across and, because of the list, well under water. Instead he found that the top was still just above the water and that in his estimation, the length of the hole was about 35 feet. He then boarded

Blue. When the destroyer cast off from alongside, she moved out ahead of *Canberra* and turned to starboard—thus allowing St George another look which confirmed what he had seen from the water.[20]

Among those survivors who would have given evidence supporting the claim that *Canberra* had been torpedoed and who did not appear before the Board was Seaman 1st Class Whitmire, an American on loan to *Canberra*. He was standing at the rear of the bridge on the starboard side watching *Chicago* for possible signals when, he stated:

> a shell struck the port side of the Compass Platform . . . At this moment a torpedo struck starboard side amidships, entering Boiler Rooms and disabling ship's power and control. I saw two torpedoes pass astern on the starboard side. From where they came I do not know.[21]

Whitmire was probably the only person in the vicinity who was not looking in the other direction for the Japanese. In his short time in *Canberra*, the American had impressed those who worked with him. Mesley, in his own survivor's report, wrote that Whitmire had been of great assistance in every way and was calmness itself. He requested that a mention of his merit be forwarded to *Chicago* for report to Admiral Leary on whose staff he really belonged.[22]

There seems no reason now to doubt that *Canberra* was torpedoed starboard side amidships. The only question remaining to be answered is by whom?

18
Friendly fire?

The Japanese had fired salvoes of torpedoes at *Canberra* at the following times and ranges:

Chokai: four at 0138 at a range of 10 000 yards.
Furutaka: four at 0143 at a range of 9000 yards.
Aoba: four at 0144 at a range of 4200 yards.
Kako: three at 0146 at a range of 3600 yards.
Kinugasa: four at 0153 at a range of 2000 yards.

These torpedoes would have passed their target at approximately 0143, 0148, 0146, 0148 and 0155 respectively. Because *Chokai*'s were seen to pass down either side of *Canberra* and *Kinugasa*'s were fired well after *Canberra* had been disabled, only those from *Furutaka, Aoba* and *Kako* could possibly have found their mark. The War College Analysis found, however, that these ships were all on the cruiser's port bow when they launched their torpedoes, and at no time during the torpedoes' running time did *Canberra* present her starboard side to them.[1] This finding is supported in a negative sense by witnesses at the Board of Inquiry, for none reported seeing a Japanese cruiser to starboard. It follows, therefore, that *Canberra* could not have been hit on that side by a Japanese torpedo.

The Japanese cruisers were not the only ships to fire torpedoes at that time that night, however, because *Bagley* also launched four at about 0147. This destroyer had been to starboard of *Canberra* when she sighted the leading Japanese cruisers fine on her port bow, probably having been alerted by the same explosion heard on board *Canberra* at about 1043. *Bagley* turned under full wheel to port—that is, towards *Canberra*—apparently with the intention of firing a salvo of four from the starboard torpedo tubes, but

191

this proved to be impracticable. At the same time speed was increased to 25 knots.

In his report of the battle, *Bagley*'s commanding officer, Commander George Sinclair, gave no reason for the failure to illuminate the enemy with starshell or searchlight, or to raise the alarm by radio. He explained that the torpedoes could not be fired to starboard because there was insufficient time to insert the primers used to ignite the explosive charges that discharged the torpedoes.[2] This is disputed by the sailor in charge of the port forward torpedo mounting, Torpedoman 3rd Class Eugene McClarty, who remembers that the primers were always in place whenever *Bagley* was at sea; he believes the real reason was that the ship was swinging too fast to allow the tubes to be aimed in the right direction.[3]

Bagley's turn to port was continued. As soon as the port tubes would bear on the enemy, the ship was steadied briefly and four torpedoes fired at *Kako* and *Kinugasa*, then only just visible in the hazy conditions. According to the destroyer's action report, the torpedoes headed just to the right of the summit of Savo Island which bore about 320 degrees.

At the same time that *Bagley* was turning to port and increasing speed, *Canberra* was turning to starboard towards the destroyer and accelerating to full speed. Whether or not *Canberra* would have crossed *Bagley*'s line of fire depends on the positions of the two ships relative to each other when they started their respective turns. For example, if the ships passed port side to port side there was no chance of an accident because *Bagley* was initially well forward on *Canberra*'s bow. But if they passed starboard to starboard, then *Bagley*'s position relative to *Canberra* at about 0144 is of critical importance in determining whether an accident could have occurred.

None of the survivors from *Canberra* reported seeing *Bagley* at any time during the action. Sinclair's reports made no mention of the position of *Canberra* relative to *Bagley* while the latter made her turn and fired torpedoes. However, two seamen in *Bagley* remember seeing *Canberra* to starboard. A bridge lookout, Signalman 2nd Class Raymond Orr, recalls seeing *Canberra* on an opposite course to starboard of *Bagley* at a range of no more than 1500 yards.[4] Electrician 2nd Class John Williams, the search-light operator who had an unrivalled view of proceedings, has stated that just before the battle started he saw *Canberra* on the port beam; later, as *Bagley* was turning, he saw *Canberra* 'loom to starboard' as *Bagley* safely cleared her.[5]

It has been generally accepted that *Bagley*'s screening station was 45 degrees on *Canberra*'s starboard bow, but there is disagreement over the distance she should have been from the cruiser. Sinclair maintained that it was between 1500 and 1800 yards[6], which is curious as it was contrary to the practice in those days of describing a screening station as a position rather than an arc or area to be patrolled (the normal practice today). Though in 1943 Hepburn accepted *Bagley*'s statement, the analysts at the Naval War

College revised the distance outwards to about 2000 yards.[7] This was twice that given by Australian sources, since both Wight, *Canberra*'s Principal Control Officer, and Gregory, the Officer of the Watch, believed that the true distance was only 1000 yards.[8] The latter saw *Bagley* at 1200 yards a few minutes before the battle started.[9]

The tracks followed by both *Canberra* and *Bagley* have been estimated, using the results of *Canberra*'s turning trials carried out when she was completed in 1927 and the turning data obtained from the trials of *Blue* (*Bagley*'s sister ship) in 1938. Neither information is exact, as trials were not carried out to assess the effect of acceleration on turning circles. Moreover, *Canberra*'s draught in 1942 was 10 per cent greater than during her trials, and *Bagley* had only two of her four boilers connected at Savo while *Blue* had full power available when the data for that ship were obtained.

Nonetheless, the tracks used in Diagrams 1, 2 and 3 are believed to be sufficiently accurate for the purposes of this study. All three diagrams are based on the assumption that both ships began altering course at the same time, that *Canberra*'s swing to starboard was delayed one minute by Wight's original order of 'hard a port' and that she was slowed in the process by the movement of the rudder from one side to the other. All three diagrams also show the arc that Gregory searched with binoculars in an attempt to find the source of the explosion which occurred at about 0143.

Diagram 1 shows the tracks that the ships would have followed in two situations. One assumes that *Bagley* was in the centre of her station as reported by Sinclair, and the other that she was in the station which both Wight and Gregory believed to have been correct: namely, 45 degrees on the starboard bow at 1000 yards. The diagram shows that the ships could only have passed starboard-to-starboard if the true distance was 1000 yards, but then only just! It is inconceivable that such a situation could have been allowed to arise. Even if *Bagley* had been 1500 yards or more from *Canberra*, she must have been seen from the cruiser's bridge. Since the destroyer would have been well within the arc being searched by Gregory (at one time being within 500 yards of him), he could not have missed seeing her.

The diagram shows, in effect, that *Bagley* could not have been in her station when the battle began—or even close to it. But then, in the circumstances, this was not surprising. Both *Patterson* and *Bagley* had experienced difficulty in maintaining station that night, and in fact *Bagley* had earlier failed to alter course when the cruisers had done so.[10]

If *Bagley* was not where she was supposed to be, where was she? The possibility that she was ahead of station can be ruled out for two reasons. Firstly, though the destroyer would have been within Gregory's arc of search and virtually between *Canberra* and the enemy, she was not seen from *Canberra*. Secondly, the Japanese obviously did not see the destroyer

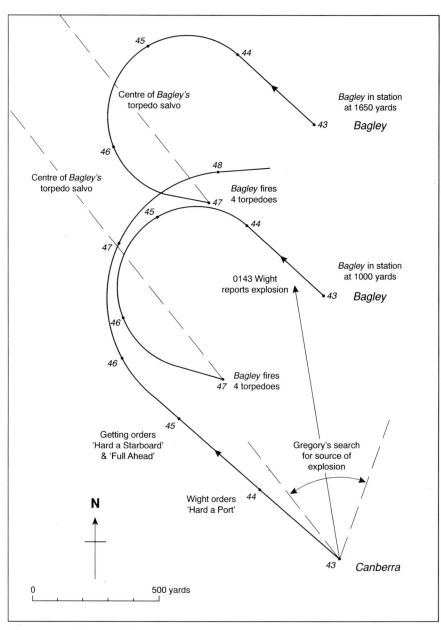

45

44

Centre of *Bagley's*
torpedo salvo

Bagley in station
at 1650 yards

43   *Bagley*

46

48

Centre of *Bagley's*
torpedo salvo

Bagley fires
4 torpedoes

47

45

44

47

Bagley in station
at 1000 yards

0143 Wight
reports explosion

43   *Bagley*

46

46

Bagley fires
47 4 torpedoes

45

Getting orders
'Hard a Starboard'
& 'Full Ahead'

Gregory's search
for source of
explosion

N

44

Wight orders
'Hard a Port'

43   *Canberra*

0   500 yards

Movements of Canberra/Bagley *0143–0148: Diagram 1*

because they maintained their course and speed. Had they seen her turning rapidly to port from such a position, they could only have assumed a torpedo attack and opened fire while taking avoiding action.

There remains only the possibility that *Bagley* was astern of station and, indeed, there is evidence that this was so. Not long before the Japanese were sighted, Gregory saw *Bagley* astern of station by as much as 15 degrees and outside her proper distance of 1000 yards. Through his binoculars, he judged the distance to be about 1200 yards.[11] Diagram 2 depicts the situation that would have developed had *Bagley* started to turn from the position in which she was last seen by Gregory. This shows that *Canberra* would have been in a perilous situation, but—as in the first diagram—*Bagley* would have been in the arc searched by Gregory and, again, should have been seen.

Bagley was, obviously, even further aft of her proper station, having continued to lose bearing on *Canberra* after being seen by Gregory, because Williams (the searchlight operator on the destroyer) saw *Canberra* on *Bagley*'s port beam as the action began. Diagram 3 illustrates this situation and shows that *Bagley* would have been outside Gregory's arc of search, which explains why he did not see her. *Canberra* was indeed standing into danger.

Diagram 3 does not prove beyond question that *Bagley*'s torpedoes hit *Canberra* since it is not possible to be precise on the information available. What is clearly shown, though, is that circumstances were such that this could have happened. How was it then that *Bagley*'s command team and torpedo tube crews did not appreciate the hazard posed to *Canberra* when the decision was made to fire torpedoes?

In the case of the tube crews, the explanation is comparatively straight-forward. Assuming that the situation was as shown in Diagram 3, *Canberra* was almost astern of *Bagley* when the torpedoes were fired. The cruiser would not always have been visible from the location where the tubes were mounted for some time before firing. The view of *Canberra* would have been intermittent, at best, while the destroyer swung to port because of the obstructions caused firstly by the forecastle, then by the large funnel uptakes, the midships deckhouse supporting the searchlight, and finally the after superstructure and two aft gun mountings. All of these, coupled with the factor of poor general visibility, would have prevented the tubes crew from keeping *Canberra*'s movements under observation. Furthermore, personnel would have been disoriented—in much the same way as *Canberra*'s command and gunnery control teams were—by the lack of any discernible background.

Sinclair recorded in his report submitted on 13 August that an explosion was observed in 'enemy area' about two minutes after firing, and that a sonar operator heard four explosions about two minutes after firing followed by two intense explosions in the same area.[12] He also stated that shell hits

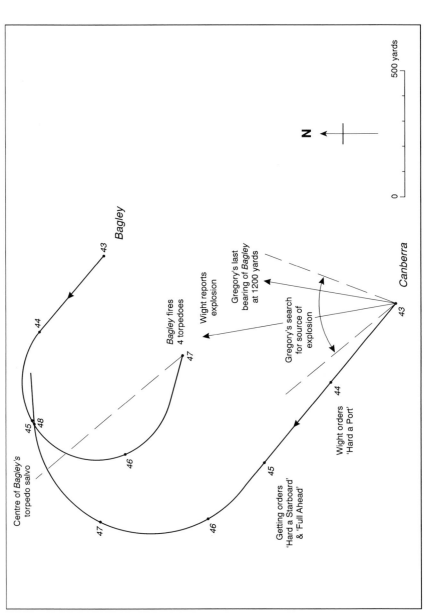

Movements of Canberra/Bagley 0143–0148: Diagram 2

Bagley

43

44

45

48

Centre of Bagley's
torpedo salvo

47

46

45

46

44

Getting orders
'Hard a Starboard'
& 'Full Ahead'

Wight orders
'Hard a Port'

47

Bagley fires
4 torpedoes

Wight reports
explosion

Gregory's last
bearing of Bagley
at 1200 yards

Gregory's search
for source of
explosion

Canberra

43

N

0   500 yards

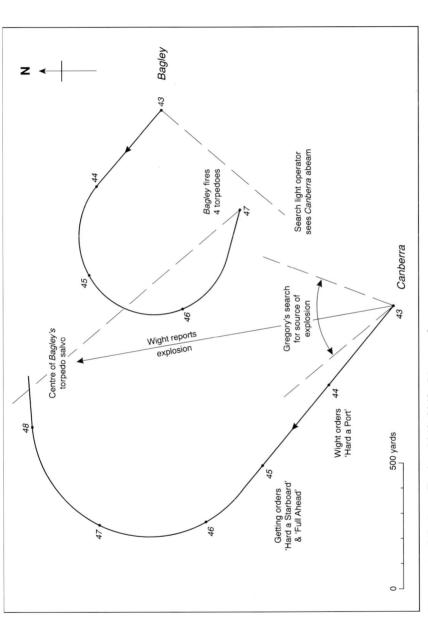

N

Bagley

43

44

45

46

47

Bagley fires
4 torpedoes

Search light operator
sees *Canberra* abeam

Centre of *Bagley's*
torpedo salvo

Canberra

43

Wight reports
explosion

Gregory's search
for source of
explosion

48

44

Wight orders
'Hard a Port'

45

46

47

Getting orders
'Hard a Starboard'
& 'Full Ahead'

0   500 yards

Movements of Canberra/Bagley 0143–0148: Diagram 3

were observed on *Canberra* by the second or third enemy salvo. The inference is that *Canberra* was under observation from *Bagley*'s bridge the whole time. This may have been so, but had *Canberra*'s position relative to *Bagley*, her turn to starboard and rapid acceleration all been taken into account by the destroyer's command team when the decision was made to fire torpedoes?

The attention of those on the bridge of *Bagley* would have been focused on the approaching enemy, then only about two miles away. The command team on *Bagley* were inexperienced and unpractised in night action and there is a possibility that they failed to appreciate the potential danger to *Canberra*, which was approaching fast from the left of the intended line of fire. In a well-controlled and experienced command team the likelihood of this occurring would be slight. There may, however, have been a measure of disorder on *Bagley*'s bridge that night, because some members of the ship's company recall having heard stories to that effect.[13] These accounts, all second-hand from men who were widely dispersed throughout the ship, vary both in detail and credibility: two even describing how Sinclair panicked when the Japanese were first sighted, how he turned *Bagley* away from them and how the Executive Officer, Lieutenant Commander Thomas Chambers, forcibly took control by threatening his Captain with his pistol.

The gist of several accounts, however, is that *Bagley*'s initial turn to port was too rapid to allow the starboard torpedo tubes to be fired: not because the primers had not been inserted but because the rate of swing was too great to allow the torpedo tubes to be aimed properly. The attack was completed by Chambers who carried on with the turn, steadied the ship and fired four of the eight port side torpedoes.

Sinclair was apparently a highly nervous man who, before assuming command of *Bagley* towards the end of 1940, had undergone postgraduate training in engineering design, graduating from the University of California, Berkeley, in 1934 with the degree of Master of Science. The following six years had been spent in engineering positions ashore and afloat. Lacking any ship-handling experience before taking up his first command, he clearly had no confidence in his ability to control the destroyer. As a result, it was normal in *Bagley* at that time for Sinclair to hand control of his ship to his Executive Officer in awkward situations and this was surely one such.[14] Therefore the mere fact that Sinclair gave control to Chambers on that night should not have been the basis for the rumours that arose after the battle. It is clearly the manner in which Chambers assumed control that was unusual, for if the transfer had been done in an orderly manner it would not have been remarkable. The fact that such rumours *did* arise is an indication that the transfer was not orderly and that at least some form of altercation took place between the two senior members of *Bagley*'s command team at a time when cool heads and sound judgments were called for.

The situation was one in which even experienced men could have made mistakes—and indeed mistakes were made. *Bagley* did not raise the alarm, did not illuminate the enemy with either starshell or searchlight, did not maintain contact and moved away from rather than toward the anchorages. In such an environment, which would have inhibited the making of rational decisions, a command to fire torpedoes without proper consideration of all the circumstances could have been given.

The reports of *Bagley*'s movements after firing torpedoes are conflicting. The ship's Deck Log recorded that she retired to the east for about ten minutes before heading for the destroyer rendezvous north-west of Savo. On the other hand, *Bagley*'s Action Report states that the turn to port was continued, and that the ship passed astern of *Canberra* and scanned the passage between Savo and Guadalcanal before proceeding to the rendezvous. The latter version is preferred, as this fits in with *Helm*'s sighting of *Bagley* at 0200 and *Chicago*'s sighting at 0217.

There are various reports of torpedoes having passed *Bagley* after the turn to port was started, leading to the suggestion that these could have hit *Canberra*. Williams, from his position on the searchlight platform, saw them passing to starboard on a course which he estimated to be about 190 degrees. As the ship was turning rapidly he was unable to be precise about their heading.[15] They were probably those fired by *Aoba* on a south-easterly heading, and had been seen earlier by Mesley approaching from *Canberra*'s port side while the ship was turning to starboard. These torpedo sightings are consistent with the situations portrayed in the diagrams.

Probably the last opportunity to prove beyond any doubt whether or not *Canberra* was torpedoed occurred when a survey of wrecks on the bed of Iron Bottom Sound was carried out in 1991–92 by an expedition led by Dr Robert Ballard for the National Geographic Society. The wreck of *Canberra* was one of fourteen identified and was videotaped on 7 August 1992—50 years to the day after the launching of Operation Watchtower. The ship was found lying upright in position 09 12.5 North 159 54.8 East, buried in silt up to about the waterline. Extensive video recordings and many still photographs of the ship were taken from both a small submarine and a remote-controlled vehicle but unfortunately the starboard side amidships was not covered.[16] As visual confirmation is lacking, reliance must be placed on other available evidence which has been described in the preceding chapter. As indicated, this overwhelmingly supports a finding that *Canberra* was torpedoed starboard side amidships at about 0147.

On the basis of the analysis outlined above, it must also be accepted that *Bagley* inadvertently torpedoed *Canberra*.

More than half a century has passed since the battle and the question may reasonably be asked as to why the possibility that the disabling of *Canberra* was due to 'friendly fire' was not examined in the intervening years. So far as the Royal Australian Navy is concerned, the answer lay in the lack of action by the Naval Board on the recommendation of the

USS Bagley *pictured in Sydney Harbour in early 1943. Strong reasons exist to believe that this destroyer fired torpedoes which accidentally crippled* Canberra *during the opening moments of the Savo Island battle, and caused the Australian cruiser's destruction.* (J. L. Williams)

Canberra Board of Inquiry for a second inquiry. This was to have examined why such a well-armed and highly-trained ship should be put out of action by 24 shells from a destroyer or medium cruiser, which was—as we shall see—all that was initially believed to have comprised the enemy force.[17] Adoption of such a course would at least have led to a resolution of the question as to whether or not *Canberra* had been torpedoed, and might have prompted an examination of the possible part played by *Bagley*'s actions, even though an analysis based on Japanese information would have had to await the end of the war.

As it was, the terms of reference of the Board of Inquiry had been limited to an examination of the conduct of the ship's company and the readiness of the ship for battle. It was convened and held in considerable haste and before details about the enemy forces involved were known. Even when the Board's findings regarding the number, size and movements of the enemy forces had been invalidated by the Hepburn Report, which was received in Navy Office in October 1943, there was apparently no will to re-examine the matter. The facts seemingly spoke for themselves. *Canberra* had been sunk in humiliating circumstances, having failed to fire a shot in her own defence. It may well have been a case of 'least said soonest mended'.[18]

Any research done in Australia after the war would have been hampered by the lack of knowledge of the analysis carried out by the War College, the results of which were neither made public nor widely distributed. The contents of the analysis probably first became known to Australians in 1958 when officers of the RAN began attending the Naval War College, and the document became the basis for a series of lectures on the Principles of War. But it seems that Gatacre, as the Australian Naval Attache in Washington in 1954, became aware of its existence because, in the middle of that year, a request was made to the Americans for it to be released to Australia. Curiously Bates did not want Australians to receive a copy 'for a number of reasons'. These reasons, which have not been made public, he gave personally to the Director of Naval Intelligence during a visit to Washington made specifically for that purpose. As a result, the Australian request was refused, no explanation being given.[19]

Because he had no knowledge of the analysis, the author of the naval section of the Australian official war history made no use of it when writing his two volumes. Confining himself to a brief statement of the Board's findings and Crutchley's rebuttal of these, he made no attempt to deal with the question of torpedoing.

For their part, the Americans have had no reason to open up old wounds. Their allies had, after all, accepted without demur the comments made by various American flag officers, and Hepburn's findings too. In September 1943, with a war still to be won, King reported to the Secretary of the Navy that:

> the deficiencies which manifested themselves in this action with particular reference to communications and the condition of readiness, together with erroneous misconceptions of how to conduct this type of operation, have long since been corrected. Furthermore adequate administrative action has been taken with respect to those individuals whose performance of duty did not measure up to expectations.
>
> For the forgoing [*sic*] reasons and because I see nothing to be gained thereby, I contemplate no further action.[20]

King went on to recommend that no part of the Hepburn Report be made public before the end of the war, and so it came to pass.

One wonders, however, if King's attitude would have been the same had Ramsey, Hepburn's assistant, had his way. In studying the evidence of *Bagley*'s part in the battle, Hepburn had found that the destroyer had fired torpedoes to the north-east towards the *Vincennes* group, rather than to the north-west. He also found that *Bagley* would have passed uncomfortably close to *Canberra* if she had turned so as to fire torpedoes within three or four minutes. He therefore believed that the interval between the sighting of the enemy and the firing of torpedoes was longer than the period estimated by *Bagley*.[21] As a result he concluded that *Bagley* had swung in a circle ahead of *Canberra* and clear of her.

Hepburn gave no reason for rejecting the claim by the Captain of *Bagley*, which had been supported by a sketch, that the torpedoes had been fired to the north-west towards Savo Island. Possibly he believed that the Japanese cruisers were further into the sound than was actually the case, and therefore that if *Bagley* fired at the tail end of the Japanese column then the line of fire must have been towards the north-east. There is, however, nothing in the report or its annexes to support such a belief.

Given Hepburn's finding, there was nothing which raised the possibility that *Bagley* had torpedoed *Canberra*, particularly as there was no mention in his report of the possibility that the cruiser had been torpedoed. But Ramsey may have had other views. In correspondence with Morison during 1949, when the latter was collating material for his book on the struggle for Guadalcanal, he revealed that—because of the restrictive nature of King's directive for Hepburn's informal inquiry—information of vital interest had been excluded from the report. He had originally drafted the report for Hepburn, and included in it data gleaned from conversations with some of the participants which he doubted whether anyone save himself could have used effectively.[22]

In their book *Disaster in the Pacific*, the Warners assumed that Ramsey was referring to the circumstances surrounding the handling of aircraft reports of the sighting of Mikawa's force.[23] But Ramsey was neither an airman nor a communications specialist, and had no special knowledge in either field. What he did possess was detailed knowledge of destroyer operations gained through three years' experience in command of a destroyer, USS *Hughes*, with characteristics similar to those of the ships of Destroyer Squadron Four.

Hepburn did not record any interviews with destroyer personnel and, for his description of the part played by destroyers at Savo, relied on the initial action reports of the commanding officers of the destroyers involved in the battle—with just one exception. For a reason that was not explained, Ramsey asked Sinclair, Captain of *Bagley*, for an amplification of his original report. Before doing so he had seen the first report of the *Canberra* Board of Inquiry and therefore was probably aware of the Australian cruiser's movements.

Because of Ramsey's experience in destroyers, there can be little doubt that the information of vital interest which he had drafted for Hepburn (but which was excluded from the report) concerned at least one of the destroyers at Savo. Of the seven involved, only two—*Patterson* and *Ralph Talbot*—had been handled aggressively. Two more—*Helm* and *Wilson*—had performed less than satisfactorily but their conduct had not materially effected the course of the battle. Each of the remaining three—*Jarvis*, *Blue* and *Bagley*—had contributed in no small way to the disaster as each had failed to provide any warning of the enemy's approach though each had been presented with an opportunity to do so.

Ramsey could not have gleaned any information from officers in *Jarvis*, as that ship was lost with all hands. It is unlikely that he was able to discuss the battle with any from *Blue*, as her officers had been widely dispersed after that ship was sunk in August 1942. Only *Bagley* survived when Hepburn carried out his inquiry. The ship was still with Task Force 44 and, with *Australia*, had been alongside Station Pier in Port Melbourne on 22–23 February when Hepburn, accompanied by Ramsey, interviewed Crutchley in his flagship.[24] It would be most surprising in the circumstances if Ramsey had not taken the opportunity to visit *Bagley* also, to talk with her officers about their experiences at Savo.[25] His subsequent request to Sinclair for amplification of his original action report is an indication that he was not satisfied with it, very likely as a result of information he received in Port Melbourne.

If this was so, why did Hepburn ignore the data which Ramsey presented to him? The answer was, in part, provided by Ramsey when he encountered Gatacre in Washington in May 1960. Gatacre was then a rear admiral and Head of the Australian Defence Staff in the American capital. In a letter reporting the conversation to Crutchley, Gatacre wrote that Ramsey had told him that:

> Admiral Nimitz had convinced himself that such was the case [i.e. that a RN officer was not capable of exercising command of ships of the USN in battle and that this had caused the defeat at Savo] and had formed doubts about your plan (in some respects) to fulfil the tasks given you as Commander of the Screening Force. Ramsey went on to say that his inquiries with Admiral Hepburn had been most comprehensive and that they had convinced Hepburn and himself that your command of the forces under you had left no room for any criticism whatever and that the dispositions you formed and the orders you issued were sound and indeed most intelligent.
>
> Ramsey told me that Nimitz was so sure that the findings of the Report would be other and that they would support what he, Nimitz, had been judging without a full knowledge of the facts, that Nimitz hasn't spoken to Ramsey since then. Hepburn is dead of course. Ramsey said that the true facts have never been published, that he has all the papers and supporting facts ascertained post war from the Japanese and that only consideration for the feelings of Nimitz has so far delayed him in publishing a book with the full true story.[26]

Ramsey's remarks answer those who argue that Hepburn and he had taken part in a conspiracy with Turner, Crutchley, Morison and others to conceal the truth regarding the handling of Stutt's report of his sighting of Mikawa and his raiding force. He had gone out of his way to compliment Crutchley on the manner in which operations off Guadalcanal had been conducted.

But in destroying the theory of a 'cover-up' related to the receipt of intelligence, Ramsey revealed that he had taken part, albeit reluctantly, in another 'cover-up'—one related to the conduct of American forces. It is possible that Ramsey had gleaned only information concerning the conduct of Sinclair on *Bagley*'s bridge that night. Such conduct would not, in itself, however, have altered the course of the battle sufficiently to have warranted Ramsey's remark that one day he would tell 'the full true story'. It must be presumed therefore that he had something more serious in mind, such as the possible disabling of *Canberra*.

But it was Hepburn and not Ramsey who was ultimately responsible for the preparation of the report. Having himself been severely critical of the handling of *Chicago* and the conduct of Bode, he would no doubt have appreciated that a report which attributed the disabling of *Canberra* to American action could have damaged relations within the alliance and affected morale. Hepburn therefore had a powerful inducement to restrict the scope of the findings in his report to the conduct of the cruisers, and to suppress any discussion of the part that *Bagley* may have played. This would explain the absence of any mention in the report of the belief in some quarters that *Canberra* had been torpedoed, although the first report of the RAN Board of Inquiry was attached as an annex, and Hepburn had held discussions with Turner and Crutchley—both of whom certainly believed that the ship had been torpedoed.

Though Hepburn seems to have been guilty of withholding information on Savo, whether or not he went so far as to distort his findings regarding *Bagley*'s turn to port, to deliberately conceal her part in the loss of *Canberra*, remains a matter for conjecture. It would seem, though, from Ramsey's expressed desire to shield Nimitz, that Hepburn kept to himself any doubts he had regarding the conduct of at least *Bagley*, and a loyal assistant would have done the same. Thus Nimitz would not have been a party to any cover-up.

As the author's attention was first drawn to the possibility that *Bagley* had been responsible for disabling *Canberra* by a diagram in the Naval War College Analysis, it is not easy to understand why it was that the War College failed to investigate the matter. The War College Analysis criticises *Bagley* for turning to port towards the cruisers but does not discuss the hazard posed to *Canberra* by the firing of torpedoes—this in spite of the fact that Diagram F of the analysis document showed that *Bagley* turned to starboard of *Canberra* and that the torpedoes were fired to the north-west towards the tail end of the Japanese column.[27] That diagram thus contradicted Hepburn's finding, but no comment to this effect was made.

It would be surprising if the officer responsible for the analysis, Commodore Richard Bates, a naval officer of considerable experience, did not also see the possibility. He was known to the author during a year spent at the War College in 1959–60 and perceived to be a highly intelligent and knowledgeable officer with a forceful personality. But the analysts—Bates included—apparently preferred to shelter behind Hepburn and the findings of the *Canberra* Board of Inquiry, even though Hepburn's annexes and the minutes of the inquiry were available to them, and the analysis shows evidence of minute attention to detail.

Friendly fire?

It is not unlikely that one of the reasons that Bates had for refusing the Australian request in 1954 for a copy of the analysis was his realisation that it could lead to an investigation of *Bagley*'s torpedo attack.

19
Actions of the southern group survivors

While the Japanese were engaging *Canberra*, the American destroyer stationed on her port bow, *Patterson*, had not been idle. Commander Walker, alone of all the Allied captains, having assessed that the Japanese could arrive during the night, was ready for them in all respects. Walker was on his bridge, his officers of the watch had been directed in his Night Order Book to be particularly alert and to see that a proper lookout was maintained. Moreover, the primers had been inserted in all sixteen torpedo tubes and communications between the bridge and torpedo tubes were manned. The ship was all set to go.

Possibly alerted by the same explosion which had been observed from *Canberra*, at about 0143 *Patterson* sighted a ship dead ahead at a range estimated to be about 5000 yards. This was probably the fourth ship in the Japanese column, *Kinugasa*. *Patterson* was in an almost perfect position for a torpedo attack, being about 30 degrees on her target's bow and within torpedo range. Walker immediately turned his ship to port to make such an attack.

Mindful of his responsibility to inform all ships in the force of the presence of the enemy, Walker instructed his signalmen to pass an enemy report by flashing light to both *Canberra* and *Chicago*. He himself broadcast a warning on TBS, the voice radio, that three enemy ships were inside Savo Island. This message was received in *Vincennes* and *Quincy* but not in *Astoria*, and in several destroyers including *Ralph Talbot* and *Wilson* (with *Vincennes*'s group). *Wilson* reported hearing the warning immediately after the first flares were seen.[1]

There is no record that *Patterson*'s flashing signal lamp was seen in *Chicago*. But in *Canberra*, Wight, who had observed the destroyer altering course after he had heard the torpedo explosion at 0143, saw her commence

206

signalling as she was turning.[2] The Naval War College Analysis would have it otherwise, assessing that *Patterson* sighted *Furutaka* at 0146—that is, after *Chokai* had opened fire, *Canberra* had commenced her swing to starboard and Kiyose had dropped his flares. The basis for this assessment was said to be Walsh's original report on the battle dated 12 August,[3] but in that report and in his subsequent evidence at the Inquiry, he mentioned neither *Patterson*'s turn nor enemy report.

Because of the analysis, Walker has not received the credit he deserves for his conduct in the opening moves of the battle. His reactions had been quick and correct. His ship's company—who were in action for the first time—had responded well, for *Patterson* fired starshell as she was turning. If all his fellow commanding officers had reacted as positively and ships' companies as quickly, the result of Savo could have been very different. *Patterson*'s efforts did not, however, reap the reward they deserved, because the noise of the guns drowned Walker's order to fire torpedoes so that it was apparently not heard by the Torpedo Control Officer. Had *Patterson* succeeded in launching a spread of eight torpedoes, she could not have missed hitting at least one Japanese cruiser and probably, because they were in column, more than one. Walker apparently was not satisfied with the performance of his Torpedo Control Officer that night, for two days later it is recorded in *Patterson*'s Deck Log that he was suspended from duty for ten days for 'aggravated and indifferent performance of duties' and relieved of his duties as Torpedo Control Officer.

The opportunity did not reoccur, as *Patterson* then became involved in a gun battle with the two light cruisers, *Tenryu* and *Yubari*. This went on for several minutes as *Patterson*, after initially heading west away from *Canberra* and the anchorage, turned back to the east. Both sides suffered damage, *Patterson* being hit aft. The two after 5-inch guns were disabled and a large fire started, but the fire was soon extinguished and one of the disabled guns brought back into action. *Patterson* continued to engage as she swung back towards the anchorage but eventually, at about 0150, Walker lost sight of his two opponents when they proceeded to the north-east along the eastern shore of Savo.[4]

Tenryu and *Yubari* had left the Japanese column as *Chokai* opened fire on *Canberra* and headed for the Tulagi anchorage. According to the commander of Cruiser Division Eighteen, Rear Admiral Matsuyama, his division was acting in accordance with the basic plan, which was for the heavy cruisers to attack the transports off Guadalcanal and for his division plus the destroyer *Yunagi* to attack those off Tulagi.[5] Because the light cruisers were unable to listen to the tactical frequency in use in the heavier ships to report their enemies' movements, Matsuyama was unaware of Kiyose's sightings or of *Chokai*'s sighting of *Canberra*'s group. He was also unaware that *Vincennes*'s group barred his way to Tulagi until he sighted them soon after 0146. As a result, after he broke off contact with *Patterson*, he headed north to keep between Savo and *Vincennes*. By this time his division had been joined by *Furutaka*.

Furutaka had been having steering problems which began as fire was opened on *Canberra* soon after 0143. The shock of the after turret firing caused the steering motors to fail and for a short time she was steering by main engines. She veered to starboard and for a while it appeared not unlikely to those on board that she would collide with *Canberra*. By the time steering control had been re-established she had dropped astern of the remainder of her division, which had followed *Chokai* into the sound, and as a result decided to follow on astern of *Yubari*. During the period when she was having steering problems she sighted *Patterson* and fired a torpedo at her which only just missed.[6]

The enemy cruisers were now operating in two groups and the destroyer *Yunagi* was acting independently, having reversed course after passing *Jarvis*. It will not have gone unnoticed by the reader that the Japanese were having the same kind of control and communications problems that Crutchley foresaw when he decided to split his force of heavy cruisers; this in spite of the fact that they were thoroughly versed in the art of night fighting and shared a common doctrine.

Yunagi was apparently acting on her own initiative when she closed *Jarvis* and opened fire at about 0155. *Jarvis* was seen by *Chicago* to return her fire and possibly proved more than a match for her because, after five minutes, *Yunagi* broke off the action and headed off to the north-west towards *Blue* and *Ralph Talbot*.[7]

Almost as *Chokai* opened fire on *Canberra*, Mikawa ordered *Chokai* to lead round to the north-east to close *Vincennes*'s group, then about seven miles distant. As the four cruisers remaining with Mikawa filed past *Canberra* they each, for varying periods during the next eight minutes at ranges that were never much more than 4000 yards, gave her their undivided attention. Only *Kinugasa* paid any attention to *Chicago* when, for a few moments, she shot at her with her starboard 4.7-inch dual purpose guns.

The Allied force guarding the southern entrance to the sound had been swept aside, never having functioned as a cohesive force although three of them remained effective fighting units. None of them were to re-establish contact with the Japanese heavy cruisers that night, and the question must be asked as to how this came about. The answer lies in the conduct of Captain Bode and *Chicago*.

Captain Howard Bode, aged 53, had been in command of the battleship *Oklahoma* but was ashore when she was sunk at Pearl Harbor. He seemed assured of promotion to rear admiral and was apparently well regarded by Rear Admiral Crace, Crutchley's predecessor. His subsequent poor performance at Savo is therefore difficult to understand.

Details of *Chicago*'s part in the battle are drawn from Bode's report of the action and from papers relating to Hepburn's interview with him at

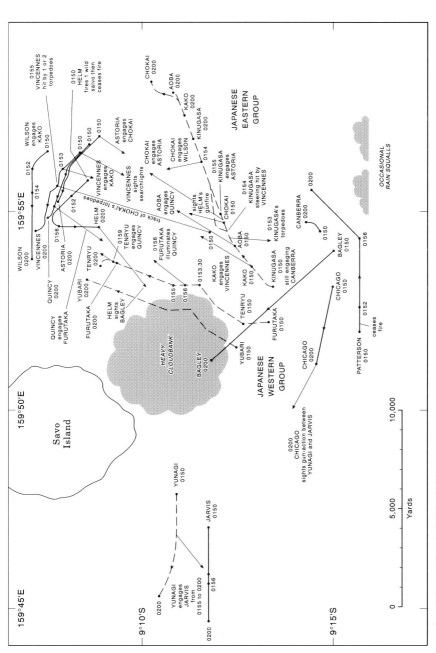

Battle of Savo Island: 0150–0200

Corpus Christi, Texas, in early April 1943. The only other source of information on the conduct of *Chicago* is the record of Hepburn's interview with the navigating officer, Commander Irish, in Honolulu. The amount of material available from *Chicago* is therefore in marked contrast to that from the other four cruisers, the survivors of which submitted a large number of reports of their recollections and, in some cases, their opinions on what happened in the battle.

Chicago had been a member of the Anzac squadron on its formation in February 1942, originally replacing *Canberra* while she refitted. She had been with *Australia* and *Hobart* at Coral Sea and was with *Canberra* in Sydney when the Japanese midget submarine attack took place. The torpedo which sank the accommodation ship and old Sydney ferry, HMAS *Kuttabul*, alongside Garden Island is thought to have been aimed at her.[8] Like the Australian cruisers, she had no TBS radio so, to improve tactical communications, signalmen were exchanged between *Chicago* and the Australian cruisers. The absence of TBS did not, however, rule out the use of radio for passing instructions and information between the ships, as they and the two destroyers were guarding the H/F morse net used for such traffic within Turner's task force. *Chicago* had taken part with the Australian ships in a number of tactical and communication exercises, including some at night. Her visual signalling at night was on a par with that of the Australian ships and to all outward appearances she was a smart and efficient ship which was always handled well.

When Crutchley in *Australia* moved inshore to confer with Turner, Bode became the senior officer of the ships patrolling the southern entrance to the sound. Initially he thought of leading *Canberra* and moved to take the lead but changed his mind because he thought that there would be less confusion when *Australia* rejoined. *Chicago* therefore remained 600 yards astern of *Canberra* and Bode went to his sea cabin, very close to the bridge, at about midnight.

Bode was sleeping fully clothed when *Chicago*, at 0142, sighted two flashes near the surface of the sea. They were probably from the discharge of *Furutaka*'s torpedoes, but no action was taken as it was thought that they were fires ashore on Savo Island which lay beyond *Furutaka*. A minute or so later Kiyose's flares ignited on the starboard quarter, towards the transports, and as a result the captain was called to the bridge and the ship went to general quarters. Johnson's red signal lamp was seen but the message was not understood and appeared to *Chicago* to have been broken off when *Canberra* turned to starboard and was hit.[9] A repetition of the message was not called for.

Chicago recorded that *Canberra* turned to starboard at 0145 but her increase in speed went unnoticed. Bode might well have thought that Getting was making the reversal of course to starboard, scheduled for 0200, a little early and no doubt would have queried the move but the reason for

USS Chicago, *pictured shortly after her less-than-outstanding role during the Savo action, carrying damage to her bow caused by a Japanese torpedo. Plainly visible at her main masthead is the massive antenna of the air warning radar she carried.* (J. Langrell)

Canberra's unheralded alteration soon became apparent when two 'dark objects' were seen ahead in the gap between *Canberra* and *Patterson* and one just to the right of *Canberra*.[10] These shapes were probably those of *Chokai, Aoba* and *Kako*.

The situation then developed rapidly and, for a short time Bode was forced to concentrate on the safety of *Chicago* when the starboard bridge lookout reported torpedo tracks. Bode responded by ordering 'full right rudder' though no tracks could be seen from the bridge. Almost immediately afterwards those on the bridge saw torpedo tracks approaching from fifteen degrees on the port bow so that the rudder was reversed and the ship swung to comb the tracks. Then Bode became aware of what he took to be a destroyer fine on his port bow, which he regarded as being in a torpedo firing position. He recommenced the turn, finally steadying on a course of 283—all the time moving away from *Canberra* and the anchorages.

At 0147 two of the four torpedoes fired by *Kako* struck *Chicago*, one hitting abreast the starboard engine room which, most fortunately for *Chicago*, did not explode. The second hit the stem causing no change in the ship's trim and, apart from hull damage right forward, had no appreciable effect on the ship though the shock damaged the ship's two gyro compasses. Within five minutes, after the bulkheads forward had been examined, it was decided that the maximum safe speed would be 25 knots.

At about the same time as she was torpedoed, *Chicago* observed a ship on her port bow exchanging shots with two ships on her starboard bow. She was watching *Patterson* engaging *Tenryu* and *Yubari*. To clarify the situation starshell were fired to port to illuminate the ship that was *Patterson* and, at the same time, to starboard to illuminate a ship that was 45 degrees on the starboard bow and shooting at *Canberra*. All starshell failed to provide any illumination. However, advantage was taken of *Patterson*'s brief illumination by searchlight of *Tenryu* and *Yubari* to open fire with the starboard 5-inch gun, with the result that a hit was obtained on *Tenryu*. The 8-inch guns did not open fire.

At this stage *Chicago* was in a position similar to that of *Canberra*: her main armament was ready to open fire but could not acquire a target against the pitch black background even though, unlike *Canberra*, she was on a steady course. Soon after *Patterson* doused her searchlight, *Chicago* lost sight of the two light cruisers when they altered course to the north to keep between the *Vincennes* group and Savo Island. No attempt was made to follow them nor was *Patterson* instructed to rejoin *Chicago*.

When *Kinugasa* briefly engaged *Chicago* she obtained one hit on her foremast which caused a little superficial damage and some casualties, including one dead, but the cruiser's fighting capability was unimpaired. Thereafter the Japanese ignored *Chicago* and she gave them no reason to do otherwise as she plodded on.

After losing contact with *Tenryu* and *Yubari* at about 0150, *Chicago* saw nothing to seaward for another five minutes. As course was continued away from the transports, *Chicago* ignored the evidence of aircraft flares, heavy and continuous gunfire and burning ships which indicated that a major battle was in progress, not too far away to starboard. At 0150 Mikawa had ordered *Chokai*, then 6000 yards from *Chicago*, to open fire on *Astoria*. *Aoba* and *Kako* followed suit, firing on *Quincy* and *Vincennes* respectively. *Kinugasa*, 3000 yards away, was firing on *Canberra*. The noise of gunfire must have swelled when the three American ships opened fire after 0152, and again when *Furutaka* and the two light cruisers engaged *Vincennes*'s group at 0157.

Yet *Chicago* was apparently distracted by a minor skirmish some 5000 yards distant and away from the anchorages! She was distracted for a second time at about 0155 when she witnessed the five-minute gun duel between the two lightweights, *Yunagi* and *Jarvis*, which took place about 13 000 yards fine on her starboard bow. Speed was increased to seventeen knots and starshell fired to clarify the situation without success. That speed was maintained until 0213 when it was reduced to twelve knots.

Curiosity may have got the better of Bode because at 0205 he fired starhell set to burst at 11 000 yards towards the noise of battle. When these revealed nothing he decided that the ships concerned were out of range. They may have been out of range but any Japanese ship in that direction

Chicago *at* Cockatoo
Island dockyard in
Sydney, being readied for
repair of torpedo damage
to her bow, sustained
during the Savo Island
battle. (AWM neg.
305782)

was a threat to the transports—yet he still headed west. Visibility was not then his problem because a ship on fire was seen at 18 000 yards. Finally, at 0228 he altered *Chicago*'s course to the east.

When *Chicago* had been torpedoed, *Canberra* had been about a mile to starboard of her, on fire and clearly in need of support against the ships that were seen from *Chicago* to be shooting at her from the north. The Australian ship received no help from Bode, who maintained his westerly course for 40 minutes before he headed back towards the anchorages. *Chicago* was then some ten miles west of *Canberra*, had made no report to Crutchley, had not sought to warn Riefkohl in *Vincennes* and had not communicated with his destroyers, either visually or by radio, even though he had had glimpses of both of them.

Why had not Bode 'marched to the sound of the guns' or at the very least headed towards the transports which it was his bounden duty to defend? He had no answer, and the two memoranda that he submitted to Hepburn— one before and one after his interview with him—show that he became increasingly aware of that fact as time went by. His explanations became confused and sometimes contradicted the report which he and his officers had compiled immediately after the battle.

In his first memo to Hepburn, Bode explained that he assumed—having observed nothing to the contrary and having received no reports—that *Patterson* and *Bagley* had resumed screening *Chicago* and that, after all sign of activity in the vicinity had ceased, *Bagley* had continued to screen *Canberra*. Regarding his failure to send any reports to Crutchley, he rather lamely asserted that he had 'no desire to use visual signals or to use radio unnecessarily because of the possibility of disclosure of position or revealing information indirectly'.[11] Was he hiding? Does this explain the lack of any information to Crutchley and Riefkohl? If so, it does him no credit. It was an extraordinary statement for a cruiser captain to make.

Historically, cruisers have had two roles: the defence of shipping and, more importantly, the task of scouting ahead of the battle fleet to find and report the enemy. Both roles called for rapid and accurate enemy reporting and this was practised in the Commonwealth navies whenever opportunities occurred. This explains why it was that Getting was so quick off the mark when he ordered an enemy report to be sent to his senior officer, Bode, immediately he sighted the Japanese and why Mesley almost immediately afterwards ordered an enemy report to be sent by radio.

The speed with which the radio organisation in *Canberra* responded is evidenced by the fact that the main radio set had started to transmit before all power was lost.[12] The possibility of compromising the ship's position was not, for obvious reasons, a consideration. What mattered in *Canberra* was the provision of information to other naval forces and authorities without delay, and it continued to be uppermost in the minds of both Getting and Walsh after the ship was immobilised and they had been wounded.[13] Efforts continued to send an enemy report and the communications staff eventually succeeded in repairing an emergency transmitter and rigging a jury aerial so that at about 0215 a report was transmitted. This was followed by other messages.[14]

But *Canberra*'s efforts were all to no avail because the information was not received in *Australia* and Crutchley remained in ignorance of events. He had watched as the battle moved away from where *Canberra* and *Chicago* had been operating towards the *Vincennes* group and was confident that he had sufficient forces in the area to deal with any enemy. Whether he associated the attack with the force sighted earlier in the day off Kieta is not known, but if he did he would have assumed that five Allied heavy cruisers and four destroyers would have been more than a match for the reported three cruisers and three destroyers.

Nevertheless, Crutchley moved *Australia* out from behind the destroyers screening the transports off Guadalcanal to a position seven miles west of those transports, into a position where he could intercept any enemy break-through. He also ordered his destroyers to concentrate on *Australia*. Unfortunately the position given for the concentration was not enciphered in a system familiar to the Americans, so that they assumed the rendezvous was the one specified in Crutchley's instructions for the screening group and headed for a position north-west of Savo.[15] In the end this was of no consequence, but it is further evidence of the difficulties the two navies were experiencing in operating together.

At 0226, having heard nothing and watched the tide of battle ebb away to the north-west, Crutchley sought information by asking the three group commanders in *Chicago*, *Vincennes* and *San Juan* if they had been in action. In retrospect a signal better designed to adduce information could have been sent, but clearly Bode had no conception of Crutchley's needs for he replied 'Were but not now'.[16] He seems to have been determined to give nothing away! Scott in *San Juan* gave a little more useful information when he replied, 'This force not in action. Appears to be surface force between Florida Island and Savo.' No reply could be obtained from any of the *Vincennes* group.

Crutchley, after that exchange, was no better informed so, having observed three ships on fire between Savo and Florida Island, at 0242 he ordered Bode to report his situation. Bode's second attempt was only a little better than his first, for at 0245 he replied, 'We are now standing toward Lengo on course 100'. Crutchley's first message probably had caused the reversal of course by *Chicago* at 0228. Finally at 0249, over an hour since he was first engaged, Bode told Crutchley that *Chicago* was south of Savo, had been torpedoed and was down by the bow, that enemy ships were firing to seaward and that *Canberra* was on fire on a bearing of 250 degrees, five miles from Savo. *Patterson* was standing by *Canberra*. He could not tell Crutchley any more because that was the limit of his own knowledge. Even then his information was misleading because *Canberra* actually lay about nine miles east of the position given.

It is a measure of the paucity of information available to Crutchley that when he sent his first report to Turner there was very little to tell him which the latter had not been able to see for himself. All that Crutchley could say was that there had been a surface action near Savo and that the situation had yet to be determined.[17] The time was 0310. It must have been a long 100 minutes for both admirals since aircraft flares had first been sighted, but even longer before they were aware of the magnitude of the disaster that had occurred.

In the meantime the situation to the south and west of Savo Island continued to develop. It will be remembered that *Yunagi*, after a brief brush with the crippled *Jarvis*, had headed north and west—towards *Blue* and *Ralph Talbot*. About ten minutes after leaving *Jarvis*, that is at 0210, she used her searchlight and briefly illuminated *Ralph Talbot* as *Blue* was approaching the north-east end of her patrol in visibility which she estimated as being 8000 yards. Probably aided by *Yunagi*'s use of her searchlight, *Blue*'s gunnery officer in the director and the starboard torpedo tubes crew saw *Yunagi* at 5000–6000 yards on the starboard side. Both the gunnery officer and the tubes' crews requested permission to open fire but this was refused by the Captain, who was uncertain whether the target was friend or foe. His attention had just been diverted by a sonar contact to the south-east which, after course had been reversed to the south-west, was sighted at 2000 yards and identified as a 'harmless' two-masted schooner with an auxiliary engine heading east at slow speed.[18] *Blue* did not send a report of the sighting of *Yunagi*, and in fact no mention was made of the sighting in the subsequent report of the battle.

While *Yunagi* continued to the north-west, *Blue* carried on with her patrol until at 0250, when at the south-western end of her patrol line she sighted a ship rounding Cape Esperance and heading away from her. This was the injured *Jarvis* who had continued to the south-west after *Yunagi* had given up the fight. *Blue* spent about half an hour trailing *Jarvis* at twelve knots and then overhauling her at twenty. *Jarvis*, having made good about ten knots after departing from the anchorage, apparently increased to a moderate speed to escape from the unidentified ship bearing down on her.[19]

It was not until 0325 that *Blue*—having closed to within 500 yards of *Jarvis* and exchanged identities with her by signal lamp[20]—turned back towards her patrol line, which she regained at the leisurely speed of twelve knots, according to her own report, at about 0400. She had been off station for about an hour. But in the event this was unimportant as she had already 'sold the pass'.

20
Annihilation of the *Vincennes* group

When *Chokai* led the Japanese column round to the north-east to close the three American heavy cruisers, *Vincennes* was about 13 000 yards ahead of her and had just altered course to the north-west. *Quincy* and *Astoria* followed her round so that by 0144 the *Vincennes* group was crossing Mikawa's 'T'. How pleased Crutchley would have been had he still had an overview of the scene of action, particularly as at the same time *Canberra* seemed to be leading *Chicago* in a turn to starboard to engage the enemy, who were breaking into two groups of cruisers. The Japanese would have appeared to be between the jaws of a nutcracker.

But how quickly his mood would have changed to one of apprehension as both *Canberra* and *Chicago* failed to open fire, as *Canberra* caught fire and stopped, as *Chicago* wandered off to the west and as *Chokai* altered course to starboard so as to pass astern of the Americans. As a result, the Japanese would be able to bring all their main armament to bear, thus negating the advantage that the Americans had held. In fact, it would have been apparent to Crutchley that Mikawa was turning the tables on Riefkohl and unless the Americans turned to port soon they would find themselves at a considerable disadvantage. Then *Chokai* capped it all by firing four torpedoes at *Vincennes* which made it imperative that the Americans altered course, one way or the other, so as to avoid them.[1]

Crutchley's anxiety would have deepened as the Americans held their course and speed and, one by one, the three leading Japanese cruisers, on a course to pass astern of *Astoria*, first illuminated by searchlight their opposite numbers in the American column and then opened fire on them soon after 0150; *Chokai* on *Astoria* at 7700 yards, *Aoba* on *Quincy* at 9200 yards and *Kako* on *Astoria* at 10 500 yards.[2] And how concerned he would have been to watch the delayed response of the Americans. At that moment he might well have despaired for the survival of the three ships, being aware, as Hepburn later wrote, that:

> It has long been recognised that lightly armored ships of any type not designed for 'corresponding protection' can only exert their designed offensive power before they have received substantial damage . . . It means that, other things being equal, victory rides with the first effective salvo.[3]

Crutchley's feelings would no doubt have been similar to those he expressed some years later when he wrote to Gatacre that 'I felt like a gamekeeper who puts the pheasants over the guns and the guns don't even bother to shoot at them!'[4] It was the Americans who were then between the jaws of a nutcracker as *Tenryu*, *Yubari* and *Furutaka* continued their course to pass to the west of them.

In *Vincennes*, starshell and gunfire were observed to port at about 0145, some six minutes before the Japanese opened fire. The officer of the watch informed Riefkohl, who was then sleeping fully clothed in his sea cabin adjacent to the bridge. In his initial report of 14 August, Riefkohl described how, when he came to the bridge, his Executive Officer told him that he had seen some firing and silhouettes of ships that he recognised as *Canberra* and *Chicago*. Riefkohl then saw three or four starshell and a ship firing on the port beam and, 30 degrees to the left, another. He saw no (other) ships, heavy gunfire or searchlights though the Gunnery Officer told him that he had seen other gunfire in the same direction and that he thought that *Australia*'s group were engaging shore installations.[5]

Visibility was far from good to the south and it is possible that the Japanese heavy cruisers and the burning *Canberra* were hidden from Riefkohl, but it is difficult to accept this as his force was visible to the Japanese—at least to *Chokai*, who was able to fire torpedoes with *Vincennes* as the target. It is also difficult to accept that the noise of the cannonade which destroyed *Canberra* escaped him. Be that as it may, Riefkohl assessed that the ship to the right was a destroyer and part of a ruse to draw his group from the northern entrance to the sound. As a result he also assessed that the main attack force would come through the northern channel into the sound.

Riefkohl was apparently unaware of the receipt in *Vincennes* of *Patterson*'s warning message, though it had been received in the central radio office before the ship went to general quarters.[6] He assumed that, if the southern group were engaging heavy ships, they would illuminate them and 'the situation would soon be clarified'.[7] In the absence of such clarification, he rejected the idea of supporting the group of Allied cruisers to the south in favour of maintaining his postion astride the northern entrance. When he was interviewed by Hepburn at Corpus Christi on 3 April 1943 he apparently gave the impression that he was waiting for orders from Crutchley. From the tone of his questions, Hepburn thought this unreasonable and a poor excuse for inaction, possibly because he knew of Ramsey's doubts regarding Riefkohl's statement that he was unaware that Crutchley and *Australia* had left the southern group.[8]

Riefkohl considered firing starshell to the south but rejected the idea in order not to give away his position[9]—a forlorn hope since he had already been in view of the Japanese for more than ten minutes. Most importantly, having made his own assessment of the situation and his own ship having assumed the first degree of readiness, he took no steps to alert the other ships under his command or to inform Turner or Crutchley of the situation.

The only positive action he took in the five or six minutes he spent on the bridge before the Japanese opened fire was to increase the speed of his group to fifteen knots. Whether he would have been more decisive had *Canberra* succeeded in passing Mesley's enemy report of the sighting of three cruisers or whether he would have had sufficient warning had *Chicago* reported her initial sighting of three ships can only be the subject of conjecture. His subsequent handling of the situation, however, indicates that the outcome for *Vincennes* would not have been very different.

At what time *Vincennes* went to general quarters is not entirely clear. Many survivors' reports gave the time as 0145, when starshell and gunfire were first observed. However, the War College analysts and Hepburn both found that *Vincennes* went to general quarters three minutes after Riefkohl reached the bridge, or at about 0148.[10] This would help to explain why no reports had reached the Gunnery Officer of any of the armament being in the first degree of readiness for action when the ship was illuminated by *Kako*'s searchlight soon after 0150.[11]

Quincy was following 600 yards astern of *Vincennes* when, at 0145, the same flares or starshell which had been observed from *Vincennes* were seen from the forward gunnery control position. The Gunnery Control Officer thought that they were starshell being fired by destroyers off Tulagi to assist in the location of the aircraft which had been flying over the force since midnight; he did not connect them with any other enemy activity.[12] The bridge was informed but there was no reaction.

At about 0147 *Patterson*'s warning message was received on the bridge, the Captain was called from his sea cabin and the ship went to general quarters. Two or three minutes later, the silhouettes of three cruisers reportedly having three turrets forward were sighted from the bridge 'rounding Savo Island'. But neither the information from *Patterson* nor the sighting of the three cruisers were promulgated within the ship so that, three minutes later, the gunnery control positions were thoroughly in the dark regarding the reasons for the sounding of the alarm until *Chokai* illuminated *Astoria*.[13]

Captain Moore's reaction to being illuminated by searchlight was to order the cruiser's fighting lights to be turned on. He did not survive the battle, so that his reasons for doing so are unclear, but USN doctrine called for such action when the situation was confused and there was a chance of being fired on by friendly forces.[14] He could not have remained in doubt as to the identity of his attackers for any length of time, as he very quickly ordered fire to be opened on the searchlights.

It was several minutes before Moore's orders were carried out and he grew increasingly impatient as time went by. Like *Vincennes*, *Quincy* was caught in the process of assuming the first degree of readiness from the second degree. This could take up to eight minutes because it involved the movement of personnel off watch to their action stations from their bunk spaces or cabins and, in a significant number of cases, the changing of positions of those on watch at the time.

The situation was apparently exacerbated in *Quincy* by adherence to a task force instruction (presumably of Task Force 18 to which *Quincy* was attached for her passage from the east coast of the United States) which required that both anti-aircraft directors be fully manned in the second degree. This could only be done by using officers and men whose normal function was to take part in the control of the main armament.[15] The result, in *Quincy* at least, was a slow and disorganised change to the first degree at a time when seconds counted. Confusion was compounded by the rapid response of damage control parties in closing watertight doors thus preventing men from moving freely to their stations.

From the report of *Quincy*'s senior surviving officer, the Gunnery Officer Lieutenant Commander Heneberger, it can also be gleaned that the passing of information and orders suffered during this crucial period because the ship's organisation involved the changing round of men manning the many telephone systems.[16] This requirement probably contributed to the failure of the bridge to keep the gunnery control positions informed of events.

Astoria, the third ship of the American column, had just steadied on the new course of 315 at about 0144 when the Supervisory Officer of the Deck (*Astoria*'s equivalent to *Canberra*'s Principal Control Officer), Lieutenant Commander Topper, felt an underwater explosion which he took to be from depth charges.[17] Nothing more was seen from the bridge or from the gunnery control station until about 0148 when both Topper, on the bridge, and the Gunnery Officer, Lieutenant Commander Truesdell, in the forward gunnery control station, saw four aircraft flares to the south. Truesdell immediately alerted the armament and requested permission to open fire when *Chokai* was seen, almost as *Astoria* was illuminated.[18]

In the meantime Topper had Captain Greenman called from his sea cabin and warned the quartermaster, Petty Officer 2nd Class Radke, to stand by to sound the action alarm. Radke had himself seen the flares, however, and on his own initiative sounded the alarm.[19] Before it had stopped ringing *Astoria* fired her first salvo and at that moment had every chance of hitting her opponent with the first 'effective salvo'.

220

Thus *Astoria* began her fight with *Chokai* while in the second degree and with the Captain absent from the bridge. This does not appear to have slowed her initial reactions and, as will be seen, she was the first of the group to open fire. *Astoria* that night was no sitting duck and, without doubt, would have benefited from any warning received of the approaching enemy. Unfortunately, she did not receive *Patterson*'s warning, did not see the first aircraft flares, and neither saw nor heard the Japanese attack on *Canberra* and *Chicago*.

The War College Analysis attributes these failures to a preoccupation with activities within the ship and her group. The bridge personnel were more than likely absorbed in their tasks of altering course and remaining in station behind *Quincy*. The gunnery control station might well have been distracted by the activities of radar maintainers who were endeavouring, ultimately successfully, to repair the gunnery radar.[20] Certainly the TBS operators were trying to receive a message from *Vincennes* which was amending the time for the next alteration of course; they subsequently blamed this transmission for their failure to hear *Patterson*.[21] What is difficult to understand is why no signs of the battle to the south were seen or heard by lookouts, but the analysis suggests that they were distracted from their surface searches by looking for the aircraft which was operating nearby.

Though *Vincennes* and *Quincy* had had what *Canberra* and *Chicago* were not given, namely warning of the enemy's presence inside Savo some minutes before they were fired upon, they failed for various reasons to take advantage of it. In the case of *Vincennes*, this was largely because of poor judgment on the part of Riefkohl, and in *Quincy* because of poor internal organisation. *Astoria* was in a different category. Principally because a proper lookout was not being maintained at the time the Japanese attacked *Canberra* and *Chicago*, virtually no warning was obtained. That this occurred in a ship as well organised for war as *Astoria* is probably testimony to the debilitating effect of the tropical heat on personnel, such as lookouts whose duties required them to be alert throughout their watch.

The fate of the three American cruisers was decided in the next five minutes as *Chokai*, *Aoba*, *Kako* and *Kinugasa* closed *Vincennes* from the south at 26 knots on a course to pass about four miles astern of the American column. For the first three or so of those five minutes, Riefkohl maintained his north-westerly course and his leisurely speed of fifteen knots as Mikawa took his ships between the American cruisers and the anchorages. His three leading ships had fired their opening salvos to find the ranges of their respective targets in almost ideal conditions. The ranges were short, the targets were on a steady course and speed and, most importantly, clearly illuminated. Furthermore there was nothing, at least initially, to unsteady the nerves of Japanese gunnery control teams as their enemy did not fire back.

USS Astoria *recovering her aircraft during tactical exercises in Hawaiian waters on 8 July 1942. She did best of any of the Allied cruisers at Savo, firing thirteen salvos at Admiral Mikawa's raiding force. Hit repeatedly by enemy shells though not torpedoed, she suffered 216 officers and men killed: another 186 of her crew were wounded. Attempts to salvage her in the hours after the battle were unsuccessful, and she finally sank at about midday on 9 August—the third American heavy cruiser lost through the action.* (US National Archives neg. 80–G–10125)

It is not surprising therefore that *Kako* and *Aoba* obtained hits on *Vincennes* and *Quincy* with their third salvos. *Chokai* took a little longer to hit *Astoria*, but once that was achieved the issue was never in doubt. Firing slowly and deliberately at a range of a little over three miles, *Chokai* found her mark on the fifth salvo. The first was short and to the left. The second and third were in line with the target but still short. The fourth was a straddle, and the fifth scored four hits which left *Astoria* a flaming beacon amidships as the ship's aircraft and their fuel caught fire. There was no further need for illumination.[22]

In *Vincennes*, the gunnery organisation was clearly in some disarray as the change was made from the second to the first degree of readiness. The result was that, although the Japanese opened fire about three minutes after the ship went to general quarters, the first salvo in reply was not fired until after *Kako* had set *Vincennes* afire amidships.[23] Like Bode in *Chicago*, Riefkohl's first consideration became the safety of his own ship.

Hepburn was of the opinion that Riefkohl was sufficiently experienced to carry out the function of a group commander at the same time as fighting his own ship, but generally speaking American naval opinion did not (and still does not) agree and remains critical of the lack of a flag officer in

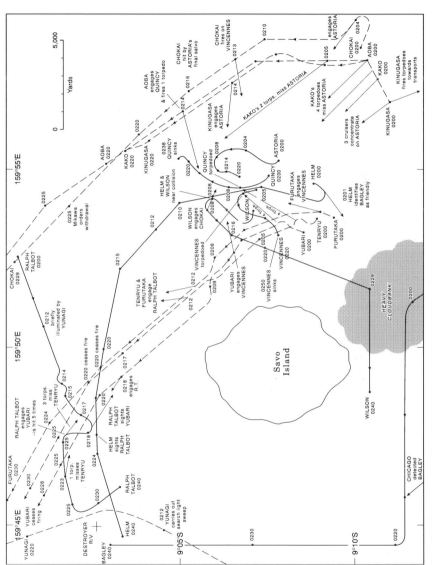

The final phase—Battle of Savo Island: 0200–0240

USS Vincennes *pictured on 8 July 1942 during the same exercies off Hawaii which involved* Astoria. *At Savo she was able to fire only five salvos at her Japanese attackers before being overwhelmed by at least three torpedoes and as many as 74 shell hits. She capsized with the loss of 332 of her officers and men.* (US National Archives neg. 80–G–10116)

Vincennes. British opinion tends to support Hepburn, based largely on the many occasions on which senior officers of groups of destroyers also fought their own ships in complicated tactical situations. The best example would be the night action fought on 15 May 1944—the last surface action of the Pacific War—in which the Japanese heavy cruiser *Haguro*, a sister ship of *Chokai*, was sunk by five destroyers led by Captain Power of HMS *Saumarez* in a torpedo attack which required a great deal of coordination.[24]

But that be as it may, Riefkohl that night was presented with two problems that demanded rapid resolution and he failed to come to grips with either of them. The Japanese were passing between his force and the ships he was there to defend, and his own ships were not yet fully ready for battle. British and American doctrine at that time was to turn away if surprised at night to gain time. Such a turn by Riefkohl coupled with a large increase in speed would have given at least *Vincennes* time to get organised and moved his force towards the anchorages. There were other advantages in such a turn and speed increase for, as *Canberra* had already shown, drastic manoeuvring reduced the enemy's hitting rate even at very close range and a turn away would have reduced the dangers from a torpedo attack.[25]

But Riefkohl did neither and maintained his course and speed. Having received no information from the southern force and not having received *Patterson*'s warning, he was not convinced that the ships firing on him were hostile. Three years later he was to recall how his first reaction had been to broadcast a message on TBS radio for friendly forces to stop illuminating *Vincennes*. This message was broadcast continuously until the TBS failed at about 0215, thus preventing it being used for manoeuvring signals or for passing other information.[26] When illumination continued, he instructed his force to open fire on the searchlights but was still not convinced of the presence of the enemy. This in spite of his reputed assessment that the Japanese could arrive during the night.

Kako's second salvo landed only just 100 yards short and by that time Riefkohl coud see a number of ships firing from his port beam to his port quarter. These would have included *Tenryu* firing at *Bagley* and *Kinugasa* firing at *Canberra*. Riefkohl finally accepted that the ships firing at his group were hostile and ordered *Helm* and *Wilson* to attack with torpedoes.[27]

By then it was apparent that a turn to port was necessary, to allow all turrets to fire at the enemy ships as they continued on their course to cross *Vincennes*'s stern. By that time, however, all radio communications from the bridge had been lost, and all visual signalling equipment had been destroyed by several hits in the bridge area. Nevertheless Riefkohl altered course 40 degrees to port and ordered an increase in speed to 25 knots in the expectation that the other ships would at least turn with *Vincennes*. He was pleased to see that they did, but it was quickly apparent that the manoeuvre provided only a temporary respite as the Japanese maintained their course. He then realised that the only way out of his predicament was to reverse course to starboard, but he had lost control of his force and was unable to order such a move.[28] In any case his command was by then in no condition to comply.

Vincennes was being hit repeatedly, with fires amidships raging out of control due to damage to the fire mains and with internal communications badly damaged so that the bridge was unable to communicate with the engine rooms. At 0155, before the ship could make more than eighteen knots, she was struck port side amidships by one and possibly two of *Chokai*'s torpedoes which had been fired seven minutes previously.[29] In the four minutes before she was disabled, *Vincennes* had succeeded in firing just two full 8-inch salvos. The first had missed *Kako* but the second, delayed by damage caused by *Kako*'s fourth salvo, hit *Kinugasa* aft and damaged that ship's steering engines so that for some time she was forced to steer by main engines.[30] Towards the end of the period, *Kinugasa* had also opened fire on *Vincennes* and obtained early hits.

Quincy had been hit by at least four salvos from *Aoba*. The bridge was hit several times, ready use ammunition for the port 5-inch guns amidships was exploding and those guns were unusable, and the cruiser was burning fiercely as aircraft in the hangar caught fire. Although eight minutes had elapsed since the alarm was sounded, the ship had not yet opened fire with her main armament as the movement of men to their general quarters had been impeded by the closing of all watertight doors.[31]

Any chance of *Astoria* being able to hit *Chokai* with an effective salvo before *Chokai* hit her was lost when Captain Greenman arrived on his bridge after starshell had been fired by the port 5-inch and as her second full 8-inch salvo was fired. *Astoria* had practised changing from second to first degree in such circumstances and this was paying off as the gunnery department quickly settled down to do its job. Without waiting to be briefed on the situation that had led to fire being opened without his permission, Greenman uttered the now immortal words 'Topper, I think we are firing on our own ships. Let's not get excited and act too hasty! Cease firing!'[32]

Topper agreed with his captain's decision, as he had seen no enemy ships and told him that he thought that they were firing on friendly ships. The Gunnery Officer, however, was in no doubt as to the real situation, having seen his targets from his position above the bridge and recognised

Captain W. G. Greenman receiving the Legion of Merit from the Assistant Secretary of the Navy, H. S. Hensel, in Washington on 25 May 1945. In command of Astoria *at Savo Island, Greenman initially stopped his Gunnery Officer from replying to Japanese fire because he thought they were salvos from friendly ships engaging him by mistake.* (US National Archives neg. 80–G–49290)

them as Japanese cruisers, and having observed two enemy salvos fall short. He pleaded, 'For God's sake give the word to commence firing'.[33]

Still Greenman hesitated. He did not see *Chokai*'s third salvo, which landed 500 yards short. He could not miss seeing the fourth salvo though, which straddled the ship and scored one hit in the bows. With the comment 'Whether our ships or not, we will have to stop them', he ordered firing to be resumed.[34] But it was too late, as *Chokai*'s next two salvos destroyed the forward turret, temporarily disabled the after turret and set the boatdeck, hangar and aircraft on fire. *Chokai* had landed the first effective salvo.[35]

At much the same time as *Vincennes* altered course to port and increased speed, Greenman decided that he must alter to port to allow his one remaining turret to continue the battle. He also increased *Astoria*'s speed to twenty knots. At 0155, the three ships were apparently still a cohesive force manoeuvring together. That this was an illusion soon became apparent, as *Vincennes* turned to starboard and was torpedoed, *Quincy* maintained her course westwards and *Astoria* altered to port and increased speed. They were no longer able to defend the anchorages and the way was open for Mikawa to destroy the Amphibious Group. But Mikawa had other ideas. His force continued to engage the *Vincennes* group—*Tenryu*'s group from the west as they headed north along the coast of Savo, and *Chokai*'s group from the east as they swung to the north.

The action continued for another twenty minutes, during which *Vincennes* received the attention not only of *Kako* but, at various times, of each of the other four heavy cruisers and the light cruiser *Yubari*. Still not totally convinced that the ships firing on his port beam (the Japanese western group) were hostile, Riefkohl ordered an American flag to be hoisted at the yardarm and illuminated.[36] One by one the 8-inch turrets and 5-inch guns were put out of action until, about eleven minutes after being lit by *Kako*, only one 5-inch gun was firing. One by one also the four boiler rooms flooded until, at 0203 or about thirteen minutes after being illuminated, a torpedo from *Yubari* hit the last remaining serviceable boiler room. *Vincennes* slowly came to a halt, on fire almost everywhere and with a list to port that was steadily increasing.

Throughout the action *Vincennes* was only able to fire five salvos, of which only the first two were from all nine guns. Two more were from six guns and one from three, making a total of 33 eight-inch shells fired.[37] Her output in the early stages of the engagement had been severely restricted not only by delays in assuming the first degree of readiness but also by the poor visibility, exacerbated by smoke from her own fires which she inadvertently laid between herself and the enemy.

The Japanese ceased fire at 0216, at which time Riefkohl—realising the situation was hopeless—gave the order to abandon ship. This was done in an orderly manner as the wounded were lowered over the side onto the life rafts. At 0240 Riefkohl, believing that the ship might sink at any minute, left the bridge and ordered all personnel remaining on board into the water. *Vincennes* finally capsized at 0250, taking with her 332 officers and men. The ship had suffered at least three torpedo hits and received damage from as many as 74 shells. The USN's Bureau of Ships stated that damage had been so extensive that her loss was inevitable. In the Bureau's opinion, it was not possible for any lightly protected ship to take such punishment and survive.[38]

At 0156 *Quincy* had not yet got a shot away, and was still under heavy and accurate fire from *Aoba* on her port quarter, when a new threat appeared on her port beam. This was *Furutaka*, the rear ship of the Japanese western group, which illuminated the American cruiser with a searchlight and opened fire. Ranging on the searchlight, *Quincy* fired her first salvo from all nine guns at 0158 before Moore decided to alter course to starboard, to avoid the threat of torpedoes from *Furutaka* and to use his forward turrets against the ship firing at him from astern. As the turn was commenced, *Furutaka* scored a hit which knocked out the after turret. For the next two minutes *Quincy* enjoyed a temporary break while *Aoba* and *Furutaka* engaged other targets. Their place, however, was taken by *Tenryu*, also of the western group, which opened fire at the same time as preparing to fire torpedoes.[39]

The glow of the fires in *Astoria*, then between *Quincy* and the eastern group of Japanese ships, made it difficult to acquire a target in the latter group. Because of this, and the fact that the Japanese were not at that moment using searchlights, *Quincy* fired three groups of starshell. None of these provided any illumination, however, as they burst above the low cloud. It was then found that communications between the bridge and searchlights had failed. Unable to acquire a target, *Quincy*'s two remaining turrets remained silent.

Aoba then illuminated *Quincy* by searchlight and opened a devastating fire which knocked out all four starboard 5-inch guns and their control position. But *Quincy* had a target at last and succeeded in firing one six-gun salvo at *Aoba* before the searchlight was extinguished.[40] Another searchlight was seen and *Quincy* was able to fire what turned out to be her last salvo, three shells of which hit *Chokai*, damaging the aircraft crane and destroying the flag plot situated just behind the bridge.

In the meantime, at 0204, two of *Tenryu*'s torpedoes exploded on *Quincy*'s port side, one of which put out of action two of the three boiler rooms still serviceable (the fourth having earlier been put out of action by shellfire).[41] The end was near for *Quincy* as *Aoba* scored hits which knocked out the forward turrets, all remaining gunnery control positions and killed almost everyone on the bridge, including Captain Moore, whose last order was that the ship should be beached.

Down below in the machinery spaces an epic struggle to keep the ship moving was being gradually lost. Although both engine rooms were intact and all four sets of turbines were still providing power, the remaining boiler

Captain S. N. Moore, photographed about 1941 while serving in the Navy Department in Washington. Commanding the cruiser Quincy *at Savo, he was killed on the bridge by shellfire after ordering that the ship be beached. Further salvos delivered by* Aoba *left his ship dead in the water and sinking.* (US National Archives neg. 80–G–K–13910)

room was slowly flooding. At 0210 the port boiler had to be shut down when the level of water reached the fire box as the list to port increased. At about that time, conditions forced the after engine room to be abandoned,[42] but the ship was still being driven by one boiler and the forward turbines in a gradual turn to the right towards the retiring Japanese, one of whom described the scene in the following terms:

> From a group of three enemy ships the center one bore out and down on us as if intending to ram. Though her entire hull from midships aft was enveloped in flames her forward guns were firing with great spirit. She was a brave ship, manned by brave men.[43]

Finally at 0216 *Aoba* delivered the *coup de grâce* when one of her torpedoes hit *Quincy*'s starboard side. Down below, in the surviving boiler room, water rose to the fire box of the remaining boiler so that it had to be shut down. Without power, *Quincy* slowly came to a stop:

> She lay helplessly in the water listing heavily to port and sinking by the bow. She had not only suffered heavy material damage but also by far the heaviest personnel casualties sustained by any of the Allied ships in this night action.[44]

The cruiser finally sank by the bow, rolling over to port and disappearing with 370 officers and men. She had been hit by as many as 54 shells and three torpedoes, and in addition had suffered an explosion in the forward 8-inch magazine. As in the case of *Vincennes*, the Bureau of Ships found

USS Quincy *off New York in May 1942. The American cruiser sustained the heaviest personnel loss of any of the allied ships engaged at Savo, 370 of her officers and men going down with her after she had been pounded by 54 enemy shells and three torpedoes. In reply she managed just three salvos.* (US National Archives neg 19–N–30731)

that no lightly protected ship could have survived the punishment which she sustained.

Throughout the action *Quincy* had managed only three salvos, firing a total of 21 shells. Though originally hampered by difficulties in assuming the first degree of readiness from the second, the principal reason for the poor output was an inability to acquire a target in conditions of poor visibility exacerbated by flames and smoke from her own fires and from those of her consorts.[45]

After *Vincennes* was torpedoed, Greenman continued to act independently. With the repair of power supplies to the after turret, *Astoria* was still an effective unit and maintained a steady rate of fire against *Chokai* without obtaining a single hit. Unfortunately, the gunnery radar was again defective so that, in the existing visibility, ranges used were estimated rather than measured by rangefinder and, because of the visibility, spotting the fall of shot to correct the range was impracticable.[46]

In anticipation of rapidly overhauling *Quincy* because of the unilateral increase in speed, Greenman altered to starboard to avoid passing across *Quincy*'s line of fire. But it took longer to get clear of *Quincy* than anticipated as *Astoria* was unable to accelerate as quickly as Greenman planned. One boiler room had been damaged by shellfire and the boilers in two of the remaining three boiler rooms were not yet connected as they had been at fifteen minutes' notice to provide steam when general quarters was sounded.[47] The state of *Astoria*'s boilers is a strong indication that Greenman had not expected the Japanese to arrive during the night.

Chokai was also maintaining a steady rate of fire and, just before 0200, hit *Astoria*'s bridge killing the navigator and the helmsman. *Chokai* 'had found the range' and many more hits would have been made had not the Japanese column become disorganised as *Chokai* continued to the north-east while Cruiser Division Six altered course to the north. The result was that *Aoba* fouled *Chokai*'s range, causing her to check fire. Eventually *Chokai* also turned to the north but the Japanese line was further disorganised. It is tempting at this stage to argue that there was a disagreement between Mikawa in *Chokai* and Goto in *Aoba* as to whether the force should withdraw before the transports were attacked, but there is no evidence of this. Bates thought it possible that *Chokai* was experiencing a steering problem and that Goto was merely carrying out his Admiral's wishes in continuing the engagement on a retirement course.[48]

Astoria enjoyed no prolonged respite because the remainder of the Japanese column shifted targets on passing through the Americans' wakes and for a short time *Aoba*, *Kinugasa* and *Kako* all concentrated on the target nearest to them, namely *Astoria*. As Greenman wrote in his report 'From this time until about 0206, the ship seemed to be under the heaviest concentration of enemy fire. Shells were falling on both sides and the ship was hit repeatedly from the foremast aft.'[49]

Kinugasa obtained a most damaging hit on *Astoria* at 0203 when a kerosene fuel tank was ignited, the smoke from which forced the abandonment of the after engine room and caused a further loss of speed to a maximum of eight knots.[50] At 0215 the forward engine room had to be abandoned and the ship came to a standstill. Fortunately the Japanese ceased fire at much the same time, allowing Greenman to take stock of his situation in comparative quiet.[51]

All radio and telephone communication systems from the bridge had been destroyed and the entire upper deck aft of the foremast was on fire. All 5-inch guns and their control systems were out of action. The gunnery officer reported that, although two of the three 8-inch turrets were serviceable, all control and communication systems had been destroyed so that they could only be fired in local control. As if to demonstrate this point, when *Kinugasa*'s searchlight illuminated the ship at 0216 the after turret was fired in local control by the communication officer 'who climbed up on to the trainer's sight and coached the turret on to the light'.[52] The three shells missed their target but one went on to hit *Chokai*'s forward turret, after which *Astoria* saw no more of the Japanese cruisers as they moved away to the north-west.

Greenman decided that *Astoria* could fight no more and ordered all hands to assemble on the forecastle. At the same time, the Executive Officer ordered all those who could do so to muster aft. The damage to communications was such that neither group knew of the existence of the other.[53] *Astoria* had fired thirteen salvos totalling 53 eight-inch shells and also 59 five-inch shells; she had been hit up to 63 times (although 34 hits was the officially accepted figure) and had lost 216 officers and men, another 186 being wounded. That casualties on this ship were lighter than her two sisters was probably due to the fact that she was not torpedoed.[54]

21

After the deluge

Both of the destroyers with *Vincennes*—*Helm* to port and *Wilson* to starboard—had seen the first flares released by Kiyose and had gone to general quarters. When the Japanese illuminated the three American cruisers both destroyers were able to open fire on the searchlights at once, but *Helm* ceased fire after only one salvo as she lacked a clearly defined target. *Chokai* was at that time about 7000 yards from *Helm* and saw her open fire but took no action against the destroyer.

Commander Carroll in *Helm* waited for instructions from Riefkohl while he spent the next four minutes maintaining a course which was taking him further away from the ships firing on the cruisers. He did not have long to wait as at 0152 Riefkohl ordered the destroyers to attack with torpedoes. As the senior officer of the two, Carroll should then have coordinated the movements of *Helm* and *Wilson*, but he made no attempt to do so. His immediate response should have been to turn towards the searchlights and gun flashes, and to increase speed for an immediate torpedo attack while ordering *Wilson* to do the same. Between them, the two ships possessed a considerable striking force of 32 torpedoes and might well have inflicted sufficient damage on the enemy to have altered the balance in the Allies' favour. Another opportunity had been missed.

Carroll should have appreciated that there was no time to be lost if he was to move between the enemy and the transports. But instead of taking positive action, he maintained his heading for another two minutes before turning to the south at 0154, still maintaining fifteen knots even though the enemy were already to the south-east of him and moving further to the east towards the Tulagi anchorage.

During that run to the south, *Helm* was seen and fired upon by both *Aoba* and *Kinugasa* but neither were seen by *Helm*—nor did *Helm* see

233

Tenryu or *Furutaka* of the western group who must have passed about a mile from her on a northerly course, perhaps because they were against the inky background of Savo.

At about 0200, *Helm* sighted a ship on her starboard bow at a range of about four miles. Judging this vessel to be part of the enemy force, the destroyer altered course towards it, increased speed to twenty knots and prepared to attack with torpedoes. Fortunately, before the attack was made, the ship was momentarily illuminated by lightning and identified as friendly. The target was in fact *Bagley*, which did not see *Helm* but continued to the west.

At 0201 *Helm* reversed course and increased to 25 knots. Passing between *Vincennes* and *Quincy*, by then widely separated, *Helm* almost collided with *Wilson* without seeing her. At this point, the ship's aimless wandering was halted by the receipt of Crutchley's message for destroyers to rendezvous north-west of the Guadalcanal anchorage. Unfortunately, the position of the rendezvous could not be decrypted, so that *Helm* headed for the destroyer rendezvous north-west of Savo which had been given in Crutchley's Special Instructions. Five minutes later she saw an action in progress to the north-west and increased speed to 30 knots to investigate. At 0225 *Ralph Talbot* was identified but, as all firing soon ceased, *Helm* continued towards the rendezvous, passing close to the badly damaged destroyer without asking if any assistance was required.[1]

The second destroyer, *Wilson*, did not receive Riefkohl's order to attack and remained for some time on the starboard bow of *Vincennes*. Heading generally westward, she shot at various ships in the Japanese eastern force whenever a target was seen, at times firing over her own cruisers. No attempt was made to mount a torpedo attack. *Wilson* was seen from *Chokai*, which opened fire with her secondary armament of 4.7-inch guns and narrowly missed the American ship on several occasions. Though the destroyer approached to within a mile and a half, she failed to spot the western Japanese group—despite *Tenryu* opening an accurate fire on her and obtaining some near misses. *Wilson*, not seeing *Tenryu*, assumed that the shells were from the eastern group.

At about 0208, as *Helm* passed between *Vincennes* and *Quincy* on a northerly course, *Wilson* had to take violent action to avoid a collision as *Helm* crossed ahead without seeing her. *Wilson* made no move to join *Helm* but, still acting independently, shot at *Chokai*'s searchlight when that cruiser illuminated *Astoria* for the last time. When *Chokai* extinguished her light at 0216, *Wilson* headed for the rendezvous at a leisurely fifteen knots, passing south of Savo Island. She arrived at about 0400 and eventually, at 0430, joined *Helm*.[2] Thus both *Helm* amd *Wilson* had been totally ineffective in the defence of the cruisers they were screening. When they proceeded independently towards the rendezvous, passing each side of Savo, the Japanese eastern group was between them and the Tulagi anchorage.

Furthermore *Helm* had passed through the wake of *Furutaka*, then about a mile ahead as the Japanese western group withdrew to the north-west at high speed, without seeing her.

USN doctrine called for screening destroyers in such circumstances to attack,[3] but was imprecise as to the manner in which such a response should be carried out. Because of this, the Naval War College Analysis was critical of Crutchley for not having stipulated in his Special Instructions what the screen should do. Hepburn, though, took a very different view when he wrote that:

> I cannot give much weight to the criticism that no special battle plan was prescribed for night action. Under the existing circumstances, where the approximate contact conditions governing gun and torpedo action, that is to say ranges, courses, relative bearings and visibility could not be predicted, only one plan of action was practicable, viz., bring batteries to bear as quickly as possible on a course that would interpose between enemy and transports or at least bring about decisive action before the enemy had the transports under fire.[4]

Hepburn had the conduct of the cruisers in mind but the principle applied equally well to the destroyers.

The criticism Hepburn referred to had been expressed first by Ghormley in a report he submitted to Nimitz on 17 October 1942, the day before he was relieved of his command by Halsey. Ghormley, who had a good knowledge of the Royal Navy and its methods, believed that Crutchley's instructions may have been adequate for units of the Royal Navy (and by extension the RAN too) but did not consider the phraseology and the terms used were definitive enough to convey to USN units a clear-cut picture; nor did they reflect the commander's scheme of manoeuvre or battle plan to meet the approach of an enemy force. Ghormley felt that there would always be difficulties whenever units of two different navies operated in close cooperation without a period of training and indoctrination. He also believed that the lack of such a period had been an important fundamental factor contributing to the Savo defeat.[5]

Ghormley's view on the need for training before units of different navies could work together is now widely accepted, and the same criticism could not be made of operations in, for example, the Gulf War. But his opinion that the lack of such training was a basic reason for the defeat at Savo is arguable, because no amount of joint training by units of Turner's amphibious force and its screening force would have prevented the Japanese from achieving surprise—the prime reason for that defeat. That hypothesis can be tested by replacing Crutchley, *Australia* and *Canberra* with an American rear admiral and two American heavy cruisers.

Such a change would not have affected the situation before Mikawa sighted *Blue*, or improved *Blue*'s performance. It would not have prevented

Turner calling his meeting which resulted in the withdrawal of a heavy cruiser and, even more importantly, a flag officer from patrol. It also would not have prevented Bode's decision to lead from the rear, and most certainly would not have prevented *Chicago* from wandering off to the west. Joint training, in itself, would not have altered *Bagley*'s conduct or prevented the mishandling of the *Vincennes* group, which was an all-American affair.

On the other hand, the various situations would have been handled very differently had the USN had a fleet-wide night-fighting doctrine and practised it. As it was, lacking any detailed directive from Crutchley on what to do in a number of differing circumstances, the American commanding officers had very little to fall back on except their own initiative and professional expertise, and these were lacking in a number of individuals. Generally speaking, they were tactically unaware, as evidenced by the many incidents in which they failed to pursue the simple plan of action described by Hepburn: to place themselves between the enemy and his objective.

The final phase of the battle began soon after the Japanese western group ceased fire on *Vincennes* and headed off to the north-west, where *Ralph Talbot* was halfway down the south-westerly leg of her patrol. This destroyer had watched the battle between the *Vincennes* group and the eastern Japanese group, but had not seen their western group which was approaching her from the south. At 0212 the destroyer *Yunagi*, then to the north-west of Savo, briefly illuminated *Ralph Talbot* by searchlight. *Tenryu* and *Furutaka* saw the American destroyer about 4½ miles north of them, illuminated her and opened fire. *Ralph Talbot* did not return the fire, thinking the firing ships were friendly, and instead, switched on fighting lights to identify herself. In this phase of the encounter the American ship was hit only once before the Japanese ceased fire, but this single shell disabled a set of torpedo tubes on the starboard side.[6]

Lieutenant Commander Callahan's doubts about the identity of the ships that had shot at him were resolved when *Yubari* was sighted and recognised as being Japanese. As all three of the eastern group opened fire on *Ralph Talbot*, Callahan altered course to starboard, opened fire on *Yubari*, fired three torpedoes and immediately turned back to port to fire the starboard tubes. In the meantime, the ship had been hit many times by *Yubari* and both the torpedo tubes and their control systems were damaged. The result was that only one torpedo was fired by local control, and this missed (as had the previous three).[7]

The three Japanese cruisers continued firing on *Ralph Talbot* until Mikawa, at 0220, ordered his force to break off the engagement and withdraw. Only *Yubari* continued the action as she withdrew to the north-west, the final shots of the battle of Savo being fired at about 0230. *Chokai* and the eastern group were about five miles east of *Tenryu*, while the destroyer *Yunagi* was leading the way having achieved nothing during the entire battle except to harass *Jarvis*.[8] The cruisers' aircraft were instructed to proceed to the Shortland Islands where they landed at 0600. Kiyose had dropped nine parachute flares and ten floating flares.[9]

Ralph Talbot had done her best against very heavy odds but had only succeeded in inflicting minor damage on the enemy. The ship was now in dire straits. Listing 20 degrees to starboard and on fire, she could make only five knots and was unable to steer. Without a serviceable radio set, she was unable to send reports on either her position or condition. Callahan decided to head for Savo Island where his ship lay close offshore effecting repairs.[10]

As the battle ended, the Allied screening force was scattered all round Savo. *Jarvis* was limping towards Cape Esperance apparently on her way to Sydney. *Blue* was maintaining her patrol. *Chicago* was south-west of Savo, having just altered course back towards the anchorage off Lunga Point. *Bagley* was west and *Patterson* south of Savo, both proceeding towards the destroyer rendezvous north-west of the island.

Canberra was stopped and on fire south-east of Savo, *Vincennes* was abandoning ship east of the island, while *Quincy* was about to sink in waters north-east of Savo. *Astoria* was stopped and on fire about 5000 yards east of *Vincennes*. *Helm* and *Wilson* were to the north-east of Savo *en route* to the rendezvous, and *Ralph Talbot* was slowly moving towards the northern shore of Savo. Only *San Juan* and *Hobart*, with their two escorting destroyers, were in a formed state as they maintained patrol between the anchorages off Tulagi and Guadalcanal. *Australia*, meanwhile, was setting up a patrol to the north-west of the Lunga Point anchorage and calling for destroyers to rendezvous in the vicinity.

The Allied ships had suffered a comprehensive defeat, not only because they had been surprised but also because they had been out-fought by a better trained, offensively minded enemy. And yet, the Japanese were the losers in the long term, because they failed to destroy the Amphibious Group on which the future of Guadalcanal depended. For as long as the Battle of Savo Island is remembered, people will query Mikawa's decision to withdraw at the moment when he had the opportunity to deliver a crushing strategic defeat on the Allies.

There can be no doubt that if Mikawa had attacked the Amphibious Group that night, the Marines could not have held on to their gains—let alone develop them for future operations. The new-born American counter-attack could have been brought to a sudden stop, for it depended on the setting up of an airfield in the southern Solomons and the denial of that area to the Japanese. As it was, the success of the whole campaign was a near-run thing.

According to Ohmae, the decision to withdraw was made at a meeting on the bridge of *Chokai* at about the time that the western group opened fire on *Ralph Talbot*. Mikawa and some members of his staff were for attacking the anchorages but eventually opinion for withdrawal prevailed.

The reasons for the choice were summarised by Ohmae in the following terms:

1. The force at 0230 was in three groups, each acting independently with the flagship in the rear. To reform in the darkness, it would have been necessary to slow down considerably. It was estimated that from their position north-west of Savo, it would take half an hour to slow down and assemble, another half hour to reform and yet another to regain speed, and they would still have required another hour to reach the anchorages. They estimated therefore that they could not resume the attack until 0500 or an hour before daylight.
2. To remain in the area at daylight would be to invite destruction.
3. If they withdrew immediately they might still be attacked but they might also lure the carriers to within reach of their shore-based aircraft.[11]

In these days of radar, the time allowed for reforming and regaining 'battle speed' seems excessive, but it says a lot for the difficulties that even the fully trained and experienced Japanese had in operating together at night. In spite of the white pennants at the yardarm, they clearly had no liking for the prospect of an old-fashioned mêlée.

Ohmae also explained the decision in terms of the Japanese 'decisive battle' doctrine, which held that destruction of an enemy's fleet brought an automatic constriction of his command and therefore his use of the sea. In other words, the destruction of the screening force off Guadalcanal would lead to the withdrawal of the transports. In a sense this view was right, for the defeat did lead to the withdrawal of the transports. But that defeat had only been a local one, and in no way constituted the decisive battle sought by the Japanese. American naval surface and air reinforcements allowed the transports to return, and—in view of the resources available to the Americans—this outcome was inevitable.

Ohmae was probably getting nearer to the truth when he also wrote that Mikawa, as he did not command the Japanese naval air forces in the Rabaul area, could not count on air cover being available if he were caught in daylight within striking distance of American carrier aircraft. Mikawa was an experienced flag officer with an experienced staff, and it must be assumed that all discussions on the subject would have taken into account the probability, if not certainty, that the American carriers would close on the area as soon as news of the cruiser force's presence was received. On the information available, therefore, the Japanese could make no appreciation of their situation other than that, if they carried on with their attack, they would suffer very heavy losses. If they withdrew at once, however, they might lessen the scale of air attack, and there was the very inviting possibility that they might even draw the American carriers within range of Japanese shore-based aircraft.

A commander can only appreciate his situation on the basis of the intelligence available to him, and he should be judged accordingly. There can be no doubt that Mikawa's assessment of the threat was right. If subjected to repeated attacks by the aircraft of three carriers, his force would almost certainly have been very badly damaged—if not totally destroyed. If his fears seem extreme in retrospect, it would be as well to remember the fate of the small carrier HMS *Hermes*, the heavy cruisers HMS *Cornwall* and HMS *Dorsetshire* and the destroyer HMAS *Vampire*, when these ships had been caught without air cover in the Bay of Bengal by Naguno's carriers. Mikawa had been present at the time and would have known that the two heavy cruisers had a much heavier anti-aircraft armament than the ships of Cruiser Division Six. Mikawa also had the example of the severe mauling that the modern heavy cruisers *Mogami* and *Mikuma* received after the Battle of Midway when, caught without any air cover, *Mogami* received damage which put her out of the war for more than a year and *Mikuma* was sunk.

Mikawa was apparently faced with the choice of ensuring that the American assault would fail and losing perhaps his entire force, or permitting the Americans to set up a major base in the area and conserving his force to fight another day. But did he see it quite like that? He could have had no doubt about the importance of an airfield on Guadalcanal to either side, but it would seem unlikely that he would, at that stage of the war, have written off the possibilty of Japan quickly regaining control of the island. He had, after all, been reassured by the Army before he left Rabaul that they would have no difficulty recapturing it.

The choice confronting Mikawa may not, therefore, have appeared as being between Guadalcanal and his cruisers. If that is so, then his problem became tactical rather than strategical and he was left weighing up the advantages of enlarging on what was already a major victory against the almost certain loss of his force if he persisted with his attack.

In 1957, when reviewing Ohmae's article, Mikawa was to admit that, had he known the transports were so vital to the Americans, that the Japanese Army would fail to dislodge the Marines, and that the carriers would be unable to strike him, it would be easy to say that another decision would have been correct. As it was, on the information then available to him, he still believed that he had made the right decision. As his command contained a third of the heavy cruisers available to the Japanese and as their building capacity was considerably less than that of the Americans, for there were no heavy cruisers in the new construction pipeline, it would seem that he was right to withdraw.[12] In this regard it is significant that, while there was a chance that they could recapture Guadalcanal, the Japanese high command agreed to his withdrawal.

For this reason, as has already been stated, it is believed that the US Naval War College analysts were unfair when they wrote of Mikawa that:

Content with a tactical victory he failed to exploit the strategical situation by destroying the transports and cargo ships. He had such apprehension of carrier based air power as to allow it to seriously effect [*sic*] his judgement . . . He did not seem able to evaluate properly the possible loss of his ships in accomplishing his objective against the adverse effect which the failure to disrupt the Allied operations might have on the Japanese strategical plans.[13]

What a wonderful thing is hindsight and the possession of almost unlimited resources! It would seem doubtful that those senior American officers who were operating on a shoestring in the South Pacific in 1942, and who at one time were down to their last carrier, would have been, in 1950, quite so unsympathetic and critical of the man who gave them all a very sharp lesson in how to conduct an offensive cruiser operation.

For the Allies, realisation of what had been achieved was slow in coming. Of immediate concern to Turner and Crutchley was not only the need to secure the footholds on Tulagi and Guadalcanal but also the re-establishmant afloat of a semblance of order, the rescue of men in the water, the treatment of the wounded and the possible salvage of *Canberra*, *Astoria* and *Ralph Talbot*. After that would come the post-mortem.

22
A sort of ghastly situation

Canberra came to a halt listing about 8 degrees to starboard and on fire amidships. The Captain was still conscious and insisting that he would be all right, but when the Executive Officer, Walsh, arrived on the bridge from his position in the after control, Getting told him to carry on and to do the best he could. Walsh did so, but kept his captain informed of the situation as it developed for as long as Getting was conscious. The worst news was provided by the Engineer Commander, McMahon, who reported that the ship could not steam, that there was no electrical power and no water pressure for fighting the fires. The petrol tanks full of aviation fuel had been released, the magazines flooded and all torpedoes fired.[1] Walsh himself was suffering from a severe head wound which affected his eyesight but he continued in command until the ship was abandoned.

The ship's company was employed fighting the fires as best they could with buckets and blankets; throwing overboard the ammunition stowed in lockers on the upper deck; moving the wounded onto the forecastle and quarterdeck; searching the ship for other wounded and lowering all boats and floats into the water. An attempt was made to smother the fires amidships by closing all ventilation openings, doors and hatches, but this seemed to have little effect. As has already been told, a jury radio aerial was rigged and several unsuccessful attempts made to pass situation reports to Crutchley.

It was a long night for those in *Canberra*. An able seaman was to recall many years later that:

> By this time it was raining and there was lightning. All in all it seemed as if the meteorological situation had been scripted for the morning as it all fitted into a sort of ghastly situation all round. Even the weather helped to give you the impression that all was not as it should have been.[2]

241

The heavy rain assisted fire fighting and there were times when the fires on the upper deck appeared to be under control. But the fires between decks were another matter. The Senior Engineer Officer, Lieutenant (E) Williams, volunteered to enter a boiler room to ascertain the extent of the damage but was prevented from doing so by McMahon who considered that, because of the fires burning in the vicinity of the fan flats above the boiler rooms, such a move would be suicidal.[3]

Canberra was on her own until about 0300 when *Patterson* approached. On instructions from Walsh, the American ship passed a report of *Canberra*'s condition to Crutchley and then prepared to go alongside the port side amidships. However, as Walker began his approach, he was warned by *Canberra* to wait until the danger from exploding ammunition had eased.

Patterson eventually went alongside at 0408 and remained there for an hour, during which time some wounded were transferred and a petrol-driven pump and hoses passed to assist fire fighting. Unfortunately the pump could not be started, and it soon became apparent that the hoses were not long enough to fight the fires below decks. The problem of how to join *Canberra*'s and *Patterson*'s hoses, which were incompatible, was solved by the improvisation in *Canberra* of canvas sleeves to effect the joins. In all, four hoses were provided—one of which was used with good effect on a fire burning in a ready use ammunition store on the upper deck in which ammunition was exploding. The remainder were played on fires between decks without much success.

Despite the gravity of the situation, *Patterson*'s assistance raised morale in the stricken cruiser. Men had begun to believe that the ship could be saved when, at about 0500, their hopes were dashed by a signal received in *Patterson* from Turner addressed to Crutchley. This stated that, 'If *Canberra* cannot join retirement in time, she should be destroyed before departure'. After consulting McMahon, Walsh reluctantly accepted that the ship could not be under way by 0630 and ordered all hoses to be returned to *Patterson* and preparations made to abandon ship, if necessary using boats and floats and anything else that was available.[4]

The transfer of wounded continued until, at about 0510, *Patterson* detected a ship approaching from the east which failed to respond to her challenges. All lights in both ships were extinguished and *Patterson* went ahead from alongside as securing lines were either cast off or cut. The destroyer illuminated the stranger with her searchlight and had fired three four-gun salvos before recognising *Chicago*.[5] *Chicago* had recognised *Patterson* but, without authority from the bridge, the starboard 5-inch guns opened fire and loosed several shots before Bode's order to cease fire was obeyed. Fortunately neither ship obtained a hit.[6]

The behaviour of *Canberra*'s ship's company when *Patterson* left from alongside in response to the approach of what was believed to be an enemy ship was specially commented upon by Walker. Writing to Crutchley four days later, he recorded the admiration of all in *Patterson* for the calm, cheerful and courageous spirit displayed by officers and men of *Canberra* at the moment of *Patterson*'s departure: 'There were no outcries or entreaties—rather a cheery "Carry on *Patterson*—Good luck"—and prompt and efficient casting off of lines, brows etc. Not a man stepped out of line.' Walker concluded with the comment that everyone in *Patterson* felt 'privileged to have served so gallant a crew'.[7] This was a most gracious gesture, coming as it did from the captain of a ship which was herself damaged and had lost ten men.

Once again *Canberra* was on her own, but not for long, as *Blue* appeared—having been summoned from her patrol by *Patterson*—and went alongside forward to take off 343 survivors (including eighteen seriously wounded). Evacuation of the forecastle area was completed by 0640 when *Blue* cast off and proceeded into the anchorage area to transfer her load to USS *Fuller*. *Patterson*, when she returned from her affair with *Chicago*, went alongside aft to embark the remainder of *Canberra*'s ship's company and subsequently transferred 398 officers and men to USS *Barnett* of whom 46 were seriously wounded. Both *Fuller* and *Barnett* had extensive medical facilities, including fully-equipped operating theatres, so that the wounded received all possible care within the limitations imposed by the large number of casualties. These included many from the three American cruisers and Marines wounded in the fighting ashore.

Of the seriously injured casualties from *Canberra*, three died before they could be transferred to *Barnett* and three—including the Captain—died of their wounds in the transport.[8] Getting had been taken on board *Patterson* when she first went alongside *Canberra*. An emergency operation had been performed on him, but the double shock of his wounds and the loss of his ship proved too much.

Photographs taken as *Canberra* was abandoned show her listing about 20 degrees to starboard with all her turrets trained on the port quarter. Smoke rising from the area of the boiler room fan flats is the only visual evidence of the fires that caused her to be abandoned.

For an understanding of what then happened in the sound, it is necessary to look at the situation as Turner and Crutchley saw it. At 0430 Turner had instructed Crutchley that *Canberra* was to be destroyed if she was unable to withdraw with the remainder of the Amphibious Force. At the same time, Turner sent a message to all ships informing them that it was urgent that the force depart at 0630.[9]

An hour later, having heard nothing more from *Patterson*, Crutchley ordered the Commander Destroyer Squadron Four (COMDESRON 4) in *Selfridge* to investigate the state of both *Canberra* and *Patterson*. He was worried about the destroyer because the message reporting *Canberra*'s condition had read, 'Disabled on fire in position seven miles south east of Savo'. As received in *Australia*, the message did not mention *Canberra* and

This dismal scene, with Canberra *crippled and listing in the wake of the surprise Japanese raid, was taken from* Chicago *about 6.30 a.m. on 9 August. The American destroyer* Blue *is alongside* Canberra's *bow, removing survivors, while* Patterson *approaches the cruiser's stern.* (US National Archives neg. 80–G–13488)

could have been describing *Patterson*'s condition. COMDESRON 4 was instructed to sink both *Canberra* and *Patterson* if they could not join in the retirement plan.[10]

At about that time, Turner was informed by Vandegrift—who had completed his visit to the Tulagi area—that there were only one and a half days' supply of ammunition and three days' of rations ashore, that the island had not been completely secured, and that the Amphibious Group should not sail until more stores and ammunition had been landed. He urged Turner to allow six more hours of unloading before departure.[11]

Up to that time Turner had insisted on a departure soon after sunrise, even though he knew that unloading had stopped because the transports and store ships had got under way when the battle commenced and were only then returning to the anchorages. But faced with Vandegrift's plea, which could not be ignored, he decided to delay his departure until the afternoon. He accordingly cancelled his orders for departure at 0621. *Canberra*, however, was not to be granted the reprieve that this delay would have allowed.

In accordance with Crutchley's instructions, *Selfridge* had moved towards *Canberra* and, on the way, came across the burning *Astoria*. Her report, made at 0644, giving the cruiser's position and stating that four destroyers were picking up many survivors, was the first news that Turner received of the fate of the three American cruisers. He passed on the information to Crutchley, telling him that the captain and crew of *Astoria*

244

This badly waterstained photograph shows Canberra *just before American destroyers used torpedoes and gunfire to send her to the bottom at 8 a.m. How necessary was* Canberra's *sinking, however, once the Allied withdrawal which initially prompted the order for her to be destroyed was postponed?* (RAN Photographic Unit)

were trying to save their ship, that *Quincy* had apparently been sunk and he had no news of *Vincennes*, and that he believed that *Ralph Talbot* had also been sunk.[12]

Selfridge came upon *Canberra* deserted, listing and on fire. It must have been clear to COMDESRON 4 that she would be unable to get under way in the immediate future. Whether or not he knew of Turner's decision to delay the departure is not clear, for the signal cancelling it had only been addressed to Crutchley and the senior transport commander. There was, however, some doubt in his mind as to whether he should proceed with his task of sinking her because he asked Turner if he should carry on with it.

Without consulting Crutchley, Turner replied in the affirmative so that at 0710, *Selfridge* opened fire. While *Selfridge* was firing, the destroyer USS *Ellet* approached and—seeing *Selfridge* shooting at what was taken to be a damaged Japanese cruiser—she, too, opened fire at a range of 5000 yards. Before *Selfridge* could tell her that she was firing at *Canberra*, *Ellet* had expended 106 rounds of 5-inch and had obtained several hits.[13]

At 0747 *Canberra* was still afloat, although *Selfridge* had expended 263

USS Selfridge, *pictured in the Solomon Islands in August 1943, was the leader of Destroyer Squadron 4. She was given the task of sinking the crippled and abandoned* Canberra *on the morning after the Savo action.* (US National Archives neg. 80–G–266036)

rounds of 5-inch and four torpedoes (only one of which exploded). COM-DESRON 4 then called in *Ellet* to finish the job. The destroyer fired a torpedo at close range which exploded on the starboard side abreast the bridge.[14] This was too much for *Canberra*. At 0800 she sank, taking with her the bodies of the nine officers and 64 men who were subsequently posted as missing believed killed.

Canberra was obviously not in a sinking condition when she was abandoned. The question must therefore be asked whether or not she could have been salvaged if advantage had been taken of the extra time available as a result of the postponement of departure. As was the case with *Astoria*, it would have been possible to get one or two destroyers alongside to provide hoses and portable pumps to put out the fires and correct the list. The ship could then have been towed at a good speed, as the machinery provided for controlling the rudder in the event of an electric power failure was undamaged.

But was she worth saving? This must remain a matter for conjecture. She was certainly very severely damaged in the vicinity of the boiler rooms, but the remainder of the ship does not seem to have suffered to the same extent. The engine rooms and main armament had suffered comparatively minor damage so that she was scarcely a burnt-out shell. Facilities sufficient to carry out the repairs existed in the Sydney area, though these were later to be stretched to the limit with the need to repair several American cruisers

The US destroyer Ellet, *shown here at New York in April 1939, was called upon to deliver the* coup de grace *to* Canberrra *after* Selfridge *and* Ellet *between them had fired 370 five-inch rounds and four torpedoes without sinking her. A torpedo from close range finally sent the wreck to the bottom at 8 a.m.* (NHC neg. NH67739)

and *Hobart*, which were severely damaged in operations in the Solomons subsequent to Watchtower.

Her future value was not, however, a factor that morning; at least, not until she had been inspected to ascertain the extent of her damage. What was required was a decision as to whether or not she could be prevented from sinking and towed clear of the operational area. By mid-morning the tactical situation was no longer a factor in that decision, because Turner had decided to attempt to save *Astoria* and requested air cover to cover her withdrawal. He was apparently being inconsistent in his decisions regarding the two damaged cruisers.

Astoria had been abandoned at about 0445 with the assistance of *Bagley*. That destroyer, after spending an hour alone in the rendezvous position, had investigated a ship on fire north-east of Savo Island which was soon identified as *Astoria*. Extensive fires throughout the cruiser prevented *Bagley* from going alongside. As a result the executive officer, who was handling the destroyer, placed her starboard bow alongside *Astoria*'s starboard bow. In all, Captain Greenman and about 450 of his ship's company, including 185 wounded, were embarked before *Bagley* cast off to pick other men from the sea.[15] At the request of Greenman, *Bagley* then stood by *Astoria* until dawn with the intention of returning alongside to allow an inspection of the ship in daylight.[16]

Just before daybreak, a small group of survivors was seen aft. This group included the executive and engineer officers and when *Bagley* nudged up to the stern, the two officers convinced their captain that there was a chance that the ship could be saved. A salvage party of about 325, including all unwounded officers, was then immediately placed back on board. An unsuccessful attempt was made to raise steam while the fires were tackled—as in *Canberra*—with buckets, but her list was slowly increasing due to the ingress of water through shell holes on the water line.

Soon after 0900, Greenman ordered the destroyer minesweeper *Hopkins* to take *Astoria* in tow. *Hopkins* did so, after placing a portable pump on board, and by 1100 slow progress was being made towards Guadalcanal.[17] Greenman then told Turner, through *Hopkins*, of his situation and suggested that *Astoria* might be salvaged if power and water to fight the fires could be provided.[18] As a result *Wilson* was ordered by Turner to assist and went alongside, provided fire hoses and put men on board to assist. However fires below decks, including one in the second turret, continued to burn fiercely and at about 1100 an explosion forward was followed by an increase in the list to port.[19]

At 1119, Turner ordered the destroyer *Buchanan* to take the place of *Hopkins* and *Wilson*, so that those ships could take their survivors from the three cruisers to the transports off Guadalcanal. He also ordered the transport *Alchiba* to take *Astoria* in tow.[20] At 1145, *Hopkins* cast off the tow and *Wilson* left from alongside.

As the list steadily increased, by 1200 it was apparent to Greenman that their task was hopeless and that *Astoria* was sinking. He therefore ordered the ship to be abandoned and the 382 survivors were picked up by *Alchiba* and *Buchanan*. *Astoria* had been hit at least 34 times, though not by torpedoes, and in return had fired a total of 53 8-inch and 59 5-inch shells. In commenting on her loss, the USN's Bureau of Ships found that structural damage was not such that loss was inevitable but that fires had prevented effective damage control.[21] The same could have been said of *Canberra*.

If such an effort could be made to salvage *Astoria*, why not *Canberra*? Part of the answer could well be that, having made his decision to accept the risk of staying another day, Turner became progressively bolder—particularly when no morning air attacks developed. But the principal reason probably is that no one suggested to Turner that *Canberra* might be salvageable. Greenman, unlike Walsh, was not presented with what amounted to an ultimatum—raise steam within two hours or abandon ship. Because of the absence of that time constraint, he was able to suggest that, with help, *Astoria* could be saved. Had Walsh made a similar suggestion there is no reason to think that an effort similar to that made for *Astoria* would not have been made.

This does not excuse Turner from destroying a potentially valuable asset without further investigation when time to do so was available. And it does not explain why Crutchley was not more inquisitive about *Canberra*'s state when it became apparent that the departure had been delayed, or why Turner did not refer *Selfridge*'s query to him for comment. Turner had no knowledge of the Australian ship, or the extent of repair facilities available in Australia.

At 1030, *Selfridge* was ordered to go to the assistance of *Ralph Talbot*. Since 0515, Turner and Crutchley had been aware of the condition of the destroyer and that she was effecting repairs close to the north-west coast of Savo. Her ship's company, using their own resources, had been successful in their efforts. An intense fire which was burning in the bridge structure had been extinguished by 0900, the list of 20 degrees to starboard had been corrected by jettisoning (among other things) the starboard torpedo tubes, and all flooded compartments had been pumped out. *Selfridge* stood by her when, at 1315, she was able to proceed at twenty knots to the Guadalcanal anchorage, where she arrived at 1420.[22]

During the morning and early afternoon, *Bagley*, *Helm*, *Wilson*, *Patterson*, *Blue*, *Buchanan*, *Ellet* and *Mugford* transferred their loads of survivors to the now empty transports off Guadalcanal. The destroyers then resumed screening operations off the beachheads.

Practically the only ships not affected by the signs of battle were the light cruisers *San Juan* and *Hobart* screened by the destroyers *Monssen* and *Buchanan*. Rear Admiral Scott had maintained his ships on their patrol between the anchorages, making no move to proceed to a position from which he could cover the transports should any Japanese ship approach them. Indeed at 0200, as the battle was nearing its climax, Scott had reached the northern limit of his patrol, reversed course and stood away to the south. At that moment *Chokai* was within gun range of Group X-ray, being just eight miles to the west and heading towards the anchorage off Tulagi. Scott could see the three burning American cruisers, but neither *San Juan* nor *Hobart* could see the Japanese. *Hobart*, at least, was aware from the direction in which the American ships were firing that their target was between them and the Allied cruisers. *Canberra* was clearly visible.[23] Scott apparently obtained no information from the centrimetric radar, type SG, fitted in *San Juan*.

Crutchley's special instructions to the screening group ordered that, in the event of an attack by day, the light cruisers were to act as backstop and protect the transports if the heavy cruisers became engaged.[24] It is a weakness of those instructions that no mention was made of the use of the light cruisers in a night attack on the heavy cruisers. Nevertheless, this does not excuse Scott from failing to take the elementary precaution of remaining between the enemy and his likely targets, particularly when it became clear to him that the American cruisers were being severely punished. The War College Analysis makes no comment on Scott's conduct.

In accordance with the original operation orders, the group broke up after dawn—*San Juan* moving to the Tulagi anchorage and *Hobart* joining Crutchley off Guadalcanal. During the morning, the surviving cruisers and destroyers in the sound were kept on their toes by a number of reports of submarine contacts, all of which were false, and by air-raid alerts. The first of these was the result of a report from Read, the coastwatcher on northern Bougainville, that aircraft had been heard heading towards Guadalcanal. Unloading was suspended and ships got under way, but no attack developed and at 1100 the transports returned to their anchorages.[25]

The aircraft which Read had reported included sixteen torpedo bombers and fifteen fighters. *En route* to Guadalcanal these aircraft were diverted to attack what the Japanese believed was an Achilles-class cruiser which had been reported by a Japanese reconnaisance aircraft earlier in the day. Their target was in fact *Jarvis*, which was sunk, but not before she had shot down two and damaged four of her attackers.[26]

At about 0915 *San Juan* detected an aircraft circling the Tulagi–Guadalcanal area. This was one of seven long-range reconnaissance aircraft from Rabaul whose primary task that morning was to locate the American carriers. The Japanese believed these were operating near Guadalcanal but they were actually well south of San Cristobal Island and outside the coverage of the Japanese aircraft. *San Juan*'s contact spent almost an hour in the vicinity of the anchorages unmolested by fighters or anti-aircraft fire.[27]

And what of Fletcher and the Air Support Force? The record shows that operations of this group on 9 August included combat air patrols and aircraft reconnaissance in support of the carriers and a flight to Tulagi to drop some photographs for the Marines.[28] Not a single sortie was flown in support of the Marines or the ships in the sound. No attempt was made to relocate the Japanese force that had done so much damage during the night, though there was no intelligence until mid-afternoon that it was returning at high speed to the Rabaul area and would not be in position to re-attack the next night.

Fletcher and Noyes had both received a radio report at about 0300 of a surface action off Guadalcanal to the north-west, but no action was taken to close Savo at high speed although Mikawa's raiders were well within strike range. Instead, course was altered to the south-east at 0430. Notwithstanding *Wasp*'s night-flying capability, no aircraft were flown off until 0600 when eight were launched to search to the west of Guadalcanal. The search's only value was to ensure that a surface force was not approaching the carriers, as it was limited to a depth of only 175 miles and its northern limit scarcely reached Savo. One of these aircraft saw and reported *Jarvis*, still on course for Sydney. The aircraft flying the photos to Tulagi returned at 1100 and reported that all seemed quiet in the sound and that they had seen no enemy ships.[29]

During the night, after the report had been received, the commanding officer of *Wasp*, Captain Forrest Sherman, had estimated that if *Wasp* proceeded to the north-west at full speed she could strike the retiring Japanese. They could launch at once, as *Wasp*'s air group was fully qualified in night operations. Sherman and at least one staff officer made three

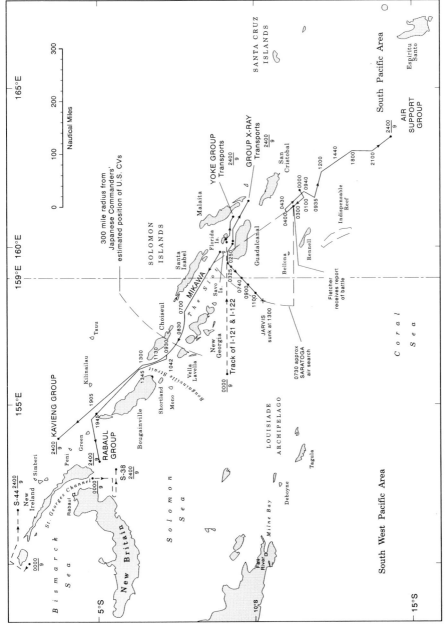

Allied and Japanese naval movements—9 August

separate recommendations to that effect to Noyes, but the Admiral rejected these proposals explaining that Fletcher had all the information and would order such an attack if he thought it best to do so.[30] He was mirroring Fletcher's attitude at the Battle of the Coral Sea, when he waited for Rear Admiral Fitch to make a decision to strike the Japanese carriers which were known to be close.

Similar pleas were made by the Air Group Commander in *Saratoga* to Fletcher himself, but he would have none of it.[31] Course was maintained to the south-east throughout the day, in spite of a plea from Turner for air cover for *Astoria* as she withdrew to the south-east. The result was that the Japanese went virtually scot-free until the old submarine *S-38* torpedoed and sank *Kako* as she was about to enter Kavieng Harbour.

Mikawa had made his withdrawal from Savo Island at high speed so that by dawn *Chokai* was about 110 miles north-west of Savo Island. At 0930, when Vella Lavella was abeam to port, feeling that he was safe from carrier aircraft attack, Mikawa ordered a lower state of readiness and a reduction in speed to twenty knots. Half an hour later he split his force into two groups, Cruiser Division Six being ordered to Kavieng while *Chokai* proceeded with the remainder to Rabaul.[32]

At 1405, when off Kieta, *Kako* and other members of her division sighted a Hudson which remained in view for 45 minutes.[33] This was Hudson 157, flown by Flight Lieutenant Milne, who first saw the cruisers at 1415 at a range of three miles. He made an immediate enemy report, presumably to Fall River, which arrived in ACH Townsville an hour and a half later— that is, at 1543. There was then little more than three hours of daylight remaining, making it impossible to organise and launch a strike from Port Moresby.[34] After sending an initial report Hudson 157 suffered a radio failure, so that it was not until Milne landed at Fall River at 1730 that he was able to report that, three-quarters of an hour after sighting Cruiser Division Six, he had seen a heavy cruiser and a destroyer (*Chokai* and *Yunagi*) and that the latter had opened fire on him.

Of the three Hudsons which reconnoitred Area B on the 9th two experienced radio failures, which is further evidence of the maintenance difficulties being experienced by the Hudsons as a result of Fall River's environment and the lack of maintenance personnel. Milne accurately described the type and tonnage of the ships he saw, thereby underlining the effect of the lack of experience among the crews of Stutt and Willman. It is tempting to wonder what would have been the result of the battle if Milne had flown either one of the search tracks which he had allocated to Stutt and Willman the previous day.[35]

Meanwhile, back at Guadalcanal, having made his decision to delay departure, Turner was able to take a careful look at his situation. He still believed that the risk of remaining for longer than was absolutely necessary off the beach was unacceptable, particularly as a plea to Fletcher for air cover had gone unanswered. He had made this request twice, the first time at 0305 when he informed Fletcher of his intention to depart on the morning of the 9th. The second time was at 0641, when he told the Expeditionary Force commander that he had had to delay his departure.[36]

Turner's position had deteriorated with the loss of the four cruisers and he now had four damaged ships, whose capability in one way or another had been seriously affected. There was also the large number of wounded men in overcrowded hospital facilities; these needed to be put ashore as soon as possible, or at least into the hospital ship, USS *Solace*, in Noumea. For various reasons, however, unloading was still unsatisfactory on Tulagi, and more time would be necessary if the Marines were to be left with their minimum needs.

During the morning, after a brief conference with Vandegrift who had called in on his way from the Tulagi transports to his headquarters on Guadalcanal, the Admiral decided to depart in two groups. The first group would leave at 1500 and would consist of the damaged ships and the transports and store ships off Guadalcanal. The second would consist of the ships off Tulagi and would depart about two hours later, just before dark, escorted by the remaining cruisers.

And so it came to pass. *McCawley* cleared the channel between Guadalcanal and Florida Islands and set course for Noumea just before midnight. The 'meeting engagement' of the Solomons campaign was over. Any doubts Turner may have had that he was now without any carrier support and, indeed, that he was on his own in so far as command of the expedition was concerned, were dispelled when *McCawley* intercepted a radio message at 1435 from Fletcher to Ghormley. This communication summarised the reports which Fletcher had received from Turner before telling Ghormley that he was unable to provide Turner with any protection, and concluded with 'Direct Turner to make reports direct to you, info to me'.[37]

And that was that so far as Fletcher was concerned. He had washed his hands of the whole affair and nobody—not Ghormley, Nimitz or even King—had a word to say about his conduct. It was as if the horror of Savo had paralysed the desire of those flag officers to assert themselves against a fellow officer who had just simply walked away from his responsibilities in the face of the enemy and left a substantial part of his command in jeopardy. It is fitting that this account of the operations associated with Watchtower should end with that extraordinary message, typifying as it did everything which was wrong with the command structure which planned and executed that operation.

23

The verdict

Examination of the causes for the defeat began early on the afternoon of the battle, when Turner asked Crutchley for details of the instructions given the previous evening to his screening group. The next day, Crutchley followed up his signalled reply with a preliminary report of the action based on his own observations, together with information gleaned by a medical officer from *Australia* who had treated *Canberra*'s wounded in the transport *Fuller* and from reports received from *Chicago*, *Blue* and *Helm*. It is interesting, in view of the controversy which was to follow, that the doctor reported that *Canberra* had been hit by a torpedo in the boiler rooms. Though the preliminary report linked the raiders with the force sighted off Kieta on the morning of 8 August, no comment was made on the delay which had occurred in passing the news of that sighting.[1]

The report was accompanied by a personal letter to Turner in which Crutchley expressed the opinion that:

> There is certainly a great deal to be cleared up such as:
> Why no warning from radar of *Blue* or *Ralph Talbot*?
> Why no enemy report from anyone?
> The fact must be faced that we had adequate force placed with the very purpose of repelling surface attack and when that surface attack was made, it destroyed our force. Why [the] enemy did not come on and attack the convoy, I do not know.
> The only thing that can be said is that the convoy was defended but the cost was terrific and I feel that it should have been the enemy who should have paid, whereas he appears to have got off free.
> I know that at night, the odds are heavily in favour of the attacker and by the very nature of things, our people in this case had to be in the position

of defenders; our only chance of reversing that position was warning of
the attack by outlying destroyers.[2]

That same day Crutchley also wrote to Admiral Sir Guy Royle, the
Chief of the Naval Staff at Navy Office in Melbourne, to put on record a
description of events as he then saw them and to forward a copy of his
letter to Turner. Written as it was in the loneliness of his sea cabin in
Australia so soon after the battle, and before he had had a chance to examine
events in detail, it reveals a great deal of the admiral's character. His head
was 'bloody but unbowed' and already he was looking ahead rather than
back. It was certainly not the letter of a man who was seeking to cover up
mistakes, for he told Royle that the whole matter should be thoroughly
investigated.[3]

Crutchley was saddened by the loss of *Canberra*, but obviously puzzled
that three other fine 8-inch cruisers could be surprised and destroyed even
though a measure of warning had been given to them. On these matters he
expressed himself in the following terms:

> It is very sad but one must expect losses and if that was all I should not
> complain but the other division [of cruisers] a few miles away and who
> saw this action and should therefore, inspite of any fatigue from previous
> hard times which might be used as some excuse for others [presumably
> *Canberra*, *Chicago*, *Blue* and *Ralph Talbot*] have been thoroughly alert
> allowed themselves to be destroyed—3 eight inch cruisers! Each division
> had two destroyers with them [but] none claim to have fired their tor-
> pedoes!! A grim tale.[4]

He went on to emphasise the need to improve the Allies' night-fighting
capability if the Japanese were to be beaten ('don't let anyone tell me that
the Japanese are inefficient at night operations'). He also stressed the need
for an exercise area in which to train, and the need to retain men in ships
once they had been trained. He was to find it necessary to state this latter
requirement time and time again during his service in Australia as, almost
inevitably, experienced men were drafted from his cruisers to meet the
trained manpower needs of a rapidly expanding navy.

Regarding his Australian ships' companies he wrote that:

> their conduct and efficiency in air attack is magnificent. The reason is that
> they have had practice, both exercise and real. It is not their fault that they
> have not had it in night action. It is the service that they have been on and
> something had to be given up. I must emphasise that if we are going to
> be offensive, this must be put right. I hope we can trust our allies to put
> their house in order.

In two years of serving with American forces, this was the nearest Crutchley
ever came, at least in correspondence, to criticising the Americans' conduct
of operations.

He concluded his letter with a plea for more balanced reporting of the air effort in support of naval forces, saying that:

> I have heard a certain amount of sarcastic comment about the subsequent broadcast on the part played by shore based aircraft. How their interdiction of Rabaul aerodromes helped the show and what wonders they had performed! I did not hear the broadcast but I did see the aircraft that came from Rabaul. The puffing of the air trumpet is not good for naval morale nor does it create mutual confidence between the Services.

When Turner replied to Crutchley on 12 August, he had some information on the part played by the American cruisers and, in what amounted to a preliminary report, gave a remarkably accurate reconstruction of events. He did not attempt to analyse the causes of the defeat but ventured the opinion that the Japanese had an excellent radar-controlled gunnery system.[5] They in fact had no radar, having relied entirely on well-trained human eyes for the detection of their enemies and the control of their guns. They were to show in future battles that their ability to see at night was on a par with the performance of the radar sets then fitted in American ships. Turner followed that letter with a personal note to Crutchley in which he commented that it was difficult to understand how events could have happened as they did, but that facts had to be faced.

On 13 August Crutchley completed his Report of Proceedings for Operation Watchtower. By that time he had received reports from all ships which had survived the battle and from the senior surviving officers of those that had been sunk. He was able to give what Hepburn was later to describe as the most complete and lucid report of the entire operation. Believing that the picket destroyers' radars had a reliable detection range of six miles, he surmised that the enemy must have outflanked them by keeping close to Guadalcanal and, once again, he commented on the high standard of night fighting demonstrated by the Japanese.

He correctly assessed the Japanese reaction to the capture of Tulagi and Guadalcanal when he concluded that:

> There is no doubt that we have annoyed the enemy to such an extent that he is almost certain to attempt to recapture what he has lost. The success or failure of this operation cannot yet be judged as it depends on our ability to hold what we have taken and to make use of it for further offensive operations.[6]

Neither Crutchley's letter to Royle nor his Report of Proceedings had been received in Melbourne when, on the strength of the information contained in Crutchley's signalled reports, the Naval Board decided on 20 August to convene a Board of Inquiry to undertake a full and careful investigation into the circumstances attending the loss of *Canberra*. Rear Admiral Muirhead-Gould, Rear Admiral in Charge of HMA Naval

Establishments at Sydney, was appointed president of the Board.[7] Among other matters, this body was tasked with examining the state of readiness in *Canberra*, whether a good lookout was being maintained, whether there had been any reports of an enemy in the vicinity, the cause of damage and whether everything possible had been done to save the ship.

When considering the Board's findings it should be noted that, at the time of the Board's first report, no Australian authority had been informed officially of the loss of the three American cruisers. As late as 28 August, Royle was to remark in a letter to Admiral of the Fleet Sir Dudley Pound (then First Sea Lord in London) that he had only received word of the American losses through private American sources.

Undoubtedly *Canberra* survivors, who had arrived in Sydney on 20 August, were well aware of events off Savo. Initially they had been ordered that reference to the battle was to be confined to 'I have been taking part in the operations in Solomon Islands about which you will have heard and read'.[8] This was relaxed to a degree when the loss of *Canberra* in waters adjacent to the Solomon Islands was announced the day they arrived in Sydney, but no mention was made of any other Allied losses.[9] This was not unusual as the Americans had not yet announced the loss of *Yorktown* at the Battle of Midway. It was to be months before the American public heard of the loss of the three heavy cruisers.

A search of all survivors' reports, evidence given to the Board and the Board's reports show the extent to which security restrictions were observed, because the only mention made of the presence of the three American cruisers in any of those documents was by *Canberra*'s senior surviving officer, then in Sydney. Lieutenant Commander Plunkett-Cole, in his written report to the board, described how *Vincennes*, *Quincy* and *Astoria* were patrolling an area adjacent to that patrolled by *Canberra* and *Chicago* without mentioning their part in the action.

The deliberations of *Canberra*'s Board of Inquiry were therefore confined to matters relating solely to the loss of the ship. They were in no way part of a wider examination of the events which led up to that loss so that, for example, the adequacy or otherwise of aerial reconnaissance and the splitting of the heavy cruisers into two groups were not discussed.

The Board lacked information not only on the participation of other friendly forces, but also the composition of the enemy. It was to be some time before it was known that the damage had been inflicted by five 8-inch cruisers and that no light cruiser or destroyer had fired upon *Canberra*.

In their first report, dated 23 August, the Board was of the opinion that *Canberra* should have been in the first degree of readiness all night, that there was an awareness among her senior officers that radar could not be relied on because of the proximity of land and that therefore more than four surface lookouts should have been on watch, that the report of Mikawa's force had been received after dark, and that it was improbable the ship had

Survivors from Canberra *return to Sydney in the transport* President Grant *on 20 August 1942. Scenes connected with their arrival probably prompted the commander of naval establishments at Sydney, Rear Admiral G. C. Muirhead-Gould, to tell later returnees (including the author) that they should feel ashamed for having lost their ship without firing a shot at the enemy.* (AWM neg. 305628)

been torpedoed. The Board also found that the ship could not have been saved without outside assistance and that the decision to withdraw at 0630 prevented such assistance being given. The Board also expressed their opinion that, had outside assistance been available, 'there would have been a possibility of extinguishing the fires'. They envisaged the ship being taken in tow and beached. The report concluded by proposing that another Board of Inquiry be convened to: 'consider the reason why such a well armed and highly trained ship should have been put out of action by twenty four shells from a destroyer or medium cruiser'.

The Board gave no reason for its assessment that the damage had been done by a destroyer or small cruiser but obviously relied on the navigating officer's report that he had seen a ship firing at *Canberra* that was either a small cruiser or a destroyer. They may have taken into account that the gunnery control officer and the gunnery director's crew saw only one cruiser just as all power was lost. They were obviously influenced by the evidence of witnesses that the ship had only been hit by shells of up to 5.5 inches in diameter. Captain Getting's assessment, based on reports made to him by the Principal Control Officer, Wight, and the Yeoman of the Watch, Webster, that three cruisers were present was apparently ignored. Be that as it may, that finding had a profound effect on the way the sinking of *Canberra* was regarded within Navy Office and no doubt influenced Muirhead-Gould's view that the survivors should feel ashamed of themselves.

The Naval Board sent the report to Crutchley who disagreed with much of it. He emphatically disagreed with the finding that the ship should have been in the first degree at night while relaxing by day. He pointed out that, though it was true that they had had some valuable early warning of two of the big air attacks:

> we had a dive bombing attack with no warning and in the Torpedo Bomber attack all we knew was that 40 large twin engined planes had been seen some 400 miles away. The actual attack came from low over the land and good lookouts happened to see them coming over the skyline and cruisers just had time to get off two broadsides of main armament barrage which were largely instrumental in breaking up the attack. It was absolutely necessary for Captains of ships to make some modification to the first degree and, apart from the guns being unloaded, the degree of readiness ordered in *Canberra* was not, in my opinion, unreasonable. Half the armament would have been manned and ready instantly, the other half at about twenty seconds notice.

The Board found that the cause of the list and the cause of the fires were too complicated to be covered by the inquiry. But, because he found it difficult to believe that shellfire could have disabled *Canberra* in the manner described, Crutchley felt that it was important that they be fully investigated.[10] The Naval Board agreed and on 12 September ordered Muirhead-Gould to complete his investigations and to ascertain whether the ship had been torpedoed and the calibre of shell used against her.[11]

The second report was completed on 30 September and, as has already been described, found that *Canberra* had not been torpedoed.[12] This induced Crutchley to write a detailed reply refuting the Board's findings, a stance in which he was supported at Navy Office by Collins and Dowling.[13] The members of the Board reported that they were unable to establish the calibre of the shells that had struck *Canberra* but they believed that they were no more than 5.9 inches.

No Naval Board decisions were promulgated on either matter, as they got on with the war. The recommendation that a second Board of Inquiry be convened to investigate why *Canberra* had been disabled by a destroyer or small cruiser was forgotten—presumably when the size of the raiding party was established.

There was concern in Australian government circles lest the Royal Australian Navy be held responsible by the Americans for the defeat at Savo. On being informed in January 1943 of the impending visit of Hepburn to Melbourne to call on Royle and to interview Crutchley, Prime Minister John Curtin (who was also Minister for Defence) sought assurance from his colleague the Minister for the Navy, Mr Norman Makin, that no blame could be attached to any officer of the RAN. The Prime Minister felt that three matters ought to be considered:

- whether the screening dispositions had allowed the best use to be made of 'the RDF apparatus' (radar)
- the preparedness of the ships for immediate action (it worried him that *Canberra* was not at action stations and that her guns were not loaded)
- the effectiveness of the RDF apparatus (he was concerned at the opinion expressed by the Board of Inquiry that it would have been possible to have detected the Japanese approach had an experienced operator and an accurate plot of the movements of friendly ships been available).

Curtin called for advice as to where responsibility lay for each of the three matters.[14] Makin passed the request on to the Chief of the Naval Staff for action.

In his reply to Makin, Royle supported Crutchley's arrangements and told him that in his opinion 'there was nothing in the disposition of our forces which should have prevented the effective use of their RDF provided it was used with good judgement and common sense'.[15] Regarding the ship's preparedness, Royle said that if it had been up to him he would have allowed some men to sleep at their guns as was done in *Canberra* but that he would have had the guns loaded. He considered that:

> There was a definite lack of immediate readiness on the bridge of *Canberra*. The delay caused by this lack of immediate alertness and the absence of sufficient warning to permit the Captain and Specialist Officers reaching the bridge earlier, may have made all the difference between success and failure.
>
> It must be realised that the advantage will always be with the attacking force which at the moment of attack will be in a state of 100 per cent readiness.

Royle then made clear his opinion as to who was to blame for the loss of the American cruisers when he wrote that:

> It is understood from information received from survivors of the three American cruisers which were sunk that their state of readiness was less than the *Canberra*'s and that the men not actually closed up at the guns were asleep down below in their bunks, in spite of warning that should have been given by the *Canberra*'s action.

The admiral believed that the failure by *Canberra* to obtain early warning of the approach of enemy ships could only be attributed to the lack of experienced officers and men in the tactical use of RDF and to an inexperienced operator.

Of course, Royle at that time had no knowledge of the part played in the debacle by inadequate aerial reconnaissance and the inefficient use of communications. He knew nothing of the lamentable failure of *Blue*, and he was in no position to judge the part played by the inexperience of his American allies or the ineptitude of many of their senior officers. Unlike Nimitz, he gave no credit to the Japanese for a brilliantly conducted operation and, equally, he knew nothing of the Japanese long-range torpedo. There can, however, be little dissent from his concluding comments on the loss of *Canberra* itself when he wrote: 'It must be accepted that more efficient operation of the RDF and more alertness on the bridge might have produced victory instead of disaster. For these, circumstances only and not persons can be blamed.'

But the Australian sailors had no doubt as to the cause of the defeat. They had no feeling of shame, some of them being worried only by the problem of explaining how it was that they had been sunk without firing a shot. They had been well and truly beaten and as one them was later to write, their feeling was, in the rough and often racist vernacular of those war years: 'Clever little yellow bastards. Maybe we'll get you next time.'[16]

And of course many of them did so, because *Canberra*'s survivors formed the nucleus of the ship's company that commissioned HMAS *Shropshire*, Churchill's gift to replace *Canberra*. *Shropshire* formed part of the force that sank two battleships on 25 October 1944 in the Battle of Surigao Strait, firing 36 broadsides at the battleship *Yamashiro* and claiming many hits.[17]

But what of the American debate? On his arrival in Noumea Turner gave Ghormley his preliminary report on Watchtower, together with the reports that he had received from ships and the senior surviving officers of the cruisers lost. He asked that his appreciation be expressed to the coastwatching organisation for the warning which had been provided of the approach of the torpedo bomber attack on 8 August, and he estimated that the attacking force comprised three cruisers and four destroyers.[18]

Ghormley was quick to pass on Turner's report to Nimitz and, in doing so, he cautioned that it was subject to errors and omissions as accurate data had not been obtained. He informed Nimitz that he had not yet received any report from Fletcher or McCain. The size of the attacking force was reassessed as three heavy cruisers, two light cruisers and five destroyers which Ghormley believed had approached Savo through the Solomon Islands. A copy of this letter was not passed to Crutchley and, indeed, after the initial exchange of messages and letters between Turner and Crutchley, there was no further comparing of views between Americans and Australians until Hepburn interviewed Crutchley in Melbourne in February 1943.[19]

By 23 August Nimitz had completed his preliminary report on

Watchtower and forwarded it to King in Washington. He considered that the outstanding features of the operation were:

> the excellence of the approach and initial operations against strong shore and air resistance, the little damage incurred from large scale air attacks and [the] large losses on the night of 8 August when the Japanese delivered their highly successful night surface attack.

He was critical of the failure of reconnaissance aircraft, which at that time he thought were American B-17s and not RAAF Hudsons, to track the force sighted off Kieta. He assessed that it was that force which had later attacked the Allied force off Savo Island.[20] Like Crutchley, Nimitz thought that all the advantage lay with the raiding force and he acknowledged that *Vincennes*'s group had not been ready when they were first fired upon. In analysing the results of the operation he asked that Ghormley answer several pertinent questions in his final report, for example:

1. Would it have been practicable to have withdrawn and refuelled the carrier groups one at a time?
2. Should it not have been possible for shore based aircraft to attack the Japanese as they withdrew?
3. Were radar conditions such that complete reliance could be placed on it for detecting an enemy's approach?
4. Was consideration given to the possibility of a surface attack that night?
5. Was the best use made of the available cruisers and destroyers?

In conclusion he hoped that the Americans would benefit from the Japanese example of boldness and resolution, and in future turn against them the lessons they had so ably taught his forces.[21]

King made no reply, presumably because he was waiting for Nimitz's final report. Nimitz, in his turn, was waiting for Ghormley's, but Ghormley was very busy fighting a determined and aggressive enemy in the Solomons so that it was not until 16 October 1942—that is, the day before he was relieved by Halsey as the Commander South Pacific—that he sent to Nimitz what amounted to an 'interim report'. He explained that his comments were submitted without the detailed and exhaustive analysis which the subject warranted. 'There has not been sufficient time available under the press of continuing combat operations with the enemy to make such an analysis at present'—a fair comment in the circumstances. Nimitz's questions went unanswered.[22]

Ghormley listed eight reasons for the excessive losses suffered at Savo, the first three of which were attributable to Crutchley. These were:

1. The Special Instructions to the Screening Group were too indefinite in regard to what the units of that group were to do and how they were to accomplish their tasks.

2. No special plan was prescribed to cover the possibility of a surface ship night attack [on] 8–9 August.
3. The night disposition relied principally on radar to detect the approaching enemy.

These were probably the basis for Nimitz's pre-Hepburn opinion that Crutchley was largely to blame for the whole affair and would explain Ramsey's remarks made to Gatacre in Washington in 1960. As has been shown, however, Hepburn demolished the first two and the third was irrelevant as the Japanese almost collided with *Blue* on their way into the sound. Crutchley's estimation of the reliable detection range of the destroyers' radar may well have been optimistic, but it had nothing to do with the defeat.

Other reasons advanced by Ghormley were the absence of Crutchley and *Australia*, the failure to realise the significance of the presence of the aircraft, the surprise achieved by the Japanese, the tactical requirement of being on the defensive and the cruisers' state of readiness. Although he did not list it among the reasons for the excessive losses, Ghormley introduced a new factor into the debate when he reported that:

Detailed plans and orders for the Watchtower operation were of necessity prepared in a short space of time immediately prior to its execution, giving little, if any, opportunity for subordinate commanders to contact commanders of units assigned to them for the purpose of indoctrination.

Nimitz forwarded Ghormley's second report to King on the first anniversary of the attack on Pearl Harbor with the remark that, while the only new lesson to be learnt from the defeat was that radar could not replace alert lookouts, many old lessons had been relearnt and he listed a few. He once again showed his respect for what the Japanese had achieved when he commented that: 'The basis of the Japanese victory, which is the basis for most victories, was their bold offensive spirit and alertness'.[23]

King was not satisfied with the inadequate and piecemeal manner in which his admirals had reported on the defeat and it was for that reason that he instructed Hepburn, on 20 December 1942, to carry out his informal investigation in which he was to act as an agent for Nimitz. King instructed him to examine the circumstances attending the loss of the four heavy cruisers. His report to Nimitz was to include, in addition to the facts he established, his opinion as to the primary and contributing causes of the losses and whether any individual had been culpable.

Informal though it may have been, Hepburn's inquiry was nonetheless thorough. It lasted almost five months and involved the Admiral, and his assistant Ramsey, in travel as far afield as Melbourne. His report, which was submitted to Nimitz on 13 May 1943, was of 56 pages and was supported by 713 pages of annexes.[24] Hepburn found that the fundamental cause of the defeat was surprise and listed the causes for the defeat, in order of importance, as follows:

(a) Inadequate condition of readiness on all ships to meet sudden night attack.
(b) Failure to recognise the implications of the presence of enemy planes in the vicinity prior to the attack.
(c) Misplaced confidence in the capabilities of the radar installations on *Ralph Talbot* and *Blue*.
(d) Failure in communications which resulted in the lack of timely receipt of vital enemy contact information.
(e) Failure in communications and standard practice resulting in failure to give timely information of the fact that there had been practically no effective reconnaissance covering [the] enemy approach during the day of 8 August.

As a contributory cause of the disproportionate damage incurred must be placed the withdrawal of the carrier groups on the evening before the battle. This was responsible for Admiral Turner's conference, which in turn was reponsible for the absence of the *Australia* from the action. It was, furthermore, responsible for the fact that there was no force available to inflict damage on the withdrawing enemy.

Regarding culpability, Hepburn was of the opinion that Bode of *Chicago* deserved censure for not having taken the lead from *Canberra* when *Australia* left the formation. He also found that *Chicago*'s behaviour in standing to the west for almost forty minutes was inexplicable. He was not impressed with the leadership of Riefkohl and criticised his choice of patrol courses. Hepburn's thought on the need for a flag officer in the *Vincennes* group was that one was certainly needed there but that 'it was impossible to say, however, that lacking foreknowledge of the event, any flag officer should have been shifted from his assigned task to take this command'.

Nimitz agreed with Hepburn's findings but felt that the inadequate condition of readiness played only a part in bringing about that surprise. In his letter forwarding Hepburn's report to King, he listed the following as the causes of the defeat:

(a) Communication weaknesses.
(b) Failure of either carrier or land based air to conduct effective search and lack of co-ordination of searches.
(c) Failure to track after contact by RAAF planes based on Milne Bay and resultant lack of utilisation of our air striking power.
(d) Erroneous estimate as to the probable intentions of the enemy force, possibly based on the lack of appreciation that the enemy would be bold enough to attack with inferior surface forces.
(e) Over dependence on ineffective radar scouting, obviously based on

inadequate appreciation by commanders involved of the limits of the sets.

(f) Failure to take action when unidentified planes were sighted (neither R.Adm Turner or R.Adm Crutchley were notified of the presence of these planes).

(g) Lack of flag officers in the cruiser forces engaged.

Before finalising his comments on the report, Nimitz asked Turner for his remarks. Turner was almost entirely satisfied with what he regarded as an admirable report. He considered it to be accurate, fair, logical and intuitive. His only significant disagreement concerned the fate of *Canberra* for Hepburn had accepted, without reservation, the finding of the Board of Inquiry. Turner found it difficult to believe that 5-inch shells had done the damage and told Nimitz that he still believed that *Canberra* had been torpedoed.[25]

Turner also suggested that one important cause of the defeat had not been identified by Hepburn: namely, the psychological factor. Experience in Watchtower and subsequent operations had convinced him that the US forces had not been 'battle-minded'. He pointed out that none of them had been in a surface action of any kind and that few had experienced action against aircraft or submarines. He believed that the problem had been exacerbated by the lack of both tactical and weapon training since Pearl Harbor. He concluded that:

> The Navy was still obsessed with a strong feeling of technical and mental superiority over the enemy. In spite of ample evidence as to enemy capabilities, most of our officers and men despised the enemy and felt themselves sure victors in all encounters under any circumstances. Accentuating this was a mental uncertainty as to the methods and capabilities of fellow members of this heterogeneous force.
>
> The net result of all of this was a fatal lethargy of mind which induced a confidence without readiness and a routine acceptance of outworn peacetime standards of conduct. We were not mentally ready for hard battle. I believe that this psychological factor as a cause of our defeat was even more important than the element of surprise.

Nimitz recognised the truth in what Turner had said and as a result ended his endorsement of the Hepburn Report with: 'Finally there is the probability that our force was not psychologically prepared for action and that they were not sufficiently "battle minded" '.

This was the case in the American cruisers and destroyers (with the possible exceptions of *Patterson* and *Ralph Talbot*) and to some extent in *Canberra*, with the notable exception of Walsh. It certainly did not apply to *Australia* and *Hobart*, both of whom had been operationally active in the 27 months which preceded the entry of the US into the war, *Hobart* being a survivor of operations against the Japanese in the Java Sea. With Bode,

Riefkohl, Greenman and Moore all aged in their 50s, these officers must have found it difficult to break the habits acquired during 23 years of peacetime routine.[26] There can be no questioning of Nimitz's list with one exception. For reasons which have already been explained, it is now known that reliance on the picket destroyers' radar was not a factor in the defeat.

King agreed that surprise was the immediate cause of the defeat and was more inclined to accept Nimitz's list of causes than Hepburn's, but considered that no one officer should be blamed for failing to anticipate the attack. It was, he wrote:

> the first battle experience for most of the ships participating in the operations and for most of the flag officers involved and that consequently it was the first time that most of them had been in the position . . . They simply had not learned how and when to stay on the alert.

King accepted that the planning and, to a lesser degree, the exercise of command reflected the urgency with which the operation had been undertaken, and that these aspects fell short of the usual standards. He also accepted that inexperience had played a part in this. Although he planned no disciplinary action against officers who had performed badly, administrative action had already been taken against a number. These included Ghormley, Fletcher, Noyes, Riefkohl and Greenman, who were prevented from again exercising operational command at sea. Any action contemplated against Bode had been forestalled by his suicide soon after he was interviewed by Hepburn.

Regarding the future of McCain, the officer who reviewed the Hepburn Report for King, Captain Russell, remarked in a memorandum to his chief that: 'In view of subsequent developments concerning Admiral McCain, any such action now would be most awkward, to say the least'.[27]

McCain had been awarded the Distinguished Service Medal for his service in the Solomon Islands, the citation for which included the comment that 'his tireless energy and extraordinary skill contributed greatly to occupation of the Guadalcanal–Tulagi area by our forces. . .'! What was potentially even more embarrassing to King was that McCain had been nominated for promotion to vice-admiral and was to become King's Deputy Chief of Naval Operations (Air) in August. Thus McCain, who must be regarded as being one of the architects of the defeat and as one of those who put the success of the whole operation at risk, escaped any censure at all and was rewarded with further promotion and command of a carrier task force.

Two officers were, however, commended for their part in the operation: Turner and Crutchley. King recorded his approval of their performance in the following terms:

> I deem it appropriate and necessary to record my approval of the decisions

and conduct of Rear Admiral R.K. Turner USN and Rear Admiral V. Crutchley RN. In my judgement those two officers were in no way inefficient, much less at fault, in executing their parts of the operation. Both found themselves in awkward positions and both did their best with the means at their disposal.

Russell's memorandum to King is of considerable interest, not only because it was the basis for King's decision not to seek retribution from those who were responsible for Savo, but also because it explained with unusual clarity the thinking that lay behind that decision. The features of the action which impressed Russell the most were the simplicity of the Japanese attack, the combination of circumstances which permitted the surprise and the command 'set up'. With regard to the latter he admitted to King that he did not know what Fletcher had contributed to the operation. His conclusion is noteworthy:

> It does not necessarily follow that because we took a beating, somebody must be the goat. The operation was undoubtedly hastily planned and poorly executed, and there was no small amount of stupidity, but to me it is more an object lesson in how not to fight than it is a failure for which someone must hang. The best thing to do, in my opinion, is to accept the report and to take whatever corrective action is indicated administratively, by which I mean, cash in on the lessons learned. To a large extent we have already done so.

The final act in the Allied admirals' debate took place in Australia. On receipt of a copy of King's letter to the Secretary of the Navy on 8 October, Royle sent a personal signal to Crutchley with the comment that he was glad to pass on King's remarks as they bore out views that he had always strongly held.[28]

There was very little debate concerning the victory among the Japanese admirals. Initially it was acclaimed as a great victory and Yamamoto signalled to Mikawa:

> Appreciate the courageous and hard fighting of every man of your organisation. I expect you to expand your exploits and you will make every effort to support the land forces of the Imperial army which are now engaged in a desperate struggle.[29]

The euphoria disappeared, however, to be replaced by bitter criticism when the effect of Mikawa's withdrawal before destroying the transports became apparent, especially when it was realised that the American carriers had not been in a position from which they could have attacked him.[30] It soon became apparent to the Japanese that there was an opportunity for the 'decisive battle' for which they craved, and on 12 August units of the Combined Fleet under Yamamoto began moving south. Yamamoto saw the impending battle as a competition between Japanese discipline and American scientific technology,[31] but in reality it became a war of attrition which, because of immeasurably greater American resources, Japan could not win. No one was more conscious of this than Yamamoto.

Although his report was accepted by King in 1943, Hepburn has since been criticised for its concentration on the events of the battle itself. He had not examined the reasons for inadequate reconnaissance and communications, though he noted problems arising from them. He is reputed to have deliberately limited the scope of his inquiry because of his wish not to offend Nimitz. He was less than forceful in his examination of the activities of MacArthur's Allied Air Forces, probably because his authority stemmed from King and not from the United States' Joint Chiefs of Staff. He therefore had no mandate to inquire into the activities of forces under the command of MacArthur, for MacArthur was responsible only to the Joint Chiefs. He failed to review the adequacy or otherwise of McCain's plans for aerial reconnaissance. He noted Turner's request for additional searches without commenting on the shortcomings of the search plan that led to that request, and he did not establish whether the searches had been carried out. He did not compensate for the lack of any report by Fletcher, McCain or Noyes on the activities of their commands by interviewing those Admirals or members of their staffs.

Thus the performance of elements of MacArthur's Allied Air Forces, led first by Brett and later by Kenney, and the performance of McCain and his reconnaissance aircraft, and of Fletcher and Noyes and their aircraft carriers, were not subjected to the critical examination that was merited, probably because neither Hepburn nor Ramsey had any expertise in air operations. In retrospect therefore, Hepburn's report was far from satisfactory. In the light of the failure to closely examine many aspects of the operation, it is not surprising that Watchtower and the Battle of Savo have provided a breeding ground for rumour and misinformation, the best example of which is the rumour that the crew of the aircraft that first sighted Mikawa went to tea before reporting what they had seen. Much of this misinformation persists to this day.[32]

Seven years after Hepburn completed his report, the Naval War College's analysis of Savo covered most of the ground missed by him—albeit some of it imperfectly. The analysts had access to all Japanese and American records and to surviving personnel. It is disappointing to note however, that, concerning *Canberra*'s part in the battle, they apparently examined no Australian documents that had not been available to Hepburn and neither wrote to nor interviewed any Australian personnel. No approach was made to Crutchley for amplification of his reports and his discussions with Hepburn, an omission which could at least be labelled as discourteous. Because of this lack of a fresh Australian input, the Naval War College was unaware of the second report of *Canberra*'s Board of Inquiry and of the correspondence between Crutchley and the Naval Board.

If proof is needed that the analysis is far from being a dispassionate review of an Allied operation, it is to be found in the refusal by Bates to release the document to the Australian Government in August 1954. Its findings must therefore be reviewed in the knowledge that it was an American study for American eyes only.

Generally speaking it reiterated the opinions of Nimitz and King, though it tended to be more critical of Crutchley's actions and in particular did not accept the generally supportive views of Turner and Hepburn on Crutchley's disposition of the cruisers and destroyers.

The Naval War College analysis, however, made one important contribution to the debate on the causes of the defeat, pointing out for the first time the part played by command inadequacies. One of its conclusions was that the group commanders and commanding officers of ships, who were probably as proficient as any of their contemporaries and who had met all the essential peacetime tests, had, once they were caught by surprise, almost invariably made the wrong decisions. This was a damning indictment of the state of readiness of all commanding officers at Savo, including Getting of *Canberra*. He was found to have made no attempt to originate an enemy report: this allegation being made in spite of the evidence to the contrary contained in the report of the Board of Inquiry which is known to have been examined by the analysts. Getting and his ship's company, though surprised, had in fact reacted quickly and correctly to the emergency. The criticism therefore can only be accepted as an indictment of American officers.

A Board of Review of several USN captains, assembled at the Naval War College in January 1950 to make detailed comments on the analysis, supported its findings. After stating their belief that it was incredible that after eight months of war senior officers could be so unready for night action, they suggested that there had been something radically wrong with the USN's pre-war system of training and in the selection of officers for high command.[33] This was widening the debate well beyond the bounds of Savo, but there is no doubt that events in August 1942 justified such an extrapolation. How else can one explain Fletcher's conduct throughout Watchtower, Ghormly's decision not to place land- and shore-based aircraft under the command of Fletcher, McCain's inadequate air plans, Turner's rejection of intelligence, Noyes' failure to keep control of flight operations on the morning of the torpedo bombers' attack, the lack of a fleet-wide night fighting doctrine and the many failures in communications.

There was indeed something wrong, and surface actions in the Solomons subsequent to Savo were to emphasise that point. But there is no substitute in war for the brain tempered by experience and eventually the deadwood in the command structure was weeded out and the lessons of Watchtower, Savo and later battles were put to good use.

Savo has been called many things: a galling defeat, a debacle, a shameful defeat, a bloody shambles and an object lesson in how not to fight, to name just a few. It was in fact all those things and this should never be forgotten. But it was also the catalyst for the remarkable rejuvenation of the United States Navy which cannot be explained only in terms of growing numbers and new technology. The study of the lessons from Savo enabled better use to be made of the new ships as they entered service and also enabled operational techniques to be developed to take advantage of the growth in technology. Savo, shameful though it was, was a vital stepping stone on the road to victory.

Appendix 1

SHIPS INVOLVED IN WATCHTOWER

Akitsushima (IJN)—a tender designed to handle a single large flying boat; 4650 tons; 387 feet x 52 feet; armament included 4 x single 5-inch.

Aoba (IJN)—heavy cruiser very similar in appearance to *Furutaka*, *Kako* and *Kinugasa*, all four being completed between March 1926 and September 1927; 10 341 tons full load; 607 feet 6 inches x 57 feet 9 inches; speed 35.5 knots; armament included 3 x 2 8-inch, 4 x single 4.7-inch, 2 x 4 24-inch torpedo tubes (16 torpedoes were carried); 1 Alf and 1 Jake reconnaissance aircraft. *Aoba* was wearing the flag of Rear Admiral Goto, commander of Cruiser Division Six, at Savo.

Astoria (USS)—heavy cruiser of New Orleans class, which included *Quincy* and *Vincennes*; built to conform to 10 000-ton limit of the Washington Treaty, the design was so tight (from the point of view of displacement) that none could be fitted as a fleet flagship; completed 1934; 12 463 tons full load; 588 feet x 61 feet 9 inches; speed 32.7 knots; armament included 3 x 3 8-inch, 8 x single 5-inch; 4–5 Curtis SOC aircraft.

Australia (HMAS)—completed 1928 by John Brown and Co. Ltd of Clydebank as identical twin to *Canberra* but underwent a major modernisation which was completed as war broke out in 1939. Whereas *Canberra* had no side armour, during her modernisation *Australia* was fitted with a 4-inch armoured belt from just forward of the boiler rooms to aft of the engine rooms which extended 6 feet below the water line. The sides of the fan flats above both boiler rooms were similarly armoured. The same armour in another ship of this class (*Berwick*) deflected an 8-inch shell by the German

271

heavy cruiser *Hipper*. The single 4-inch guns were replaced with twins and a second anti-aircraft fire control system was fitted. Perhaps the most significant additions, in view of *Canberra*'s fate, were two diesel generators to provide power in the event that steam was not available. These had been considered in the original design but not fitted to save weight, so as to keep within the Washington Treaty limit of 10 000 tons standard displacement. During her modernisation, displacement was increased to 14 900 tons full load.

Bagley (USS)—name ship of a class of eight destroyers completed in 1936–37 (the others being *Patterson*, *Helm*, *Jarvis*, *Blue*, *Ralph Talbot*, *Henley* and *Mugford*) which, together with the large destroyer *Selfridge* as squadron leader, comprised Destroyer Squadron Four; 2245 tons full load; 341 feet 4 inches x 35 feet 6 inches; speed 38.5 knots; armament included 4 x single 5-inch, 4 x 4 21-inch torpedo tubes.

Blue (USS)—see *Bagley*.

Canberra (HMAS)—heavy cruiser built by John Brown and Co. Ltd of Clydebank, and completed July 1928; 13 630 tons full load, 630 feet x 68 feet 4 inches; speed 31.5 knots; armament included 4 x 2 8-inch, 4 x single 4-inch and 2 × 4 21-inch torpedo tubes; 1 or 2 Walrus aircraft.

Chicago (USS)—heavy cruiser completed 1931; 9006 tons full load; 600 feet 3 inches x 66 feet 6 inches; speed 32.5 knots; armament included 3 x 3 8-inch, 4 x single 5-inch; 4 Curtis SOC aircraft.

Chokai (IJN)—one of eight similar heavy cruisers, completed June 1932; 12 781 tons full load; 668 feet 6 inches x 59 feet 2 inches; speed 35.5 knots; armament included 5 x 2 8-inch and 4 x single 4.7-inch, 4 x 4 24-inch torpedo tubes; 2 Alf and 1 Jake reconnaissance aircraft.

Curtiss (USS)—large seaplane tender capable of handling 25 aircraft; completed 1940; 8625 tons; 527 feet 4 inches x 69 feet 3 inches; speed 18 knots; armament included 4 x single 5-inch.

Ellet (USS)—one of ten Benham class destroyers, completed 1938; 340 feet 9 inches x 35 feet 6 inches; speed 38.5 knots; armament included 4 x single 5-inch, 4 x 4 torpedo tubes.

Enterprise (USS)—completed 1938; 25 484 tons full load; 824 feet 9 inches x 83 feet 2 inches; speed 32.5 knots; armament included 8 x single 5-inch; aircraft carried for Watchtower: 36 fighters, 36 dive-bombers, 16 torpedo bombers/reconnaissance aircraft.

Furutaka (IJN)—see *Aoba*.

Hobart (HMAS)—light cruiser, completed 1936; 9150 tons deep load; 562 feet 3 inches x 56 feet 8 inches; speed 32.5 knots; armament included 4 x 2 6-inch, 4 x 2 4-inch, 2 x 4 torpedo tubes; 1 Walrus aircraft.

Jarvis (USS)—see *Bagley*.

Kako (IJN)—see *Aoba*.

Kinugasa (IJN)—see *Aoba*.

Mackinac (USS)—purpose-built small seaplane tender capable of handling one squadron of aircraft; completed 1942; 1695 tons; 310 feet 9 inches x 41 feet; speed 20 knots; armament included 2 x single 5-inch.

McCawley (USS)—completed 1928; 7712 gross tons; speed 16 knots; formerly named *Santa Barbara*.

McFarland (USS)—small seaplane tender capable of handling one squadron of aircraft, converted from a four-funnelled destroyer; completed 1920; 1190 tons; 314 feet x 30 feet 8 inches; armament included 2 x single 4-inch.

Mugford (USS)—see *Bagley*.

North Carolina (USS)—completed 1941; 44 377 tons full load; 729 feet 9 inches x 108 feet 4 inches; speed 28 knots; armament included 3 x 3 16-inch, 10 x 2 5-inch; carried 7621 tons of oil fuel giving range of 15 000 miles at 15 knots.

Patterson (USS)—see *Bagley*.

Platte (USS)—a good example of the fast fleet replenishment tankers produced to service the Pacific Fleet, completed 1940; 16 375 dead weight tons; speed 19 knots.

Quincy (USS)—see *Astoria*; completed 1936.

Ralph Talbot (USS)—see *Bagley*.

San Juan (USS)—completed February 1942; 8340 tons full load; 541 feet 6 inches x 53 feet 2 inches; speed 32.5 knots; armament included 8 x 2 5-inch (broadside of 14 x 5-inch).

Saratoga (USS)—laid down as a battle cruiser and completed as an aircraft carrier in 1927; 43 055 tons full load, 888 feet x 105 feet 5 inches; turbo-electric drive, speed 33.25 knots; armament included 12 x single 5-inch; survived the war to be sunk as a target at the Bikini atom bomb tests; aircraft carried for Watchtower: 36 fighters, 36 dive-bombers, 18 torpedo bomber/reconnaissance aircraft.

Selfridge (USS)—one of Porter class, completed in 1936; 2597 tons full load; 381 feet × 37 feet; speed 37 knots; armament included 4 x 2 5-inch low angle, 2 x 4 torpedo tubes.

Tenryu (IJN)—a small light cruiser (by Allied standards), completed in November 1919; 3230 tons; 458 feet x 40 feet 6 inches; speed 33 knots; armament included 4 x single 5.5-inch, 2 x 3 18-inch torpedo tubes; wore the flag of Rear Admiral Matsuyama, commander of Cruiser Division Eighteen, at Savo.

Tsugaru (IJN)—a single-funnelled minelaying cruiser used principally for escort duties; 4000 tons; 408 feet x 51 feet; speed 20 knots; armament included 2 x single 5-inch.

Vincennes (USS)—see *Astoria*; completed 1937.

Wasp (USS)—completed 1940; 18 700 tons full load; 720 feet x 81 feet 7 inches; speed 29.5 knots; armament included 8 x single 5-inch; sunk south of Guadalcanal 15 September 1942; aircraft carried for Watchtower: 27 fighters, 28 dive-bombers, 6 torpedo bombers/reconnaissance aircraft.

Wilson (USS)—Benham class destroyer (see *Ellet*).

Yubari (IJN)—a small light cruiser completed in July 1923; 3780 tons; 450 feet x 39 feet 6 inches; armament included 2 x 2 and single 5.5-inch and 2 x 2 24-inch torpedo tubes.

Yunagi (IJN)—a destroyer completed in April 1925; 1300 tons; 327 feet x 32 feet; speed 35 knots; armament included 3 x single 4.7-inch and 3 x 2 18-inch torpedo tubes.

Appendix 2

ALLIED AND JAPANESE AIRCRAFT TYPES

Allied reconnaissance aircraft

B-17E (Boeing Flying Fortress)—had range of 2500 miles in reconnaissance role, 1200 miles as a bomber carrying maximum load of 4000 pounds; maximum speed 295 mph; ceiling 36 600 feet.

Hudson (Lockheed)—range 1355 miles in armed reconnaissance role carrying load of 900 pounds; maximum speed 222 mph at 7900 feet; ceiling 24 500 feet. A very versatile aircraft which the RAAF also used as a bomber and as a transport aircraft.

PBY-5 (Consolidated Catalina)—reconnaissance patrol bomber with range (in reconnaissance role) of 3100 miles; maximum speed 189 mph at 7000 feet, crusing speed 115 mph; ceiling 18 100 feet; armament included 2 x fixed .3 machine-guns, 2 x .5 flexible machine-guns; carried up to 4 x 1000-pound bombs. Also used as a night bomber.

Allied carrier and cruiser-borne aircraft

F-4F (Grumman Wildcat)—fighter which made its operational debut at Midway; range with two wing tanks 1275 miles; maximum speed 320 mph at 18 800 feet; ceiling 34 000 feet (12.4 minutes to climb to 20 000 feet); armament 6 x .5 machine-guns. Inferior to the Japanese Zero in speed, rate of climb and range but a much more rugged aircraft, enabling it to absorb considerable damage.

SPD-3 (Douglas Dauntless)—dive-bomber; crew of 2; range 1100 miles; maximum speed 245 mph at 15 800 feet, cruising speed 144 mph; ceiling 24 300 feet; armament included 2 x fixed .5 machine-guns, 2 x flexible dorsal .3 machine-guns; carried up to 1000 pounds of bombs under fuselage and 2 x 325-pound bombs under wings.

TBF-1 (Grumman Avenger)—reconnaissance, low-level and torpedo bomber aircraft; range 1215 miles; maximum speed 271 mph at 12 000 feet, cruising speed 145 mph; ceiling 22 400; armament included 1 x fixed .3 machine-gun, 1 x dorsal .5 machine-gun, 1 x ventral machine-gun; carried up to 1600 pounds in bomb bay.

SOC (Curtiss)—cruiser-borne reconnaissance aircraft with range of 675 miles; maximum speed 165 mph at 5000 feet, cruising speed 133 mph; ceiling 14 900 feet; armament included 1 x fixed .3 machine-gun, 1 x flexible .3 machine-gun aft; carried 2 x 325 pound bombs.

Walrus (Supermarine Seagull V)—cruiser-borne reconnaissance and sea–air rescue amphibian; range 600 miles; maximum speed 135 mph at 4750 feet, cruising speed 95 mph; ceiling 18 500 feet; armament 2 x .303-inch machine-guns; carried 760 pounds of bombs or depth charges under wings.

Japanese shore-based aircraft

Betty (Mitsubishi G4M1)—twin-engine bomber also known as the Navy Type 1 Land Attack Aircraft; range 3250 miles; maximum speed 266 mph at 13 780 feet, cruising speed 196 mph at 10 000 feet; ceiling 28 200 feet; could carry 2200 pounds of bombs or a 1760-pound torpedo over 2600 miles—a performance which came as a complete surprise to the Allies. The aircraft was, however, very vulnerable as it was not armoured and its large internal wing tanks were unprotected, a weakness demonstrated at Guadalcanal in the torpedo attack on the Amphibious Force on 8 August.

Zero (Mitsubishi A6M3)—fighter with range 1870 miles; maximum speed 338 mph at 20 000 feet; ceiling 38 000 feet (7.3 minutes to climb to 20 000 feet); armament 2 x 20mm cannon, 2 x .7 machine-guns. This version of the Zero had virtually no armour to protect the pilot and no protection for the fuel tanks. Lightly constructed, it was unable to withstand the same amount of damage as the US Wildcat.

Val (Aichi D3A)—carrier-borne dive-bomber also known as the Navy Type 99 Carrier Bomber; range 1250 miles; maximum speed 240 mph at 9850 feet, cruising speed 184 mph; ceiling 30 050 feet; bomb-load 1 x 550 pound under fuselage, 1 x 132 pound under each wing.

Japanese cruiser-borne aircraft

Alf (Kawanishi E7K-2)—also known as the Navy Type 94 Reconnaissance Seaplane; twin-float; crew of 3; endurance up to 11.5 hours; maximum speed 171 mph at 6500 feet, cruising speed 115 mph; ceiling 23 165 feet.

Jake (Aichi E13A-1)—also known as the Navy Type O Reconnaissance Seaplane; single-float; crew of 3; range 1298 miles; maximum speed 234 mph at 7155 feet, cruising speed 138 mph; ceiling 28 640 feet.

Endnotes

Books and articles cited are in an abbreviated form. Full details can be found in the bibliography.

Chapter 1

1 Howarth, *Morning Glory*, p. 252.
2 ibid. p. 243.
3 Marder, *Old Friends, New Enemies*, vol. 1, p. 511.
4 Howarth, *Morning Glory*, p. 240.
5 ibid. p. 239.
6 Marder, *Old Friends, New Enemies*, vol. 2, p. 372.
7 Ohmae, 'The Battle of Savo Island', p. 1263. This article also appears in Evans, *The Japanese Navy in WW II*, a collection of accounts by former Japanese naval officers of their war experiences. Captain Ohmae was serving on the staff of Mikawa in *Chokai* at Savo.
8 Ohmae, 'The Battle', p. 1264.
9 ibid. p. 1264.
10 As far as the Americans were concerned, this policy was first postulated in Plan Dog drawn up in November 1940 under the auspices of Admiral Stark, the Chief of Naval Operations. See Reynolds, *The Creation of the Anglo-American Alliance 1937–41*, p. 185.
11 Dyer, *The Amphibians Came to Conquer*, vol. 1, p. 234.
12 Larrabee, *Commander in Chief*, pp. 173–4.
13 Dyer, *The Amphibians*, p. 246.
14 Vandegrift, *Once a Marine*, p. 100.
15 King and Whitehall, *Fleet Admiral King*, p. 176.
16 ibid. p. 178.
17 Message from C-in-C US Fleet to C-in-C Pacific, 242306Z June 1942, NWC Archives, Research Group 23, box 46, Savo Island folders 1–4.

Chapter 2

1　Joint Directive of US Joint Chiefs of Staff, NWC Archives, Research Group 23, box 46, item 4, Savo Island folders 1–4.

2　Churchill, *The Second World War*, vol. 3, p. 119.

3　Transcript of Recordgraph made by Vice-Admiral Ghormley for the Office of Naval Records and Library on 22 January 1943, NHC, Morison Papers, box 24.

4　Gatacre, *Report of Proceedings*, p. 159.

5　Marder, *Old Friends, New Enemies*, vol. 2, p. 23.

6　Leahy, *I Was There*, p. 85.

7　NWC study entitled 'The Battle of Savo Island, 9 August 1942, Strategical and Tactical Analysis', by Commodore Richard Bates and Commander Walter Innis (hereafter referred to simply as Bates), p. 17.

8　Dyer, *The Amphibians*, vol. 1, p. 303.

9　ibid. p. 303.

10　Layton, *And I Was There*, p. 344.

11　Dull, *The Imperial Japanese Navy 1941–45*, p. 25.

12　A full account of that interview was given by Potter in *Nimitz*, p. 86.

13　ibid.

14　Captain Forrest Biard, unpublished manuscript dated 20 June 1985.

15　The policy of severely restricting the numbers of people who knew of Allied signals intelligence was continued well into the postwar era. For example, the author was unaware of any details of such activities until especially briefed on assuming his first command in 1957, even though he had served on the staff of the Flag Officer Commanding the Australian Fleet for two years. Intelligence gleaned by this means was passed on in terms which would not reveal its source; if this could not be done, it was not passed on.

16　This account of Fletcher's behaviour is repeated in Layton, p. 399. Layton died before completion of *And I Was There*, which was finished by Roger Pineau and John Costello. They had been instrumental in Layton's decision to write the book and were closely associated with him in its compilation until he died suddenly in April 1984, by which time the portion of the manuscript covering up to the Battle of Midway was almost complete. It is said to be difficult to differentiate between Layton's work and that of his co-authors. There is, however, very little doubt that references to Biard's account of the conduct of Fletcher are Layton's own work, since Biard had written to him in August 1980 sending the first third of his account in which he described his experiences in the Battle of the Coral Sea and expressed extreme bitterness towards Fletcher. See Layton, p. 509, and letter, Biard to Layton, 4 August 1980, NWC, Edwin T. Layton papers, box 40, folder 1.

17　Letter, Nimitz to King, 31 October 1942, PRO, ADM 199/1323.

18　Marder, *Old Friends, New Enemies*, vol. 2, p. 33.

19　For further discussion of Fletcher's performance see also M. E. Butcher, 'Admiral Frank Jack Fletcher. Pioneer Warrior or Gross Sinner?' Naval War College *Review*, Winter 1987.

20　Dyer, *The Amphibians*, p. 384.

21　ibid. p. 302.

Chapter 3

1 Slessor, *The Central Blue*, p. 355.
2 Vandergrift, *One a Marine*, p. 118. Yet another opinion of Turner is that of Rear Admiral Edwin Layton whose objectivity is, however, questionable as he was Nimitz's Combat Intelligence Officer and had a poor opinion of Turner's use of intelligence. To him, Turner was 'aggressive, abrasive, opinionated but a brilliant officer. No one ever questioned his bravery. He never got on with anyone least of all his superiors. He bullied his juniors and licked the boots of his superiors.' NWC, Edwin T. Layton Papers, box 30, folder 2.
3 Reminiscences of Rear Admiral Arthur McCollum, USNI, p. 307. McCollum was Head of the Far East Desk in ONI from November 1939 to October 1942. Born in Nagasaki, the son of Baptist missionaries, he was an interpreter and translator of Japanese and spent a total of four-and-a-half years in Tokyo. He was also a submarine specialist.
4 In the event they were to make their move in July.
5 McCollum, reminiscences, p. 309.
6 ibid. p. 312.
7 ibid. p. 315.
8 ibid. p. 321.
9 Layton, *And I Was There*, p. 274.
10 McCollum, reminiscences, p. 329.
11 ibid. p. 330.
12 Dyer, *The Amphibians*, p. 1168.
13 ibid. p. 243.
14 Letter, Turner to Rear Admiral Charles Welborn, Deputy CNO (Administration), NHC, Morison Papers, box 27.
15 Layton, *And I Was There*, p. 459.
16 From conversations and correspondence with Lieutenant Commander William Crutchley, RN, son of Admiral Crutchley.
17 *London Gazette*, 28 August 1918.
18 *Diomede* was in Sydney for ceremonies related to the opening of the Sydney Harbour Bridge in March 1932. Crutchley was therefore close by when Major De Groot gatecrashed the opening ceremony on horseback and slashed the symbolic ribbon with his sword! In 1933 *Diomede* provided emergency services for the town of Napier, New Zealand, after it had been destroyed by an earthquake.
19 Task Force 44—Sweep into the Coral Sea, AWM file 78, item 393/1.
20 HMA Squadron War Diary, May–July 1942, AWM file 78, item 393/1.
21 The S class of submarines, built in 1924–25, displaced 850 tons and were armed with only four torpedo tubes. Their surface speed was eleven knots and they were not airconditioned.

Chapter 4

1 Commander South Pacific's Operation Plan 1/42 dated 16 July 1942, Hepburn Report (hereafter referred to simply as Hepburn), Annex E1. Admiral Arthur

J. Hepburn, a former Commander-in-Chief US Fleet, was instructed by King on 20 December 1942 to carry out an informal inquiry into the loss of *Canberra*, *Vincennes*, *Quincy* and *Astoria* and to report his findings to Nimitz. He completed this task on 13 May 1943. In the course of his inquiry, Hepburn interviewed many witnesses, including Turner, Crutchley and the three surviving American cruiser captains. He had access to all survivors' reports and to the report and minutes of the RAN Board of Inquiry held in Sydney in August 1942 into the loss of *Canberra*. Nimitz described the report as an exhaustive study and analysis which represented months of skilful investigation.

2 Gillison, *Royal Australian Air Force 1939–1942*, p. 524.

3 Manchester, *American Caesar*, p. 300.

4 Bates, p. 27.

5 ibid. Diagrams C and D.

6 Message 0820Z on 4 August to RAAF No. 32 Squadron, ACH Townsville Signal Log, RAAF Miscellaneous Operations Records, AWM file 66, item 18/2/4.

7 Bates, p. 28.

8 Gill, *Royal Australian Navy 1942–45*, p. 133.

9 Letter, Crutchley to Vice-Admiral Sir Guy Royle (CNS Melbourne), 10 August 1942, a copy of which is in the possession of the author.

10 General Headquarters Operation Instruction No. 14 of 26 July 1942, AWM file 54, item No 519/4/13.

11 Bates, p. 29.

12 Joint Directive of US Joint Chiefs of Staff dated July 1942, NWC Archives, Research Group 23, box 46, item 4, Savo Island folders 1–4.

13 AAF Signal Instructions, Annexure B to Operation Instruction No. 18 dated 31 July 1942, and a personal message from Brett to the Area Commands, 0209Z of 2 August, AA (Canb), MP 1196/2, file 60/501/103.

14 Correspondence and conversations with Mr Wilbur Courtis, navigator of Hudson 218 of No. 32 Squadron, RAAF.

15 ibid.

16 From conversations with Air Commodore Deryck Kingwell.

17 From records in RAAF Historical Section, Air Force Office, Canberra.

18 From conversations with Air Commodore W.H. Garing.

19 AAF Headquarters message to ACH Townsville, serial No. A191 of 2/7, RAAF Historical Section records, Air Force Office, Canberra

20 Deane-Butcher, *Fighter Squadron Doctor*, p. 120.

21 AAF Headquarters message 0810Z of 4 August, ACH Signal Log, AWM file 66, item 18/2/4.

22 From conversations with Mr W. Stutt.

23 Commander Aircraft South Pacific Op Plan 1–42 dated 25 July 1942, pp. 5–6, Hepburn, Annex E8.

24 ibid., p. 4.

25 ibid., p. 8.

26 The PBY flying boat, also known as the Catalina, was used to search to a depth of up to 900 miles and the B-17 Flying Fortress up to 800 miles. Both were fitted with an early form of radar which provided a search beam of about 30 degrees ahead of the aircraft with an effective detection range of about 25

miles. While offering no advantage over visual search in good visibility, this provided a search capability by night in areas free of interference from land echoes but only in clear weather, as it was very susceptible to interference from cloud, rain and sea returns. In the environment of the Solomons it was invaluable as a navigation aid.

27 Expeditionary Force Commander (Commander Task force 61) Op Plan 1–42 dated 25 July 1942, Hepburn, Annex E9.

28 Admiral R.K. Turner's comments on Morison's volume, *The Struggle for Guadalcanal*, NHC, Morison Papers, box 27. The comments were made in a letter to Rear Admiral Charles Welborn, Deputy CNO (Administration), dated 20 August 1950, and were in response to a request by Welborn.

Chapter 5

1 Part 4 of message from MacArthur and Ghormley to the Chiefs of Staff, 081012 July, NWC Archives, Research Group 23, box 46, Savo Island folders 1–4.

2 Task Force 62 Tentative Operation Plan A2-42 dated 22 July 1942, AA (Vic), MP 1290/1, file 29.

3 Task Force 62 Operation Plan A3-42 dated 30 July 1942, Annex E—Intelligence, Hepburn, Annex E.

4 Captain J.G.P. Vivian's report 'Efficiency of the Japanese Navy' dated 18 February 1935, PRO, ADM 116/3862.

5 Letter, Captain Shin Itonaga to author, 15 October 1990. Captain Itonaga, a retired officer of the Japanese Maritime Self Defence Force (JMSDF), was a member of the staff of the National Institute for Defense Studies, Tokyo.

6 *Conway's All the World's Fighting Ships 1922–1946*, p. 6.

7 Dull, *Japanese Navy*, p. 60.

8 Rawling's reports on the Imperial Japanese Navy for the years 1937 and 1938 were equally devoid of information on weapon training, AA (Vic), MP 1049/5, file 1877/13/161.7.

9 McCollum, reminiscences, p. 353.

10 ibid. p. 147.

11 The risk was probably considered unacceptable in view of an improved engine that had been developed for the orthodox 21-inch torpedoes, see *Conway's*, p. 6.

12 Gatacre, *Report*, p. 141.

13 McCollum, reminscences, p. 147.

14 Marder, *Old Friends, New Enemies*, vol. 2, p. 45.

15 ibid. p. 8.

16 Sir Frederick Dreyer to the Admiralty, 10 February 1939, PRO, ADM 1/11326.

17 Turner's 'Comments on Hepburn Report' dated June 1943, on NHC microfilm of Hepburn (NRS 1976).

18 McCollum, reminiscences, p. 331.

Chapter 6

1 Letters, Commander Task Force 62 to Commander South Pacific, 16 August 1942, and Commander-in-Chief Pacific Fleet to Commander-in-Chief US Fleet, 25 September 1942, Hepburn, Annex T.
2 Naval Staff Minute by the Fifth Sea Lord, PRO, ADM 199/1323.
3 Letter, Commander-in-Chief Pacific Fleet to Commander-in-Chief US Fleet, 25 September 1942, Hepburn, Annex T.
4 Partial Summary of Communications of 8–9 August 1942, relative to Savo Island Action during Early Morning of 9 August 1942, prepared by Commander D.J. Ramsey, Hepburn, Annex T.
5 COMAIRSOPAC Operation Plan 1-42, Annex D, AA (Vic), MP 1290/1, file 29.
6 Operation Instruction No. 18/1942 from Headquarters AAF to Headquarters North Eastern Area, Annexure B—Signal Instructions, AA (Canb), A1196/2, file 60/501/103 Part 1.
7 Bates, p. 101.
8 Feldt, *The Coast Watchers*, p. 285.
9 A good description of the development of the coastwatching service is contained in the foreword by Hermon Gill to the 1946 edition of *The Coast Watchers*.
10 Feldt, *The Coast Watchers*, p. xxi.
11 Naval Staff Minute by the Director of Naval Intelligence dated 21 December 1939, AA (Vic), MP 1049/5, file 1840/2/80.
12 Naval Board Minute No. 31 dated 26 January 1940, AA (Vic), MP 1049/5, file 1840/2/80.
13 Gill, *Royal Australian Navy 1942–45*, p. 123.
14 Task Force 62 Operation Plan A3-42 dated 30 July 1942, Annex H. AA (Vic), MP 1290/1, file 29, and Hepburn, Annex E10(f).

Chapter 7

1 Vandegrift, *Once a Marine*, p. 99.
2 ibid. p. 101.
3 ibid. p. 102.
4 ibid. p. 103.
5 Griffith, *The Battle for Guadalcanal*, p. 51. As a lieutenant colonel, Griffith was commander of the First Marine Raider Battalion which distinguished itself in the two-day fight for Tulagi. His book was described by Nimitz as being the most realistic and interesting book written on Guadalcanal.
6 Vandegrift, *Once a Marine*, p. 109.
7 Part 6 of a message from MacArthur and Ghormley to the Chiefs of Staff 081012 July, NWC Archives, Research Group 23, box 46, Savo Island folders 1–4.
8 Commander-in-Chief U.S. Fleet's message, 102100Z July, NWC Archives, Research Group 23, box 46, Savo Island folders 1–4.

9 Letter, Leary to Crutchley, 10 July 1942, a copy of which is in the possession of the author.
10 Bates, p. 41.
11 Commander South Pacific Op-Plan 1–42 dated 16 July 1942, AA (Vic), MP 1290/5, and Hepburn, Annex E1.
12 Griffith, p. 55.

Chapter 8

1 Dyer, *The Amphibians*, p. 364fn, and Hepburn, Annex T.
2 The history of the development of the 271 and the tactical use of radar in the RN is well documented in Howse, *Radar at Sea*. For information on the fitting and use of radar in *Canberra*, the author is indebted to Dr David Medley, now of Los Osos, California. After the war, Medley spent a year lecturing at Sydney University before joining the Department of Civil Aviation. Within ten years he had risen to the position of Director of Engineering in the department before spending five years in Montreal as Australian Representative on the Council of the Internatival Civil Aviation Organisation. In 1962 he and his family moved to America where he has resided ever since, becoming an American citizen in 1968.
3 Conversation with Rear Admiral H.A. Showers, August 1990. The two officers he sent, Lieutenants J.P. Stevenson and R.A.H. Miller, did very well on their course. Illustrating further the attitude to radar at that time, in August 1992 Vice-Admiral Sir Richard Peek told the author that during one of the periods he spent at Navy Office he had sighted a memorandum in which the statement was made that radar would not last.
4 The ships having been identified as an armed raider accompanied by a tanker, Captain Farncomb, then in command of *Canberra*, decided to engage at long range to remain outside the enemy's possible gun and torpedo range. He was later censored for wasting ammunition but his caution was justified, as eight months later *Sydney* unwisely closed a merchant ship which proved to be the German armed merchant cruiser *Kormoran* and was sunk with all hands by gunfire and torpedoes.
5 Captain Frank Getting was born in 1899 and graduated from the Royal Australian Naval College, Jervis Bay, in 1917. Qualified to command submarines from 1926, he became the first RAN officer to do so when he was made captain of HMAS *Oxley* in 1928. After attending the Naval Staff College and the Imperial Defence College, London, in 1934, he was appointed captain of HMAS *Kanimbla* in 1939. Promoted Captain in 1940, he was Deputy CNS at Navy Office, Melbourne, the following year before becoming captain of *Canberra*. Throughout his career Getting had impressed his superiors by his personal qualities, and his 'blue jacket' (file of commanding officers' reports) shows that he was consistently well regarded. In August 1940 Admiral Sir Percy Noble, Commander-in-Chief of the RN's China Station where *Kanimbla* was then serving, described him as 'a smart, efficient and hardworking officer' possessing 'imagination and courage . . . [and] a fine power of command'.
6 *Canberra* War Diary, 1 March–31 May 1942, AWM file 78, item 82/3.

7   The transmitted power of the original 271 was little more than 5 kW and because of this the length of cable between the aerials and the transmitter/receiver had to be kept to a minimum to reduce the amount of power lost. For this reason, the transmitter and receiver 'cheese' aerials, mounted one on top of the other, were directly above the radar office. This six-foot-square space contained the receiver, the display unit and the mechanical aerial rotation gear, leaving very little room for an operator's chair. To make the assembly watertight, the radar office was surmounted by a lantern-like structure of teak pillars which served as frames for flat plastic windows. Later 271s transmitted about 70 kW, permitting the use of waveguides and separation of the aerial assembly from the radar office. *Canberra*'s 271 was supplied in a prefabricated package which necessitated little more than the manufacture of a platform on which to bolt the radar office with the aerial assembly above, and provision of power supplies, before the set was operational. Although a truly agricultural piece of equipment by today's standards, it nonetheless worked. Reliable detection range of a destroyer was in the order of nine miles.

8   *Suffolk*'s captain had been confronted with the same problem when radar was first fitted to that ship. He later recorded that when he took command he found a newly installed radar outfit: 'Not a soul could tell me a thing about its tactical implications. I had to figure it out for myself from such basic knowledge as I had or could add to experimentally at sea.' Unfortunately for *Bismarck*, he had the time to figure it out before *Suffolk* made contact. See Howse, *Radar at Sea*, p. 98.

9   Dyer, *The Amphibians*, p. 302.
10   Griffith, *The Battle*, p. 58.
11   Dyer, *The Amphibians*, p. 300.
12   Vandegrift, *Once a Marine*, p. 120.
13   Dyer, *The Amphibians*, pp. 300–02.
14   Griffith, *The Battle*, p. 58, quoting from the unpublished 'United States Naval Administration in World War 2: Commander in Chief Pacific Fleet Amphibious Force', vol. 1.
15   Dyer, *The Amphibians*, p. 301.
16   NHC, Morison Papers, box 27. Turner's remark was included in notes that Hepburn's assistant, Ramsey, prepared for Morison's use in writing *The Struggle for Guadalcanal*. Ramsey did not reveal who his source was, but did say that Callaghan had been aware of the remark. These were strong words for anyone to use to a holder of the highest American decoration for courage, the Congressional Medal of Honor, and must therefore be taken as an indication of the extent of the anger that Turner felt at Fletcher's proposal.
17   NHC, Morison Papers, box 25—Record of CINCPAC's conference in *Argonne*.

Chapter 9

1   Commander Task Force 62, Operation Plan A3-42 dated 30 July 1942, in Hepburn, Annex E10.
2   Hepburn, Annex B2.
3   ibid. p. 44.

4 There were four publications used throughout the Royal Navy: *Fleet Signal Book* (FSB), *Conduct of the Fleet, Fleet Tactical Instructions* and *Fighting Instructions.*

5 Statement submitted by Crutchley regarding the Savo Island battle dated 21 February 1943, in Hepburn, Annex B1.

6 NHC, Morison Papers, box 27.

7 Statement by Crutchley regarding battle of Savo Island, 21 February 1943 (in which he discussed fully the philosophy behind his dispositions), in Hepburn, Annex B1.

8 ibid.

9 'Watchtower—The Capture and Occupation by United Nations Forces of Tulagi and Guadalcanal', Hepburn, Annex B2, and AA (Vic), MP 1587/1, file 105E.

10 Griffith, *The Battle*, p. 64.

11 Bates, p. 36.

12 The differences between the two systems were fully discussed by Hepburn, p. 48 *et seq.*

Chapter 10

1 Bates, p. 35.

2 Griffith, *The Battle*, chap. 4.

3 Vandegrift, *Once a Marine*, p. 124.

4 Griffith, *The Battle*, p. 76.

5 ibid. p. 79.

6 Vandegrift, *Once a Marine*, p. 12.

7 Feldt, *The Coast Watchers*, p. 115.

8 The author remembers the broadcast as 'Do you hear there. The force will be attacked by enemy aircraft at about 1300. Hands to dinner.'

9 Bates, p. 47.

10 ibid. p. 48.

11 ibid. p. 66.

12 ibid. p. 66.

13 Vandegrift, *Once a Marine*, p. 123.

14 Hepburn, p. 11.

15 ibid. p. 42.

16 Dyer, *The Amphibians*, p. 371.

17 Hepburn, Annex T, p. 677.

18 Deck Log HMAS *Australia*, August 1942, AA (NSW).

19 Feldt, *The Coast Watchers*, p. 144, and Griffith, p. 77.

20 Bates, p. 84.

21 Hepburn, Annex B2, and AA (Vic), MP 1587/1, file 105E.

22 This and other information on carrier operations has been extracted from NWC Archives, Research Group 23, box 35, item 5.

23 ibid.

24 This account of the failure to provide adequately for the air defence of the forces off Guadalcanal is, in places, contrary to Bates' NWC Analysis, which

found that the first eight fighters from *Saratoga* arrived in time to join in the defence—thus contradicting the statement of the leader of those aircraft. It is by no means the only example in that document which took the soft option when the performance of American units was in question.

25 Commander SWPA message 071219Z, Hepburn, Annex T, p. 671.
26 Hepburn, p. 11.
27 Commander SWPA message 081130Z, Hepburn, Annex T, p. 674.

Chapter 11

1 Bates, p. 94.
2 CTF 61's message 080707Z, Hepburn, Annex T, p. 659.
3 Bates, p. 94.
4 Message from CTF 61 to TF 61.1 080317 August, NWC Archives, Research Group 23, box 46, Savo Island War Diaries.
5 Vandegrift, *Once a Marine*, p. 129.
6 Griffith, *The Battle*, p. 80.
7 Comments by Turner to Morison, NHC, Morison Papers, box 24, folder 'The Battle of Savo Island 1943'.
8 Evidence of Lieutenant Commanders Plunkett-Cole and Mesley, minutes of *Canberra* Board of Inquiry, pp. 3, 9.
9 Transcript of a talk given by Captain Riefkohl in the Pentagon, 26 January 1945, NHC, Morison Papers, box 26.
10 MacArthur's headquarters sent Ghormley a message at 1817 that day giving their appreciation that the cruisers and seaplane tenders were probably engaged in setting up a base in the Shortland Islands.
11 'Ramsey on Savo', NHC, Morison Papers, box 27, folder 'Savo Island and Cape Esperance'.
12 Turner's answers to Hepburn's questionnaire, Hepburn, Annex F, p. 272.
13 ibid.
14 A copy of Walker's night orders for that night is held by the author. Walker was to serve under Crutchley's command for another nine months and was held in high regard by him.
15 Bates, p. 136.
16 Vandegrift, *Once a Marine*, p. 128.
17 ibid. p. 129.
18 Operation Watchtower—The Capture and Occupation by United Nations Forces of Tulagi and Guadalcanal, para 92, Hepburn, Annex B2, and AA (Vic), MP 1587/1, file 105E.
19 This account of the circumstances in which *Jarvis* left the sound is based on that given by Turner in his letter to Rear Admiral Welborn dated 20 August 1950, commenting on Morison's *The Struggle for Guadalcanal* (NHC, Morison Papers, box 27). He contradicts Gill's statement in *Royal Australian Navy 1942–45* (p. 142) that *Jarvis* was bound for Vila. Gill was apparently unaware that *Jarvis* had been seen by *Blue* off Cape Esperance and that she had been sunk to the south of Guadalcanal.

Chapter 12

1 Ohmae, 'The Battle', p. 1264.
2 Letter, Captain Itonaga to author, 21 June 1991.
3 Bates, p. 168.
4 Ohmae, 'The Battle', p. 1267.
5 ibid. p. 1268.
6 Bates, p. 10.
7 ibid. p. 7.
8 ibid. p. 8.
9 This move by native labour had taken Clemens, the coastwatcher in eastern Guadalcanal, some days to accomplish; 'The Battle of Savo Island', a paper delivered to the Naval Historical Society of Australia (Victorian Chapter) by Major W.F.M. Clemens.
10 Bates, p. 10.
11 ibid. p. 44.
12 Ohmae, 'The Battle', p. 1269.
13 Nevertheless a Japanese unit *did* sight the carriers: a coastwatching station on Cape Hunter on the south coast of Guadalcanal. An attempt was made to report the sighting at 1035 of a large force consisting of a battleship, two aircraft carriers, five cruisers and approximately ten other ships. The course of Watchtower might have changed dramatically had that station been able to contact its controlling station on Lunga Point, but it had been knocked out by the landings and the coastwatchers' radio lacked the power to pass the message direct to Rabaul. It was not until a submarine contacted the post on 12 August that the report could be passed. See p. 92 of a partial translation by Rear Admiral Layton of the Japanese Defence Agency's War History Publications, Naval Operations in the South East Area, vol. 1; NWC, Edwin T. Layton Papers, box 34, folder 9.
14 ibid. p. 1270.
15 ibid. p. 1278. The statement was made by Mikawa after he had read Ohmae's article in which he testified to the completeness and accuracy of it.
16 Mikawa's statement on Ohmae's article; Ohmae, 'The Battle', p. 1278.
17 Ohmae, 'The Battle', p. 1270.
18 Dull, *The Japanese Navy*, p. 184.
19 Itonaga letter, 3 October 1991.
20 The War College found that *I-122* was delayed for 24 hours in Rabaul, but research of Japanese records by Captain Itonaga revealed that the two submarines left together from Rabaul and arrived off Guadalcanal on the afternoon of 9 August. These were the two submarines attacked by Hudson 218 (flown by Sergeant Stutt) to the west of Guadalcanal on 8 August.
21 Bates, pp. 78–80.
22 *Kako* War Diary, 7–10 August 1942, NHC, Morison Papers, box 27, folder 'The Battle of the Eastern Solomons, 1942–43'.
23 Bates, p. 73.
24 Itonaga's letter, 15 October 1990.
25 Itonaga's letter, 16 July 1990.

26 Captain Emile Bonnot's unpublished paper, p. 4. Itonaga's letter of 16 July
    1990 also quotes from *Chokai*'s War Diary.
27 Itonaga's letter, 15 October 1990. No further sightings of Allied aircraft were
    made that day.
28 Ohmae, 'The Battle', p. 1271. *Aoba*'s operations officer had been a member
    of the crew of the aircraft, which probably accounts for the quality of the
    report.
29 ibid.
30 Itonaga's letter, 16 July 1990.
31 ibid.
32 Mikawa's intentions and instructions were contained in his Signal Order No.
    25 which he originated at 1640 and passed by semaphore (Bates, pp. 75–6).
33 *Canberra* defuelled her aircraft at dusk as a matter of routine but the fuel was
    stowed in tanks on the upper deck either side amidships beneath the 4-inch
    gun deck which was to take very heavy punishment in the action. The fuel
    tanks were, however, safely jettisoned.
34 Ohmae, 'The Battle', p. 1272.
35 See Marder, *Old Friends, New Enemies*, vol. 1, pp. 265–84, for a summary
    of the training that a Japanese officer underwent at Eta Jima and a comparison
    between that training and the training afforded young Royal Naval officers at
    Dartmouth.
36 Itonaga's letter, 16 July 1990.

Chapter 13

1   Hepburn, p. 11.
2   Bates, p. 68
3   Hepburn, p. 10.
4   Layton, *And I Was There*, p. 458.
5   Extracted from 'The Role of Communications Intelligence in the American
    Japanese Naval War—Volume 3. The Solomon Islands Campaign. 1. Back-
    ground of the Landings on Guadalcanal Island and the Battle of Savo Island
    (July 1— August 9 1942)' dated 23 June 1943, National Library of Australia,
    Canberra.
6   ibid.
7   Hepburn, Annex T, p. 674.
8   COMAIRSOPAC Op Plan 1–42 of 25 July 1942, Hepburn, Annex E8.
9   Hepburn, p. 42 para 85, and Bates, p. 98.
10 Dyer, *The Amphibians*, p. 371.
11 Gill, *Royal Australian Navy*, p. 13.
12 Bates, p. 99.
13 NHC, Morison Papers, box 24, folder 'The Battle of Savo Island 1943'. Turner
    was responding to a request from the Deputy CNO (Administration) in Wash-
    ington for his comments on Morison's book.
14 Hepburn, Annex T, p. 648.
15 NHC, Morison Papers, box 26, Savo Island.
16 Hepburn, Annex F.

17 Bates, pp. 95–6.
18 COMSOPAC's Op Plan 1–42 of 16 July, Annex A.
19 Bates, p. 97.

Chapter 14

1 This and subsequent information on the sortie of Hudson 218 was obtained
   from conversations and correspondance with the pilot and captain (Sergeant
   Stutt), navigator (Sergeant Courtis) and radio operator (Sergeant Geddes), as
   well as from the Daily Record and Signal Log of ACH Townsville now held
   by the AWM.
2 Gill, *Royal Australian Navy*, p. 50.
3 Coulthard-Clark, *Action Stations Coral Sea*, p. 136.
4 These submarines were *I-121* and *I-122*, *en route* from Rabaul to Guadalcanal
   where they arrived on the afternoon of 9 August.
5 Denis and Peggy Warner, with Sadeo Seno, *Disaster in the Pacific*, (hereafter
   referred to as Warners), p. 240.
6 Hepburn, Annex T, p. 655.
7 The author first heard this rumour while serving in HMAS *Arunta* immediately
   after the war, probably from Gatacre who was then captain of the ship.
8 Letter, Captain Itonaga to author, 8 August 1990.
9 Hepburn, p. 55, para 139d.
10 Geddes was replying to a request for information from the General Editor of
   the *Official War History* in Canberra.
11 Hepburn, Annex T, p. 655.
12 Bates, p. 103.
13 Mervyn Willman died in October 1990 after a successful career as a barrister
   in New South Wales where he was Crown Prosecutor for a number of years.
   He joined the RAAF Reserve after the war in his wartime rank of Squadron
   Leader, a measure of the regard in which his Service held him, and continued
   in the Reserve for many years. His immediate family and Sergeant Courtis
   provided much of the information on the sortie of Hudson 185.
14 Warners, p. 17.
15 A translation by Captain Itonaga from *Kaisen* (Sea battle) by Niwa Fumio.
16 Denis and Peggy Warner, *Kamikaze*, p. 187.
17 Loxton, 'Three Cruisers, Three Destroyers, Two Seaplane Tenders', USNI
   Proceedings, August 1992, p. 80.
18 Itonaga's letter, 3 October 1991.
19 Fall River's Form White 3/8, ACH Townsville Daily Record for 8 August 1942
   held by AWM. One account of this sortie (Warners, p. 17) reports that Milne
   sighted the Japanese and shadowed them for half an hour but there is no
   mention of this in the Form White. Flight Lieutenant Milne sighted the
   Japanese the following day as they were returning to their bases. According
   to the War Diaries of *Chokai*, *Kinugasa* and *Tenryu*, summarised on microfilm
   JT1 held by the NHC, the aircraft that sighted them on the 9th also attacked
   them. It had remained in sight of them for 43 minutes. Very probably, therefore,

there has been some confusion over the dates of Milne's sighting of Mikawa's cruisers.

Chapter 15

1   Ramsey graduated from Annapolis in 1924 and after completing a postgraduate course in law at George Washington University in June 1939, he commanded the destroyer USS *Hughes* for three years before being relieved in December 1942. He was awarded the Silver Star Medal for service in the Guadalcanal area in September 1942 and the Navy Cross for his work in attempting the salvage of the carrier *Hornet* in October the same year at the Battle of Santa Cruz. In between several Japanese air attacks he had taken his ship alongside the burning carrier to assist with fire fighting but eventually had to give up the attempt to save her. Abandoned, she was later sunk by Japanese destroyers. Ramsey was therefore well qualified professionally and by experience to assist Hepburn. He retired in July 1947 in the rank of rear admiral. Biography supplied by NHC.

2   Hepburn, Annex T, p. 686b.

3   ibid. p. 41.

4   NHC, Morison Papers, box 26, 'Notes on Guadalcanal 1943'.

5   Morison, *The Struggle for Guadalcanal*, p. 25.

6   Newcomb, *Savo*, p. 74.

7   Bonnot based much of his paper on the research of Nancy Milne and on information provided by Major Martin Clemens.

8   Information provided by the Australian Ionosphere Prediction Service at Chatswood, NSW, in a letter to the author dated 23 January 1991. From the information provided by the IPS, it was also established that the message could not have been received in Sydney and probably not in Brisbane.

9   Warners, p. 11.

10   The minutes of the first report of the *Canberra* Board of Inquiry, p. 11, AA (Vic), MP 1587/1, file 105H.

11   Warners, *Kamikaze*, p. 185, and Dull, *The Japanese Navy*, p. 333

12   Hepburn, Annex D3.

13   ibid. Annex F, p. 271.

14   ibid. p. 54, para 133.

15   Warners, p. 233.

16   Hepburn, p. 41. That particular recollection of Turner's is not included in the Report or its Annexes.

17   Dyer, *The Amphibians*, p. 372.

18   The message quoted was a garbled version of what had been originated in Brisbane at 2047 as 'Air sighting 0001Z/8 position 05 42 S, 156 05 E. 2CA, 2CL, 1 small unidentified. 1 cruiser similar Southampton class. When plane attempted correct approach ships opened fire. At 0120Z/8 sighted small merchant vessel in 07 02S 156 25E course 290 speed 10.' The mistakes, resulting from attempts to fill in bits that were obviously missed by the radio operator reading the message, are interesting. They are an indication of the standard of communication personnel in the Amphibious Force and may explain why so

many messages were not logged as having been received. Perhaps they were too garbled to patch. Hepburn, Annex T, p. 665.

19 Warners, p. 234.
20 ibid. p. 245.
21 ibid. p. 236. The emphasis is the author's.
22 AA (Vic), MP 1587/1, file 105A, Solomons 'Watchtower' Ops, Crutchley's Report of Proceedings (hereafter referred to simply as Crutchley) and Hepburn, Annex B.
23 Warners, p. 234.
24 Crutchley consistently reported the time of receipt of the report received via Canberra as 0817 but this was the time at which the message was originated. *Australia* actually received that report at 1837.
25 Letter from Crutchley to Gatacre dated 30 May 1960, a copy of which is in the possession of the author.
26 Hepburn, Annex M4, p. 382.
27 ibid. Annex M1, p. 371.
28 ibid. Annex M9, p. 412.
29 NHC, Morison Papers, box 26, 'Savo Island 1942–49'.
30 Warners, p. 234.
31 ibid. p. 231.
32 Hepburn, Annex O, p. 477.
33 ibid. p. 454.
34 ibid. p. 561.
35 Warners, p. 232.
36 Hepburn, Annex I, p. 318.
37 ibid. p. 313.
38 ibid. p. 313.
39 Warners, p. 241.
40 Hepburn, Annex N, p. 452.
41 ibid. p. 422.
42 ibid. p. 441.
43 Warners, p. 239.
44 Captain Sherman's letter to Morison dated 14 February 1949, NHC, Morison Papers, Box 27, 'Savo Island and Cape Esperance 1942–49'.
45 The Report and Minutes of the Board of Inquiry are to be found in AA (Vic), MP 1587/1, file 105H. The report is also to be found in Hepburn, Annex J, together with the submissions to the Board by Commander Walsh, Lieutenant Commander Wight and Commander (E) McMahon.
46 Hepburn, Annex T, p. 686b.
47 ACH Signal Log, AWM File 66.
48 Warners, p. 11.
49 COMSOPAC's Op Plan 1–42 of 16 July 1942, AA (Vic), MP 1290/1, file 29, and Hepburn, Annex E1.
50 Hepburn, Annex T, p. 658. There is a conflict here with the Warners' statement that there would appear to have been no provision for monitoring coastwatcher frequencies (see Warners, p. 249).
51 ibid. p. 654.

Chapter 16

1 Bates, p. 90, and Hepburn, p. 35.
2 Crutchley, p. 19, and Hepburn, Annex B.
3 Evidence of Lieutenant Commander Wight, first report of *Canberra* Board of Inquiry, Question 117, and of Commander Walsh, second report of the same Board, Question 503.
4 Statement by Riefkohl, Hepburn, Annex M(4), p. 377.
5 Morison, *The Struggle for Guadalcanal*, p. 44.
6 Crutchley, p. 19.
7 Letter, Itonaga to author, 16 July 1990.
8 Layton, *And I Was There*, p. 459.
9 Biard, unpublished ms., p. 26. This is not to say that Turner's refusal to embark a signal intelligence team was justified; it most certainly was not.
10 A quotation from the Foreword, written by Roskill, to Newcomb's *Savo*.
11 C-in-C 8th Fleet War Diary cited in Itonaga's letter to author, 15 October 1990; Ohmae, 'The Battle', p. 1273.
12 This problem would have been paralleled in the Allied cruiser force had they been concentrated. See Action Report of Cruiser Division 18 in NHC, Morison Papers, box 27, folder 'The Battle of the Eastern Solomons 1942–43'. See also p. 112 of a partial translation by Rear Admiral Layton of the Japanese Defence Agency's War History Publications, Naval Operations in the South East Area, vol. 1; NWC, Edwin T. Layton Papers, box 34, folder 9.
13 C-in-C Eighth Fleet's War Diary quoted by Itonaga; also Dull, *The Japanese Navy*, p. 187.
14 From the records of Cruiser Division Eighteen and Itonaga's letter of 15 October 1990.
15 Bates, p. 110. It would seem that the analysts had no feeling for relative motion. *Chokai* was closing on *Blue* at a relative speed of only eleven knots which cannot be considered rapid.
16 Bates, p. 108. Apparently believing that *Chokai* had made the sighting on a bearing of 159, not 059 as recorded by the Japanese, the analysts identified the contact as being the same small craft that *Aoba* and *Furutaka* were to see as they moved south-east. See Bates, Diagram E. *Blue* was also to sight the schooner.
17 Bates, p. 112.
18 Interview of Mikawa by Pineau in Tokyo, 13 June 1949, NHC, Morison Papers, box 8.
19 Hepburn, p. 20.
20 Ohmae, 'The Battle', p. 1273.
21 Hepburn, Annex G2, The deck logs of American ships which took part in Watchtower are to be found in the National Archives, Washigton D.C. There was a significant difference between the type of information entered in the deck logs of American ships and that entered in British and Australian ships. In American ships, navigational details were rarely entered whereas in *Canberra*, for example, great care was taken to record such details as would be necessary to allow the track of the ship to be reconstructed in the event of a

collision or grounding. This required the entry of alterations of courses and speeds and, from time to time, geographical positions. It was noticeable that in the case of *Blue*'s Deck Log, details of courses steered were provided for the middle watch and part of the morning watch on 9 August only; that is, from about midnight to 0430. The previous night the entries had been confined to 'Patrolling on course 051 and 231' in the middle watch and 'Steaming as before' in the morning watch. On neither night were details entered for the watches between dusk and midnight.

22 MacIsaac, *U.S. Strategic Bombing Survey*, vol. 2, interrogation no. 109.
23 Gatacre, *Report*, p. 174. Just who described to him the nearness of the *Blue* in such terms is unclear, but it was probably Admiral Nobue Morishita with whom Gatacre discussed Savo. According to Itonaga, the phrase is not to be found in any Japanese official or personal record of the battle.
24 Captain Yuuji Takahashi survived the sinking of *Kako* off Kavieng on 10 August and was eventually promoted to rear admiral. In 1967 he wrote *Tettei Kaikyou: Iron Bottom Sound*, published by the Mainichi Press. Itonaga letter, 8 November 1990.
25 Gatacre, *Report*, p. 174.
26 Itonaga letter, 16 July 1990.
27 Itonaga letter, 8 November 1990.
28 ibid.

Chapter 17

1 Evidence of Lieutenant Commander Plunkett-Cole to *Canberra* Board of Inquiry, AA (Vic), MP 1587/1, file 105H.
2 Bates, p. 126.
3 This account of the Battle of Savo Island is based on the NWC Analysis except where stated.
4 Letter, Itonaga to author, 16 July 1990.
5 It was estimated by the Japanese that 40 per cent of their torpedoes exploded prematurely during the series of actions now known as the Battle of the Java Sea. The fault was not finally eradicated until mid-1943.
6 The last moments of *Canberra*'s command team have been distilled from the accounts which surviving members provided for the Board of Inquiry, AA (Vic), MP 1587/1, file 105H.
7 Evidence of Mr Andrews, Gunner, Appendix K, and of Mr Hardiman, Commissioned Gunner, Appendix H and Question 219, *Canberra* Board of Inquiry, AA (Vic), MP 1587/1, file 105H.
8 Author's conversation with the Damage Control Officer, Lieutenant (E) Mussared, 1990.
9 AA (Vic), MP 1587/1, file 105E.
10 *Canberra* was at a disadvantage vis-a-vis *Australia* in that the gunnery control position and the director were separate, only the latter rotating. As a result of her modernisation, *Australia* had a combined gunnery control position and director in a director control tower which provided the gunnery control officer with a platform which could be stabilised in azimuth. Had the DCT been given

an enemy bearing of 310, for example, the director—including the director gun sight—would have remained on that bearing as the ship altered course. This would have simplified Hardiman's task of acquiring a target.

11 Correspondence with Ordinary Seaman Warne, October 1992.
12 Evidence of Commander (E) McMahon to *Canberra* Board of Inquiry, Appendix B and Questions 563–594 listed in the Board's first report, and Questions 1–72 included in the second report, AA (Vic), MP 1587/1, file 105H and MP 1049/5, file 2026/3/501.
13 Second report of the *Canberra* Board of Inquiry dated 30 September 1942, AA (Vic), MP 1049/5, file 2026/3/501.
14 Observations by Commander Task Force 44 on Report of Inquiry regarding the loss of HMAS *Canberra*, AA (Vic), MP 1049/5, file 2026/3/501.
15 Letter dated 12 September 1942 by Rear Admiral in Charge HMA Naval Establishments, Sydney, AA (Vic), MP 1049/5, file 2026/3/501.
16 Author's correspondence with Alan Payne in 1972–73. Both as a survivor from *Canberra* and as the Director of Naval Intelligence, Canberra, the author assisted Payne in his compilation of his history of the ship. Walsh must have been disturbed by the Board of Inquiry's finding that McMahon had been the principal driving force about the upper deck after the battle. There is ample evidence that Walsh, though injured, was exercising command; this was later confirmed by Mesley in letters to Payne. The Board's high opinion of McMahon would seem to be largely based on McMahon. According to Payne, Crutchley had a poor opinion of him.
17 Evidence of McMahon to the first session of the inquiry, Question 566, AA (Vic), MP 1587/1, file 105H.
18 Loss of HMAS *Canberra* dated 8 November 1942 by Commander Task Force 44, AA (Vic), MP 1049/5, file 2026/3/501.
19 AA (Vic), MP 1049/5, file 2026/3/501.
20 Corroborative evidence of St George's sighting was provided in correspondence with Ordinary Seaman Warne in October 1992. He had heard St George tell of seeing the torpedo damage at the time. He may not have been surprised at what St George had told him, as he was among those who heard or felt something which seemed more than a shell explosion. In 1992 he recalled that 'the sounds of explosions were of two different types. Some were somewhat sharper than the extended whump that rattled my teeth after which the sudden lurch commenced.' He was not called upon to provide a written account of his experiences or to give evidence to the Board of Inquiry.
21 From a statement made by Whitmire after the sinking of *Canberra* (he did not give evidence to the Board of Inquiry), AA (Vic), MP 1049/5, file 2026/3/501.
22 Evidence of Lieutenant Commander Mesley to the *Canberra* Board of Inquiry, Appendix D, AA (Vic), MP 1587/1, file 105H.

Chapter 18

1 Bates, p. 116 *et seq*, and plates V–XIV.
2 Hepburn, Annex K, and Crutchley, Appendix 8.
3 Letter, E. McClarty to author, 24 March 1993.

4 Letter, R. Orr to author, 28 April 1993.

5 Letter, John L. Williams to author, 30 April 1993.

6 Hepburn, Annex K, and Crutchley, Appendix 8.

7 Bates, p. 55.

8 Evidence of Lieutenant Commander Wight to the *Canberra* Board of Inquiry, q.400, AA (Vic), MP 1587/1, file 105H.

9 Correspondence with Gregory dated 31 March 1992 and subsequent conversations.

10 Author's midshipman's journal.

11 Conversations with Gregory, December 1992.

12 Hepburn, p. 20 para 57A.

13 Correspondence with members of the USS *Bagley* Association, December 1992–August 1993, and 'The Six Long Years', an unpublished account of the experiences in *Bagley* of Radioman 2nd Class George Sallet.

14 Letter, Captain William Hunnicutt, USN (Rtd) to author, 5 September 1993. Hunnicutt was the Gunnery Officer of *Bagley* at Savo in the rank of Lieutenant (JG).

15 Letter, John L. Williams to author, 30 April 1993.

16 Correspondence in October 1992 with Mr Bert Warne, who represented *Canberra* survivors in the expedition's task of identifying and surveying the wreck. Also, from my own observation in Washington of both video tapes and still photographs of *Canberra* on the bottom, December 1993. Dr Ballard's expedition to Iron Bottom Sound is described in the book *The Lost Ships of Guadalcanal*.

17 The first report of the *Canberra* Board of Inquiry, p. 6, AA (Vic), MP 1587/1, file 105H.

18 This attitude still exists and may well be the reason why Getting's name was not among those to be given to the six Collins Class submarines now under construction in Adelaide. As the first graduate of the Royal Australian Naval College to command an Australian submarine, HMAS *Oxley*, his omission is especially notable.

19 Letter from Bates to Commander Dan Drain of DNI's Staff, Washington, dated 9 August 1954. NWC, Richard W. Bates Papers, box 3, folder 11.

20 Letter from C-in-C United States Fleet to Secretary of the Navy, 14 September 1943, AA (Vic), MP 1185/8, file 1932/2/226.

21 Hepburn, p. 20.

22 NHC, Morison Papers, box 24, Folder 'Acknowledgements'.

23 Warners, p. 247.

24 Williams, USS *Bagley*, p. 101.

25 Commander Sinclair had left the ship earlier in February, having been relieved by his Executive Officer.

26 Letter from Gatacre to Crutchley, 27 May 1960, a copy of which is held by the author.

27 Bates, p. 34. Part of that diagram is reproduced in the insert map on p. 179.

Chapter 19

1 Hepburn, Appendixes H, L, M, N, O and P; Crutchley, Appendix 17—a letter from *Ralph Talbot* dated 15 August 1942, amplifying original action report.

2 Wight's evidence to *Canberra* Board of Inquiry, question 400 listed in the first report of the board, AA (Vic), MP 1587/1, file 105H.
3 Bates, p. 136.
4 Crutchley, Appendix 9: *Patterson*'s Report of the Engagement with Enemy Surface Ships Night 8–9 August.
5 MacIsaac, *US Strategic Bombing Survey*, vol. 1, interrogation no. 61 (Rear Admiral Matsuyama) carried out on 31 October 1945.
6 Bates, p. 121.
7 ibid. p. 166.
8 Captain Bode was also ashore on that occasion and was dining with Rear Admiral Muirhead-Gould when the incoming midget submarines were detected.
9 Statement by Commander Irish, Hepburn, Appendix I, p. 317.
10 Crutchley, Appendix 7, and Hepburn, Annex I, p. 319 *et seq.*
11 Memorandum to Hepburn by Bode dated 3 April 1943, Hepburn, Annex I, p. 309.
12 Statement by Lieutenant (E) Mussared contained in the bundle of survivors' reports not considered by the Board of Inquiry, AA (Vic), MP 1049/5, file 2026/3/501.
13 Statement by Chief Yeoman of Signals Gunthorp, Appendix I to the first report of the *Canberra* Board of Inquiry, AA (Vic), MP 1587/1, file 105H.
14 Statements by Chief Petty Officer Telegraphist Thompson, Yeoman of Signals Webster, and Seaman 1st Class Whitmire contained in the bundle of survivors' reports not considered by the Board of Inquiry, AA (Vic), MP 1049/5, file 2026/3/501.
15 Crutchley, Annex 5.
16 ibid.
17 ibid.
18 From the unpublished memoir by Captain John Lacouture, USN (Rtd), who served as the gunnery officer in *Blue* at Savo.
19 Captain of *Blue*'s letter dated 12 August 1942, Crutchley, Appendix 6, and Hepburn, Annex G, p. 282.
20 Captain of *Blue*'s letter dated 17 August 1942, Hepburn, Annex G, p. 284.

Chapter 20

1 Bates, p. 122.
2 Bates, p. 153 *et seq.*
3 Hepburn p. 50 para 109.
4 Letter from Crutchley to Gatacre dated 30 May 1960, a copy of which is in the possession of the author.
5 Commanding Officer USS *Vincennes*: Report of Action off Savo Island, night of 8–9 August 1942, dated 16 August 1942; Hepburn, Annex M(4), pp. 382 *et seq.*; Crutchley, Appendix 14.
6 Statement by Radioman 2nd Class W.H. Franzer, excerpts from reports submitted by various officers and men attached to USS *Vincennes*, Hepburn, Annex M(9), p. 411.

7 Hepburn, Annex M(4), pp. 382 *et seq.*
8 Further interrogation of Captains Riefkohl and Bode at Corpus Christi, Texas, 3 April 1943, Hepburn, Annex M(1), p. 371.
9 Hepburn, Annex M(4), p. 384.
10 Hepburn, p. 25 para 62a.
11 Report of gunnery control officer (Lieutenant Commander R.L. Adams USN), Hepburn, Annex M(7), p. 400; Bates, p. 152.
12 Lieutenant Commander Heneberger—Preliminary report of engagement on the night of 9 August 1942 off Guadalcanal, dated 12 August 1942, Hepburn, Annex N(2), p. 425 para 2.
13 ibid. pp. 425 and 427 para 4.
14 Bates, p. 178.
15 Interrogation of Lieutenant Commander Heneberger, Gunnery Officer and senior survivor USS *Quincy*, Hepburn, Annex N(1), p. 422 para 12.
16 ibid. para 13.
17 Report submitted by First Lieutenant and Damage Control Officer USS *Astoria* (supervisory officer of the deck from 0000 to 0155), dated 17 August 1942, Hepburn, Annex O(6), p. 536.
18 Report of cruiser night action 9 August 1942 submitted by Gunnery Officer, 13 August 1942, Hepburn, Annex O(8), p. 549.
19 Statement of R.A. Radke, QM2c USN (Quartermaster of the 0000–0400 watch on 9 August), Hepburn, Annex O(10), p. 563.
20 Bates, p. 141.
21 Commanding Officer USS *Astoria* report on the Battle of Savo Island—Action Cruisers Task Group 62.3, early morning 9 August 1942—loss of USS *Astoria*, Hepburn, Annex O(3), p. 488.
22 Bates, pp. 152–9.
23 Further interrogation of Captains Riefkohl and Bode, 3 April 1943, Hepburn, Annex M(1), p. 376.
24 Dull, *The Japanese Navy*, p. 333.
25 Bates, p. 70. The information used by Bates was extracted from War Instructions US Navy 1934 (FTP 143), chap IX: Night Encounters, p. 44, and RN Fighting Instructions 1939, chapter: Night Action, para P.
26 Statement of Radioman 3rd Class Huse, excerpts from reports submitted by various officers and men attached to USS *Vincennes*, Hepburn, Annex M(9), p. 409.
27 Bates, p. 172.
28 ibid. p. 175.
29 ibid. p. 176.
30 ibid. p. 175.
31 ibid. p. 180–2. The author can personally testify to the effects of *Aoba*'s excellent gunnery, as he shared a ward in the hospital ship USS *Solace* for some days after the battle with many of the wounded from *Quincy*, the majority of whom were very badly burned as a result of those fires. It seemed at the time that *Quincy*'s ordeal had been far worse than the other ships.
32 Report submitted by First Lieutenant and Damage Control Officer USS *Astoria* (supervisory Officer of the Deck 0000 to 0155), dated 17 August 1942, Hepburn, Annex O(6), p. 537.

33   ibid.
34   ibid.
35   Bates, pp. 194–6.
36   Statements by Chief Quartermaster Stark and Quartermaster 3rd Class Petersen, excerpts from reports submitted by various officers and men attached to USS *Vincennes*, Hepburn, Annex M, pp. 409, 411.
37   Bates, p. 290.
38   ibid.
39   ibid. pp. 185–7.
40   ibid. p. 236.
41   ibid. pp. 239–40.
42   ibid. p. 241.
43   Ohmae, 'The Battle', p. 1275.
44   Bates, p. 242.
45   ibid. p. 291.
46   ibid. p. 244.
47   ibid. p. 245.
48   ibid. p. 215.
49   Commanding Officer USS *Astoria*: Report of the Battle of Savo, dated 20 August 1942, Hepburn, Annex O(3), p. 481.
50   ibid. also Annex O(3), p. 480 para 161.
51   Bates, p. 248.
52   ibid. p. 482 para 19.
53   ibid. p. 246.
54   ibid. p. 295.

Chapter 21

1   Commanding Officer USS *Helm*: Report of night engagement off Savo Island, Solomon Islands, 9 August 1942, dated 12 August 1942; Bates, p. 291, Hepburn, Annex Q(3), p. 613, and Crutchley, Appendix 12.
2   Commanding Officer USS *Wilson*: Report of action against enemy surface ships off Savo Island, night of 8–9 August 1942, dated 20 August 1942; Hepburn, Annex P(1), p. 600, and Crutchley, Appendix 13.
3   War Instructions US Navy 1934, FTP 143, and Bates, p. 199.
4   Hepburn, p. 44, para 93.
5   Commander South Pacific's Report: Cruiser Action off Savo Island on the night of 8–9 August 1942, dated 17 October 1942; AA (Vic), MP 1587/1, file 105N.
6   Commanding Officer USS *Ralph Talbot*: Preliminary report of action on 8–9 August 1942, dated 11 August 1942; Crutchley, Appendix 17, and Hepburn, Annex H(2).
7   Commanding Officer USS *Ralph Talbot*: General account of night action off Savo Island, dated 11 August 1942; Hepburn, Annex H(1).
8   Bates, pp. 263–4.
9   Itonaga letter, 16 July 1990.

10 Commanding Officer USS *Ralph Talbot*: General account of night action off Savo Island, dated 11 August 1942; Hepburn, Annex H(1), p. 285.

11 Ohmae, 'The Battle', p. 1276.

12 Before he left Tokyo for Rabaul, Mikawa was told by the Chief of the Naval General Staff, Admiral Osami Nagano, that as Japan's industrial power was small, he was to see to it that their ships were not destroyed. This warning was undoubtedly a factor in Mikawa's decision to withdraw. See p. 124 of a partial translation by Rear Admiral Layton of the Japanese Defence Agency's War History Publications, Naval Operations in the South East Area, vol. 1; NWC, Edwin T. Layton Papers, box 34, folder 9.

13 Bates, p. 368.

Chapter 22

1 Evidence of Commander Walsh to the second session of the Board of Inquiry, question 503, AA (Vic), MP 1587/1, file 105H. Also, report of the Executive Officer HMAS *Canberra* in Crutchley, Appendix 10.

2 From the transcript of a tape sent to the author by Able Seaman Hall in which he described his experiences. Hall, aged 20, whose action station was in the fore control, was involved in moving the wounded (including the author) from the bridge of *Canberra* and giving them first aid on the forecastle. Though his only medical training had been lectures in first aid, he became part of the medical team assisting the wounded in *Canberra*, and later in *Patterson* and *Barnett*. His experiences included assisting in Surgeon Commander Downward's emergency operation on Captain Getting in *Patterson* and also, for four days virtually non-stop, an American doctor in *Barnett*. He eventually collapsed from exhaustion. For this remarkable effort he was one of the few (all members of the medical parties, and the only able seaman) whose services were later rewarded by a mention in dispatches.

3 From conversations with Lieutenant (E) Williams in 1946–47.

4 Evidence of Lieutenant Commander Plunkett-Cole to the first session of the *Canberra* Board of Inquiry and of Commander Walsh to the second, AA (Vic), MP 1587/1, file 105H.

5 Report of the Commanding Officer USS *Patterson* on the Engagement with Enemy (Japanese) Surface Ships Night 8–9 August, dated 13 August 1942, Crutchley, Appendix 9. Also Hepburn, Annex L.

6 Report of Commanding Officer USS *Chicago* on the Action Against Enemy Forces 9 August 1942, dated 13 August 1942, Crutchley, Appendix 7. Also Hepburn, Annex I(3).

7 Letter, Commanding Officer USS *Patterson* to CTF 44, dated 13 August 1942, Crutchley, Appendix 21.

8 Bates, pp. 289 and 299.

9 Bates, p. 316.

10 Night Action off Savo Island, 9 August 1942—Remarks by CTG 62.6—Preliminary Report dated 11 August 1942, Crutchley, Appendix 5.

11 Bates, p. 317.

12 Night Action off Savo Island, 9 August 1942—Remarks by CTG 62.6—Preliminary Report dated 11 August 1942, Crutchley, Appendix 5.

13 Bates, p. 285.

14 *Selfridge* must have felt a little like the battleships HMS *King George V* and HMS *Rodney* the previous year in the North Atlantic when, having failed to sink *Bismarck* with gunfire, the cruiser *Dorsetshire* was called in to sink her with torpedoes.

15 *Bagley*'s rescue of over 450 men, in what must have been appalling conditions as survivors and rescuers alike were constantly menaced by flying debris from exploding ammunition, was recognised by the award of the Legion of Merit to Commander Sinclair. Undoubtedly, as *Bagley*'s captain, he merited such an award but the citation mistakenly included mention of his skill in placing his ship alongside *Astoria*. Credit for that feat rightly belonged to Lieutenant Commander Chambers. Chambers relieved Sinclair in command of *Bagley* in February 1943 and during the following twelve months he earned a Gold Star in lieu of a Bronze Star for his service in that ship. He further distinguished himself during the Okinawa campaign when the destroyer picket that he was commanding suffered a magazine explosion forward when she was hit by two suicide or kamikaze aircraft. Because the ship lost 80 feet of her bow and was flooded to the forward boiler room, she was unable to go ahead, so Chambers took her astern all the way to Guam. For this feat he was awarded a Silver Star and, for other service off Okinawa, a Bronze Star.

16 Report of Commanding Officer USS *Bagley* on the Night Engagement 9 August 1942—Tulagi Guadalcanal Area, dated 13 August 1942, Crutchley, Appendix 8, and Hepburn, Annex K(2).

17 Commanding Officer USS *Hopkins*' Report of Engagements in Guadalcanal–Florida Area 7–9 August 1942, dated 12 August 1942, AA (Vic), MP 1587/1, file 105E.

18 Report of Commanding Officer USS *Astoria*, Battle Savo Island—Action Cruisers Task Group 62.3 early morning 9 August 1942—loss of USS *Astoria*, dated 20 August 1942, Hepburn, Annex O(3).

19 Report of Commanding Officer USS *Wilson*. Report of Action against Enemy Surface Ships off Savo Island, Night of 8–9 August 1942, dated 20 August 1942, Hepburn, Annex P(1).

20 Bates, p. 294.

21 ibid. pp. 294–5.

22 Report of Commanding Officer USS *Ralph Talbot*, General Account of Night Action off Savo Island—9 August 1942, dated 11 August 1942, Crutchley, Appendix 17, and Hepburn, Annex H(1).

23 Report of Commanding Officer HMAS *Hobart*, Narrative of Night of 8–9 August 1942, Crutchley, Appendix 18.

24 Special Instructions to Screening Group and vessels temporarily assigned, Crutchley, Appendix 3, and Hepburn, Annex B(2).

25 Bates, p. 320.

26 ibid. p. 277.

27 ibid. p. 273.

28 ibid. p. 327.

29 ibid. p. 328.

30 Letter from Vice-Admiral Forrest Sherman to Morison dated 14 February 1949, NHC, Morison Papers, box 27, Folder 'Savo Island and Cape Esperance'.

31 Conversation with Captain H.G. Bradshaw USN (Rtd) in mid-1970 and letter dated 20 January 1991. As a Lieutenant (JG), Bradshaw had been a pilot in the torpedo attack squadron embarked in *Saratoga* at the time.

32 Bates, p. 268.

33 War Diary of *Kako* 7–10 August 1942, Solomons Sea Battle, NHC, Morison Papers, box 27, folder 'The Battle of the Eastern Solomons 1942–43'.

34 Log of Signals In and Out, August 1942, ACH Townsville, AWM file 66, item 18/2/4.

35 Fall River Form White 1/9, ACH Townsville Daily Record for 9 August, AWM.

36 Hepburn, Appendix T(1), p. 650.

37 Message from CTF 61 to COMSOPAC originated at 090315Z (Greenwich Mean Time), NWC Archives, Research Group 23, box 46, item 5.

Chapter 23

1 Crutchley, Appendix 5, AA (Vic), MP 1587/1, file 105E.

2 AA (Vic), MP 1587/1, file 105B.

3 Letter, Crutchley to Royle, 10 August, a copy of which is in the possession of the author.

4 Crutchley had not at that time received a report from *Bagley*.

5 AA (Vic), MP 1587/1, file 105B.

6 Crutchley, AA (Vic), MP 1587/1, file 105E.

7 The board's reports are in AA (Vic), MP 1587/1, file 105H. Statements by those survivors not interviewed by the board are in AA (Vic), MP 1049/5, file 2026/3/501.

8 AA (Vic), MP 1587/1, file 105J.

9 The survivors were greeted on their arrival with a signal from the Naval Board congratulating them on having taken part in an operation of supreme importance, as it heralded the beginning of the Allied offensive in the Pacific. This book might never have been written if the survivors who arrived from Auckland on 15 September had been greeted in like fashion. See AA (Vic), MP 1049/5, file 2026/3/501.

10 AA (Vic), MP 1049/5, file 2026/3/501.

11 AA (Vic), MP 1587/1, file 105H.

12 The report is in AA (Vic), MP 1049/5, file 2026/3/501, and the minutes in MP 1587/1, file 105H.

13 AA (Vic), MP 1049/5, file 2026/3/501.

14 Letter, Minister for Defence to Minister for the Navy, 19 February 1943, AA (Vic), MP 1185/8, file 1932/2/226.

15 Minute, CNS to Minister for the Navy, 3 March 1943, AA (Vic), MP 1185/8, file 1932/2/226.

16 From the transcript of a tape made by Able Seaman Hall for the author.

17 From Nichols, HMAS *Shropshire*.

18 AA (Vic), MP 1587/1, file 105B, and Hepburn, Annex A(4).

19 ibid. Copies of this and later correspondence between Ghormley, Nimitz and

King are held by the Australian Archives, presumably having been obtained from the Office of Naval Records and Library, Washington, by Gill during his research.

20 Nimitz attributed the sending of the report of Stutt's sighting of Mikawa to 'Melbourne radio' apparently in the belief that the RAN's naval radio station was situated near Navy Office, then in Melbourne, not where it was (and still is) at Canberra. This mistake has caused at least one researcher to attribute the report to the RAAF radio station in Melbourne and led them into the error of assuming that Stutt's message had been picked up by such a station.

21 AA (Vic), MP 1587/1, file 105B, and Hepburn, Annex A(4), p. 19 *et seq.*

22 Cruiser Action off Savo Island on the night of 8–9 August 1942 dated 17 October 1942, AA (Vic), MP 1587/1, file 105N, and Hepburn, Annex A(1).

23 Hepburn, Annex A(1), p. 1.

24 The Hepburn Report, with Nimitz's and King's endorsements of it but minus Annexes, is in AA (Vic), MP 1185/8, file 1932/2/226. The full report, with all annexes and various endorsements, is held by NHC.

25 Memo, Turner to Nimitz dated June 1943, filed with Hepburn in NHC.

26 Comparison of the ages of Allied officers at Savo.

Name	Rank	Ship	Born	Age
Ghormley	Vice-Admiral USN		15/10/83	58
McCain	Rear Admiral USN		9/8/84	58
Fletcher	Vice-Admiral USN		29/4/85	57
Noyes	Rear Admiral USN		15/12/85	56
Crutchley	Rear Admiral RN		2/11/93	48
Greenman	Captain USN	*Astoria*	26/8/88	53
Bode	Captain USN	*Chicago*	23/1/89	53
Riefkohl	Captain USN	*Vincennes*	27/2/89	53
Moore	Captain USN	*Quincy*	7/9/91	50
Farncomb	Captain RAN	*Australia*	28/2/99	43
Showers	Captain RAN	*Hobart*	24/5/99	43
Getting	Captain RAN	*Canberra*	30/7/99	43
Walker	Commander USN	*Patterson*	11/7/99	43
Williams	Commander USN	*Blue*	6/4/00	42
Carrol	Lieut Cdr USN	*Helm*	1/7/00	42
Sinclair	Lieut Cdr USN	*Bagley*	26/4/01	41
Price	Lieut Cdr USN	*Wilson*	21/12/03	38
Callaghan	Lieut Cdr USN	*Ralph Talbot*	28/6/04	38
Walsh	Commander RAN XO	*Canberra*	8/10/05	36
Gatacre	Commander RAN		11/6/07	35

27 Captain George Russell, then Flag Secretary to King, prepared a memo dated 31 July 1943 in which he summarised the report and proposed the courses of action which King accepted. It is filed with other documents relating to that report in NHC.

28 AA (Vic), MP 1185/8, file 1932/2/226.

29 Eighth Fleet War Diary for August 1942, NHC, Morison Papers, box 27, folder 'The Battle of the Eastern Solomons, 1942–43'.

30 Ohmae, 'The Battle', p. 1277.

31 Hoyt, *Japan's War*, p. 307.

Endnotes*

32 The latest addition to that misinformation is to be found in Robert Ballard's book *The Lost Ships of Guadalcanal*, published as recently as mid-1993, in which it is alleged (p. 55) that *Australia* was at anchor inside the screen of destroyers off Guadalcanal during the battle, and remained there as Crutchley sought to clarify the situation. A modicum of research would have shown that most improbable story to be utterly false.

33 Memo from Senior Member of the Board of Review, 'Battle of Savo Island' to President, Naval War College, 9 January 1950. NWC, Richard W. Bates papers, box 15, folder 10.

303*

Bibliography

UNPUBLISHED OFFICIAL SOURCES

Australia

Australian Archives, Melbourne, Vic

Most important material was found to be held by this repository, including the two reports of the Board of Inquiry convened to investigate the circumstances surrounding the loss of HMAS *Canberra*. The first report (with minutes) is at MP 1587/1, file 105H, while other valuable files in this series are:

105A—Admiral Crutchley's report as Commander Task Group 62.6 dated 13 August 1942
105B—report on Watchtower by COMSOPAC
105E—reports from ships in Tulagi–Guadalcanal area
105J—Watchtower signals
105N—report on Savo by COMSOPAC and preliminary report of C-in-C US Pacific Fleet

The second report of the Board of Inquiry, with accompanying correspondence, is contained on MP 1049/5, file 2026/3/501. An incomplete copy of the Hepburn Report (see Naval Historical Center, Washington, below) is held on MP 1185/8, file 1932/2/226. Other relevant material was located on MP 1290/1, file 29 (USN operations orders), MP1290/5 (COMSOPAC operation plan 1–42 dated 16 July 1942), and MP 1049/5, files 1840/2/80 (Navy Office minutes) and 1877/13/161.7 (reports on the Japanese Navy 1937–38).

Australian Archives, Canberra, ACT

Material located in MP 1196/2, item 60/501/103 (AAF Signal Instructions) was found to be useful.

Bibliography

Australian Archives, Sydney, NSW

This repository was found to hold the Deck Log of HMAS *Australia* for August 1942.

Australian War Memorial, Canberra

A study was made of material in the following files:
54, item 519/4/13—GHQ Operations Instructions
66, item 18/2/4—RAAF Operations records (including the Daily Log of ACH Townsville)
78, items 82/3 and 393/1—war diaries of HMAS *Canberra* and of the Australian Squadron/Task Force 44.

Department of Defence (Air Force Office), Canberra

A report on the RAAF establishment of Fall River (Milne Bay, Papua) during 1942 was consulted in the RAAF Historical Section.

Department of Defence (Navy Office), Canberra

A copy of the pamphlet 'Battle Experience—Bulletin No.2: Solomon Islands Actions, August and September 1942' (1942) is held by the Naval Historical Section.

National Library of Australia, Canberra

This institution holds a series entitled 'Copies of NSA Documents, Collection MicroFilm Set, Top Secret studies on US Comint during WW 2. Part 1. Pacific Theatre.' The most useful document here was 'The Role of Communications Intelligence in the American Japanese Naval War—Volume 3. The Solomon Islands Campaign. 1. Background of the Landings on Guadalcanal and the Battle of Savo Island (July 1–August 9, 1942)' dated 23 June 1943.

United States

National Archives, Washington, DC

The deck logs of all US ships present at Savo Island are held here.

Naval Historical Center, Navy Yard, Washington, DC

In addition to the report by Admiral Arthur J. Hepburn into the circumstances attending the loss of *Vincennes*, *Quincy*, *Astoria* and *Canberra* (1943), including all annexes and relevant correspondence (microfilm no. NRS 1976), the Center holds the papers of Captain S. E. Morison, the official navy historian, where much useful material was located in boxes 8, 24–27.

Naval War College, Newport, Rhode Island

The Naval Historical Collection holds 'The Battle of Savo Island, 9 August 1942. Strategical and Tactical Analysis' a study produced by Commodore Richard W. Bates and Commander Walter D. Innis (1950). Material in Research Group 23, boxes 27, 35 and 46 was also relevant. Also held here are the papers of Richard Bates and Edwin Layton.

England

Public Record Office, Kew, London

Relevant material was located in the following Admiralty records:
ADM 1/11326—Potential War in the Pacific: Notes and Appreciations
ADM 116/3862—1927–39, Naval arrangements in event of war in the Far East
ADM 199/1323—1942–43, Solomon Islands Campaign: Reports

PUBLISHED OFFICIAL HISTORIES

Australia

Gill, G. Hermon (1957) *Royal Australian Navy 1939–1942*, Canberra: Australian War Memorial
——(1968) *Royal Australian Navy 1942–1945*, Canberra: Australian War Memorial
Gillison, Douglas (1962) *Royal Australian Air Force 1939–1942*, Canberra: Australian War Memorial

United States

Morison, Samuel E. (1949) *The Struggle for Guadalcanal*, Boston: Little, Brown and Co. (vol.5 of *History of United States Naval Operations in World War II*)
Office of Naval Intelligence, US Navy *Solomon Islands Campaign*, vol.2, *Battle of Savo Island*

England

Historical Section, Admiralty (1956) *Naval Staff History, Second World War. War With Japan—vol.3, The Campaigns in the Solomons and New Guinea*
Tactical and Staff Duties Division, Naval Staff, Admiralty (1949) *Battle Summary No.21: Naval Operations in the Campaign for Guadalcanal August 1942–February 1943*

OTHER PUBLISHED BOOKS AND ARTICLES

Agawa, Hiroyuke (1981) *The Reluctant Admiral*, Tokyo: Kodansha International

Ballard, Robert D. (1993) *The Lost Ships of Guadalcanal*, London: Weidenfeld and Nicolson

Butcher, M. E. (1987) 'Admiral Frank Jack Fletcher: Pioneer Warrior or Gross Sinner?', Naval War College *Review*, Winter

Churchill, Winston *The Second World War*, London: Cassell and Co.

——vol.3, *The Grand Alliance* (1950)

——vol.4, *The Hinge of Fate* (1951)

Collier, Basil (1969) *The War in the Far East 1941–1945*, London: William Heinemann

Costello, John (1981) *The Pacific War*, London: Collins

Coulthard-Clark, Chris (1991) *Action Stations Coral Sea: The Australian Commander's Story*, Sydney: Allen & Unwin Australia

Deane-Butcher, W. (1989) *Fighter Squadron Doctor. 75 Squadron RAAF, New Guinea 1942*, Sydney: Kwik Kopy Printing Centre

Dull, Paul S. (1978) *The Imperial Japanese Navy 1941–45*, Annapolis: Naval Institute Press

Dyer, George C. (1969) *The Amphibians Came to Conquer: The story of Admiral Richmond Kelly Turner*, vols. 1 & 2, Washington: Department of the Navy

Evans, David (ed.) and O'Connor, Raymond (1969) *The Japanese Navy in WW II: In the Words of Former Japanese Naval Officers*, Annapolis: Naval Institute Press

Feldt, Eric (1946) *The Coast Watchers*, New York: Oxford University Press

Francillon, R.J. (1970) *Japanese Aircraft in the Pacific War*, London: Putnam and Co.

Frank, Richard B. (1990) *Guadalcanal: The Battle and the Legend*, New York: Random House

Gatacre, G.G.O. (1982) *Report of Proceedings: A Naval Career 1921–64*, Sydney: Nautical Press

Green, William (1962) *War Planes of the Second World War*, vol.6, *Floatplanes*, London: MacDonald

Griffith, Samuel B. (1963) *The Battle for Guadalcanal*, New York: Ballantine Books

Hara, Tomeichi (1961) *Japanese Destroyer Captain*, New York: Ballantine Books

Hinsley, F.H. (1981) *British Intelligence in the Second World War*, vol.12, London: HMSO

Hough, Richard (1986) *The Longest Battle: The War at Sea 1939–1945*, London: Weidenfeld and Nicolson

Howarth, Stephen (1983) *Morning Glory*, London: Hamish Hamilton

Howse, Derek (1993) *Radar at Sea: The Royal Navy in World War 2*, London: Macmillan Press

Hoyt, Edwin P. (1987) *Japan's War: The Great Pacific Conflict 1853–1952*, London: Guild Publishing

Hughes, Wayne P. (1986) *Fleet Tactics—Theory and Practice*, Annapolis: Naval Institute Press

Kahn, David (1967) *The Code Breakers*, New York: Macmillan

Kennedy, Paul (1983), *Strategy and Diplomacy 1870–1945*, London: George Allen & Unwin

King, Ernest J. and Whitehall, Walter W. (1952) *Fleet Admiral King: A Naval Record*, New York: Norton

Larrabee, Eric (1987) *Commander in Chief: Franklin Delano Roosevelt, his Lieutenants and their War*, London: Andre Deutsch

Layton, Edwin T. (1985) *And I Was There: Pearl Harbor and Midway, Breaking the Secrets*, New York: Quill

Leahy, William D. (1950) *I Was There*, New York: Gollancz

Loxton, Bruce 'Three Cruisers, Three Destroyers, Two Seaplane Tenders', USNI *Proceedings*, August 1992

MacIsaac, David (1976) *U.S. Strategic Bombing Survey (Pacific): Interrogations of Japanese Officials*, vols. 1 and 2, New York: Garland

Manchester, William (1978) *American Caesar—Douglas MacArthur 1880–1964*, Boston: Little, Brown and Co.

Marder, Arthur J. (1981) *Old Friends, New Enemies: The Royal Navy and the Imperial Japanese Navy*, vol.1, *Strategic Illusions 1936–1941*, Oxford: Oxford University Press

Marder, Arthur J. *et al.* (1990) *Old Friends, New Enemies: The Royal Navy and the Imperial Japanese Navy*, vol.2, Oxford: Oxford University Press

Morley, Walter S. and Williams, John L. (1992) *Bagley: First in her Class*, West Denis, Mass.: USS *Bagley* (DD-386) Association

Moyes, John F. (1944) *The Scrap Iron Flotilla*, Sydney: NSW Bookstall

Newcomb, Richard F. (1963) *Savo: The Incredible Naval Debacle off Guadalcanal*, London: Constable and Co.

Nicholls, Stan (1989) *H.M.A.S. Shropshire*, Sydney: Naval Historical Society of Australia

Ohmae, Toshikasu 'The Battle of Savo Island', USNI *Proceedings*, December 1957

Potter, E.B. (1976) *Nimitz*, Annapolis: Naval Institute Press

——(1985) *Bull Halsey*, Annapolis: Naval Institute Press

Pogue, Forest C. (1966) *George C. Marshall: Ordeal and Hope 1939–1942*, New York: Viking

Payne, Alan (1973) *H.M.A.S. Canberra*, Sydney: Naval Historical Society of Australia

Reynolds, David (1981) *The Creation of the Anglo-American Alliance 1937–41*, London: Europa Publications

Slessor, John (1956) *The Central Blue: Recollections and Reflections*, London: Cassell and Co.

Swanborough, Gordon, and Bowers, Peter M. (1968) *U.S. Naval Aircraft since 1911*, London: Putnam and Co.

Vandegrift, A.A. (1964) *Once a Marine: The Memoirs of General A.A. Vandegrift, Commandant of the U.S. Marines in WW II*, New York: Norton

Van de Rhoer, E. (1979) *Deadly Magic: Communications Intelligence in World War 2 in the Pacific*, London: Hale

Van der Vat, Dan (1991) *The Pacific Campaign*, London: Hodder and Stoughton

Warner, Denis and Peggy, with Sadao Seno (1983) *Kamikaze: The Sacred Warriors 1944–45*, Melbourne: Oxford University Press

——, with Sadao Seno (1992) *Disaster in the Pacific: New Light on the Battle of Savo Island*, Annapolis: Naval Institute Press

Watts, Anthony J. (1971) *The Imperial Japanese Navy*, London: MacDonald and Co.

Williams, John L. (1992) *U.S.S. Bagley (DD-386): The Waters Aft*, Decorah, Iowa: Anundsen Publishing Co.

Bibliography

UNPUBLISHED PRIVATE MANUSCRIPTS AND PAPERS

Bates, Rear Admiral Richard W., USN (Rtd), papers held in the Naval Historical Collection, US Naval War College, especially box 9 (folder 11)

Biard, Captain Forrest S., USN (Rtd), 'A Personal Account of On-the-Spot Experiences encountered by the Officer-in-Charge of the Radio Intelligence Team assigned to the Staff of Rear Admiral Frank Jack Fletcher, Commander Task Force 17 in USS *Yorktown* (CV5), from departure from Pearl Harbor 15 February 1942, through the Battle of the Coral sea and until the Return to Pearl Harbor 28 May 1942' (1985), copy in possession of Dr C.D. Coulthard-Clark.

Bonnot, Captain Emile L., USNR (Rtd), 'Were the Hudsons to be blamed for the Naval Disaster at Guadalcanal?' (1988), copy in author's possession.

Clemens, Major W.F.M., 'The Battle of Savo Island, 9 August 1942', transcript of an address given to the Naval Historical Society of Australia, Victorian Chapter, copy in author's possession.

Lacouture, Captain John, USN (Rtd), 'Remembrances of the Landings at Guadalcanal, Tulagi and the Battle of Savo Island and the sinking of the *Blue*', copy in author's possession.

Layton, Rear Admiral Edwin T., USN (Rtd), papers held in the Naval Historical Collection, US Naval War College, in particular boxes 30 (folder 2) and 34 (folder 9)

McCollum, Rear Admiral Arthur, USN (Rtd), reminiscences, vols. 1 and 2 (1973), held by Oral History Department, US Naval Institute, Annapolis, Maryland.

Sallet, George, 'Six Long Years (the experiences of Radioman 2nd Class in USS *Bagley* throughout the war)', extract in author's possession.

CORRESPONDENCE AND INTERVIEWS

Australia

Bischer, Mrs Diane Willman, Balgowlah, Sydney, NSW

Campbell, Commodore David RAN, Canberra, ACT

Caruana, Mr John (radio propagation consultant), Chatswood, NSW

Clemens, Major W.F.M., OBE, MC, Toorak, Vic.

Courtis, Mr Wilbur, DFC, Hawthorn East, Vic.

Date, Mr John, Turramurra, NSW

Deane-Butcher, Dr William, Killara, NSW

Freemantle, Mr Keith, Canberra, ACT

Garing, Air Commodore W.H., CBE, DFC, RAAF (Rtd), Turramurra, NSW

Geddes, Mr Eric, Bardwell Park, NSW

Gregory, Lieutenant Commander M.J., RAN (Rtd), Rosanna, Vic.

Hall, Lieutenant Commander Henry (Nobby) RAN (Rtd), Currarong, NSW

Kingwell, Air Commodore Deryck, CBE, DSO, RAAF (Rtd), Kenmore, Qld

McClarty, Mr Eugene, Modbury North, SA

Mann, Mrs Victoria, Balgowlah, NSW

Milne, Mr Lloyd, DFC, Melbourne, Vic.

M ray, Commander Dean, RAN (Rtd), Canberra, ACT
P ne, Mr Alan, Sydney, NSW (deceased)
J k, Vice-Admiral Sir Richard, KBE, CB, DSC, RAN (Rtd), Cooma, NSW
 se, Captain Athol, RAN (Rtd), Sydney, NSW
 anderson, Commander N.L., RAN (Rtd), Sydney, NSW
Showers, Rear Admiral H.A., CBE, RAN (Rtd) (deceased)
Smith, Admiral Sir Victor, AC, KBE, CB, DSC, RAN (Rtd), Red Hill, ACT
Snow, Commodore John, RAN (Rtd), Sydney, NSW
Stutt, Mr William, DFC, Melbourne, Vic.
Warne, Mr Bert, Sydney, NSW
White, Captain Norman (Knocker) RAN (Rtd), Balgowlah, NSW

United States

Bradshaw, Captain Harold G., USN (Rtd), Virginia Beach, Virginia
Cherpak, Dr Evelyn, NWC, Newport, Rhode Island
Connor, Mrs George R., Columbus, Georgia
Fleming, Mr Thomas, New York
Frank, Mr Richard, Annandale, Virginia
Haberlein, Mr Charles, Falls Church, Virginia
Hamilton, Commander Bruce RAN, Washington D.C.
Hilton, Rear Admiral Robert, USN (Rtd), Alexandria, Virginia
Hunnicutt, Captain W.R., USN (Rtd), Willow Hill, Pennsylvania
Lacouture, Captain John, USN (Rtd), Washington D.C.
Lloyd, Miss Kathleen M., Washington, D.C.
Medley, Dr David, Los Osos, California
Orr, Commander Ray USN (Rtd), Westport, Connecticut
Ramsey, Mrs Pamela, Potomac, Maryland
Sallet, Mr George, Clearwater, Florida
Woodson, Captain Walter B. USN (Rtd), Newport, Rhode Island (deceased)
Williams, Mr John L., Laguna Niguel, California

England

Brown, Commander David RN (Rtd), London
Crutchley, Lieutenant Commander William RN (Rtd), Mappercombe, Dorset
Dunn, Lieutenant Commander Gordon RN (Rtd), Porchester, Hampshire

Japan

Itonaga, Captain Shin, JMSDF (Rtd), Tokyo

Hong Kong

Salisbury, Commander W. RAN (Rtd)

Index

Page numbers in italics refer to illustrations

51–2, 58, 82, 109, 118, 121, 123, 135

Blue, USS, xxiv, 62, 81, 114, 118, 165, 167, 171, 173–5, 177, 189–90, 193, 202, 208, 215–16, 235, 237, 243, *244*, 249, 254–5, 261, 263–4, 272, 287

Bode, Captain Howard D., xxiv, 111–12, 151, 159–60, 168–9, 204, 208, 210–15, 222, 236, 242, 264–6, 296

Bonnot, Captain Emile L., 153, 290

Bougainville Island, xxiv, 37, 42, 53, 90, 96, 103, 109, 111, 126, 129, 131, 138–9, 142, 146–7, 157, 159, 250

Brett, Lieut.-General George H., 34, 36, 142, 268

Brilliant, HMS, 28

Brisbane, xxiv, 27, 30–1, 33–4, 36, 51, 53, 58, 62, 143, 146, 151, 158, 162, 168

Buchanan, USS, 74, 89, 248–9

Buka Island, 3, 4, 37, 42, 92, 96, 103, 125–6, 135, 149, 161

Buna, 4, 122, 166

Callaghan, Rear-Admiral Daniel J., 69, 71, 80, 284

Callahan, Lieut.-Commander Joseph W., 236–7

Campbell, HMS, 63

Canberra, xxiv, 49, 51, 53–4, 90, 96, 143, 146, 153–4, 160, 162–3, 302

Canberra, HMAS, xxii–xxvii, 30, *31*, 44, 46, 51–2, *60*, 62–8, 75, 77, 79, 82–4, 86, *87*, 90, 93, 95, 98, 108–9, 111–12, 114, 123, 142, 144, 152–3, 161–5, 167–8, 176–8, 180–93, *189*, 195, 198–202, 204, 206–8, 210–15, 217–19, 221, 224–5, 235, 237, 240–6, *244*, *245*, 248–9, 254–61, 264–5, 268–9, 272, 288, 294, 299

Canberra, HMAS (book), 189

Cape Esperance, 118, 133, 167, 169, 216, 237, 287; battle, 80

Cape Hunter, 287

Carpender, Vice-Admiral Arthur S., 158

Carroll, Commander Chester E., 233

Centurion, HMS, 28

Chambers, Commander Thomas E., 198, 300

Chicago, USS, xxiii–xxv, 15, 30, 51, 62, 67–8, 74, 77, 79, 82, 84, 95–6, 98, 108, 111–14, 130, 142, 151, 159–60, 167–9, 176–8, 181–2, 190, 199, 204, 206, 208, 210–15, *211*, *213*, 217–19, 221–2, 236–7, 242–3, 254–5, 257, 264, 272

Chitose, *141*

Choiseul, 27, 125, 131, 150, 157

Chokai, 42, 119, *120*, 122–3, 126, 129–30, 132–3, 135–6, 142, 144, 146–7, 156, 166–7, 170–1, 173, 175–6, 178, 180–3, 191, 207–8, 211–12, 217–19, 221–2, 224–8, 230–1, 233–4, 236–7, 249, 252, 272

Churchill, Rt Hon. Sir Winston, 4–5, 8–10, 19, 261

Cimarron, USS, 83

Clemens, Major W.F.M., 58, 290

coastwatchers, Australian, 52–4, 58, 90, 96, 99, 101, 107, 162–3, 250, 282; Japanese, 287

Coburg, 65

Collins, Vice-Admiral Sir John, 183, 188, 259

communications, 49–54, 62, 112, 137–8, 146, 151–64, 290, 302

Coral Sea, 3, 11–18, 22, 27, 30, 65, 92, 98–9, 119, 130, 142, 167, 210, 252, 278

Cornwall, HMS, 122, 239

Costello, John, 278

Courtis, Sergeant W., 37, 147

Crace, Admiral Sir John, 15–17, 28, 75, 119, 142, 208

Cruiser Division Six (Japan), 42, 84, 120, 123, 126, 135, 171, 231, 252

Cruiser Division Eighteen (Japan), 135, 174, 207

Crutchley, Admiral Sir Victor, VC, xxiv, xxvi, 28–30, 42, 51–2, 59, 68–9, 73–7, 79–82, 85, 89–90, 93,